PENGUIN BOOKS

EMILIE DU CHÂTELET

Originally from New York City, Judith P. Zinsser is a professor of history at Miami University in Ohio. She began her career as a women's historian as the coauthor of *A History of Their Own: Women in Europe from Prehistory to the Present*. She explored the effects of the women's movement on history in her next book, *Feminism and History: A Glass Half Full*. Zinsser has spoken widely on Du Châtelet and her articles about the marquise have appeared in edited collections and scholarly journals in the United States and Europe. For more information, see her Web site: http://www.users.muohio.edu/zinssejp.

EMILIE DU CHÂTELET

❧

DARING GENIUS
OF THE ENLIGHTENMENT

JUDITH P. ZINSSER

Previously published as *La Dame d'Esprit*

PENGUIN BOOKS

PENGUIN BOOKS

Published by the Penguin Group

Penguin Group (USA) Inc., 375 Hudson Street, New York, New York 10014, U.S.A.

Penguin Group (Canada), 90 Eglinton Avenue East, Suite 700, Toronto,
Ontario, Canada M4P 2Y3 (a division of Pearson Penguin Canada Inc.)

Penguin Books Ltd, 80 Strand, London WC2R 0RL, England

Penguin Ireland, 25 St Stephen's Green, Dublin 2, Ireland (a division of Penguin Books Ltd)

Penguin Group (Australia), 250 Camberwell Road, Camberwell,
Victoria 3124, Australia (a division of Pearson Australia Group Pty Ltd)

Penguin Books India Pvt Ltd, 11 Community Centre,
Panchsheel Park, New Delhi – 110 017, India

Penguin Group (NZ), 67 Apollo Drive, Rosedale, North Shore 0632,
New Zealand (a division of Pearson New Zealand Ltd)

Penguin Books (South Africa) (Pty) Ltd, 24 Sturdee Avenue,
Rosebank, Johannesburg 2196, South Africa

Penguin Books Ltd, Registered Offices: 80 Strand, London WC2R 0RL, England

First published in the United States of America as *La Dame d'Esprit: A Biography of the
Marquise Du Châtelet* by Viking Penguin,
a member of Penguin Group (USA) Inc. 2006
Published in Penguin Books 2007

3   5   7   9   10   8   6   4   2

The prologue in different form appeared in *Rethinking History,* issue of Spring 2003,
and later in *Experiments in Rethinking History,* edited by Alun Munslow
and Robert A. Rosenstone (Routledge, 2004).

ISBN 0-670-03800-8 (hc.)
ISBN 978-0-14-311268-6 (pbk.)
CIP data available

Printed in the United States of America
Designed by Nancy Resnick

To
Les Introductrices:

Gretel Zinsser Munroe
and
Barbara Lewis Zinsser, Esq.

Contents

PART III: APRIL 1741—SEPTEMBER 1749

Prologue: 1749*

From the window of the queen's apartments at the palace of Lunéville in Lorraine, *allées* of trees shadow the gravel walks, and borders of yellow and red zinnias brighten the vista. Fountains and the series of circular reflecting pools suggest some relief from the late summer heat, particularly in the early hours of the evening. One Saturday at the end of August 1749, Gabrielle Emilie le Tonnelier de Breteuil, marquise Du Châtelet, the forty-two-year-old *philosophe*, mathematician, and authority on Leibniz, sat at her desk by this window amid the apparent chaos of her scholar's tools. All around her, piled on the parquet floor, the bureau, and the shelves of cabinets, were the mathematical and astronomical treatises, the books of physics, and Newton's *Principia* and his *System of the World* that she had translated and on which she was now completing a commentary. Bits of paper, sealing wax, a compass, the cup of trimmed quill pens, the ink pot, the shaker of sand littered the desk. Her quarto-sized notebook lay open. She had indicated in the margins the calculations to be corrected. Now page proofs had to be revised, explanations clarified, line after line of complex equations rechecked.

On that August evening, she must have pushed all the papers aside. She found a blank sheet of her stationery with its delicate hand-painted border, folded it in half, and began a letter to Jean-François de Saint-Lambert, her young lover and the man responsible for her pregnancy. The summer light may still have been bright enough for her to write by, or perhaps she called to have the candles in the wall sconces and in the holders on the tables lit. Opening the tall casement windows that face the garden would allow for a

---

*This Prologue appeared in an earlier form in *Rethinking History* 7 (2003), pp. 13–22, and was reprinted in *Experiments in Rethinking History,* edited by Alan Munslow and Robert A. Rosenstone (New York: Routledge, 2004), pp. 195–208.

breeze, but might scatter bits of wax on her papers, and cause the tapers to burn unevenly.

In this letter, thoughts came in no particular order, but turned around her need for her lover to be "in the same place" as herself. His military duties have kept him in Nancy. She has lived two days without any word from him. She can be patient about her condition when he is with her, "but when I have lost you, I see only black." She suggests that her long letter of yesterday will please him more than this one, not because "I was loving you better, but because I had more strength to tell you."

Today, she writes, her belly has dropped so low that the "pain in my kidneys" is "unbearable"; she will not be surprised if she gives birth tonight. She reports that she walked in the garden, but her fears, the presentiments of death that color this, her fourth pregnancy, are so strong, she feels despondent in both spirit and her whole being. She began to write in smaller letters with less space between the lines, to be sure she could finish her last thought by the end of the page. Only her heart is spared, she continues—by implication, spared in order to love him. The last sentence, in even smaller script, runs along the pale-green border: "I finish because I can write no more."[1]

In less than a week, Mme Du Châtelet completed the revisions of her commentary on Newton, and in the early morning hours of September fourth, she gave birth to the baby, a daughter, Stanislas-Adélaïde, named for Du Châtelet's host and patron, King Stanislas, former king of Poland, and now duc de Lorraine. Despite the ease of the delivery, six days later, on September tenth, she died suddenly of a cause her contemporaries could not identify. The infant's baptism, and then her death a year and a half later, were duly recorded in the parish register. Although Du Châtelet's husband accepted paternity, it was widely rumored that the child was not his. And what of Du Châtelet's translation and commentary, her grand project of the previous five years? It almost died as well, unpublished until 1759—ten years after its completion, and long after the author's friends and lovers had moved on to other amusements and other concerns.

This is one possible beginning for the biography of this brilliant, unorthodox woman. But Mme la marquise Du Châtelet can be introduced in a different time and place. In Paris a few months earlier, in May 1749, she was in residence in a grand three-storied house in the rue Traversière–Saint

Honoré. She and Voltaire each had a suite of rooms, or *appartement*. The *hôtel*, as such a house was called in eighteenth-century France, was only a few blocks from the busy government offices of the Louvre, and from the royal palace of the Tuileries. In this second beginning, Du Châtelet also sits at her work, in the middle of writing what will be an eleven-page letter to her young army officer. Although Saint-Lambert's letter has been lost, he must have asked her once again to join him in Lorraine, where he was garrisoned. For in her answer she will both justify their separation and detail the sacrifices she has made in order to complete her grand scholarly project and to rejoin him before the baby arrives. She was in the sixth month of her pregnancy, when a woman usually feels strong and the baby's size does not yet cause much discomfort. Contemporaries described her as big-boned, perhaps five feet six inches, taller than many men, and since this was her fourth pregnancy she could expect all to go easily until the last few weeks and the birth itself.

On this May evening, she explains to Saint-Lambert how she has come to establish what sounds today like a punishing regimen to complete her project of the last five years, her translation of and commentary on Newton's *Principia*. In a characteristic show of intensity, self-discipline, bravado, and common sense, she writes that the imminence of her *accouchement*, or lying-in, gives her a clear deadline for its completion. She rises at eight or nine and works straight through to three in the afternoon. A *café*, and then she begins again at four. Dinner alone at 10 p.m. Soon after that, Voltaire, France's most renowned playwright, her former lover and her companion of fifteen years, comes to her rooms for conversation. Work fills the rest of the night and the early-morning hours, from midnight until 5 a.m. She has acknowledged to her lover that this "required a mind and body of iron," but finishing this book is "a frightening need." The premonitions of death that understandably plagued the thoughts of an eighteenth-century French woman pregnant well beyond the usual age of childbearing make the time even more precious. Death in childbirth with the manuscript unfinished, the page proofs unrevised, would mean, she writes, that she would lose "all the fruit of my work."[2]

Initially, Du Châtelet thought that she could manage the project by working only during the day, leaving herself free in the evening for *société:* the opera, conversation at Mme de Villars-Brancas's salon, card games with

the queen—Maria Leszczyńska, wife to Louis XV—and all the other entertainments of Versailles and Paris. But the time is too short. Continuing in
this life would mean many more weeks in Paris, probably giving birth there,
and suffering the certain ridicule of courtiers who took great pleasure in the
latest witticism about that noblewoman with intellectual pretensions, foolish enough to become *enceinte* (pregnant) at forty-two. "Why does Mme Du
Châtelet suddenly want to see her husband?" "It is," the riddle continued,
"one of those cravings of pregnant women." Even Voltaire could not resist
a *bon mot* at her expense. He told his male correspondents that this child,
given the irregularities of its paternity, must be considered one of the marquise's "Miscellaneous Works."[3] To avoid this series of "inconveniences," as
she describes them, she prefers to leave Paris for the comfort and friendship
of the duc de Lorraine's palace at Lunéville, in the northeastern part of the
country. But this means that she must have her commentary ready for publication before she leaves. As a result, she refuses dinner invitations, is
abstemious, and takes her "dark [barley] syrup." "My health takes it marvel-
ously," she announces. She only hopes that the child, who now moves frequently, takes it as well.[4]

In many ways this scene in Paris presents a more pleasing beginning, not
so somber as the first one. Those few months in late May show the marquise
at a more hopeful time, with a future to imagine. However, there are yet
other possibilities, other choices that can be made. The standard biographies
usually start very differently, not with Mme Du Châtelet, but with Voltaire.
In fact, the whole story of her death can be told from his perspective. This
more traditional introduction to the marquise's life explains that Voltaire
and Du Châtelet probably first met when she was a little girl of eight or nine
and he was in his twenties. He frequented her father's *salon* in Paris and
listened indulgently to her first translations of Virgil's *Aeneid*. As a young
man, Voltaire had achieved almost instant fame for *La Henriade,* his verse
epic on the life of Henri IV, considered proof of the superiority of French
culture over that of ancient Greece. Voltaire, the modern Homer, then
went on to be declared France's leading playwright as well. He was thirty-
eight when they first became attracted to each other in 1733; she was
twenty-six. Du Châtelet had married well, an army officer from one of the
most ancient lineages of Lorraine. By 1733, she had produced the requisite
two sons and a daughter for this kind and amiable older man, who remained

a loyal and understanding supporter of all her projects throughout her life. He expected his lively and intelligent young wife to amuse herself in Paris and even to take lovers. As an officer of the Royal Army, he was away for months at a time, as one war led to another in the middle decades of the eighteenth century.

Voltaire himself created many images of Gabrielle Emilie le Tonnelier de Breteuil, marquise Du Châtelet, in the last year of her life. Voltaire composed an epistle to Saint-Lambert, a gift from the master in the arts of love and letters to his apprentice. Portraying himself as the aged, displaced sexual partner, Voltaire offered the aspiring poet verses that would please "la belle amante de Newton" (the beautiful lover of Newton). Busy himself since 1745 with a secret affair with a younger partner, his niece Mme Denis, Voltaire could be both gracious and irreverent in his good wishes for his successor. He described "our heroine" leaving her studies, her compass, and her equations. She was dressed in "an old black apron," her fingers, as always, stained with ink. He told the younger man to "take these flowers" to her and sing for her the pretty songs "rehearsed by love, and unknown to Newton."[5] Love, Voltaire suggested, is a time of "illusion," as was his poetic version of his attitude toward the marquise's soldier-poet. In fact, he had been outraged when he learned of their love for each other.

Voltaire alluded more accurately to his feelings in his correspondence during the last weeks of August 1749. After pages describing his own activities, he ended his letter to their friends, the comte and comtesse d'Argental, with a sentence of news about her condition. On an impatient note, he added: "Madame du Chastelet [sic] still gives birth to nothing but problems." He remained self-absorbed. Even his lighthearted account of the baby's arrival, the morning of September fourth, dwelt as much on his own travails as on hers. He wrote the marquis d'Argenson, an important patron at Versailles, that, while "at her secrétaire, scratching some 'pancarte neutonienne,' she felt a little need. This little need was a girl who appeared that instant. She put it on a geometry book," and then retired to her bed. He went on to explain that he had also given birth to his newest tragedy, and that he was much more exhausted than she.[6]

Throughout their time together, Voltaire wrote about her in these ways, both appreciatively and deprecatingly. The formal dedicatory prefaces and laudatory epistles that circulated in manuscript, or that he appended to a number of his published writings, sound extravagant to modern readers in their praise of his "divine Emilie." In contrast, in letters to his friends, he made light of her activities and of her scholarly endeavors. He called her "mme Neuton [sic] Pompom," mocked her enthusiasms, and dismissed what he considered her troublesome emotional responses to everything from his own difficulties at court to her unorthodox predicament in the last year of her life.

Three possible introductions to the marquise Du Châtelet. Each is a "true," a "real" account of her last months. All are based on sources, on facts that make up the historical record, the official memory of her life. As her biographer, I can choose the time, the place, when and where to begin a narrative. With these choices historians decide which aspects of an individual's life and personality to expose, which part of her contemporary reputation to highlight. This is especially true for Mme Du Châtelet. What remains to document the marquise's life gives a wide range of often contradictory images and disparate accounts of her activities, sometimes making it hard to believe they all describe the same woman. Even in the best of circumstances, when practically every minute of an individual's life is known, biographers rely on judgment and imagination. They piece bits of knowledge, the "facts," together to fill in the interstices of an individual's recorded past, to make an apparently seamless narrative of a life. Like medieval mapmakers, they extrapolate from what they know and adapt from what they have experienced in their world to describe worlds they want their readers to envision.

The three alternative beginnings—at the palace of Lunéville, in Paris in mid-May, and during her last days as told from Voltaire's perspective—illustrate this process. For example, I chose to picture her at work, because this was the first image I wanted readers to see: Mme Du Châtelet at the height of her career, the self-proclaimed *géomètre* (mathematician) and *physicien* (physicist), the woman acknowledged in her own lifetime as a genius, accorded the title of *philosophe* by her contemporaries. To create a vivid picture, I drew on inventories of her possessions done after her death, and every kind of information about the palace and the room where she worked, including observations based on my own experience. I went to Lunéville one summer and felt the heat, saw the *allées* of trees and the flowered borders of the gravel walks. Engravings from the eighteenth century show similar, if grander, vistas. The palace itself had been converted into offices, so I relied on the Ministry of Culture guidebook for a sense of the former opulence of the interior: painted friezes, mirrored walls, parquet floors.

The scene of Du Châtelet at her *secrétaire* came from a number of contemporary accounts of the appearance of rooms she worked in. All marvel at the confusion of papers, books, and tables. Voltaire ordered "trimmed quills" in one of his letters. I liked the sharp neatness of the phrase and assumed she would have used them as well. Anyone writing in the eighteenth century would have had an ink pot, and sand to sprinkle over the finished page to absorb the inevitable unevenness of the ink on the rough stock of page proofs, and on the thinner, glossy surface of her stationery. I do not know if she was hot, but I have seen the breeze from an open window scatter the wax of the candles and make them burn unevenly. The description of her clothes is pure extrapolation. I remember my own pregnancy, contending with the summer heat, sweating no matter how thin my clothing, when I sat, as she did, for long hours at my desk.

The second beginning, the scene in Paris, relied on Du Châtelet's own letters. From them I reconstructed her state of mind, her immediate aspirations, and her own speculations about her future. Here is the practical, independent, but sensual and affectionate lover, with very little about the setting. One letter that she probably wrote in May, certainly from Paris in the middle of her pregnancy, made the narrative. Du Châtelet's letters are among the richest sources for her biographers. They fill two published volumes and cover the years from 1733 to 1749. The Voltaire scholar Theodore Besterman found them when he was scouring French archives and collections for the great man's papers. But even letters do not give a complete "reality." This is a skewed collection. Most of the letters are to the men of Voltaire's immediate circle. Hundreds, perhaps thousands of others have yet to be discovered. The marquise wrote to a wide circle of friends and acquaintances; this was how she maintained the network of influence and obligation that was part of her courtier's world. Even at their best, then, these letters tell only a small part of what could be known.

In addition, portions of letters can be quoted to highlight one sentence and not another. The words a woman writes acquire different meanings when presented in one order or another, in this and not that context. For example, Du Châtelet's love letters to Saint-Lambert have traditionally been used by her popular twentieth-century biographers and by Voltaire scholars to portray her as a foolishly passionate, semihysterical middle-aged woman. And so they seem to read, as ordered by her first editor, Besterman. In fact, the originals, now carefully preserved in a red leather quarto volume at the Morgan Library in New York City, are bound in a completely different order. Besterman himself acknowledged the tentative nature of the chronology he had set. Many of the most intensely emotional letters and notes have no date, or merely indicate the morning, the evening, or the day of the week. A third or more float free of time and place and can be arranged in an infinite number of sequences to create an infinite number of stories and images. The reconstruction of Du Châtelet's last weeks in Paris of this second beginning relies on an altogether new order and emphasizes emotions and attitudes that other historians have failed to mention. There is passion, impatience, frustration, but not the foolish rantings of the hysteric. Every biographer of Du Châtelet quotes from the letter describing her Paris regimen, but none connects her sense of urgency to her contradictory feelings about her work and her lover. Perhaps because of similar experiences in my own life, this account highlights what I hear as the conflict she felt between her project on Newton and her desire to abandon it all for the man she wanted to make the grand passion of her life. In May she wrote from Paris and assured him, "I love you," "à la folie," and "it's certainly folly, but it is for life." In another letter to Saint-Lambert, his impatience prompted her plea that he not blame her for their separation. She reassured him: "I don't love Newton, at the least I finish it for reason and for honor, but I love only you and that which connects to you."[7]

In this way, biographers use their own preconceptions to interpret and re-create an individual's unspoken feelings. This process of interposing one's own interpretation of an individual's actions and attitudes is also evident in the last version. Yes, using Voltaire's writings to introduce the marquise offered the most conventional approach. But after that, I made different choices from those of other biographers; through editorial comments, I allowed his words to reveal more about his foibles and his attitudes toward her than about the "facts" of her life.

The more we study the historical record, any historical record—sites and objects, letters, manuscripts, and memoirs—the more spaces appear, spaces between the "facts" that in turn pose questions defying simple answers. Gabrielle Emilie le Tonnelier de Breteuil, marquise Du Châtelet, exemplifies such challenges. There are so many spaces and questions. Historians have filled those spaces and answered those questions in different ways. Those of her immediate contemporaries who wrote about her, like Voltaire, either lionized her for her genius and learning or ridiculed her pretensions at inclusion among Europe's intellectual elite. Nineteenth-century writers included her in their compendia of accomplished women or ignored her in their histories of the Enlightenment. The major twentieth-century biographers of Du Châtelet and Voltaire, as well as historians of science, have minimized or dismissed her intellectual accomplishments, some even ascribing her works to others. It is a truism of historiography that each century must tell stories in its own way, that historians can write only within a framework bounded and crisscrossed with preconceptions. All have implicit or explicit agendas that determine what subjects they have chosen to research and re-create. All of us have a particular story to tell that reflects our own questions about our own times, even about ourselves.

❧

I first learned about the marquise Du Châtelet when I was thirteen or fourteen. I cannot remember exactly, because the memory comes from a period in my life when I was learning all the time: how to dress, which fork to use, the names of classical composers, which authors to read, and which to dismiss. My family had moved back to New York City from southern California, back to a culture that my parents knew but I did not. No one considered bringing my bike, and the Fifth Avenue hairdresser was instructed to cut off my long ponytail. That first summer of 1956, I spent much of my time with my cousin, Antonia, and her family. Antonia and I are the same age. Perhaps she told me, perhaps I heard talk at the dinner table: her mother had a project. Everyone believed my aunt to be the most elegant, gracious woman, in both appearance and gesture. She was a charming hostess for her lawyer husband, an attentive mother to her two daughters, and editor of the newsletter for the Legal Aid Society; she led a full and busy life. Yet there was this project. Reading her letters after her death, I found an early reference to the marquise Du Châtelet. In her late twenties and newly married, my aunt assured her writer father that she had located Du Châtelet's letters in a nearby library and would soon be working through them.

I never saw anything she wrote and forgot about her interest altogether. She died of cancer in the spring of 1962 with all of Voltaire's correspondence on the shelves above her desk: the plain French paperback books from the publisher Gallimard that leave the pages for the reader to cut. These books and all of her notes disappeared. I had to rediscover Mme Du Châtelet for myself. Almost fifteen years later, by chance, I found a popular account from the early 1970s, *The Divine Mistress* by Samuel Edwards, among the secondhand books at a Salvation Army store, a few blocks from where I lived in New York City. It was months before I made the connection between this biography and the radio play my aunt had planned to write. It is as if this gifted eighteenth-century woman challenged us both: to tell her life in new ways that do justice to all aspects of her unorthodox interests and achievements, and to explain how such genius could have been alternately admired, ridiculed, and forgotten. The original title of this biography, *La Dame d'Esprit,* was intended as a beginning, for *esprit* is one of those French terms rich in multiple meanings that, to be understood, must be translated into many words in English. The marquise Du Châtelet personified all that it conveys: she was the woman of spirit, intellect, wit, and energy, one of the great minds of the eighteenth-century "Republic of Letters"; in short, a daring genius of Europe's Enlightenment.

PART I

DECEMBER 1706—JUNE 1735

CHAPTER ONE

The Families: Daughter and Wife

An early-nineteenth-century French pamphlet of "Femmes célèbres" (famous women) gave a simple explanation for the marquise Du Châtelet's genius and her unorthodox life. According to the author, the *géomètre* and *physicien* was born to it: Gabrielle Emilie·le Tonnelier de Breteuil is described as a little girl of three who discovered how to use a large set of mathematician's dividers, the eighteenth-century equivalent of a compass. According to the story, a well-meaning servant, in an effort to make a toy for her, closed the wooden V and dressed it to look like a doll. But, unsatisfied with this gift, the remarkable little girl studied the figure and undressed it. She intuited its purpose, and used it to make a circle. It became her favorite possession. She kept it with her "day and night."[1] The popular versions of the lives of the early Christian martyrs read in the same way: St. Catherine had her wheel, St. Margaret her dragon; so Du Châtelet was associated with the symbol of her future fame. This anecdote, however, tells more about how the educated elite of nineteenth-century France wanted to remember her than about anything else. It was, the story suggests, her "nature." She was a prodigy, an anomaly, unlike any other female.

What is, in fact, known about the childhood of this extraordinary woman? What explains her exceptional talents and her unorthodox aspirations? The novelist Julian Barnes describes a biography "as a collection of holes tied together with string."[2] The holes are so wide for the first years of Du Châtelet's life that the speculations of previous biographers have proved too weak to hold the narrative together. The date and place of her birth have been established beyond dispute: in Paris, on December 17, 1706, in the parish of Saint-Roch. After that, there is an enormous gap. There are no uncontested reminiscences of a father or mother, no youthful diaries. The first letter of Du Châtelet's that we have is tentatively dated December 1734, when she was already a married woman of twenty-eight, and could have been written by any lively, privileged noblewoman of her era.

So, without direct evidence, how can the transformation—from privileged little girl to learned woman and published author, lauded by her contemporaries as a genius, and accepted as a member of Europe's Republic of Letters—be explained? Her studies in early adulthood rivaled those of her male intellectual contemporaries; she read Latin, Italian, English, and Flemish. Her writings included a translation of a controversial English work of moral philosophy, the *Fable of the Bees;* collaboration with Voltaire on the *Eléments de la philosophie de Newton* (Elements of the Philosophy of Newton); a treatise on the nature of fire; and her own work of natural philosophy, the *Institutions de physique* (Foundations of Physics). Her skeptic's commentary on the Old and New Testaments, and her translation of and commentary on Newton's *Principia,* were but the last of her projects. With such material, historians, like scientists, create hypotheses, and then test them against borrowed evidence and insights gleaned from the documented experiences of other women. Reasoning in this way, the marquise's previous biographers have suggested two hypotheses to be tested: either she had a mentor father, or she was given a formal convent education.

Daughter to the Baron de Breteuil

The best known of Du Châtelet's French biographers ascribe primary credit for her aspirations and her education to her father, baron Louis Nicholas le Tonnelier de Breteuil. They imagine a special relationship between a daughter and a narcissistic older man, with "all of the frailties" of a grandfather and the "tendernesses" of a father.[3] The evidence exists to create such scenes. The baron de Breteuil, aged sixty-seven, could have sat in front of the fireplace in his bedroom, reading a favorite novel. Though the fire was bright, he pulled the lush folds of his fur-lined robe across his legs to keep warm in this opulent world without central heating. The gray early morning light from the double set of windows was just enough to read by. The remains of his light breakfast, his *petit déjeuner,* hot chocolate and a roll, were on the folding marquetry table beside him. The clock on the chimney breast had just struck the half hour.

A little girl not yet ten, also warmly dressed against the cold and damp of a Paris winter, knocked at the door of her father's inner sanctuary. Her bold action was rewarded, and she was allowed to enter. She made a deep curtsy and then, forgetting all the lessons her mother had taught her, stepped and skipped across the parquet floor, and leaned against his crossed legs. Louis Nicholas smiled and agreed to the unspoken request. She pulled the troublesome gathers of her skirts out of the way and climbed into his lap. She arranged herself against the smooth texture of his robe and the warmth of his body and was ready to listen as he read aloud to her, perhaps from a translation of Ovid's *Metamorphoses*, often recommended for young children.

Historians' narratives can be seductive. This scene of Du Châtelet and her father is pure extrapolation. It is, however, a kind of truth, for there is a document that gives these details of the house in Paris that Du Châtelet lived in as a little girl, the inventory of her father's estate, made at the time of his death in 1728. Notaries carefully listed the furniture and decorations in his bedroom, the clock on the chimney breast, the folding table, his brocade dressing gown with its lining of Canadian fox fur.[4] The "bedroom," in fact, would have had many purposes, both private and public. This, the main *chambre,* used for sleeping and reading but also for entertaining, formed part of the baron's centrally located suite of rooms, a common arrangement of the noble *hôtels* of the seventeenth and early eighteenth centuries.[5] The inventory indicates that Louis Nicholas had furnished it with an eye to comfort and grandeur. In addition to his bed, the main room had six *fauteuils,* or large wood-and-upholstery armchairs, and numerous small decorated folding tables that could be opened and set around for his guests to enjoy a late-night supper, or *souper,* and then games such as *pharon, cavagnole,* and *piquet,* which the nobility enjoyed so much. Would this father have encouraged the unorthodox for his only daughter? As the male head of the family, he had to approve all aspects of his children's formal upbringing, including the education of his little girl. However, given the demands of his courtier's life, would he have made time to teach her himself?

Those elite men and women that Breteuil entertained knew that he came to his privileged, lucrative career late in life. Louis Nicholas's father, Louis le Tonnelier de Breteuil, was one of the most successful courtiers of Louis XIV's reign, having risen to succeed the king's principal minister, the famous Jean-Baptiste Colbert. While Du Châtelet's uncles rose to important positions as a councillor of state, a bishop, a naval captain, and a maréchal in the Royal Army, the equivalent of a five-star general, her father played the role of irresponsible youngest son well into his forties. Initially, it did not matter. His father's wealth, and his rank and position in Louis XIV's government, ensured even this prodigal son access to the court. Breteuil's intelligence and charm won him the king's continued favor. Given the title of *lecteur ordinaire du roi* (reader to the king) in 1677, an office carrying no duties but many privileges, he had, at twenty-nine, already gained an intimacy with Louis XIV usually denied to one of his birth. The title gave Louis Nicholas "le droit," the right to be among the first groups of nobles admitted to Louis XIV's presence each morning. The king began his ceremonial display at eight-fifteen when he received the "first gentleman of the bedchamber," members of the royal family, and sundry other real and titular attendants. At eight-thirty he rose from his bed and prepared to meet more of his courtiers in the adjoining larger room. Here Breteuil was privileged to witness, among other events, the "Grand Monarch" relieving himself on his *chaise de commodité,* and his barber arranging his morning wig. Then, amid the rigorous formalities and the relative crowd of the *grand lever,* he could watch the king have his breakfast of broth or herb tea, be shaved every other day, take his shirt from the dauphin, the royal heir, and his watch from the royal clock maker.[6]

French historians always suggest that the king favored Du Châtelet's father because they both enjoyed women, and had reputations for their sexuality and their appreciation of *la volupté,* "the voluptuous," a rich eighteenth-century word with connotations of sensuality, beauty, and delights in all their manifestations. Louis XIV's palaces attested to his insistence on the luxurious and magnificent: the Tuileries and the Louvre, and, outside of Paris, Fontainebleau and his special creation, Versailles. In addition to his wife and children, Louis XIV maintained an official mistress (the *maîtresse-en-titre*) and yet another set of children, proof for all to see of His Majesty's masculine prowess. Breteuil's liaisons seem disorderly by contrast. He had two notorious affairs. The first was a secret wedding against his parents' wishes to his twenty-one-year-old cousin, Anne Lefèvre de Caumartin de Mormans, which ended with her death soon after their marriage and the birth of their daughter. And, later in life, he had an adulterous liaison with a much younger woman, the brilliant Anne Bellinzani, daughter of an Italian financier from Mantua and wife of an important Parisian official.

Both liaisons enhanced his image as a seducer, but gossip about secret weddings and adulterous young wives also courted ridicule and scandal. Bellinzani gave birth to her daughter after her husband had arranged a formal separation. He refused to accept paternity, and an order of the king sent her to a convent in disgrace.[7]

This kind of reputation did not sit well with the king. Louis XIV expected discretion of his favorites, and his tolerance for their escapades had its limits. An opportune diplomatic mission after each of Breteuil's affairs undoubtedly helped to quiet the scandals, but invited other consequences. For a courtier to be away from the Grand Monarch was a kind of living death. Perhaps Breteuil's more serious and successful brothers brought pressure, perhaps the king did. When an opportune marriage presented itself, he gave up his unorthodox ways. An elderly uncle, Claude de Breteuil-Charmeaux, had recently married. This new aunt had a younger sister. Gabrielle Anne de Froullay became Louis Nicholas's wife—and mother to the future marquise Du Châtelet. This double alliance between the Breteuils and the Froullays must have pleased the king. The comte and comtesse de Froullay, Du Châtelet's maternal grandparents, had served the royal family in posts reserved to only the most elite of the nobility, posts within the royal household. Froullay's father, the comte, as *grand maréchal des logis de l'armée du roi* (literally, grand marshal for the lodging of the king's army, but entailing many more rights and duties), held one of the highest-ranking and most lucrative positions at court. His wife, Angélique de Beaudean de Parabère, was a *dame d'honneur,* a lady-in-waiting to Queen Anne of Austria, which entitled her to a handsome yearly pension, and meant that she was one of four or five women in daily, constant attendance to the queen. These women woke the queen in the morning, assisted at her toilette, sat and read with her, attended mass when she did, and stood ready to serve her at every ceremonial function. Though both parents were long dead, the Froullay sisters remained part of the network of connection and privilege created by their parents. This and the king's blessing, rather than her modest dowry, made the twenty-seven-year-old Gabrielle Anne de Froullay an exceptionally suitable partner for the forty-eight-year-old Louis Nicholas de Breteuil. They signed their marriage contract on April 16, 1697, and thus agreed to join their families and to preserve their lineages through the procreation of sons and marriageable daughters.

After the birth of their first son, René-Alexandre, Louis XIV signaled approval of Breteuil's change in condition, from errant, aging bachelor to married man. Louis Nicholas had been given to understand that his request to purchase the newly vacant office of *introducteur des ambassadeurs et étrangers,* royal master of protocol, would be favored by the king. The price had been set at 120,000 livres. The king sweetened the transaction by giving Breteuil sixty thousand livres, thus halving the price for this favored companion. On Sunday morning, November 23, 1698, Louis Nicholas assumed his new title. From January to June—six months, or one "semester," as it was called—he was responsible for all the arrangements, including housing and provisions, for the foreign dignitaries at the court of Louis XIV. An office of this sort carried with it many opportunities—fees and gifts from the ambassadors and from those hoping to advance their interests while in France—but also potential hazards: the substantial expense of a suitable wardrobe for the many court functions, of livery, horses, carriages, and servants in keeping with the new post; and, perhaps most significant, the serious risks of royal displeasure, since the king placed so much importance on ritual and precedence.[8]

The monarch found that he had not misplaced his favor. Breteuil acquitted himself well. He embarked upon his new responsibilities with an exemplary sense of duty and of the importance of his office, filling the pages of a journal as a guide for his successors. In it he described how an ambassador extraordinary should incline his head and when he should remove his hat; the changes in arrangements when the court was in mourning (less gold was to be displayed by the visiting dignitaries); the negotiations over the manner of address, and its implications of seniority or inferiority, between the king of Denmark and the king of France. Most exasperating had been the demands of the ambassador of the shah of Persia, who refused to follow protocol and the arrangements already made. His astrologers set the date for his audience, and he demanded a separate carriage for himself alone, because he refused to touch any Christians.[9]

On Tuesdays, the Grand Monarch accepted the official greetings of foreign visitors in his bedchamber, seated in a gilded *fauteuil,* his ceremonial presence framed against a covered canopy. Typically for Breteuil and his charges, a day like this began at 5 a.m., even though Versailles was only fourteen miles from Paris. Given eighteenth-century traffic to and from the capital, only such an early departure would ensure arrival in time for the audience with the king, scheduled for nine in the morning. From the central courtyard of the palace, Breteuil shepherded his visitors up the "Stairway of the Ambassadors," through the formal public *salles* (halls) to the king's presence, then to other wings of the palace and presentations to the rest of the royal family. His day was long, for, in addition to escorting ambassadors through the almost eight hours of ceremonial royal visits, Louis Nicholas had to attend to all the regular business of the courtier, dinners, receptions, and more elaborate entertainments, such as a grand masked ball in the main apartment of the king. There would have been little time for his family.[10]

What time he had would have gone not to his daughter but to his sons. A portrait of Louis Nicholas with his eldest boy, René-Alexandre, shows both dressed in the elegant laces and brocades of their rank. Despite the set of his strong features, his shoulder-length wig of tight curls, Breteuil's pose is meant to be informal and to suggest companionship. There is the father's pleased expression; the little boy's open look; the rounded, soft face of a four-year-old; his small, delicate hand pointing to the hunting dog in the bottom corner of the picture. Breteuil had important plans for his sons. He aspired to military careers for the two eldest, a leap in rank for his offspring that would require the skills of the courtier and resources equal to those of the successful financier, for every aspect of the advancement of his boys required money and connections. Granted, after the death of his king in September 1715, Louis Nicholas's daily activities changed dramatically. He sold his position as master of protocol for 250,000 livres, and in theory, now had more time to spend with his family, particularly the younger children.[11] By 1715, Du Châtelet's two older brothers would have begun their military training in earnest, and probably only she and the youngest son, Elisabeth-Théodore, remained at home. Breteuil, however, was of the same generation as the new regent, the duc d'Orléans, and enjoyed the same luxuries and amusements. The duc held court in Paris at the Palais Royal, not in Versailles, and the young Louis XV, his nephew, lived at the palace of the Tuileries, just across the rue Saint-Honoré. This was a grand era of theater and opera, and Breteuil and his wife would have continued to entertain. Once again, Breteuil's energies would have gone to these activities, rather than to his little girl.

Daughter to Gabrielle Anne de Froullay, Baronne de Breteuil

And her mother? What was she like? What was her role in Du Châtelet's early life, in the decisions about her daughter's education? The inventory made by the notaries at the baron de Breteuil's death offers insights. The differences in decor between her rooms and her husband's were striking. Unlike the opulence and grandeur of his suite of rooms, Gabrielle Anne de Froullay's single *chambre* had a modest bed and two armchairs, both in carved unpainted walnut. Still, she expected comfort and elegance; her bed had a satin coverlet with flowers embroidered in silver thread, and crimson damask draperies. Simple flowers and forest greenery filled the tapestry and the single painting on the wall, and numerous mirrors were arranged to reflect the evening's candlelight. There was a family chapel with a single prie-dieu, where she probably took communion in the mornings when she was in Paris. Perhaps some of the paintings in the two grand public salons indicate her religious sensibilities as well: the Virgin, Mary Magdalene, the Massacre of the Innocents (a gift from her mother-in-law). These are in marked contrast to the suggestively erotic classical subjects of other paintings— Andromeda, Achilles, the Danaë, Venus and Love (Cupid), Mars and Venus— that seem more in keeping with her husband's tastes.[12]

A formal portrait of Du Châtelet's mother shows a longish, pleasing face with rounded cheeks, brown hair, a straight gaze—similar, in fact, to the images of her daughter done at about the same age. She is dressed in the rich fabrics worn for ceremonial appearances before the king and queen. Although Breteuil does not mention his wife's attendance at court, it would have been expected for someone of her family background and with such an important courtier as a husband. The memoir of one of Du Châtelet's younger cousins, Renée-Caroline-Victoire de Froullay, the future marquise de Créqui, described Du Châtelet's mother as "renowned for her beauty," and always serious, smiling only as a gesture of condescension or as an act "of tenderness [when] looking at her children." Créqui listed "particular imperfections": for example, that her aunt was superstitious, but also well read, particularly in theology and astronomy. Could Du Châtelet's mother have introduced her to critical study of the Bible and to the wonders of the stars and planets? Unfortunately, Créqui's memoirs can be unreliable.

Someone else published these reminiscences for her, and there are glaring errors in dates and places.[13]

What, then, can be constructed from other sources? Initially, Froullay and her husband lived in his father's household in the rue de Paradis, now part of the rue des Francs Bourgeois. In October 1706, just before Du Châtelet's birth, Louis Nicholas purchased the Hôtel Dangeau, the four-storied house of a successful courtier member of the *haute noblesse,* the highest ranks of the nobility, for sixty thousand livres. As a child, Gabrielle Emilie le Tonnelier de Breteuil lived here at no. 12 with her parents and her brothers. Theirs was one of thirty-six contiguous *hôtels* arranged around a central square, most of which belonged to high-ranking government officials and courtiers. Du Châtelet's great friend in adult life, the duc de Richelieu, lived at no. 21. The elder Breteuils' residence was only a few streets away. The name of the square, the Place Royale, was changed during the Revolution to Place des Vosges, but it remains one of the most prestigious addresses in Paris. Once a parade ground, the vast space even today is welcoming. The Hôtel de Sully flanks one corner; the rest is a simple square on a north-south axis. The *hôtels* all have the same exterior façade. The red brick and pale-ivory sandstone still look bright, and the colors deepen in the afternoon sun. The regularity of the arches in the pavilions makes a continuous line around the square. The plane trees are carefully sculpted each spring and display regularity and symmetry, two aesthetic qualities prized by Europe's eighteenth-century nobility. Perhaps the little girl particularly loved the equestrian statue of Louis XIII. Despite her skirts and child's whalebone corset, did she try to climb the white marble pedestal to touch the hoof of the king's prancing horse?[14]

Du Châtelet's mother's responsibilities would have increased after the purchase of the *hôtel* in 1706. Breteuil's mother moved with them to the Place Royale; a succession of other relatives followed. There would have been servants to supervise, receptions and entertainments to prepare for. A family of this rank and size might easily have employed thirty people, each with his or her separate duties and special tasks.[15] Within the first year, even before she had her own household, Du Châtelet's mother had fulfilled her primary duty as a wife: she had produced a son. Five more children—two of whom died young—followed, until 1710, over the first thirteen years of her marriage. This was the pattern for a healthy noblewoman of the early eighteenth century: one to two years between births. The frequency of the births, barely a year separating each of the first three sons, suggests it was unlikely that she breastfed any of the children.

Gabrielle Emilie, the only daughter, arrived December 17, 1706. As was done for her sons, Froullay would have already chosen Du Châtelet's *nourrice,* or wet nurse, a young woman selected for her fresh appearance, her cleanliness, and the bounty of her breasts. Froullay would scrutinize her habits and appearance before hiring her, because even the most learned men and women in Europe believed that she might impart the qualities of her own character through her breast milk. Customarily, the wet nurse was a relative of servants already employed in the household, or was from the family's country estates. In 1699, in the first years of his life of respectability, Breteuil bought such an estate, Preuilly-sur-Claise, for 378,000 livres, from a noble widow in need of money for creditors. This was a princely sum, but, in addition to two châteaux, the land carried the rights to the manorial revenues of the farmlands; lucrative iron forges and charcoal furnaces; and a title, first baron of Touraine.[16] In Louis XIV's world this was how one acquired a title, just like everything else—with money and *par la grâce du Roi,* by the grace of the king, for the monarch had to give his permission for the transaction.

Although his eldest surviving son would automatically inherit this title, after her birth Breteuil gave one of the minor distinctions attached to the country property to his daughter: she became the baronne de Preuilly. At one and a half or two, the little baronne would have been weaned. In 1708, Du Châtelet and her older brothers would have filled the children's quarters on the top floors of no. 12, Place Royale. René-Alexandre, the eldest, would already have his own tutor, or *précepteur.* The younger, Charles-Auguste, age seven, probably still had his own nursemaid. When she was four or five, Du Châtelet would have had her own *gouvernante* (governess) to keep her clean and well mannered and to hear her recite her prayers. This young woman, probably convent-educated, would also teach the future marquise the basic skills of reading, writing, and simple arithmetic. First the little girl learned her letters in a *cahier,* or copybook, carefully lined by her governess. Each exercise built on the last: "a" was formed by making a "c" and then an "i" without lifting the nib of the quill. Then a word, or a phrase.[17] She recited her prayers, and these might have been among the first words and sentences she wrote. Numbers would have been part of her exercises in penmanship as well. A little girl practiced simple arithmetic on her slate and learned the multiplication tables by heart.

Du Châtelet's day, and that of her siblings, if typical of their rank, began with prayers. A walk, or games, came after breakfast—some bread, jam, and, perhaps, chocolate (though this was an expensive treat even for adults)—and then mass in the family chapel with their mother. A simple meal—perhaps soup, cheese, and bread—punctuated a day devoted to lessons, visits from teaching masters, and the like. Froullay, as the daughter of a courtier's family and wife to Louis Nicholas le Tonnelier de Breteuil, with the concurrence of her female relatives, would also have seen to it that her daughter learned the intricacies of proper female deportment and etiquette, the telltale signs of rank and privilege. Each action and word identified one's place in the hierarchy of eighteenth-century French society. It was customary for little girls and boys to join the family in the late afternoon for the main meal of the day on those occasions when their parents dined in and were not entertaining. The Hôtel Breteuil had a separate room devoted to this one function, an innovation in the early eighteenth century. The children probably sat on the tapestry-covered walnut chairs, pushed up close to the great marble table, set with all the different forks, spoons, and knives, each with a special use. One could pass a bit of cheese on the end of one's knife, eat olives with a spoon but not a fork. Bread should be broken, not cut, on the presumption that one would always be served tender, fresh loaves. Should she be spoken to, Du Châtelet would address her parents as "Monseigneur" and "Madame," as her governess had taught her. Entering or leaving their presence had its appropriate gesture. Du Châtelet later described a four-year-old little girl learning to make *la révérence,* the low curtsy, preserved in the curtain calls of prima ballerinas.[18]

Froullay would have chosen her daughter's *gouvernante* for her accent as well as her convent training and clean habits. To speak like a Parisian denoted one's place in society as obviously as actions and greetings. Du Châtelet learned to address the members of her own family with the formal "vous" form of the verb. As an adult she addressed even her lovers this way, and probably would have given offense had she not. Gradually, she acquired phrases and other ways of speaking "with taste, charm, and good manners" that identified her as a member of the elite. For example, a person of quality drank the "wine of Champagne," not "champagne." One returned to Versailles from "Paris," not from "the capital." Missing a friend's visit left one "affligé," distressed, not "désespéré," in despair.[19]

She memorized ranks and titles, her family's place in the endless orders of procession, details that her mother had learned from her family and that her father observed so meticulously in his role at court. Precedence affected every aspect of life in Du Châtelet's eighteenth-century world. Perhaps Breteuil gave his children their first lesson by explaining the placement of the figures portrayed in the picture in their dining room of an ambassadorial audience with Louis XIV. People never spoke to each other as equals; one was of a higher or lower status, from the simplest peasant girl all the way to the king. Even the poorest Parisian guarded her right to use the public fountains before someone of a lesser rank: the way she earned her wages, where she was born, whom she had married, all would indicate her place in the line. Du Châtelet's mother would also have left time in her children's day for less serious activities: an outing in one of the family carriages to the royal park at the Tuileries, an opportunity to watch Pulchinelle in a street-side puppet show, or at the Petit-Théâtre des Marionettes in the rue Vivienne, just behind the Palais Royal, the regent's official residence. In her *Discours sur le bonheur* (Discourse on Happiness), written when Du Châtelet had her own children, she remembered puppets as one of her great delights, like characters in a play or the spectacle in an opera, a reason to believe in "illusion," and thus always a source of joy.[20]

Nothing of these arrangements precluded a convent education. At seven or eight Du Châtelet could have been enrolled in one of the elite houses in Paris. The Benedictine Abbaye de Penthémenthe served the highest ranks of the nobility for a minimum of one thousand livres per year (this when the average laborer considered one livre a day a generous wage). The Ursulines, the other major teaching order for girls, defined their instructional goals in this way: "to teach the little girls Christian piety, the virtues and good morals, and the works and exercises appropriate to their sex." A Saint-Omer painting of girls in their convent school portrays one big room with children grouped by age, all soberly dressed in white-collared dark dresses, their "habits," each involved in a different activity. The Ursulines prided themselves on mixing play and study, so the members of the youngest group are engaged in a singing game, all in a circle, holding hands. The next in age receive more individual attention: one works on her embroidery, another spins, while two other girls look at a map with one of their teachers. The oldest sit in straight-backed chairs in a semicircle listening to a nun read, perhaps from one of the approved books, like the *Fables* of La Fontaine and Aesop, or a tragedy by one of France's great playwrights, such as *Athalie* by Racine. There is some evidence that Du Châtelet spent time in a nunnery— or *abbaye,* as it was called in France. A careful and credible nineteenth-century French local historian of Cirey, the Du Châtelet estate, identified Mme de Champbonin, her neighbor in Champagne, as an old friend from convent days.[21] A cousin, the future marquise de Créqui, received just this kind of upbringing.

One of Du Châtelet's own writings, her first intellectual project, indicated her disdain for a little girl's traditional education. In 1734 or 1735, in her late twenties, Du Châtelet embarked on her first translation, actually more of a retelling, of a book by Bernard Mandeville, a Dutch refugee to London. Mandeville's *Fable of the Bees,* with its assertion that the private vices rather than the virtues of its citizens explained the prosperity of a country, outraged contemporaries in England. That the book was banned in France did not stop Du Châtelet. Her "translator's preface," in addition to describing the role of translation and its proper conventions, raised questions about women's education. Why was it that, although women's and men's minds seemed so similar, only women were apparently "stopped by an invincible force" from using their intelligence? Why, she asked, had there been no great woman playwright, poet, historian, painter, scientist? Du Châtelet blamed the lack on the denial of education to her sex. "If I were king," she wrote in an early draft of her preface, "I would establish *collèges* for women."[22]

A *collège* was not a "college," as the spelling would suggest, but refers to the elite secondary schools for boys founded by the French Jesuits in the seventeenth century. Voltaire attended one of the most famous, Louis-le-Grand in Paris, from the time he was eight until just before his seventeenth birthday, and as an adult continued to correspond about metaphysical questions with two of his teachers, the masters of rhetoric and philosophy. Though bells and prayers defined the five or six hours of classes each day in this monasterylike setting, as they did in the convent schools, the education offered was very different. All subjects were taught in Latin: reading, writing, speaking, even mathematics. History, geography, and Euclid's geometry filled out the program of study. Young aristocrats destined for the military left at fifteen or sixteen to go to their own regiment, to their own tutors, or to one of Paris's academies in the *quartier* of Saint-Germain, where they perfected their horsemanship, fencing, and dancing. (In the seventeenth and eighteenth centuries, dancing was considered the way for young men to learn proper carriage and deportment.)[23] Those who stayed at the *collège*—typically, younger sons destined for a career in the church—would have continued for two more years, with studies of rhetoric, physics, and philosophy, including logic.

Did Du Châtelet's vehement attitude reflect that of her parents? Did they make less conventional choices at this point in their daughter's life when they noticed her remarkable intelligence?

A New Hypothesis

As regular participants in the intellectual culture of the period from 1680 to 1720, Du Châtelet's parents heard and perhaps took part in the arguments for and against a carefully delimited education for females, the continuation of the centuries-old *querelle des femmes*. This "argument about women" hinged on underlying premises about their "true" nature and how it affected their minds and bodies. Such traditional images of the female and their corollary, woman's preordained role, were as old as the Bible—as old as Aristotle, who described women's temperament as cool and wet, whereas men's was hot and dry. Thus for a woman a more languid, less excitable life was required, one defined by activities related to the men of her family, to whom she owed respect and obedience. This life dictated her education. The sixteenth-century French essayist Montaigne quoted an early duke of Brittany: "A woman was learned enough when she knew how to distinguish between her husband's shirt and his doublet." Although Montaigne appeared to agree with the traditional images of women and their nature, he also insisted that "males and females are cast in the same mold except for education and custom, the difference is not great." He railed against formal education and rote learning, and complimented the parents who did not send their daughters to a convent education, for "a girl who has escaped safe, bag and baggage, from a free schooling, inspires much more confidence than one who comes out safely from a severe prison-like school."[24]

Breteuil's inventory listed Montaigne among his books. What might the phrase "free schooling" have meant to Louis Nicholas and his wife? The Créqui memoir describes a scene at dinner that suggests this different approach to a daughter's education. Du Châtelet, though still a child, had the temerity to speak. She asked her mother, seated at the head of the grand dining table, "Which should one take as more certain, that Nebuchadnezzar turned into a beast, or Prince Chérie into a bird?" Froullay answered without hesitation, "Neither." Bordering on rudeness, her daughter spoke again: she "saw it in the Bible," usually an unimpeachable source in discussions with her mother. Froullay accepted the challenge to her authority but responded, "You never saw anything like that in the Bible." In a traditional noble household, this would have been sufficient to silence a child, but Froullay instructed the little girl to bring the Bible and show the place where she had found this description of Nebuchadnezzar. The little girl left the room, fetched the book, and proudly showed her doubting parent the reference to the time when the king, having gone mad, lived beastlike in the countryside, eating only grasses and allowing his hair and nails to grow. The insistent, stubborn questioning was characteristic of Du Châtelet as an adult. The mother's willingness to have her knowledge and authority tested, her apparent acceptance of her daughter's unorthodox behavior—this is just the kind of encouragement Du Châtelet must have received as a child.[25]

Voltaire once wrote a short dialogue between two women on the subject of education. Mélinde compliments her friend: "You are so reasonable for someone of your age." Sophronie accepts the praise and credits her mother for having believed her worthy of thinking for herself and able to make decisions about her own life. Since she was to live in society, her mother wanted her to learn there and not in a convent. Créqui credited her aunt with just this sentiment.[26] So, instead of contemplating long years of formal education at an *abbaye,* Froullay possibly viewed the convent as only a temporary place for her daughter's training. In the eighteenth century parents often brought girls one month and took them out the next. We know from Mme de Graffigny, a visitor at Cirey in the winter of 1738–39, that Du Châtelet treated her own daughter's convent stay in this cavalier fashion. Gabrielle-Pauline, at twelve years of age, came and went easily, leaving the nuns so that she could participate in Voltaire and Du Châtelet's theatrical productions. More than a third of the students even at the prestigious Ursuline and

Benedictine abbeys in Paris spent less than a year in the convent. Most parents seem to have viewed this time at an *abbaye* for one purpose only, to
prepare their daughters for their first communion. During a seven-week
stay, the Ursulines gave the girls an extra hour a day of catechism and arranged a general confession two days before the first communion.[27] Du
Châtelet and her Cirey neighbor Mme de Champbonin could have met in
such circumstances.

And the other aspects of Du Châtelet's education? Probably the growing
family retired in the summer—what eighteenth-century French courtiers
called *la belle saison* (the beautiful season)—to the estate at Preuilly. Coaches
and carts filled with trunks and boxes made what must have been at least a
two-day journey south from Paris, first on the main road to Orléans and
Blois, and then along single-track country roads. Perhaps Du Châtelet, at
nine or ten, eagerly joined in the lessons with her younger brother, Elisabeth-
Théodore, the only one still being educated at home. At five or six, he
was just the age when a bright little boy would customarily begin his lessons
with his *précepteur*. Breteuil had already decided on a church career for his
youngest son, so his education would have been more humanistic in content, including the reading of ancient and modern languages that characterized Du Châtelet's everyday knowledge as an adult. Perhaps their father had
hired a new tutor, or perhaps the abbé who had taught their two older
brothers returned to instruct them.[28]

On a particular summer day, while her father visited at a Caumartin
cousin's nearby château—where Breteuil and Voltaire are supposed to have
first met—and her mother supervised this second household while keeping
up with her correspondence, her reading, and her embroidery, the abbé
would have been instructing his two pupils: the little boy and the future
marquise Du Châtelet. He would drill them on their Latin declensions, listen to their recitations of Virgil's *Aeneid,* and correct their translations of
Cicero's letters from Latin into French. Another morning, Du Châtelet
might have had Euclid's theorems, propositions, and proofs to work through,
her special enthusiasm.[29] The day's lessons completed, she reached for her
own copy of Bernard le Bovier de Fontenelle's *Entretiens sur la pluralité des
mondes* (*Conversations on the Plurality of Worlds*), perhaps a gift from her father.
The description of Descartes's universe was clearly explained, and she probably laughed at the stupidity of the fictional marquise. Did she find most

exciting the idea of the infinite differences between all the possible universes? As an adult, she would speculate in her own works of science about these other worlds, hypothesize about multiple suns of different colors, and ponder the possibility that there could be someone just like herself living out an identical life.

The 1728 inventory of her father's possessions and property tells more about the château and the family's activities. The spruce bookcases in his bedroom had novels by Scarron, the *Fables* of La Fontaine, the *Essais* of Montaigne, and many other French and classical authors, there for him to read before he went to sleep, or for everyone to help pass the time when it was too cold or wet to go outside. Given her later love of theater, Du Châtelet might have insisted that her little brother learn scenes with her from the volumes of Corneille, and Racine, practicing the majestic cadences of alexandrine verse: the twelve syllables rising for six beats, then falling to the end of the line. The château had a room specifically for billiards, cards, and board games such as *trictrac,* always a favorite of Du Châtelet's when she was an adult. Learning these games was as important as acquiring other courtier's skills.[30]

Du Châtelet could have played with her father at the *trictrac* table. The board has the same markings as for backgammon; the counters move with the roll of the dice and can be eliminated from play by the opponent. But after that the game shifts in subtle and complex ways that require circuitous thinking and quick mathematical calculation. A "match" is twelve games of twelve points each. Rolls of the dice would have enabled our young player to gain points by moving her *jetons,* or counters, along the spaces on the board, but also because she saw other possible ways of moving them. These "virtual" moves, known as gaining points *par puissance* (by power), are, in fact, how the skilled player wins. Conversely, if there were multiple possible plays that she missed, points would go to her opponent. The little girl might have seized a strategic section of the board, counting up the points gained *par puissance,* and then watched in frustration as her father rolled the dice and won the match because her strategy proved naïve.[31]

Each fall Du Châtelet and Elisabeth-Théodore would have returned to Paris, to the family *hôtel* in the Place Royale. Their studies together could have continued. The center of the renovations their father made to no. 12 was the library, three rooms thrown together into one, looking out on the *place.* Once they were a bit older, Du Châtelet and her brother could have been given free access to its treasures. An eighteenth-century drawing by an anonymous artist, done in soft lines like a Watteau or a Fragonard, suggests such a scene: a boy, perhaps nine or ten, and a young girl, of fifteen or sixteen, both reading in the family library. Here Du Châtelet could continue to study the Roman authors, such as Virgil, Horace, Cicero, and Ovid. Voltaire insisted in his own memoirs that she could recite whole passages from their works, and also from Lucretius, whose *De rerum natura* (*On the Nature of the Universe*) might have introduced her to the idea of "atoms" as the basic unit of all matter. Was this when she first marked the poems she wanted her father's secretary to transcribe for her? One such extant copybook was probably begun by her father, and continued by Du Châtelet. Many of the verses come from collections of poetry that would have been in his library.[32]

Or perhaps the lessons ended when Elisabeth-Théodore reached ten or eleven and was sent to one of the prestigious *collèges* in Paris, such as Louis-le-Grand. Du Châtelet, at fifteen or sixteen, was old enough to participate in her mother and father's public life. Two rooms in the Hôtel Breteuil (including the dining room) were furnished for elaborate entertaining, with *fauteuils* covered in her father's favorite damask, a marble table, a tapestry-covered sofa, and crystal chandeliers. These would have been the sites for Louis Nicholas's *salon,* a concept that had originated early in the previous century when two women, a marquise and a successful novelist, calling themselves *les précieuses* (the valued or precious ones), established evenings when those they favored came together for conversation and pleasant, harmonious entertainment.[33]

The tradition of *les précieuses* continued into the era when Du Châtelet joined society. The *salon* of Anne-Thérèse de Marguenay de Courcelles, marquise de Lambert, began in 1705 and continued into the Regency era. On Wednesdays, at her *hôtel* on the rue de Richelieu, the *salonnière* welcomed everyone, providing guests were of a certain rank and profession. Tuesdays Lambert reserved for the male literary elite of Paris, the poets, playwrights, and *philosophes* (learned men interested in diverse subjects, from physics to a new verse form). The actress Mlle Lecouvreur and the classical scholar and translator Mme Dacier were among the few women invited to the gatherings. To the delight of Fontenelle, a regular participant in her Tuesday meetings, Lambert differentiated her *salon* from the others of the Regency period by prohibiting games and gambling. Even plays she considered too frivolous.[34] The few brief descriptions of Breteuil's *salon* suggest that he took the evenings at the marquise de Lambert as his model. The baron's guests, courtiers like the duc de Saint-Simon and the marquis de Dangeau, met with *les gens des lettres,* the men of letters from the two royal academies, the Académie française and the Académie royale des sciences, on Thursdays. A host would be careful not to set a time that conflicted with the *salons* already established.[35] For the young Du Châtelet, talk of her father's *salon* would have been an exciting part of her "life in the world." In other ways, however, as her childhood came to an end, her days probably returned to a more conventional pattern.

Is there other evidence for this final hypothesis about her unorthodox upbringing and education? Du Châtelet herself, in her translator's preface for Mandeville's *Fable,* offered a series of memories to her readers. She explained that there was a time in her life when she turned to "les choses frivoles," frivolous things. As a result, she neglected "mon esprit et mon entendement" (my genius and my understanding). Thus, she suggested studies begun and then halted, intellectual challenges enjoyed and then ignored.[36] Her parents allowed the unorthodox until the future marquise, no longer a child, had obligations to her family that had to be fulfilled—traditional obligations, which she embraced and did not question. By the early 1720s, she would be preparing for the next stage of her life: her betrothal and marriage. At fifteen or sixteen, she had become the subject of active negotiations. Just as Louis Nicholas had raised the status of his sons and of future generations of his family through the manipulation of his connections at court and the purchase of their military commands, so he would use these assets to the same purpose for his daughter. In the end, the network created by the joining of his wife's and his families meant that a mere 150,000-livre dowry purchased a marquis from one of the most ancient lineages in Europe for their Gabrielle Emilie.

Bethrothal and Marriage to the Marquis Du Châtelet-Lomont

Before her marriage, Du Châtelet knew the name of her future husband, his lineage, and his place in her world. In every other way, Florent-Claude, marquis Du Châtelet-Lomont, would have been a complete stranger. He was a very appropriate match: an older man, a colonel in one of the king's regiments, a marquis from one of the oldest noble families of Lorraine. The arrangements had probably been initiated through cousins of her mother's who had married into the highest echelons of the nobility in this quasi-independent region of eastern France. A recent popular biographer imagines the old comte de Lomont and the baron de Breteuil discussing it like a business deal. Although there is no evidence for such a scene taking place in 1725, it could easily have happened in that manner, for both families and the two participants viewed the arrangements in this way.[37]

Du Châtelet's actions in the early years of her life with Florent-Claude, marquis Du Châtelet, indicate that the marriage and its attendant privileges pleased her. She signed her letters "Breteuil Du Chastelet"—Breteuil for her father's family, Du Chastelet (the eighteenth-century spelling, before the circumflex replaced the "s") for the new family to which she had been given—that is, when she felt the need to sign them at all. In the portrait engravings that accompanied different editions of her books, she claimed all that this union represented. She identified herself by her full name, Gabrielle Emilie le Tonnelier de Breteuil, then as wife to the marquis du Châtelet-Lomont ("Lomont" to distinguish him from other branches of the family), and with all of his titles: "baron de Cirey, &c lieutenant general of the King's Armies, general of Semur, grand Bally of Artois and Sarre Louis." Thus, she preserved the prestige of her maiden name, the associations with her father's position, and the status she had gained from her husband. Of course, her correspondents would have known the name even before opening the letter, having recognized her seal in the orange-red wax pressed across the last fold, one of three, that turned the sheet of her stationery into its own envelope. The seal displayed her coat of arms, a combination of her father's and her husband's heraldic devices: a sparrow hawk on the right for her father's family, a band of three fleur-de-lys on the left for her husband, and the many-pointed crown of a marquise over the emblazoned shield. The combination of these symbols indicated her new place in eighteenth-century French society.[38]

Her culture had one word to describe these social facts: the concept of "*état*" neatly incorporates all that English requires four or five words to describe. "Estate" is the usual translation, referring to the way the kingdom of France divided its subjects into three broad categories: churchmen, the nobility, and everyone else. Neither Du Châtelet nor her husband questioned this arrangement and its inherent inequities, nor did anyone in their families. Within the ranks of the nobility, there were other distinctions, gradations that Du Châtelet learned from her mother and father. One successful courtier's memoirs identified eight levels, from the royal family to artists and "good citizens" who had been ennobled.[39] Historians of eighteenth-century France usually describe only two levels. Du Châtelet's father, the baron de Breteuil, represented the lesser nobility, who had risen to elite status through their service to the crown. He belonged to a group the marquise de Créqui disdainfully referred to as the *noblesse de robe.* Louis XIV had rewarded Breteuil with pensions, offices, and the right to buy lands carrying a title. In contrast, her husband enjoyed his titles and privileges by right of birth. He belonged to the *noblesse d'épée,* and to its highest ranks. Florent-Claude, marquis Du Châtelet-Lomont, came from one of the few hundred families who could claim direct descent in the male line back to the twelfth-century princes and nobles who had fought in the Holy Land against the Muslims.[40] As a member of this elite of the elite, her husband's family had been granted "the honors of the court," the right to attend the king, to approach the monarch, and to speak to him, a privilege jealously guarded and given in principle to only the select few, despite the thousands who thronged Versailles and Fontainebleau when Louis XV and his queen, Maria Leszczyńska, were in residence. By negotiating a marriage into the *noblesse d'épée,* the baron and baronne de Breteuil had gained these privileges for their daughter.

So significant were unions of this sort, the mixing of blood from two different *états,* that in the previous reign Louis XIV had often insisted upon giving final approval. Courtiers could be vicious about mocking a marriage in which money appeared to buy bloodlines. In 1733, the author of the *Journal de la cour et de Paris,* one of the newsletters that circulated in Paris and out to the provinces, described "a daughter of finance" metamorphosing herself into a "woman of the best class." In contrast, the future husband needed no metamorphosis. The men of the *noblesse d'épée,* like royalty, were a "race" apart. Membership passed in the male line, a father's semen imparting to his sons the warrior skills of the ancient Franks.[41] As a result, the sons of these families were guaranteed access to the highest places in the cavalry, infantry, and navy. The marquis Du Châtelet and his brother both served as officers, each rising to the highest ranks in the king's service. In turn, his son

with Gabrielle Emilie le Tonnelier de Breteuil, as the inheritor of this powerful lineage, went into the elite king's company of the Royal Musketeers as
a matter of course, a troop in the "gift of the king" reserved for the male
offspring of the highest ranks of the nobility.

Given this lineage, what caused the scion of this distinguished family to
decide on a daughter of a lesser *état* for his heir? The comte de Lomont had
decided to follow the well-established tradition. He exchanged a "beautiful
genealogy," as contemporaries described it, for money and connections.
The thirty-year-old marquis came with few financial resources. As was the
practice, the comte de Lomont had been able to purchase an infantry regiment for his eldest son to command, who then arranged, in a manner characteristic of his sense of family and loyalty, for each of his two younger
brothers to become captains in his regiment and thus to begin their own
military careers. The only significant property the marquis brought to the
marriage came from his mother, Cirey, a small château and lands in Champagne, in the eastern part of France, hectares of farm and grazing land,
forests, and iron forges that generated a very modest yearly income. The
Versailles courtier the duc de Luynes summed up the situation neatly: "M.
le marquis Du Châtelet-Lomont, homme de grande condition, mais qui
n'est pas riche [M. le marquis Du Châtelet-Lomont is a man of the highest
rank, but is not rich]."[42]

Traditionally, the couple never saw each other until called in to give
their signatures to the marriage contract negotiated by their fathers and
turned into legal documents by notaries. The document, carefully preserved
among Du Châtelet's papers, tells much about the ways in which the nobility dealt with these important financial arrangements. Breteuil promised the
Du Châtelet family a total of 150,000 livres, payable in installments from the
day of the "célébration" of the marriage, the day when the families gathered
for the nuptial mass celebrating the union. The schedule of payments
stretched many years into the future, until after the death of both her parents. The contract also provided for the young woman in case her husband
predeceased her, a real possibility given his age and profession. In the event
of her husband's death, Du Châtelet, as tradition dictated, received a
"dower," in this case, six thousand livres a year to support herself and the
children that it was assumed would result from the match. She also had access to half of what French customary law called the *communauté des biens,* or

"community property," a fund to which both fathers contributed substantial sums. Most significant for the immediate future of this new family, Lomont had sweetened the alliance with the presentation to his son of one of the military offices he held, the governorship of Semur-en-Auxois in Burgundy (and thus a formal residence), and a place in provincial society for the new couple.[43] Perhaps more important than these contractual agreements, the Breteuils brought their royal connections to the match. Any military promotion for any man, regardless of his birth and service, came at the recommendation of the minister for war, and at the whim of the king. Fortunately for a military family like the Du Châtelets, in 1725, the future bride's cousin François-Victor le Tonnelier de Breteuil, marquis de Fontenay-Trésigny, was secretary of war to the young King Louis XV.

The eighteen-year-old Du Châtelet would have had a new elegant dress for the signing ceremony, an event complete with invitations, small gifts, and a reception afterward for the guests. On that June day, a notary read out the articles of the agreement to the family members assembled to witness the ceremony. Summoned into the room, Du Châtelet would have been allowed to exchange a few pleasantries with her prospective husband. Then, by the simple movement of the quill and ink on the document, by signing her name, the baron de Breteuil's daughter became a marquise. A week later, on the twelfth of June, in Paris's main cathedral of Notre Dame, the bishop de Bourbon, one of the highest-ranking clerics in the kingdom, performed their wedding mass and gave the nuptial benediction. The marquis would have been resplendent in his full-dress uniform as a colonel of the Hénaut regiment. Du Châtelet would have worn the complete regalia of the *habit de cour*.[44]

~❧~

As for marriage itself, neither Du Châtelet nor her husband would have had any romantic illusions about the purpose or the nature of their union.[45] This was to be a practical working liaison to advance the interests of the new family. Later, in her *Discours sur le bonheur* (Discourse on Happiness) and in her letters, Du Châtelet would write of how important "passion" and "love" were to her, but no one of her rank and era expected these in marriage. Mutual respect, shared duties, and obligations characterized a couple's relationship. Perhaps companionship, but nothing more, and certainly nothing exceptional from her husband as her first sexual partner. Instead, as Montaigne explained, husbands should exemplify moderation when having intercourse with their wives and never go "beyond the barriers of reason." If Du Châtelet allowed her own sexual experiences to serve as models for her prose, then the coupling with her army-officer husband was quick and rough. Mandeville's *Fable of the Bees* gave her the opportunity to translate the Dutch doctor's cynical views of man's natural lust and to embellish them with her own additions. She drew for her readers the details of a French wedding night, perhaps much like her own. Parents and family accompanied the couple to the bed they would share for the first time; the bride's virginity was guaranteed by her education in shame and modesty. Du Châtelet continued: "The mother puts her (daughter) in the arms of her lover and strongly recommends that her daughter suffer with resignation all that the desires of her lover will require of her." The young marquise Du Châtelet would have accepted these realities, including the idea that she would seek pleasures with men other than her husband, as he would with other women. She certainly understood that her first responsibility as a wife was the birthing of children, what she later referred to in her translation of Mandeville's *Fable* as "the propagation of the species."[46]

As for so much of this part of Du Châtelet's life, even information about her husband, Florent-Claude, marquis Du Châtelet-Lomont, must be pieced together. There are his military records, preserved with those of his contemporaries in the military archives at the Château de Vincennes, and the brief mentions of him in the letters of his wife and their friends. He was twelve years her senior—considered a suitable difference in ages, for a husband was meant to be a guiding influence in the life of his young bride. He had already seen active service during the last war of Louis XIV—just eighteen then himself—as a member of the first company of the Royal Musketeers, and then as an infantry lieutenant. He led the rigorous life of a military officer from 1713 until he resigned from active service as one of eleven commanders of the Royal Army in 1749, like his father awarded first the Croix Saint-Louis, the *cordon rouge,* and then the Grand Croix Saint-Louis, France's highest military decoration. Letters that the marquis wrote to the king and the royal ministers to justify the first of these military distinctions for himself show that he placed himself in danger willingly but was aggrieved when he thought that the verbal promise of the king, his service, seniority, and birth would not be honored as a matter of course.[47]

He took his peacetime duties as seriously. Legal documents among Du Châtelet's papers included instructions to their notary to buy property and to negotiate loans and annuities with his relatives, friends, and employees. He spent time on his seigneurial lands in Champagne, usually at the beginning of the new year, when tenants owed traditional payments and services. In addition, he made periodic trips to Versailles and Fontainebleau, and to the court of Lorraine, maintaining the lineage's ties to their ancient feudal overlords. There are no portraits or physical descriptions of the marquis, only phrases and sentences that others wrote in passing to give glimpses of his character and demeanor. By all accounts, he was not an imposing figure. A visitor to Cirey in the winter of 1738–39 mentioned that he stuttered when he performed in impromptu plays with his wife, Voltaire, and their guests. Was this characteristic, or just an indication of his nervousness in an unfamiliar role? Du Châtelet often mentioned him in her letters to others, commenting on his good health, his good spirits. When bemoaning that she could not travel to England, however, she gave this picture of her husband's limitations: he would not consent "to a trip for pure curiosity; he doesn't know English, and he has not read the letters and verses of Lord Hervey."[48]

Despite his lack of interest in what she was reading, the marquis never wavered in his support of her unorthodox choices. When the titular head of her family, Du Châtelet's cousin François-Victor le Tonnelier de Breteuil, took offense at the inclusion of Voltaire in her household, seeing him as a provocative bourgeois poet and playwright, the marquis joined in the writer's defense, appealing to the king's principal minister, Cardinal André-Hercule de Fleury, on Voltaire's behalf. He often delivered Voltaire's manuscripts to publishers, and took instructions to the abbé Moussinot, the poet's man of business in Paris. Although Du Châtelet might joke flirtatiously about the "conjugal yoke" with one of her Parisian companions, she knew, as she explained to another of Voltaire's friends and protectors, the comte d'Argental, that she could always rely on her husband. "Happily, I am sure of m. du [Châtelet], he is the most respectable and most estimable man I know." He seems to have personified the ideal of her parents' generation, the *honnête homme,* the man of complete honor, civility, and discretion.[49] In addition, the marquis remained content with the differences that gradually became evident between his exuberant, gifted wife and himself. He proudly boasted of her *dissertation* on fire to the court at Lunéville, and he took her *Institutions de physique* to the printer for her. He never remarried, though he was only fifty-four in 1749, when she died.

Family and Children

The first years of Du Châtelet's marriage, from 1725 to 1733, represented the only extended period she spent with the marquis before his military duties took him regularly on campaign. She was probably already pregnant at the end of September 1725, when she and her husband made the two-to-three-day journey from Paris to Burgundy and their ceremonial *entrée* into the city of Semur. As wife to the new military governor, she sat by her husband's side in a grand carriage while drummers on the ramparts signaled their imminent arrival. Peasants, artisans, women and men, children, all crowded the bridges and streets of the ancient fortified town. The carriages and baggage train halted on the edge of the city to receive the greetings of the mayor, and for a special presentation of the relics of the town's most important church, including a ring believed to have belonged to the Virgin. The couple then proceeded to the castle at the head of a long cortège of local notables. A formal ball and a fireworks display, for which her cousin the minister of war was billed, finished the festivities.[50]

For much of these first years in Semur, Du Châtelet would have been busy with family. Two of her husband's sisters and a brother of hers married. Her father and her father-in-law died. The documents listed in the inventory done at the time of her death suggest many hours of family negotiations and arrangements, for all four events would have involved the transfer of money and property. Her sense of responsibility for the Breteuils and her obligations to her near relatives only increased into the 1730s. Her two elder brothers did not survive to realize their father's dreams. René-Alexandre, heir to the lands and title, died at twenty-two, in 1720. Charles-Auguste, the new heir, married to a wealthy Normandy government administrator's daughter, guaranteed the lineage when his son was born in March 1730, but he, too, died suddenly, a year later, leaving the family with a one-year-old as the heir to the Breteuil titles and lands. Du Châtelet's younger brother, Elisabeth-Théodore, now an abbé, became the boy's guardian; the young widow remarried, and her little girl was destined for a convent. In these new circumstances, Du Châtelet took on much of the responsibility for her mother and siblings. It was she who rushed to be with the aging Froullay when she was ill in 1734 and 1735. The dowager baronne retired to Créteil on the outskirts of Paris, and lived to be seventy, dying in the beginning of August 1740. Du Châtelet also acted as an advocate for her younger brother. She described Elisabeth-Théodore as "mon ami intime," "my intimate friend," and wrote on his behalf to her friend the comte d'Argental, nephew to the powerful Cardinal de Tencin. (In fact, her brother did well on his own, acquiring lucrative ecclesiastical posts, including, eventually, his own bishopric.) She even concerned herself with her father's illegitimate daughter's claim to an inheritance in 1736. Du Châtelet defended the fifty-year-old Michelle—who had lived her life in a convent—against François-Victor's efforts to silence this cause célèbre. The Paris parlement awarded the unfortunate woman a settlement six years later.[51]

These were also Du Châtelet's childbearing years. Her daughter, Gabrielle-Pauline, was born barely a year after her marriage, June 30, 1726. A daughter would be hailed as the means to new alliances, but, most important, the young wife had proved her ability to carry a pregnancy successfully to term. She gave birth to Florent-Louis Du Châtelet, the son to carry on the lineage, a little over a year later, at noon on the twentieth of November 1727, according to his baptismal record. A second son, born in 1733, in theory guaranteed the line. The frequency of the first two pregnancies suggests that birth control, even the usual method of withdrawal, was never considered. Du Châtelet has left no record of her feelings nor any account of her health during her first three pregnancies. Women took to wearing the robe volante made popular by the marquise de Montespan, Louis XIV's maîtresse-en-titre. With no waist, and big pleats of fabric in both the front and back of the gown, it flowed over the petticoats and paniers to make a very graceful image.[52] The births seem to have gone without incident. Like her mother, she would have been attended by the women of her husband's family, a midwife, and servants. She might have called for herbal teas, tisanes, to calm her and perhaps dull the pain of the contractions. The midwife cut the umbilical cord and tied it off with twine, or perhaps a heavy silk cord for the child of such an illustrious family.

Maids took charge of Du Châtelet's new infant daughter, and later of each of her two sons. Their father, the marquis, took them to the parish church to be baptized, customarily on the day of their birth. Du Châtelet never considered breastfeeding, but whereas most infants were sent to live with a *nourrice,* evidence suggests that the marquise followed a different practice and had the wet nurse live in the household or in lodgings nearby. Her second son was with her in Paris when he died in the late summer of 1734. She herself supervised his care during his illness. Answering a letter from a friend, she wrote, "I have lost the younger of my sons," and called the event "one of the misfortunes attached to the state of motherhood." She was, she explained, surprised at how distressed and angry she felt. This led her to speculate that "the feelings of nature" must be stronger in us than we would have suspected. Such deaths were not unusual, however. Regardless of wealth and social rank, a quarter of Europe's infants died in their first year, another quarter by their fifth birthday. Even so, Du Châtelet kept a *vermeil* baby spoon (gilded silver) with her dinner set of twelve settings of knives, forks, and spoons. The toddler who died must have been the last child to use it.[53]

❧

Du Châtelet seems to have had mixed views about the education of her daughter, Gabrielle-Pauline. Though she had bemoaned the lack of a *collège* for women, she felt protective of her daughter; a nineteenth-century local historian of Cirey places her at the convent de la Pitié, near Joinville, at the age of seven, in 1733–34, and other sources have her there again at least part of the time in 1738–39. This sentiment is also reflected in comments Du Châtelet made in her *Examens de la Bible.* There she expressed outrage at the story of Salome, that anyone would give "a little girl the head of a man on a plate to reward her for dancing well." Mme de Graffigny, a distant relative of the marquis and a visitor to Cirey in 1738, left a clear image of Gabrielle-Pauline: she "[is] not pretty, but she speaks like her mother and with all the wit and intelligence possible." During the coach ride from the convent in Joinville, she had memorized her part in the play that the household was to perform. Like her mother, she was tall. Graffigny continued her account to François-Antoine Devaux, her friend from her days as a courtier in Lorraine: the twelve-year-old "is learning Latin, likes to read, she will not fail her blood."[54] The last phrase, in all likelihood, summed up her parents' plans for their daughter: a marriage and the creation of new alliances to advance the lineage. Indeed, at sixteen, Gabrielle-Pauline married very well. Her husband, Alfonso, duc de Montenero-Carafa, was a member of an ancient Neapolitan family, with a sixteenth-century pope in his genealogy. She rose to become a *dame d'honneur* to the queen of Naples. Du Châtelet's father and mother would have been very pleased.

꩜

As might be expected, the story is more complete for Du Châtelet's elder son, Florent-Louis. His mother kept among her papers his baptismal certificate which duly recorded that both eminent grandfathers were in attendance, as well as other Du Châtelet and Froullay relatives, acting as godparents to the new heir to their bloodlines.[55] Once Florent-Louis reached educable age, Du Châtelet's letters and writings tell much about her supervision of those given responsibility for his later education, and her direct participation. Although his path in life was predetermined—a military career—and his privileges were guaranteed, for members of the eighteenth-century nobility this did not diminish the significance of the early years. Du Châtelet insisted on a rigorous education, for she saw her son as having "a pretty enough little soul to cultivate." The best inclinations of a young son had to be nurtured: the graces and sophistication of the courtier, the respect owed to parents and family. These qualities identified the *honnête homme,* the demeanor that Du Châtelet so admired in her husband. In the preface to her *Institutions de physique,* Du Châtelet elaborated on her ideal of education. Like her favorite essayist, Montaigne, she hated the idea of the pedant mindlessly filling his memory. Instead, as she explained in the preface, addressed to her son, she wished to "inspire you with love of the Sciences, & the desire to cultivate your reason." In the training of "his mind," she hoped he would experience the amusements and delights of learning. Too soon he would turn to "the passions & the pleasures" of his age, and "ambition will take possession of your soul."[56]

In 1735, Florent-Louis was eight and required a tutor, a *précepteur.* Voltaire suggested that Du Châtelet employ abbé Michel Linant, his current young protégé. As a cleric, Linant met her husband's requirements, and so the marquise brought the abbé to Cirey when she moved her family and household to the Du Châtelet country estate. She paid Linant a nice yearly salary, one hundred écus (just over three hundred livres), and gave him his own lackey (the eighteenth-century word for the lowliest of male employees); though he slept in her son's room, he enjoyed much better arrangements than any other servant. In addition, Du Châtelet accorded him a higher status within the household, in that he had *dîner*—the main meal of the day—with his pupil, and with the marquis when he was at Cirey. When asked, she brought his sister into the household as her *femme de chambre*. Normally, Linant would have served her son until it came time for him to "enter into the world" and leave for one of the military academies in Paris.[57]

Linant's letters show that nothing worked out as anyone expected. The marquise insisted on regular hours with set times for meals, as essential for her son's health. The young Florent-Louis had much energy and no desire to concentrate on his studies. Linant found his situation impossible. He had hoped that Cirey would be a pleasant retreat where he could write, but, as he complained to Pierre Robert le Cornier de Cideville, Voltaire's old friend from Rouen, this "little boy hanging all day at my belt" had to be watched over. He might fall down a well in the summer, "or in the winter into the fire." Linant wanted to be "more friend than tutor," and disliked "having to teach him things that he doesn't learn at all and doesn't want to learn." He must have surprised Cideville, his early patron and the one who had originally recommended him to Voltaire, when he wrote that he was "angry to be paid to make [the boy] unhappy." Given Linant's attitude, it is not surprising that Du Châtelet noticed his inadequacies. She soon discovered that she had to tutor the abbé in Latin so that he could teach the boy. From as early as February 1736, she, too, had complained to Cideville. She found the abbé without imagination, without invention, and ignorant. "This will always be a very mediocre man," she concluded. When she finally dismissed him and his sister in December 1737, she, the marquis, her brother, Voltaire, and his Paris friends tried to find a replacement, but without success. A solution did not present itself until June 1740, when Florent-Louis went into the Royal Musketeers, a few months before his thirteenth birthday.[58]

This series of events meant that Du Châtelet must have been her son's principal tutor for almost three years, especially in Brussels (where she had gone to defend her husband's claims to properties in Flanders), for she took both children with her. On the title page of the *Institutions,* Du Châtelet

chose an engraving that seems an uncharacteristically public gesture of affection for someone of her rank. It portrays a mother dove returning to her
nest to feed her single offspring. A ribbon banner surrounds the scene with
the Latin inscription: "Good luck, my son, raise your eyes to the stars."
Thus, she offered encouragement both for his continuing studies of the universe and for his rise within society. Later, after he was already a nineteen-
year-old lieutenant in the king's army, she completed her *Discours* on
happiness in which she listed the many possible careers open to men, open
to the son of a privileged lineage: war, government, diplomacy.[59] In fact, he
would follow all three paths: rising to the rank of maréchal de camp in the
army; serving as ambassador to England in the 1780s; and becoming one of
Louis XVI's close advisers at the end of his reign.

Households and Finances

In the first years of their marriage, Du Châtelet and the marquis made Semur
their principal residence. Since her husband's mother was dead, she must
have supervised all the details of the household, which included her father-
in-law and, until their marriages, her two sisters-in-law. On the occasions
when she or the marquis went to Paris, friends and relatives accommodated
the couple. They could live with her family at the Hôtel Bretcuil in the Place
Royale, or in the *hôtel* maintained by her husband's family. For her lying-in
when Gabrielle-Pauline was born, Du Châtelet chose the house of her husband's cousin and fellow officer in the Army of the Rhine, the marquis Du
Châtelet-Clémont. His wife, Marie Catherine Armande de Richelieu, sister
to the duc de Richelieu, one of Louis XV's favorite courtiers, expected family members from the provinces to visit and to remain for considerable
lengths of time. On other occasions, later in the 1730s, when Cirey had
become their principal residence, Du Châtelet stayed at the duc's *hôtel* in
the Place Royale, and her husband with her mother at Créteil. From 1738 to
1742, the marquis probably joined her and Voltaire at the *hôtel* she rented in
the rue de la Grosse Tour in Brussels.

At the end of September 1739, perhaps with expectations from the prospective inheritance of the Flanders properties, Du Châtelet and the marquis contemplated buying their own *hôtel* in Paris. As she explained to

d'Argental, "The care that I owe to my family makes it indispensable." The negotiations for the Palais Lambert, famous in seventeenth- and eighteenth-century guidebooks for its elegant design and elaborate interiors, continued into 1742. Du Châtelet watched the terms change, but, as she explained to a friend of Voltaire, "it is mr du Chastellet who will decide all." In fact, she never lived there. Though the marquis purchased the property for two hundred thousand livres, he sold it soon after. Instead, in 1742, acting on her husband's behalf, the marquise leased a more modest residence, a three-storied *hôtel* on the rue Traversière for twenty-two hundred livres a year.[60]

Houses had no numbers, but legal documents identified her *hôtel* as 13, rue Traversière–Saint-Honoré. Neither the *hôtel* nor the part of the street she lived on exists today; they disappeared in Baron Haussman's remodeling of Paris and the nineteenth-century creation of the Avenue de l'Opéra. From the 1739 map of Paris, the Plan de Turgot, it is possible to guess with some certainty at the location. From the rue du Clos-Georgeau, turn up the rue Traversière. On the left-hand side of the street is a continuous row of attached *hôtels* built around a number of enclosed courtyards. Du Châtelet's, like the others on the block, was U-shaped, with the arms of the U perpendicular to the street. In her *appartement* some rooms faced a small walled garden, others a main courtyard of the complex.[61]

From another document, much of the interior and the details of how she lived can be surmised, for, as with her father, notaries made an inventory of all she possessed when she died. They walked into every room, even the cellars. They valued the meters of fabric in the *commodes* (bureaux), counted the china service of fifty-seven plates and the dozens of damask napkins in the armoires and corner cupboards. They noted the number of linen sheets, satin covers, feather bolsters, and square pillows; counted the chandeliers, the candlesticks, the curtains with their rods and rings; and listed every piece of furniture, including the *chaises de commodité* (the household's toilets). According to the inventory, Du Châtelet's daily life and her tastes were rather opulent.

The inventory also gives an indication of the numbers of servants needed to maintain it all. The name Joachim François Pierre De La Croix, her *intendant de la maison,* appears on almost all of the marquis's and marquise's legal documents, including the inventory, from the time they were first married. He not only supervised the other servants but also set up accommodations for the household as Du Châtelet moved from place to place. In the late 1740s, a couple, Marguerite and Louis La Font, served the household's needs. Du Châtelet probably paid twenty to thirty sous per day to the next rank of servants, such as her *maître d'hôtel* (when she employed one), the cook, and her *femme de chambre*. They in turn gave orders to the lackeys and sculleries who performed the more menial daily tasks. These would include the *femme de change* who swept, dusted, cleaned, brushed, and polished the floors, marquetry tables, tapestry hangings, taffeta curtains, and brass chandeliers and candelabra in Du Châtelet's main room for entertaining.

With ten sous, or half a livre, the average daily wage for a common laborer, the relative stability, along with the possibility of food, lodging, and clothing, made even such arduous work seem attractive to Parisians and to the young women and men who came in from the countryside. The marquise's *femme de chambre,* her personal maid, slept on a cot in the small room on the mezzanine in Du Châtelet's *appartement.* Those lower in the hierarchy of this small world shared the dormitorylike room on the top floor with its five chairs, single armoire, one chamber pot, one camp bed, and two other beds of simple wood frames with rope webbing, thin mattresses, and wool blankets. They had a small Dutch oven that burned charcoal to keep them warm. The groom, who cared for the horses and tack, had a similar cot and bedding in the stable. The coachman, who both drove and maintained the two *berlines,* or carriages, probably lived elsewhere. In addition to their wages, the higher servants expected to make extra income out of their duties: the *maître d'hôtel* earned a percentage on provisions brought into the house (the origin of the "baker's dozen" of thirteen); the cook had the right to sell the grounds from the morning *café,* which, added to milk, sold for two sous a cup to laborers on their way to work. The *femme de chambre* had the right to her mistress's cast-off clothing and old linens. Servants at every level had another advantage: the marquise, as was the common practice, paid their *capitation,* the tax that everyone in France owed, regardless of rank. Still, the wages remained a small part of Du Châtelet's expenses; just three 1749 bills—to her enameler, a cabinetmaker, and the craftsman doing inlay work for her—totaled the equivalent of a valet's wages for an entire year.

Approximately every ten days, the courtyard of an eighteenth-century *hôtel* would be filled with activity. The big wooden doors to the street opened to admit the day laborers, hired for a few sous, with no privileges or perquisites, who did the most distasteful tasks necessary to maintain the luxurious life of even a moderately wealthy family like this one. Laundresses would be heating large tubs of water on open fires, into which they dumped all the household linens, the sheets, bolster covers, cotton *matelets* (covers), petticoats, calico curtains, shirts, chemises, napkins, tablecloths—all the washable items the staff could gather together. Women of Du Châtelet's *état* wore no underclothing, and, given the difficulty of maneuvering their skirts over an oval chamber pot, or sitting on a *chaise de commodité,* customarily relieved themselves where they stood. Other women, assisted by men—the lackeys—would do all the heavy, messy labor. Fireplace ashes needed to be taken away, wood carried upstairs, and fires reset. Water buckets had to be filled and carried from the hand pump in the courtyard to rooms throughout the residence, from the ground to the top floor, for washing, cooking, and cleaning. In winter, the buckets left full of water froze in the night.[62]

What was the marquise Du Châtelet's attitude toward this household? Like her husband, like her parents and his, she took those she employed for granted and, though rarely alone, noticed them more when they annoyed her than when they pleased her. Du Châtelet believed herself a reasonable and generous employer; even when she dismissed an employee, such as Linant, she wrote a favorable reference and solicited friends to assist him in finding a new position. She demanded absolute loyalty and appropriate respect, despised laziness, and expected servants to function without her continual intervention, as she had much more important occupations to attend to.[63] One of her servants from the 1740s, Sébastien Longchamps, left stories of his years in her employ. In all likelihood, his sister, Du Châtelet's *femme de chambre,* arranged for his post in her household. Longchamps claimed in his memoir to have worked at the court of Lorraine, but this had not prepared him for Du Châtelet's utter disregard. He was shocked the day she rang for him first thing in the morning to receive orders for the household. He dutifully appeared in her bedroom just as his sister had finished adjusting the bed curtains. Du Châtelet stepped down, took off her chemise, and put on the new one held ready for her. Embarrassed to see his employer "like a nude statue," he turned his face away and did not dare look at her. His sister's advice, that he should behave as if he had seen nothing, proved impossible for him to follow on another occasion when Du Châtelet rang: the marquise instructed him to bring the water heating in front of the fire and add it to her rapidly cooling bath.[64]

Longchamps described the sequence of events: he picked up the pitcher, he noticed that the water in the tub was completely clear, that when she parted her legs he could see "toute sa Nature" (a euphemism for her genitals); he blushed and turned his head. Du Châtelet, dismayed at his seeming incompetence in fulfilling such a simple task, ordered him to "be careful . . . you are going to burn me." In the hands of Longchamps's editor, with his embellishments, and some modern historians, with their own retellings, this incident reads like a tale of a noblewoman's promiscuity and abandon. In fact, it tells more about the character of a valet than of a marquise. She simply acted as any noble would who lived in a world where there was no privacy from one's servants. On another occasion, Longchamps told of being called upon to serve his mistress and her friends at a country outing. He remembered one woman's attitude: she "appeared to make no difference between me and the bouillon that I carried in my hand."

≈≈≈

How did Du Châtelet and her husband pay for all of this? How did they juggle their connections and their finances to maintain and improve the wealth, position, and authority of their family? Du Châtelet's accounts have no obvious columns for salary, income, bills, and expenses. And their expenses were considerable. From 1730 to 1749, they maintained a noble style of living in Paris and Versailles, at Cirey, and in Brussels, including the cost of clothing, servants, horses, and carriages. They had the expenses of the company that until 1738 the marquis recruited, armed, provisioned, and housed; they paid for their daughter's convent and for their son's education and the beginnings of his military training. And these were only the obvious costs of living for a noble family.[65] In her *Discours* on happiness, an essay she began after a decade of marriage, and, later, in the preface to her *Institutions de physique,* she suggested the financial difficulties: "What pains and what cares one takes every day in the uncertain hope of procuring honors and augmenting the fortune of one's children!" She also explained how she tried to make peace with these hopes and travails: "One of the great secrets of happiness is to moderate one's desires & to love the things that one possesses." She wrote of this in connection with one's ambitions, but also in connection with one's fortune. "One is only [made] happy by desires [that have been] satisfied; one must then permit oneself to desire only the things that one can obtain without too much care & work, & this is a point on which we can do much for our own happiness."[66]

Moderating one's desires to fit a moderate fortune: the figures from the notary's accounting at the time of her death in 1749 suggest this was her situation. In eighteenth-century France, about 13 percent of the nobility, roughly thirty-five hundred families principally from outside of Paris, were dependent for their main income on the revenues from their provincial lands, anywhere from ten to fifty thousand livres annually. This is a financial profile that fits Du Châtelet and her husband almost exactly. Cirey, with its lands, forests, and iron forges, and the small properties in other parts of France that they inherited, gave them a revenue of at least 20,500 livres a year, but the records are incomplete. They could count on the marquis's pension for his service in the Royal Army, but otherwise all was uncertainty. For example, when Marc-Antoine Honoré, marquis Du Châtelet de Trichâteau, made his cousin the marquis his heir to his Flanders properties, the assignment was contested.[67]

Even when title to lands and manorial rights had been enjoyed for generations, members of the nobility like the Du Châtelets did not collect the revenues themselves, but "farmed out" the task to someone else. This practice created other problems. From 1740 to 1744, when Pierre Chretien had the lease for their lands around Cirey, they saw almost none of that revenue and had to institute proceedings against him. Extraordinary expenses could take all that had been carefully accumulated. Between 1728 and 1740, their marriage settlement and the deaths of their fathers and of Du Châtelet's mother all gave them a considerable amount of capital, perhaps as much as two hundred thousand livres. But when the marquis inherited his father's lands, he inherited obligations to his brother and two sisters. Each rise in military rank advanced the marquis's pay—to twelve thousand livres a year by 1748, when he had become a lieutenant general—but entailed attendance at Versailles to wait on the appropriate ministers to obtain it, thus adding more expenses. The couple's success in the 1740s only brought more extraordinary expenditure: seventy thousand livres for their daughter's marriage settlement, thirty thousand livres for their son's first company. The latter was probably covered by a loan from Voltaire.[68]

Du Châtelet played a central role in these financial decisions and transactions. From 1733 to 1735, and again from 1740 to 1748, her husband was on active service with the king's armies in the Rhineland, Bohemia, Alsace, and Flanders. Though he might return in the late-fall or winter months, as was customary in the regulated world of eighteenth-century European warfare, when he was away he expected and arranged for his wife to act in his place. She had no legal status in law, but by signing a *procuration,* as he did on April 5, 1735, the marquis gave Du Châtelet the equivalent of a modern power of attorney. She arranged the sale of the Semur castle, the sale of a property of her husband's in Normandy in 1739, and a reduction in taxes on another in 1745. Though the marquis came with her and Voltaire to Brussels in 1739 and returned on other occasions, he left it to her, her legal advisers, and Voltaire to negotiate the final settlement over the contested Flanders properties. As Voltaire wrote to Cideville, Du Châtelet moved from one jurisdiction to another to prove her husband's claims, and "she did all of this joyfully because it is a duty." [69]

Still, with all their care and attention and the advice of their notary, Louis Bronod, Du Châtelet and her husband never had enough to cover their needs. All cost much more than they had at their disposal or could accumulate in new salaries and pensions. Beginning with a loan of twenty thousand livres in 1727, Du Châtelet and her husband accumulated debt. They borrowed from their family and their friends. The chevalier Du Châtelet alone made three loans to his older brother. No one escaped their notice, not even Varin, their bailiff at Cirey. Some of these debts must have been simple transactions: a sum changed hands, interest was owed, the debt retired at a fixed time. More than half of their loans, however, took more imaginative forms. Bronod arranged a number of *rentes perpetuelles,* perpetual annuities, money borrowed with no fixed time for repayment, debts that passed along to one's heirs, who continued to owe the 4 to 5 percent interest indefinitely. He also negotiated four *rentes viagères,* life annuities—debts transformed into regular payments at a higher interest rate, of 10 percent. This annuity lasted only two generations, for the life of the borrower plus that of the heir. [70] In addition, the Du Châtelets rolled their debt over. New annuities helped defray the costs of old ones, new loans financed new offices and thus access to new sources of salaries, pensions, and royal gifts. And when all else failed, Du Châtelet and her husband managed as did ·

the others of their rank: in 1748, they simply stopped paying their bills, even that of Bronod.

"Les Choses Frivoles"

These matters—marriage, the raising of children, the managing of a household and finances—would not qualify in the minds of Du Châtelet and her contemporaries as "les choses frivoles." Quite the reverse, these would be seen as the serious business of creating and maintaining the lineage. "Les choses frivoles" that the marquise referred to in her preface to Mandeville's *Fable,* such as the "too careful attention to my hair and teeth," which led to "the neglect of my mind and understanding"—meant a whole range of activities that could only be enjoyed in Paris or at the court of the king. This would be, as she described it in May 1735 to her relative the duc de Richelieu, to live "au milieu du brouhaha du monde."[71] The Paris that Du Châtelet delighted in looked very different from today. Delicate Gothic spires made the skyline. The ancient walls still encircled much of the city, having been rebuilt in the seventeenth century. Fortresses like the twelfth-century Châtelet, just across the Seine from the Conciergerie (on the Ile de la Cité), were imposing presences and reminders of the sieges that still characterized warfare in Du Châtelet's time. The Bastille, built in the fourteenth century to command approaches along the river, was only a few blocks from the Place Royale, where Du Châtelet and her brothers grew up. With more than six hundred thousand inhabitants, Paris was one of Europe's largest cities, and one of the most crowded. Its networks of narrow streets, some barely three meters across, were usually strewn with refuse, wet with mud, and dark, even in the daytime, with overhanging second or third stories.

The city had begun to install street lanterns along many of the more traveled avenues such as the rue Saint-Honoré. Given the cost of candles, however, they were only lit on moonless nights. Advertisements and endorsements covered the walls of the buildings: "Rolland tailleur des princes" (Rolland, tailor of princes); announcements of concerts, a royal lottery, the sale of a house; a police ordinance against eating melons too late in the season. And it was a violent place. Men and women shouted, argued, were quick to take offense, to push, slap, and hit one another. Approximately eleven thousand soldiers, either those garrisoned and on duty or those on leave from the regular army, lived in Paris, and were no more restrained than other citizens. In theory the king's red-and-blue uniformed *gardes fran-çaises* (French guards), roughly thirty-six hundred men, kept the peace. However, many had other jobs, and even their own criminal records. The city paid for its own guard, but these men worked only every other day.[72] Noblemen wore swords and not just for display.

⚜

The noises from the street, the courtyard, and the stairway of her *hôtel* would have been part of Du Châtelet's morning as she prepared for her day's activities. Her *femme de chambre* awakened her by opening and tying back the green taffeta curtains that encircled the bed, a massive piece of furniture six feet by six feet with a white satin embroidered counterpane. According to Longchamps, Du Châtelet liked cream with her *café,* and a roll. The approximately six thousand members of Du Chatelet's *état* living in the city called these hours "la jeunesse de la journée" (the youth of the day) a time to make one's toilette and to receive friends. *La toilette*—bathing, dressing, and having one's hair and makeup done—was a major activity for a woman of this elite world. Du Châtelet had a special table in her bedroom for the last step in these preparations; drawers opened on either side, and the top lifted up to reveal a mirror on its underside. No one has left descriptions of the young marquise's appearance in her early twenties, but the portraits commissioned later in her life show pale, almost ivory skin, a slight blush to the cheeks, the merest bit of color on her lips. This suggests a minimum of makeup, in an era when courtiers, both male and female, used rouge to create bright-red circles of color on their cheeks. The marquise's inventories, in both Paris and Lunéville, list decorated boxes for powder and for *mouches,* the black beauty marks favored at court, and a crystal flacon for perfume. In her portraits, her hair has always been carefully coiffed. Sometimes one ringlet, probably pomaded to hold its shape, rests on her right shoulder. Her hair is powdered—or, rather, floured (since flour was mixed with the powder)—a soft light gray. This would have been the last part of Du Châtelet's preparations. Her maid would carefully place the thin *dessus de toilette* around her shoulders to protect her clothing during the dusting.[73]

Preparing her mistress's clothing, assisting in her bath, dressing her to go out—these tasks were undertaken by Du Châtelet's *femme de chambre.* Having already seen to the brushing, steaming, or washing of the marquise's clothes, now she selected what was needed for the first of the day's outings from the folded garments in the large oak armoire in her mistress's bedroom. First came a *chemise,* a very fine triangular-shaped linen undergarment, gathered at the neck with a ribbon to tie it at the back, and with gussets under the arms to make it fit a bit more closely. A young woman was supposed to have numerous *chemises* in her trousseau, with the idea that cleanliness meant clean linen. Du Châtelet had a modest thirty, for, unlike her contemporaries who sponged off with a basin of water brought by a servant, she preferred to bathe her entire body. For the purpose, she had a new bright-red copper bath, valued at more than the year's salary of the priest at Cirey.[74]

The *chemise* was a very versatile item of clothing, used for sleeping and as the only article of clothing worn under the various pieces of a dress. The lace half-sleeves and the lace decoration at the top of the bodice that formed part of formal dress would be attached to it. Over the *chemise* went other articles of underclothing—"under" in the sense that they were under the final outer garment. For a formal event at court, Du Châtelet would wear a set of *paniers,* elliptical hoop skirts in damask, taffeta, or linen, each with whalebone supports threaded through the fabric to give the skirt its shape. A linen-covered whalebone corset would have been the next undergarment for formal occasions. Some came in decorated fabrics and formed the top of a dress; others required corset covers, which transformed them for the same purpose.

These stiff bodices held in the waist and pushed up the breasts. They were V-shaped in the front, with lacing in the back for the maid to do up. When Du Châtelet was pregnant, she wore bodices with lacing on the sides as well. The corset had the tabs on either side of the waist with eyelets or buttonholes on them, to which the underskirt of the formal gown would be attached. This *jupon,* or skirt, showed in the V-shaped opening of the sleeveless *robe* (dress) that went on next and formed the back and sides of the outfit. Next came the sleeves, which for all but the simplest everyday dresses to be worn at home had to be sewn on. For court, Du Châtelet had a set trimmed in ermine, another in marten. Thus, each time the *femme de chambre* dressed her employer, perhaps three or four times in a day, she literally pieced and stitched the gown together. She matched sleeves to bodices, attached skirts to the tabs on the corset, and arranged fabric over hoops or *paniers* and petticoats in contrasting colors and patterns. Du Châtelet might instruct her to change the lace trim, add satin bows or a favorite fur border. The overlapping hems of the multiple skirts could be worn in different ways: gathered in one fashion today, in another tomorrow.

Was this a luxurious wardrobe? Du Châtelet had more than thirty outfits, depending on how separate skirts, corsets, and sleeves are counted, and she took great care to be stylish. Gauze fabric became very fashionable later in the century, but Du Châtelet already had three such dresses in her wardrobe. She went to three separate *marchandes de mode,* the women who supervised the creation of such a wardrobe, including even the ribbons, lace trimmings, and shoes. Not surprisingly, the *marchande de mode* represented the real cost of being fashionable. In 1749, the year she died, Du Châtelet had outstanding bills to them that totaled just over a thousand livres, when a *robe* cost an average of forty to fifty livres.[75]

∼✤∽

When Du Châtelet went out, she moved about the city in a sedan chair. Women of rank did not expect to walk. She and her husband had one such conveyance, lined in crimson velvet, that could have belonged to her father. Paintings of Paris often show two or four liveried servants carrying their mistress or master, holding the poles on either side that kept the enclosure off the ground. While she visited the shops on the rue Saint-Honoré or paid calls during other noblewomen's *toilettes,* the porters (hired because they were the right size for the coat, vest, and breeches that identified them as servants to the marquis and his wife) waited on the street or in an antechamber until summoned to take her to her next destination. All of the tradesmen and -women Du Châtelet frequented had their shops in a large rectangular section of the area around the Louvre, the Palais Royal, and the palace of the Tuileries, roughly bounded by the rue Saint-Honoré, the rue Saint-Martin, the boulevard Saint-Denis, and the rue des Petits-Champs. Luxury shops had signs that clattered in the wind, façades in carved and painted wood, and sometimes even glass windows. Her two *parfumeurs,* Du Lac and Vigier, mixed a scent for her and sold her mixtures of herbs and flower petals for the basins and potpourris that she placed around her *appartement* to mask the unpleasant smells of the old walls and corners of the *hôtel.* Visiting fabric sellers, or mercers, must have consumed hours of the marquise's mornings or early afternoons, for her armoires contained me-

ters and meters of many different satins, velvets, and cottons valued at hundreds and even thousands of livres. An outstanding bill from 1746 of almost
six thousand livres—an exorbitant sum, half of what her husband would
have had as his military salary—was for decorative lace that she had purchased at Dentelle Beauvin.[76]

In her additions to her translation of Mandeville's *Fable,* Du Châtelet
described the pleasures of shopping: "when we have persuaded ourselves that
the shopkeeper gained little or even lost on what he has sold us." She called it
"a type of vanity" to believe one has found a bargain. But she assumed that the
merchant would "invent any lie and use any stratagem to give us this idea."
When she thought of a bargain, however, it was not for clothing or fabric.
Her passion, her weakness, seems to have been for what modern museums
call "the decorative arts," anything from little boxes, urns, and goblets to a
lacquered or varnished night table, an inlaid bureau, or a set of *fauteuils.* The
majority of her outstanding bills at her death were to *bijoutiers,* who traded
not in jewelry, as the name would suggest, but rather in porcelains and
furnishings of all sorts. She owed over twenty-two thousand livres to
L'Empereur and to Hebert, who specialized in export porcelain from China
and Japan—cups, saucers, and vases—and figurines mounted on bronze or
porcelain bases or sometimes combined into groups to increase their price.

Although Du Châtelet had some figures from China, the many items in
one armoire of the *hôtel* indicate that she loved Meissen ware—or "porce-
laine de Saxe," as it was called in eighteenth-century France. There were
two cows, many little dogs, a child on a monkey, a goat, sheep, four more
dogs, an inkstand with its containers for the ink and the sand, a candlestick,
and a porcelain bell, all from the German factories. In this armoire she also
kept a remarkable collection of snuffboxes, including a fanciful one from
Meissen in the shape of an artichoke. In her *Discours* on happiness, Du Châtelet wrote of her delight in this collection and also of the sadness that can
come with a surfeit of luxury. One might have so many snuffboxes that the
joy of possessing would be lost—the difference, she explained, between the
thirtieth and the thirty-first snuffbox. She continued: "Our tastes easily lose
their sharpness with satiety, and we should thank God for having given us
the privations necessary to preserve them." One would find it hard to define
the "privations" of Du Châtelet's life, especially in comparison with most
French women and men of her century.[77]

꙳

A visit with a friend, or a promenade in the Luxembourg Garden, might fill an afternoon, but attendance at court would be a daylong enterprise. One of the earliest extant letters of Du Châtelet was written from Versailles. In the 1730s, neither she nor the marquis was part of the royal family's immediate circle, as her father had been, but by virtue of their birth and rank they had the right to attend the royal palaces and to be present for the more public activities, like the concerts or fireworks. Louis XV was a pleasant-faced, heavyset young man now in his twenties, and the father of three children, twin daughters and a son. He paid occasional attention to the administration of the kingdom, and he loved hunting. He had moved the court back to Versailles and, with the help of some of the older courtiers, such as the duc de Luynes, reinstituted many of the rituals and customs of his great-grandfather. Du Châtelet, however, even when at court, seems to have preferred activities similar to those she enjoyed with her friends in Paris. They met, ate and drank, and gambled at cards. "Ennui," as she and Voltaire would later insist, was the enemy. Paris was the cure, not the royal palaces of Versailles, Fontainebleau, and Chantilly.[78]

On a typical evening in Paris, Du Châtelet joined her friends at their *hôtel* or went with them to another of the frivolities offered in the city, such as the annual Opéra Ball on the evening of the festival of Saint Martin. Du Châtelet would have worn a mask and a "domino," a hooded cape to cover her hair and her dress. Most dominos were black; Du Châtelet had a yellow silk one that she took with her to Lunéville. In her writings, Du Chatelet made clear the lessons she had learned from these first years in this exclusive world of "late nights" and "excesses," as she described it. She had discovered that she could not drink wine or liqueurs. She never lost her passionate love of fine food, but had found a practical solution for its unfortunate consequences. "Do not complain," she advised her readers in her *Discours* on happiness, "that you are so very fond of your food, for this passion is a source of continual pleasures; but you should know how to make it serve your happiness; this will be easy if you stay at home, & only order your servants to bring you what you want to eat." This kind of diet—this "abstemiousness"—she discovered, made even less sought-after dishes give pleasure when one became truly hungry.[79]

In Paris in the late 1720s and early 1730s, the entertainments and excesses took place in the grand *salons* of the very rich and well-connected. Du Châtelet's letters mention evenings at a number of these lively *hôtels,* her hosts all related in one way or another to the family of the Villars-Brancas. Du Châtelet was probably introduced to them by Louis François Armand Du Plessis, duc de Richelieu, but they were contemporaries of her parents, and she may have met them at her father's *salon.* The duchesse de Brancas, Elisabeth-Charlotte de Brancas-Villars, and her husband, Louis Bufile, marquis de Brancas-Céreste, had two sons closer in age to Du Châtelet, and the three became friends. It was she who kept them informed about activities in Paris when they, like her husband and the duc de Richelieu, went on campaign in 1734: "nouvelles à la main," news by hand, as she and her contemporaries called it. One son, the comte de Forcalquier, had an older woman as a mistress. Marguerite Thérèse Colbert de Croissy—niece of Colbert, the very capable first minister to Louis XIV, and now duchesse de Saint-Pierre—became Du Châtelet's most frequent companion.

Du Châtelet felt at home in these surroundings, and the duchesse de Saint-Pierre was a generous friend. She had married first a marquis and then, when he died, the duc de Saint-Pierre. Widowed for the second time in 1727, when she was in her late forties, she had money, rank, and thus independence. Madame de Graffigny described the duchesse during this period of her life as "silly, but a good woman, kind, gay, loving every kind of pleasure." Du Châtelet's letters from the early 1730s mention spending a morning receiving visitors, then taking an afternoon trip with Saint-Pierre to the Jardin du roi (now the Jardin des plantes, Paris's botanical garden and the site of the royal collection), and returning home in time to dress for the theater at six. Paris offered the young marquise three choices: the royal opera company in the Palais Royal, also the site for performances of the Académie royale de musique; the Comédie française, the royal acting company; and the Comédie italienne in the Hôtel de Bourgogne, near Les Halles, the troupe known for its performances of works by Italian composers and playwrights. Either Saint-Pierre or the duchesse d'Aiguillon, another Richelieu cousin and an active courtier and hostess of her own *salon,* came to pick up Du Châtelet in the ducal carriage. Afterward, at eight-thirty or later, they gathered at the Villars-Brancas *hôtel.* Another evening, Du Châtelet dined as the guest of Cardinal Fleury, went to the theater and then on to "la petite Crevecoeur," who was married to Saint-Pierre's son by her first marriage.[80]

The theater and the opera were as important to her as the gatherings afterward. Always when she returned to Paris she included news of these evenings in her letters, such as the performance of Corneille's *Héraclius* in May 1735. Du Châtelet had decided preferences in composers and performers. She loved Destouches's *Issé* "a hundred times better" than Lully's *Athys,* though a favorite singer did the main role: "Even her beautiful voice . . . could not prevent [the opera] from being boring." In August 1735, she wrote of her enjoyment of Jean-Philippe Rameau's *Les Indes galantes;* it was Marie Sallé who made the difference. As part of her performance as the Rose Queen, she choreographed the dances so that, unlike conventions set when Louis XIV performed these opera ballets, she, not the male lead, became the center of the carefully measured movements.[81]

In the *Discours,* Du Châtelet included pages not only on the hazards of food and alcohol, the delights of the theater and the opera, but also on her passion for "le jeu," gambling. She had learned many of the games as a child and mastered others as they became the craze in Paris or at court. On any given evening, more than twenty different games might be played, some still familiar, others found only in histories of gambling. In 1733, one played *pharon.* At the court at Lunéville, she would try *comète,* played with two packs and jokers. Perhaps because she had lost in these games herself—for example, in a notorious run of bad luck she had to borrow money from Voltaire and a friend from Semur, Mlle de Thil—Du Châtelet wrote with humor and understanding of the customs and tricks of "the players" in her translation of Mandeville's comments on "gamesters." She observed, again probably from her own experience, that winners hide their gains to avoid borrowers, whereas those who lose flaunt it to take on an air of magnificence, to enjoy being envied by those who have much to lose, and to give pleasure to those who have lost so much. Here, certainly, was the world of "les choses frivoles" that so tempted her, and that she later described as taking her from more serious intellectual challenges.[82]

Victor Esprit

How, then, did Du Châtelet come to question this life? Why would she embark on a program of study worthy of the learned elite, the men of the Republic of Letters? She has left only the slightest hints. Her father-in-law,

the comte de Lomont, died at the end of January 1732, and she and the marquis must have been called away from Paris to Semur to deal with all that
such a last illness and death entailed. Her husband became the head of the
family. Financial settlements had to be prepared, the rituals of homage made
to liege lords, and a period of mourning observed. While at Semur, perhaps
because of the death and their new importance to the continuation of the
family line, Du Châtelet and her husband may have agreed to another child.
She conceived in the summer of 1732, at the end of the required months of
mourning. Some sources give an exact date for the birth of her second son,
April 11, 1733; others mention only the year.

It would be tempting to imagine that the baby's baptismal name, Victor
Esprit, symbolized Du Châtelet's rejection of "frivolous things," the literal
"victory" of the "mind." Such thinking would have astonished and amused
Du Châtelet. Her son's name, like those of his older siblings, declared his
lineage and was meant to flatter those who could help advance him as an
adult. "Victor" tied him to François-Victor, Du Châtelet's cousin, secretary
of state for war from 1723 to 1726, who, though not serving as a royal minister when the boy was born, remained an important member of Louis XV's
and the queen's inner circles. "Esprit" united the infant boy to his father's
family, to Melchior-Esprit de la Baume, comte de Montrevel, huband to the
marquis's sister, Florence. These men and their wives probably served as
the boy's godparents.[83]

Nothing about these events or decisions, however, leads to a life of
learning. The moralists of Du Châtelet's era would have applauded a young
woman's decision to turn away from the excitements and liberality of Paris.
However, they would expect family duties and increased demonstrations of
religious devotion to replace the vanities and frivolous entertainments of
her former life, not studies rivaling those of male contemporaries. The que-
relles des femmes of her parents' era, the argument over women's roles and
capacities, continued into her day. This is the wonder of Du Châtelet: she
saw no contradictions in the two images of a woman's life and their underlying assumptions. She accepted both, but not all of their intended consequences. She did not argue with the Aristotelian description of women's
temperament as cool and moist, but merely noted that she was different:
her hot and thus masculine temperament meant that she could pursue a life
beyond that of wife and mother. She extolled the ideal of her circle, the

quality of *bienséance,* or "propriety," as it is usually translated, behavior appropriate to one's *état. Etat* for Du Châtelet meant not only her elite status, but also the fact of her sex. Because of their *état,* she explained in her *Discours* on happiness, women were "condemned" to exclusion from war, government, and diplomacy, and to "dependencies" that she did not enumerate. Still, as she also explained in the essay, this left other avenues of activity. She sought fame, "la gloire," as a man would, but she accepted that she would have to seek it by other means. Study offered the answer: the cultivation of "my mind and my understanding."[84]

As early as 1732, when Du Châtelet had returned to Semur, she could already have contemplated the necessary changes in her habits. She expanded upon an idea of Mandeville's about the passions in her translation of his remarks: "How few men reflect, and even among those who pay attention to themselves, scarcely any have [found] the thread for the labyrinth of our passions." This lack of reflection, this surrender to the passions, was, she believed, a particular fault of the younger generations of her rank. The solution, she later explained, the thread to lead one out of the labyrinth of one's passions and the irresolution this produced, was "to know what one wants to be." Without such a decision, "one swims perpetually in a sea of uncertainty; one destroys in the morning what one made in the evening; one spends life doing stupid things, repairing them, and repenting them." Du Châtelet's moments of resolution brought excitement.

The Semur that Du Châtelet returned to that winter of 1731–32 was a provincial garrison town that made a striking contrast to the life she had been living in Paris. Fulfilling her duties as the wife of the new head of the family, and then awaiting the birth of her child, would have kept the lively twenty-five-year-old marquise confined to a small circle of friends and activities very different from those she had so recently enjoyed. This circle included Muguet de Mézières, one of the most revered members of the Académie française, who had retired to Semur to devote all his time to *belles lettres.* Was it he who encouraged her to begin a new copybook, filled with sonnets, rondeaux she had memorized, and pages of seventeenth-century literary criticism? He and a number of other *gens des lettres,* though not famous outside their own time, must have provided Du Châtelet with new distractions. There was Président Lemulier and his wife; Conseiller Leclerc, the poet (father of the naturalist the comte de Buffon, later a favorite author of Du Châtelet's); and the Chevalier Bonnard. Mlle Marie-Victoire Eléonore de Sayvre de Thil remained her loyal friend and companion throughout her life, and gained her own reputation for her mathematical knowledge.[85] In addition to distractions, these companions must have given Du Châtelet the attention and encouragement she needed to revive her excitement about reading and study. As she later explained, "by chance" she encountered "gens qui pensent," people who think, who brought her to the important realization that she, too, was "a thinking creature."

What other evidence supports this explanation for the beginning of Du Châtelet's transformation? After her death, in the next king's reign, a courtier insisted that Mézières, her grandfather, "gave [Du Châtelet] all the material for the works she later published." Du Châtelet certainly felt affection and respect for the elderly Academician, whose death she would mourn in the fall of 1734.[86] Perhaps Mézières, who also had a reputation as a *géomètre*, described the mathematics of probability in the card games she loved, took her to the writings of René Descartes, and introduced her to Cartesian analytical geometry. Was it under his tutelage that she learned to follow what Descartes called "the itinerary" of an equation, marking the changes as one number and then another acts as the unknown? A new edition of Pierre Coste's French translation of John Locke's *Essay on Human Understanding* was published in 1729. Locke could have given her a new respect for her own observations, the use of her senses to perceive and describe the world around her. Did it become the subject of conversations in Semur? Add to this her revived study of mathematics, and she had a rational method by which to measure and quantify those perceptions.

⁓⁂⁓

At twenty-six in the late spring of 1733, after the birth of her son, Du Châtelet returned to Paris. Her letters indicate that she continued to enjoy her previous activities: the visits, the promenades, attendance at the theater, the opera, and evenings at the Villars-Brancas'. However, much had changed. The war to protect the claim to the Polish throne of the queen's father, Stanislas, meant active service in the Army of the Rhine for her husband. These same letters reflect other feelings and demonstrate other interests, showing Du Châtelet's gradual shift away from a life devoted exclusively to "les choses frivoles." She had returned to more serious intellectual endeavors in Semur. Now, in Paris, she focused on a particular subject: mathematics. She began lessons in advanced geometry and algebra with the Academician Pierre-Louis Moreau de Maupertuis.

So important to her was this new activity that Du Châtelet made it part of the portrait she and her husband commissioned at about this time. Her unpowdered hair and the roundness of her face indicate her youth. She is dressed formally; the *paniers* of her gown make the rich brocade of her skirts gather and billow out over the arms of the *fauteuil*. Ribbons decorate the stiff bodice, cut low to show the fullness of her breasts. Lace runs across the top of the bodice. It falls from the ends of the long matching satin sleeves. A thin, dark piece of decorative fur begins at her waist and follows the V-line of the bodice up around the back of her neck and then down the other side. Du Châtelet looks to the right, beyond the painter, as if someone has just come into view. She has a small book in her left hand; her gloved finger holds her place. One might presume this to be a religious or moral text but for the sheet of geometric drawings she holds in the other. The marquise Du Châtelet signified her exceptionality and her new passion by the objects she chose for her portrait.

Historians write of the significance of Voltaire in the next decade of her life, and his importance cannot be denied. But another man, Maupertuis, had an equally profound effect.

CHAPTER TWO

The Republic of Letters: The Prodigy

The marquise Du Châtelet, the young noblewoman who chose to have her portrait painted in an unconventional manner, with the geometric drawings in her lace-gloved hand, returned to many of her usual activities in Paris in the late spring of 1733, but with a significant difference. She sought out the *gens qui pensent* and especially Pierre-Louis de Maupertuis, her new tutor in mathematics. In a letter written in 1748, she also described this as the time when she was first attracted to Voltaire, the beginning of what would become a lifelong affair of love, collaboration, and companionship.[1] How nice it would be to arrive at a simple story of their 1733 meeting, their subsequent courtship, and Du Châtelet's decision to join him at Cirey in June 1735. Unfortunately, nothing about this part of her life is simple or self-evident. Both aspects of her decision were unorthodox: to abandon her traditional life in Paris for one of study and amusement at a distant country château; to take as a lover a man of lower rank who, despite his reputation as France's greatest poet and playwright, had been periodically imprisoned and exiled for his daring, ill-considered irreverence toward his betters.

At last, however, there is Du Châtelet's own voice to listen to. The two volumes of her correspondence begin in December of 1733. Though few in number, the letters, if read carefully, set parameters and offer probable sequences of events, just as the 1739 map of Paris showed the boundaries of the city's walls, the names of streets, and the shapes of buildings.

The Meeting

By tradition, Du Châtelet and Voltaire remet in the spring of 1733, in Mme de Saint-Pierre's loge at the Opéra. "Remet" because historians assume that the poet knew her briefly as a little girl, when he visited with her family near

Preuilly and attended her father's *salon* in Paris. As with so much else in Du Châtelet's life, however, even this simple tradition leads to no clear narrative. Some biographers credit François Augustin Paradis de Moncrif with making the new introductions. Du Châtelet had Moncrif's verses in her copybook, and certainly knew him from the late-evening gatherings she enjoyed so much. Voltaire was helping Moncrif with changes to the libretto for his opera *L'Empire de l'amour* (The Empire of Love). Authors customarily continued to alter lines, scenes, and characters even after the first presentation, especially when revenues did not meet expectations, as was the case with Moncrif's opera in May 1733. Voltaire scholars, however, believe that it was a different librettist, Jean Dumas d'Aigueberre, who reintroduced them that spring evening. The source of this alternate story is a letter from October 1749. Voltaire, anguished by Du Châtelet's death, reminded d'Aigueberre in an almost accusatory tone: "My dear friend it was you who renewed my acquaintance [with her] more than twenty years ago."[2]

But twenty years before Du Châtelet's death in September 1749 was 1729, not 1733. Perhaps Voltaire just could not remember; he was, after all, fifty-five, old for the eighteenth century. Yet he repeated the number in other letters: to Mme Du Deffand, the *salonnière;* to Mme Denis, his niece and lover: "I have lost my friend of twenty years."[3] In fact, the year 1729 makes sense. For it would have been 1728 when Voltaire returned to France from his exile in England. Once he was back in Paris, Du Châtelet and he would have frequented some of the same circles. For example, Voltaire accompanied the duc de Richelieu to the Villars-Brancas'. Du Châtelet certainly attended performances of Voltaire's *Œdipe* at the Comédie française. So, whichever librettist accompanied Voltaire to Mme de Saint-Pierre's loge in 1733, this could not have been their first meeting.

What if tradition elided two separate events? Could there have been two "introductions"? In July 1729, d'Aigueberre's greatest success, *Les Trois Spectacles* (a tragedy, a comedy, and a pastoral opera) premiered. The proud younger poet took this occasion to bring his now famous friend, Voltaire, to Mme de Saint-Pierre's loge at the Opéra. This fits the first version of Du Châtelet's and Voltaire's meeting and accounts for the "twenty years" of their friendship mentioned by Voltaire in his 1749 letters. But this was not the beginning of their affair and was perhaps no more than an exchange of pleasantries. In the summer of 1729, if Du Châtelet had been seeking a lover, she would not have chosen the bourgeois Voltaire, who, though gifted, was notorious for his difficulties with the government. At that time, she was an excited young noblewoman enjoying all that her *état* entitled her to, as she rushed from the theater to yet another gathering hosted by her friends of the *haute noblesse*. Nor would Voltaire have courted her, having women of more influence and beauty to choose from. He had a history of cultivating such associations, not for sexual reasons necessarily, but because these associations gave him access—*entrée,* as he would have said—to elite circles. His most successful liaison of this sort was with the marquise Agnès de Prie. She brought him to court at the time of the young Louis XV's marriage in the summer of 1725, and won inclusion of three of his pieces as part of the festivities.

What of the second meeting, then? On April 11, 1733, Du Châtelet gave birth to Victor Esprit. Although her later writings suggest that she questioned Catholic doctrine, she performed all of the expected rituals. For example, when she and Voltaire were in Cirey, a priest said mass every Sunday in the chapel of the château. A woman who gave birth, according to Christian custom in France at the time, remained in seclusion for approximately six weeks after experiencing the "unclean" act of childbirth. Then she would be readmitted to society at a religious ceremony known as "churching." Living in Semur, as the wife of the military governor, Du Châtelet would have honored this religious practice. Even if in Paris, she would have returned to her public life only toward the third or fourth week of May 1733. This would be just when Moncrif allegedly reintroduced the marquise and the playwright.

Perhaps on that particular afternoon Mme de Saint-Pierre collected her young friend, as she had on so many other occasions, to go to the Opéra in the playhouse of the Palais Royal. For this outing, Du Châtelet dressed with particular care, because after the performance the two noblewomen planned to go on to the Villars-Brancas' for supper, cards, and conversation, or perhaps to another relative of Saint-Pierre. Delayed by a confusion of carriages on the rue Saint-Honoré and then in the square of the Palais Royal, they had to rush along the colonnaded entryway to the playhouse and across the noisy vestibule, crowded with food sellers and last-minute patrons for standing room in the parterre. Up the marble stairs, in the corridor outside the duchesse's *petite loge,* rented for the season, an attendant opened the door for them. Du Châtelet maneuvered the wide *paniers* of her skirt between Saint-Pierre's other guests to sit at the front of the box. The duchesse joined her there and greeted friends in another loge across the theater. Du Châtelet was excited, impatient for the music to begin; she had missed these entertainments during her confinement and her months in Semur. The footlight lanterns were lit, the curtains parted and rose, the opera began. All too quickly, the prologue and the first arias and ballets finished. Just as at the Comédie française, numerous entr'actes defined the performance. As usual during the interludes, she and her hostess chatted with the other guests and with visitors to the box. Moncrif knocked and entered with Voltaire.

How did Voltaire appear to her? A pastel of him from this period softens the lines of his pointed nose; an uncharacteristically warm smile plays around his eyes and mouth. All of his portraits show him as a slight figure; he was perhaps about five feet three. Du Châtelet would have looked tall next to him. Contemporaries commented on how thin Voltaire was, that he "looked as if he had consumption." For the twenty-six-year-old Du Châtelet, it would have been Voltaire's words more than his appearance that charmed her. As Charles Jordan, a visitor to Paris from Berlin in 1733, described him, "he is polite; his conversation lively, engaged, full of sallies."[4]

How would Du Châtelet have appeared to him, and how differently would she have spoken with him? She might take no time reminiscing about her father, their earlier encounters when she was growing up, or gossiping about the friends they shared. Perhaps she offered a few polite words to Moncrif about his new opera and tonight's performance, and then, without any prefatory remarks, she spoke enthusiastically about her lessons in mathematics with Maupertuis. Voltaire responded with equal enthusiasm for the *géomètre,* and mentioned his own studies with the Academician. Du Châtelet galloped on to tell him she had read Locke and insisted that Voltaire explain his own views on the nature of the soul. She questioned him about the Englishman's contention that knowledge comes from the senses, filtered through reason's reflections. Voltaire began to answer, but the opera was about to resume. He promised to send her a book. Amazed at her energy and intelligence, in the next weeks he sought her out.

From all subsequent evidence, this is what happened. Voltaire's letters indicate that he had never seen such an incredible creature before.

The Prodigy and the Mathematicians

Du Châtelet, not Voltaire, had changed. With the birth of her second son and the excitement of her renewed interest in study, and particularly Descartes's analytic algebra, she moved in her familiar circles but with new confidence. When Maupertuis took Du Châtelet as a pupil in 1733, he was thirty-five, almost nine years her senior. He already had achieved the highest rank at the Académie royale des sciences. In addition, he had become the darling of the *salons* she frequented, with connections at court through Cardinal Fleury's adviser Jean-Frédéric Phélypeaux de Pontchartrain, comte de Maurepas. Maupertuis also had independent means, always an advantage, particularly given his provincial Breton origins. With his compact figure and lively eyes, Maupertuis seems to have commanded attention when he entered a room. He certainly charmed both the men and women of the elite circles that controlled advancement. Every later reminiscence mentioned his wit, his amiability, his good spirits, his "passion" to learn.[5] Among the first poems that Du Châtelet had arranged to have transcribed into the copybook she inherited from her father was some light verse by Maupertuis: one on a cat, another on a dog, and an ode assumed to be addressed to the duc de Richelieu.

In 1723, as a young man of spirit and intelligence, Maupertuis had first introduced himself to the elite company at Paris's leading cafés. Men of varied interests and talents gathered to enjoy coffee, the new drink from Africa, to read the latest gazettes and journals, and to indulge in conversation. Voltaire favored the Café Procope, on the rue des Fossés–Saint-Germain, across the street from the Comédie française. When at her most enthusiastic about her lessons, Du Châtelet waited for Maupertuis in her carriage in the street outside his favorite meeting place, the Café Gradot, so that he could come and work with her all the sooner, for the serving girls were the only women allowed inside.[6]

The Café Gradot, on the quai du Louvre, Maupertuis's usual choice, was presided over by one of the seventeenth and early eighteenth centuries' most famous "men of letters," a regular member of the most important intellectual *salons,* the blind and aging Antoine Houdar de la Motte. Du Châtelet knew him as the librettist of *Issé,* the opera she loved. Maupertuis knew him as one of the influential *savants* whose approval and patronage he sought to win. Charles-Marie de La Condamine, Maupertuis's close friend in the 1730s, remembered their daily routine. They met at the Café Gradot about noon, and then for another two hours in the evening, after a walk, a dinner somewhere, or the theater.[7] Maupertuis caught the attention of influential mathematicians and physicists such as those who would sponsor him at the Académie des sciences. When Houdar de la Motte died in 1731, Maupertuis replaced him as the leader and central figure of these daily gatherings.

The Académie des sciences was founded by Louis XIV and his principal minister, Colbert, to make the new experimental approach to knowledge serve the practical military, navigational, commercial, and manufacturing needs of the state, activities considered appropriate concerns only for men, and men of a certain *état*. It had no place for women except as spectators at the twice-yearly public meetings: the week after Easter in the spring, and after St. Martin's Day in the fall. Originally, the Académie met in the royal library, on the rue Vivienne, in the Hôtel Mazarin (today the Bibliothèque Nationale), but after its reorganization in 1699 by the abbé Jean Paul Bignon, members assembled in what had been the king's antechamber at the royal palace of the Louvre.[8] The "sciences" cultivated by the members of the Académie in the seventeenth and eighteenth centuries fell into two categories: those associated with mathematics and those associated with the physical world. In the Académie, six achieved formal status: geometry, astronomy, and mechanics as the mathematical sciences; chemistry, anatomy, and botany as the physical sciences. This meant admission of a total of forty-two official state-supported members at different levels of expertise: three *pensionnaires,* two associates, and two adjuncts for each of the six sciences. Men gained admission by election of the members, but nominations came from the king, who usually, though not always, accepted the suggestions of his principal minister. Similarly, Louis XV named the presiding officers and the twelve honorary members, men of the *haute noblesse,* such as his favorite and Du Châtelet's relative, the duc de Richelieu.[9]

Maupertuis's choice of mathematics as his specialty had more to do initially with prospective vacancies than with his expertise. He, like Fontenelle, author of the *Entretiens* (*Conversations*), was elected to the Académie française as well as the Académie des sciences. Perhaps Fontenelle, the "perpetual secretary" or executive director of the scientific academy, encouraged Maupertuis to return to the study of analytic algebra and abstract mathematics. Sadly, the subject never came easily to him, even though he had a gift for finding the apt subject within his competence that enabled him to shine at the Académie over the years. Between his first presentation to the Académie in December 1723 and his elevation to *pensionnaire* in 1731, Maupertuis studied the standard texts, ones that he would later recommend to Du Châtelet: the French translation of Nicolas Guisnée's *Application de l'algèbre à la géométrie* and the explanation of calculus in French, the marquis de l'Hôpital's *Analyse des infiniment petits*. Maupertuis's mentor at the Académie, François Nicole, tutored him. He traveled to London, and in the three months of his stay was introduced to the principal Newtonian natural philosophers, such as Henry Pemberton, Samuel Clarke, and Colin Maclaurin, who, despite his inability to speak English, saw to his election to the Royal Society. Most significant to his mathematical education, he went to study with Johann Bernoulli, professor of mathematics at the University of Basel in Switzerland. From September 1729 until July of 1730, he lived and worked with this almost legendary senior *géomètre*.[10]

The elder Bernoulli was described by contemporaries as jealous, irascible, ambitious, and difficult. He understood Leibniz's calculus, and formulated the equation for *forces vives* (kinetic energy) that Du Châtelet would later defend against the attack by another Academician, Jean-Jacques Dortous de Mairan. And Bernoulli, though a staunch adherent of Descartes's system of the universe, was also one of the few men outside of England who understood Newton's *Principia* and could explain its mathematics of "fluxions"— Newton's name for the calculus—to others. The authors of the texts Maupertuis labored to understand, such as l'Hôpital, and the eminent mathematicians with whom Du Châtelet would later correspond—Jacob Hermann, Leonhard Euler, Gabriel Cramer, and Bernoulli's own three sons—all studied with the Swiss professor. Bernoulli's son Johann II became Maupertuis's close friend. The renowned *savant* enjoyed the younger man, and was "charmed by his conversation." For the rest of his career, Maupertuis sought out Bernoulli for counsel, corrections, and approval. This was, in fact, how he formulated his most difficult Académie presentations. So close were Maupertuis's ties to this family that he returned to live with them during his final illness in 1759.[11]

When Du Châtelet returned to Paris in May 1733, Maupertuis had become the talk of the cafés and *salons*, both those of the intellectual and the social elite. After demonstrating his hard-won mastery of aspects of Newtonian mathematical analysis with a long *discours* read before the Académie on attraction and spherical bodies, in which he presented Newton's geometrical representations from Book I of the *Principia* translated into Leibnizian integral calculus, he published a more popular discussion of this new view of the solar system. As Fontenelle in his *Entretiens* had shown the viability of Descartes's explanation of the mechanics of the universe, so now Maupertuis, in his *Discours sur les différentes figures des astres* (Discourse on the Different Shapes of Celestial Bodies), proved its weaknesses.[12]

Maupertuis did not explicitly break with his French colleagues and their adherence to Descartes's explanation of the universe; instead, he argued that, given the laws of planetary motion formulated by Kepler, Isaac Newton's explanation could be equally valid, "neither impossible nor contradictory."[13] He diplomatically left it "to the reader to examine if attraction is sufficiently proved by the facts or if it is only an unfounded supposition that one can pass over." He avoided overt disagreement by asking not "Why do the planets move as they do?" but, rather, "Which set of supporting mathematical calculations, Descartes's or Newton's, best fits the recorded observations, and the laws that had been deduced from them?" Thus, he never engaged in the metaphysical argument on the causes of celestial movement that so concerned his colleagues. He agreed that Descartes's mechanical universe of "impulsion," where material particles became swirling *tourbillons* or vortices that carried the planets in their orbits, had "the advantage of simplicity; but, he continued, "in the details of phenomena, one finds great difficulties." For example, no adherent of the Cartesian system had yet found a way to explain how the vortices carrying a comet could pass through the vortices of the planets without disrupting the whole pattern of orbits. These problems disappeared with the concept of "attraction." In combination with centrifugal force, this action through space created Kepler's elliptical paths of the planets and the comets around the sun, and thus "gave new confirmation of the System of M. Newton."[14] With his *Discours,* Maupertuis turned a scientific dispute into a topic for the *gens qui pensent* of the cafés and *salons,* and took the very public lead for the new, younger members of the Académie who admired the mathematical and philosophical writings of the two Englishmen Newton and Locke. They met at dinners before the weekly sessions, and, from 1734 to 1735, at Mont Valérien, Maupertuis's retreat on the outskirts of Paris, where others with mathematical and scientific interests joined them.[15]

Du Châtelet's principal women friends, the duchesses de Saint-Pierre and d'Aiguillon, and the duchesse de Chaulnes, whose husband owned one of Paris's most complete scientific-instrument collections, or *cabinet de physique,* viewed themselves as Maupertuis's patrons and may already have been his pupils when Du Châtelet asked for her first lesson. He corresponded with these women and Du Châtelet even when he led the Académie expedition to Lapland. He journeyed to the Arctic Circle to measure degrees of latitude to match those his friend La Condamine was making at the equator, meant to prove or disprove Newton's hypothesis about the shape of the earth. The lessons he gave may initially have had more to do with *galanterie* than pedagogy. A short note from Voltaire to Maupertuis in September 1733 about arranging a meeting of the three of them suggests that both he and Du Châtelet were then studying with the Academician. The first extant letter from Du Châtelet to Maupertuis, tentatively dated January 1734, shows her already eagerly involved in her lessons and worried that he will not find time enough to continue them. Probably initially flattered and intrigued by Du Châtelet's enthusiasm for the subject, he may have been surprised, confused, and even annoyed by her eagerness, her aptitude, and her insistence on his tutelage.

Du Châtelet corresponded with Maupertuis throughout the 1730s. At times, they were both in Paris with its three mail deliveries a day, and servants to carry messages when needed. She told him where she would be, what she was doing, and when and where to meet, always hoping to fit in time for him around her other activities at court or in town with her friends, and hoping that he, busy at the Café Gradot or the Académie, would likewise accommodate her. When she was away from Paris, Du Châtelet wrote at greater length. In May 1734, she traveled to Montjeu, the Guise family château in Burgundy, for the duc de Richelieu's wedding, and later that fall to Cirey, the Du Châtelet family château, to see Voltaire. The two-to-three-page letters show the same combination of flirtatiousness, imperiousness, and eagerness for tutelage as her notes in Paris. She apologized for not writing, chided him for the same offense, or scolded him for paying more attention to Mme de Lauraguais (another Brancas relative). Other biographers of both Du Châtelet and Maupertuis have assumed that the extravagant language and compliments in these letters indicate the writers' sexual involvement with each other. And some of her correspondence with him, especially when they were both in Paris, can be interpreted that way. Usually, however, the context suggests otherwise. Du Châtelet sounds more melodramatic than sexual. Throughout her life, she wrote in similarly affectionate language to her friend and adviser the comte d'Argental. Moreover, the other noblewomen and -men of her circle wrote in equally suggestive and lavish phrases to their friends. It was the style of the era. The duc de Luynes included a letter to his brother the archbishop of Sens from the dauphine, wife to the heir to the French throne, in his journal of the court of Louis XV; she began: "Adieu, my cardinal; I love you with all my heart, despite the respect that I owe Your Eminence."[16]

More interesting than speculating on whether or not Du Châtelet had sexual relations with Maupertuis, something the written evidence does not tell us, is the extent to which they both understood the possibility of and contributed to this image of themselves. To their circle, natural philosophy taught by a male mentor to a female student invited sexual connotation. Maupertuis actively encouraged the image of himself as the adventurer philosopher, for whom amiability and sexuality were key elements. His was a rougher, less refined version of the *philosophe* of Fontenelle's *Entretiens*. With his 1738 expedition to Lapland and the publicity it generated, he ensured this more rakish reputation for himself, the man of action and of intellect. Du Châtelet expressed the common awed and admiring reaction in her *Institutions de physique*: "One cannot read of these dangers without fear." On his return, Mme de Saint-Pierre teased him about his newfound success at court: "Vous êtes extrêment à la mode," which loosely translates as, "You are all the rage." In the portrait he commissioned to commemorate his journey, he wears a Laplander's embroidered sealskin coat and fur hat and is framed by scenes of ice, snow, a smoking volcano, and a reindeer pulling a sledge. His right hand rests on a flattened globe, an obvious indication of the physical truth his arduous expedition proved.[17]

These same letters and notes from 1734–35 between the young marquise and her *philosophe* adventurer also give glimpses of her lessons. Along with the day's gossip, she mentioned her "devoirs" (homework), the "binomes and trigonomes," as she referred to them coyly one night after returning from the opera. Maupertuis assigned her the textbook by Guisnée, his old tutor, and sent her problems to solve. She reported to him on what she had done and not done. In June 1734, she apologized from Montjeu: "I am remiss these days with mathematics. You will find me precisely as you left me, having forgotten nothing but having learned nothing, and (with) the same desire to make progress worthy of my *maître*." Du Châtelet did not like the textbook. She complained here, as she would again: only with him could she "learn with pleasure" the abstract concepts such as "*an a less four a*." Then, using a metaphor she later favored in many of her writings, she explained: "You sow the flowers on the path where others find only brambles, your imagination knows how to embellish the driest materials without diminishing their accuracy or their precision."

Du Châtelet's letters indicate that Maupertuis did not respond as readily as she hoped and needed. In a January 1734 letter, Du Châtelet insisted that he give her tasks so that she could continue. In another, no longer coy or flirtatious, she offered different arguments to prompt his attention, his willingness to teach her "truths so sublime." Writing from the Guise wedding festivities in April 1734, she used flattery: "It is not for me that I wish to become a mathematician, it is out of my respect for you." She continued, in a modest tone that she must have hoped would accomplish her purpose: "I know that it is not permitted for someone who has you as a master to make mediocre progress." By implication, not to succeed would be shameful.[18] Given these difficulties, as early as the fall of 1734 Du Châtelet probably had already turned to Maupertuis's young protégé, Alexis-Claude Clairaut, for additional instruction.

Although there are no extant letters between Du Châtelet and Clairaut from the 1730s to describe the gradual shift from one tutor to another, two other sources give an idea of their time together as *maître* and pupil. In the 1740s Clairaut published his textbooks, *Elémens de géometrie* and *Elémens d'algèbre*. The dates of publication are misleading, for, even in their day, contemporaries knew them to be based on lessons with the marquise.[19] "Petit Clerau," as Du Châtelet called him, was six years her junior, just twenty-one in 1734, but already recognized as a mathematics prodigy. Clairaut had presented his first paper on differential calculus to the Académie just four months short of his thirteenth birthday. Only his age had kept him from membership in the Académie until 1731, and then the requirement was waived by two years. With abbé Bignon as his first mentor, he rose to associate in less than two years and to *pensionnaire* in May 1738. In 1734 and 1735, he lived with Maupertuis at Mont Valérien, and was an active member of the Anglophile, Newtonian group of young followers. At some point during that time he must have started to give Du Châtelet—and perhaps also her friend from Semur, Mlle de Thil—lessons in advanced algebra and analytic geometry.[20]

Although Clairaut did not use the conventional device of dialogues in his textbooks, one can almost hear Du Châtelet asking questions, seeking clarification, alternately protesting and then delighting in some new understanding of a complicated proposition or formula. The approach, the tone, and the overall style are very similar to Du Châtelet's own writing on scientific subjects. It can be presumed that both learned from these lessons an effective way to present difficult information for beginners. Before their publication, Du Châtelet used these lessons for her son as well. It is easy to see why. The sequence is so neat, so clear, with each of the sections building on the last and increasing in complexity. In the geometry text, one would measure a field, then discover obstacles such as a rock or a tree, and thus the pupil would learn to break up the space into geometric shapes that could in turn be measured as rectangles, triangles, circles, and polygons. From there the lessons became more abstract. Curved spaces were the prelude to what Clairaut called "geometry of the infinite"; this was the mathematics of Descartes and Newton, needed to find distances for multiple objects in different relationships to one another. The last section of the geometry text taught the student how to measure in three dimensions, everything from the practical number of stones in a wall and water in a trench to ideal shapes, prisms, pyramids, and circular solids like cylinders and spheres.[21]

Just as Clairaut sought in his geometry lessons to take his reader from the commonsense situation to its general formulation as a theorem, so he did the same in his algebra text. He began by using regular numbers for hypothetical problems, and only after giving a few examples did he suggest the mathematical generalization underlying the results obtained. The eighteenth-century images are different, but the problems sound familiar to a modern reader. "Two couriers fifty leagues apart," one in Lille, the other in Paris. The first leaves Lille at eight in the evening for Paris, traveling at four leagues an hour. The second, leaving the same day from Paris at 11 a.m., travels at three leagues an hour. "One asks, at what distance from Paris they will meet?" Of course Paris would be the reference point. It is easy to see why Du Châtelet preferred Clairaut's lessons to Guisnée's more traditional text.[22]

Clairaut structured the algebra book to reflect not only the increasing complexity of the abstractions but also the order of their invention by the first men to think in this way. "The first Algebrists" found ways to write that shortened the operations; for example, "aacc" became a^2c^2. Clairaut then took his pupil from simple equations with two unknowns, to "the apparent contradiction" of negative numbers. Again he found the practical approach from a student's own experiences, and certainly within Du Châtelet's. For example, two people combine their fortunes, but one man's debts diminish the wealth of the other. The last parts of the textbook Clairaut devoted to the intricacies of equations he dubbed "of the third and fourth degree," operations with multiple unknowns and complex operations in the division and multiplication of square roots. These lessons are the ones Du Châtelet would have needed to understand Maupertuis's discourses on Newton's *Principia*.[23] Paris gossips in late June 1735 told of Du Châtelet's making a visit to Mont Valérien, probably just before she left for Cirey to be with Voltaire. In the story, this unorthodox journey was assumed to be evidence of an affair with Maupertuis and mocked her pretensions as a student of mathematics. Perhaps Du Châtelet made no secret of these visits, and was welcomed for a more prosaic reason. Another source suggests that this may not have been her only trip, and that it was not necessarily to see Maupertuis. In the *éloge* for Clairaut, delivered before the Académie at a November 1765 meeting, as a tribute after his death, the perpetual secretary, Jean-Grandjean de Fouchy, made Clairaut Du Châtelet's principal teacher, and in passing mentioned that he was the one that she often rode to Mont Valérien to visit.[24] The young marquise did not need sexual relationships with them to find these mathematicians exciting.

For her, as for Clairaut, the subject brought wonder in and of itself. She later described this grandeur in her *Institutions de physique*. Mathematics was the true underpinning of all knowledge and of all creation. Its laws and equations gave certainty in a world where the senses could often mislead even the most rational of *philosophes*. She came to see Newton as the master of this universal series of connections; he formulated the law of attraction that could be mathematically demonstrated in an infinite number of variable situations, with one single law for motion on earth and in the skies, a single equation that described the mechanics of the entire universe. Though French Academicians did not necessarily agree with Newton's application of his law, men like l'Hôpital and Fontenelle came to the same excitement about abstract mathematical modeling. This was a tradition that had begun in the last century with Descartes's *Géométrie*. Newton himself first read Descartes. A particular event could become a generalization for actions of its kind; similarly, a mathematical generalization could be applied to a particular phenomenon to quantify its actions. A formula could be constituted from variables with both fixed and unfixed values that gave an idealized mathematical representation of all that could be observed.[25]

When did Du Châtelet come to this realization? In Semur, in her reading with Mézières? Puzzling over "binomes and trigonomes," as she described it in her letter to Maupertuis? Or was she simply trying to concentrate on the dry pages of Guisnée before dressing for the opera? Perhaps on such an afternoon she was preoccupied or bored, and looked out the window. She saw a branch move in the wind, contemplated the colors of the leaves against the sky, noted the dove on the sill, heard the sound of a cart passing in the street. It was then that she realized that what she had been studying could describe all that she had seen and heard, and describe it in the abstract language of mathematics. The dove could fly at many speeds, and Du Châtelet knew that she could calculate its pattern of flight; she could make an equation to measure the force of the wind needed to bend the branch; she could draw the angles of refraction and reflection that would always produce the colors of the leaves and the sky. For her the whole world became reducible to geometric figures, to mathematical analogies and formulas, and to the certainty and predictability they represented.

Clairaut remained committed to Du Châtelet and her projects throughout her life. He wrote to a friend when he first began giving lessons to her and to Voltaire that she was "altogether remarkable," while he could not even make the other understand what mathematics was. When, in the 1740s, Du Châtelet decided to do her translation of and commentary on Newton's *Principia*, it was Clairaut who checked her figures and with whom she discussed what she had written. For she had, by this time, surpassed the understanding of Maupertuis, her first *maître*. Maupertuis, by his own admission in his correspondence with Bernoulli, found Newton's calculus difficult to follow. Perhaps more significant, he did not have Du Châtelet's and Clairaut's same love of and excitement about mathematics.[26]

Even so, and despite a brief period of estrangement in the 1740s, Du Châtelet's relationship with Maupertuis was one of affection and respect. Maupertuis had been among the first of the *gens des lettres* to recognize her unusual intelligence. When Du Châtelet embarked on her own projects, she wrote to Maupertuis, as he wrote to Bernoulli, for information, correction, and approval. In many ways, he also became her intellectual model, his writings "full of wisdom and fine calculations." As Fontenelle's approaches and literary devices influenced Maupertuis's writings, so the *géomètre*'s influenced hers. Du Châtelet indicated how important he was in her life: she had a framed engraving of his portrait hung in her bedchamber in the *hôtel* in Paris where she did her writing, one presumes for inspiration. In 1738, as she read and reflected, Maupertuis's breadth of interests—from mathematics to metaphysics, from Newton to the nature of human generation—contributed to her own continuing exploration of the most inclusive meanings of "natural philosophy." At the beginning of that same year, in a letter to him, she had described them both as "heretics in philosophy," a position that each cultivated and enjoyed.[27]

The Courtship: 1733–34

On that early evening in May 1733 when Voltaire came to the duchesse de Saint-Pierre's loge, the marquise Du Châtelet had not yet assumed this mantle or discovered this role. However, that night and in the next months, her obvious intelligence and newfound enthusiasm for learning, her conversation, and her imagination entranced the older man. And Du Châtelet mentioned Voltaire to her correspondents in these months, but gave no hint of the affair to come. They shared interests: the mathematics lessons and fascination with Newton. Perhaps Voltaire recommended to her Jonathan Swift's *Tale of the Tub,* which appeared in a new French translation in 1733, and which she would later read and enjoy. Fresh from his success with his last play, *Zaïre,* Voltaire was already at work on *Adélaïde Du Guesclin,* a historical drama. By June, he was reciting the verses for friends and giving copies to them, including the young marquise. In December, she wrote a mutual friend, the abbé Jacques François Paul Aldonce de Sade, of how charmed she was that he, too, was pleased with the new play. She herself had been affected by it: "I found it tender, noble, touching, well written, with an especially charming fifth act." She speculated about the actress who should play the heroine. She gave news of Voltaire: he had been unable to go out for three weeks, but the illness had not made "his imagination any less lively or less brilliant." She boasted that he had also completed two operas. Her tone was light, affectionate, admiring.[28]

In contrast, Voltaire's letters of that summer and fall reveal the quick evolution of his feelings. The first, a note in connection with their encounter at the Opéra, is brief. Overwhelmed by his move from the Palais Royal to the *appartement* near the Place de Grève, opposite the great Gothic church of Saint-Gervais, and ill with "colic," he explained that he could not send Du Châtelet what he had promised—undoubtedly, the book they had spoken about during the entr'acte. He suggested in a flirtatious way that she come to visit. Already his playful words revealed the disparity in their feelings: "I have more desire to see you than you have to console me." Then two letters to Mme de Saint-Pierre in July and November indicate that he and Du Châtelet saw each other again at his lodgings, even though he remained ill for much of the summer with what he described as "inflammation of the intestines."[29]

On one such evening, dressed fashionably, confident of herself, and eager to enjoy her new flirtation, Du Châtelet might have arrived with her friends—"the three angels," as Voltaire dubbed Saint-Pierre, her lover the comte de Forcalquier, and the baron de Breteuil's daughter. They came from the Opéra, expecting to amuse and be amused. The playwright's cook had prepared chicken *fricassée* (a stew) for his guests. The lodgings would be stuffy with the summer air of the city. Du Châtelet might sit by his bedside, her youthful energy almost too much for the modest spaces. There was no impropriety about these visits. One of the most famous of the seventeenth-century *précieuses* could not tolerate direct heat, so she received the members of her *salon* far from the fireplace, in her bed, covered with furs. Another night, "the good company" played cards while Voltaire began his "Epître sur la Calomnie [Epistle on Calumny]," verses designed to praise Du Châtelet despite unflattering popular gossip about her, perhaps already mocking her aspirations as a *géomètre*.

Voltaire mentioned these verses, dedicated to a "very amiable and much maligned woman," to his dear friend Cideville, a *conseiller* to the Rouen *parlement*. To another intimate, Nicolas Claude Thieriot, he gave her name, "Mme Du Châtelet." Voltaire circulated the poem freely after he finished it in August, and thus signaled the beginning of his public courting of Du Châtelet's favor. Contemporaries would have seen little to differentiate the poet's writing appreciatively and in accepted tropes to "Emilie" from Voltaire's relationships with other noblewomen. Only by referring to her by her first name—as he did when writing to Cideville and to another Rouen friend, Jean Baptiste Nicolas Formont—did he exceed the usual boundaries of such a flirtation.[30]

These signs of intimacy in August 1733 seem to have been part of the beginning of serious courtship. As one historian described it, "He seduced her, she astonished him."[31] That she astonished him is evident in numerous letters to his friends. Voltaire's remarks indicate just how unorthodox and extraordinary she was. Du Châtelet admired his works, but she also offered suggestions and criticisms as he revised *Adélaïde Du Guesclin*. After a few months, he realized that she, not he, was the *géomètre*. She joined in his re-reading of Locke and, possibly at his recommendation or that of Mauper-tuis, took on other English and French philosophers and mathematicians, such as Samuel Clarke and Malebranche. When Voltaire began his *Traité de métaphysique* (Treatise on Metaphysics), a formal exploration of questions about the nature of God, the origins of society, and the reasons for human behavior, it is thought to have been at her request. In June of the next year, 1734, Voltaire wrote to Formont, his principal correspondent on philosophical questions, "There is a lady in Paris, named Emilie, who, in imagination and in reason, surpasses the men who like to think they know a lot about the one and the other." In the flattering words that he would in the future repeat about her knowledge of other authors, he continued: "She understands Locke better than I." At the beginning of November 1733, Voltaire had marveled to the abbé de Sade that she had learned English in fifteen days. An Irish military officer had been her tutor, and after five lessons she could read fluently. "Truthfully," he concluded, "madame Du Châtelet is a prodigy."[32]

Despite his obvious admiration, the disparity in their feelings continued. He had what he later referred to as his "amorous fantasies." She, however, he confessed to Sade at the end of August, was a "tyrant." He explained that one must pay court by speaking of metaphysics when one wanted to "speak of love." Voltaire's "Epître à Uranie" (Epistle to Urania) dates from this period. Here the poet was even more explicit about his lack of success. The lover wishes this "goddess," Uranie, the muse of astronomy, to choose "his system, that of Ovid," over her studies of the skies and measurements of the earth.

> Listen to love's lessons, from the country of dreams,
> Allow yourself to be guided to the country of desires.
> I will teach you its mysteries;
> Happily, if you want to learn its pleasures from me.

The poem also offered a picture of Du Châtelet at her studies. Voltaire complimented her charms, but asked what purpose they served. Such beautiful hands were not meant for a mathematician's compass or a physicist's lens, nor such charming eyes for observing the orbit of a planet. "No, the hand of Venus is made to touch the lute of Love." Her eyes were themselves the stars "here on earth." "Leave then," he importunes, "all systems, / Sources of errors and debates, / And choosing Love as your master teacher, / Enjoy delight in place of knowing."[33]

Voltaire did have reservations; perhaps he had never felt such strong feelings and such attraction to a woman. He mentioned "love" in verses sent to Cideville in late August 1733 but hoped that the gods would help him avoid it. Though love could bring much that pleased, it was a "dangerous madness." Still, he could not resist a description of this remarkable woman: "Here is what Emilie is. / She is beautiful, and knows how to be a friend, / She has imagination. . . ."

There was her "lively and sublime reason." "She has," he assured Cideville, "a genius / Worthy of Horace and Newton." Still, he preferred "amitié" to love. The word "amitié" could have many meanings in eighteenth-century French: from affection occasioning reciprocal obligations to love in our more modern sense of an "affair." It was the word Voltaire used to indicate his devotion to his male friends. Cideville, in fact, was envious of Du Châtelet. Perhaps in response, Voltaire ended the letter with a tribute to his longtime companion: "Goodbye. You are Emilie as a man, and she is Cideville as a woman." This juxtaposition and mixing of the sexes explains another interesting verse sent to Cideville, a few months later, in October 1733. All of Du Châtelet's and Voltaire's biographers assume that they became lovers in that first summer and fall—but with no real evidence. These October verses, despite the reference to her as "ma maîtresse" used the term in a context that suggests otherwise. Voltaire wrote of his happiness as being more than he deserved, admitting he had given in to the emotion he wished to avoid: "My heart even sometimes abandons itself to love." In the next line he explained,

> I have too little sexual desire,
> But my mistress pardons me,
> And I love her more tenderly.[34]

There is another factor to consider when thinking about Voltaire's sexual advances. During that fall of 1733 and throughout their life together, Voltaire used this same kind of language and wrote with equal if not more ardor of his affections for his male friends, such as Cideville, Sade, Formont, and Thieriot, to name only the most frequent among his correspondents. At the time Du Châtelet first came to visit him with the other two "angels," Voltaire was exchanging admiring verses from Horace with these men and writing to them explicit words of love. In one letter, Voltaire interrupted his "agony" to tell Sade that he was "a charming creature." He wrote to Thieriot, who as his closest companion in the 1720s nursed him through smallpox, and with whom he shared his royal pension, that the "idea of being loved by you sweetens all my bitternesses." He asked Formont to "love me, write me often." He closed his letter to Moncrif, the courtier, poet, and playwright, "I love you with all my heart." Having received suggestions for *Adélaïde Du Guesclin* from Cideville, his particular intimate during this period, Voltaire imagined how agreeably they would pass the time when together and compared their situation to "two lovers condemned to make love from afar."[35]

Historians have suggested that the young Voltaire was molested at his *collège* by the Jesuit instructors. Voltaire also could have had his initiation in the libertine circles he frequented when his father sent him to study law in Rouen, or when he first arrived in Paris. During the years of the Regency, Voltaire was invited to La Source, the château of the English political exile Lord Bolingbroke, and probably to his gatherings in Paris as well. Bolingbroke was openly homosexual, modeling himself on Alcibiades and Petronius as the wise elder man schooling his young protégés in political philosophy and erotica. Voltaire was sixteen when they first met.[36] Intimate male friendships, perhaps some having a sexual aspect, were characteristic of the Republic of Letters. Voltaire and Maupertuis, for example, were part of a network of young men of intellect, in a sense a coterie within the Republic of Letters, who wrote letters of introduction for each other, entertained one another, and perhaps exchanged sexual favors, just as they exchanged their verses, plays, treatises, and books.

This network made Voltaire's exile in England particularly rewarding. He met men like the authors Pope and Swift, the politician Sir Robert Walpole, and Sir Everard Fawkener, the son of a rich Levant Company merchant, who later became his lifelong friend. He dedicated his play *Zaïre* to Fawkener. Voltaire also maintained his ties to Lord Hervey, the courtier and confidant to Queen Caroline of England. In September 1733, Voltaire recommended the English version of his *Lettres philosophiques* to him and asked the "charming lord," known for his relationships with women and men, to "remember a Frenchman who is devoted to yr [sic] lordship for ever with the utmost respect, and loves you passionately."[37] In Paris, a *nouvelliste* like Commissaire Dubuisson reported the young men that Voltaire took under his wing, including abbé Linant, who lived with the older man off and on in the fall of 1733. Like Linant, each aspiring poet came from the provinces, sent his verses to Voltaire, and then received encouragement and an invitation to come to Paris.[38]

Would Du Châtelet be aware of all of this? Yes. Men's bisexuality was an open part of the *salons* she frequented. She knew of Maupertuis's dinners at Mont Valérien and of the young men he favored—Clairaut, La Condamine, and Francesco Algarotti. Algarotti visited Voltaire and Du Châtelet at Cirey and went on to be introduced to similar circles in London and at the English court, where reputedly both Lord and Lady Hervey found him seductive. Du Châtelet could not help knowing of speculations about these relationships among the members of the Republic of Letters. And the only time in her correspondence when she showed jealousy of another claimant on Voltaire's affections, it was not of a woman, but of a man, Frederick of Prussia, a man openly homosexual in his preferences. The only friend of Voltaire that she distrusted and actively disliked was Thieriot.

For these men, neither marriage nor liaisons with a woman posed any conflict. Voltaire's name was linked with women before Du Châtelet. She probably appreciated her exceptional status in the gatherings of bright men. She enjoyed receiving their flattering verses, perhaps written more for Voltaire's amusement than to please her. Cideville, in requesting a copy of the "Epître sur la Calomnie" from Voltaire, addressed Du Châtelet in terms as extravagant as those used by Voltaire. When he wrote a few weeks later to thank Voltaire for the epistle, he compared Du Châtelet favorably to Venus. Toward the end of August 1733, he confessed, "Without knowing you I adore you," and in the enclosed poem likened her complexion to the goddess Aurora, her genius to that of Minerva. She surpassed Venus. It was two close male friends playing at flirtation, vying for each other's affectionate appreciation and for that of this younger, aristocratic woman. Voltaire encouraged his other close male friends, like Formont, to seek out this "philosophe."[39]

However, perhaps most seductive for Du Châtelet, although Voltaire probably did not realize it, was his enlisting her help in research for his tragedy *Alzire*. This, more than anything, would have made her feel "a thinking creature." In October 1733, Dubuisson reported in his newsletter to those living far from Paris that Voltaire was working on a new play based on the history of Mexico. The playwright was ill, so perhaps he sent Du Châtelet to the Bibliothèque du roi (King's Library) to borrow books. Du Châtelet read aloud to him, did research, and marked passages for his attention. The evidence for this intellectual seduction is in St. Petersburg. Among the volumes in Voltaire's library, bought by Catherine the Great of Russia after his death, there is a French translation of Antonio de Solís y Rivadeneira's history of the Aztecs and of the Spanish conquest of Mexico. In that multivolume history of sixteenth-century Mexico, Du Châtelet made marginal comments, noted useful passages, and left small torn bits of paper to indicate pages for future reference. Their reading together probably continued into the fall of 1734, when Du Châtelet spent a few months with Voltaire at Cirey.[40] In the final version of *Alzire,* Voltaire altered the location from Mexico to Peru and fashioned their researches into the faintest backdrop for a tragedy about the clash of Indian and Spanish cultures, with an underlying theme that Voltaire would explore in other writings and that often posed problems with the royal censors: which of the characters was the true Christian? Although it was not evident to either of them at the time, this play and these months set the pattern for future collaborations, not only on dramas, but also on moral, philosophic, and scientific writings.

Voltaire in Danger: April 1734

Through these months in 1733 and into 1734, Du Châtelet's letters identify Voltaire as a delightful and challenging intellectual companion, not as a lover. They offer nothing to explain her dramatic decision to join him at the Du Châtelet family château in Champagne only a year later. When the moment came, in June 1735, even her friends doubted her resolve for what appeared to be unorthodox behavior at best, irresponsible and scandalous at worst. That June, Maupertuis reported to La Condamine, already on his way with the expedition to measure the earth at the equator, that the marquise had said she planned to be away for three or four years, but "happily one cannot believe her capable of this"—meaning that one would miss her were she away so long, and that she could resist the life of Paris for only a short time. Du Châtelet's previous biographers see only the hero of the 1789 Revolution, the great man, Voltaire. They cannot imagine any woman resisting his attentions, or delaying a moment to join him in his exile. But this is not how it would have appeared to Du Châtelet or her contemporaries.

When they first began their flirtation in that spring of 1733, Du Châtelet was a young woman of privilege and position. Voltaire was years her senior, a wealthy man, a literary star, but he had no claim to social distinction, and had a history of trouble with the king's government. At nineteen, for example, Voltaire had taken refuge at the country estate of one of her father's cousins. So the young man met the baron de Breteuil and, supposedly, the precocious seven-year-old Gabrielle Emilie as well. As the son of a notary, Voltaire cultivated connections with the nobility throughout his life. His father's well-born clients aided in his advancement. Admission to the prestigious Jesuit *collège* Louis-le-Grand in Paris linked the boy then known as François-Marie Arouet to René-Louis de Voyer de Paulmy, marquis d'Argenson, a future minister of war to Louis XV; René Hérault, the man who would later be in charge of the Paris police; and, perhaps his most sincere and steadfast friend among the nobility, Charles-Augustin de Ferriol, comte d'Argental, nephew to the *salonnière* Mme de Tencin.

However, Voltaire rejected the careers his parent chose for him: diplomacy, and then the law. His first trouble with the royal authorities came because his own father arranged a *lettre de cachet,* an order for his arrest and

imprisonment. By 1714, he had already begun to submit his poems to the
Académie française. Back in Paris, introduced into the world of the *salons*
and the court of the prince regent, Voltaire delighted the members of these
circles with his gift for satiric verse and his lively parodies of the august and
venerated. The *garde des sceaux,* keeper of the seals, the government official
responsible for protecting the public morals through censorship, watched
for such attacks on what the royal government defined as sacred institutions: the family, the Church, and the King. Inevitably, in May 1717, the
brash young bourgeois found himself in the Bastille. Du Châtelet's father,
the baron de Breteuil, spoke on the poet's behalf, and along with his
Caumartin cousin negotiated the young man's release, but not until almost
a year later, in April 1718.

The young Arouet emerged unchastened but a bit more circumspect. He
had been disinherited by his father, decided to take the name Voltaire, and
completed his first play.[41] The Comédie française performed *Oedipe* in November 1718, and with its publication the following January, he had made
his own fame. Members of the *haute noblesse* sought his company. He traveled with the duc de Richelieu when his estates or his military obligations
took him away from Versailles. The marquis d'Argenson, his friend from
Louis-le-Grand, probably aided in the first introductions to these elite circles. Now he would be received at Mme de Tencin's literary *salon*, and by
Anne Louise Bénédicte de Bourbon-Condé, duchesse du Maine, at the court
this member of the royal family had created for herself at Sceaux. In addition, though Voltaire received nothing from his father's death and his subsequent contest of the will, he already had a modest royal pension and had
embarked on his epic poem about the reign of Henri IV.

Despite periods of discouragement and a case of smallpox, Voltaire persevered, and *La Henriade* appeared in April 1723. Four or five pirated versions attested to its immediate success. Though the numerous cantos can
seem endless to a twenty-first-century reader—a mixture of Voltaire's own
voice with borrowings from Virgil and two Italian poets, Tasso and Ariosto—
La Henriade was applauded in the journals of the Republic of Letters, such as
the *Mercure de France* and the *Journal des savants.* In the next decades, Voltaire
oversaw many publications of the work, which always sold, and gained him
yet more acclaim. Even his most public enemies, like the courtier Maurepas, and the king's principal minister and former tutor, Cardinal Fleury,

acknowledged Voltaire's gifts. In his memoirs, Maurepas described Voltaire as "a writer facile, ingenious, elegant." Maurepas meant this as a criticism, but he had identified what both delighted and infuriated contemporaries.[42]

For the Voltaire that Du Châtelet knew, *La Henriade* defined his genius. He once explained to a correspondent that he had written the epic "to be immortal." Unlike those who would later glorify his memory, he saw himself first as a poet and second as a playwright.[43] Like his readers, he believed that this story in alexandrine verse about France's sixteenth-century religious wars compared favorably with the classical works from which he borrowed so freely. To leading figures of the Republic of Letters, Voltaire became proof that, in the battle between the "ancients" and the "moderns," this poet of the modern era had won. Not only did the verses surpass those of the ancients, but his epic was of far more use to contemporary society: a Christian exemplary history, not a pagan one; a work in the spirit of Horace but one that united poetry and philosophy in contemporary terms and in the French language. As the presiding authority of the Café Gradot, Houdar de la Motte, noted in his formal approval for the publication of *Oedipe,* Voltaire was "the successor of Corneille and Racine."[44]

In the course of his long life, Voltaire wrote a total of twenty-six tragedies and two dozen more plays, some performed by the Comédie française, others in amateur productions in which he himself often took one of the roles. When Voltaire and his contemporaries thought a playwright exceptional, it was because of his ability to write a tragedy. Jordan explained that, despite any faults in these plays, in the case of Voltaire, "there is always an infinity of beauty that charms and delights."[45] "Faults" in the eyes of an educated eighteenth-century playgoer meant a break with traditions. For drama, especially tragedy, was, like epic, a classical form. The Jesuits at Louis-le-Grand had taught Voltaire the Greek theatrical "unities" of time, action, and place, and in his desire to surpass the "ancients"—whether Greek, Roman, or French—Voltaire held to these and other rules, at least in principle: a story spanning twenty-four hours, a single day and night; a minimum number of settings; no comic scenes to alter the impact of the tragic, complicated personal dramas.

Initially, like Corneille and Racine, Voltaire drew his subjects from classical and ancient sources. *Oedipe* (1718) recalled the *Oedipus Rex* of Sophocles; *Mariamne* (1725) used the Biblical characters Herod and his wife; *Brutus*

(1730) and *La Mort de César* (1731) depicted the last years of the Roman Republic. Like other playwrights throughout Europe, he also copied and adapted plots and characters from more recent sources. After his return from exile in England in 1728, he borrowed from Shakespeare: *Eriphyle* (1732) had bits reminiscent of *Hamlet* and *Macbeth*. However, more significantly, his time in England inspired a daring break with French tradition. Voltaire did not like the messy, bloody style of English drama, the passions and violence, but, having seen the plays about Britain's kings by Marlowe and Shakespeare, he decided that the history of France offered similarly exciting plots for tragedy. He set *Zaïre* (1732) in the twelfth-century Jerusalem of St. Louis to tell the story of a Muslim ruler and a Christian slave girl. The Hundred Years' War gave him the scene for *Adelaïde Du Guesclin* (1734), which, with its star-crossed lovers caught in the politics and changing allegiances of France and England's fourteenth-century conflict, echoed *Romeo and Juliet*. When Voltaire and Du Châtelet began to spend time together in 1733, he was at the height of his form.[46]

Du Châtelet and her friends literally sobbed at the revelations of these conflicts, at the tragic turns of fate, the misplaced jealousies, the needless suicides and murders of heroines and heroes. A twenty-first-century reader might find it hard to conjure such emotions, and the plays are rarely performed today. The speeches of the stereotypical principals read stiff and lifeless, despite Voltaire's facile genius with the majestic cadences of the French alexandrine, and the neatness of his rhymed couplets. The verse, in fact, was one of the reasons for his success, because of the eighteenth century's sheer appreciation of language. Audiences reveled in the grandeur of the soliloquies, the melodrama of the extended dialogues. Voltaire's characters examine their motives, discuss their possible actions, react to what has happened offstage, speculate about what others might or might not do. People die onstage, but the real drama is the discussion that precedes or follows the action that brought tears to the eyes of Voltaire's spectators. This is a theater of familiar images and characterizations, of predictable outcomes. The virtuosity of the actors and the brilliance of the playwright lay in the manner of manipulating traditional forms, and in the studied presentation of what the elite of Paris accepted as the "universals" of the human condition.

From Voltaire's first production in 1718 at the Comédie française, he was a favored author of the royal company. Many of his tragedies brought in revenue and could be counted upon to do so whenever the company chose to play them. As author, Voltaire could name the actors he wanted, and he and the company set a date for the first performance. Jeanne-Françoise Quinault, the oldest daughter of a successful theatrical family, an actress, and a key member of the company, often read drafts of Voltaire's plays even before he formally submitted them, and her suggestions could be vital to their acceptance. Customarily, two plays were performed in an evening, and the Comédie française usually paired a tragedy with a comedy. Voltaire's *Zaïre*, his great success of 1732, however, drew audiences so successfully that sometimes it was played alone. In one particularly profitable year, it made the company twenty thousand livres in revenues.[47]

Du Châtelet's admiration for Voltaire, the man she called "the most eloquent pen of his century," knew no bounds. He was for her the personification of the highest form of genius as a "metaphysician, a historian, a great philosopher, but one who preferred to be a poet, and thus was known as France's greatest poet." She proudly told his friends that she had known his epic *La Henriade* "by heart even before knowing its author."[48] Even so, neither she nor her family would forget Voltaire's bourgeois origins. Her relatives, such as the marquise de Créqui and François Victor, the titular head of the Breteuil family, were highly critical of him, both before and after the beginning of their liaison. That Voltaire made a living from the theater and investments, had been twice incarcerated in the Bastille, and had been sent into exile made him all the more undesirable for a young woman of Du Châtelet's rank.

Even in the supposedly egalitarian gatherings of the Paris *salon* of Mme Du Deffand, customs dictated acknowledgment of difference and hierarchy. In the 1740s, a Dr. Fournier attended one of her evenings. He greeted her, a marquise, and the other nobles—Président Hénault (so called because of his office); Pont-de-Veyle, d'Argental's older brother—in the appropriate phrases, "I have the honor to present my very humble respects. . . . I am your very humble servant." When he came to greet the mathematician d'Alembert, another *salonnière*'s illegitimate son, he said simply, *"Bonjour, monsieur."* Perhaps these rigid practices and attitudes explain much of Voltaire's rebellious behavior as a young man, his challenges to these realities of French society throughout his life. In Semur in 1726, Du Châtelet probably heard the story of Voltaire's encounter with the chevalier de Rohan-

Chabot. Voltaire had responded to the nobleman's insults with quips of his own, an outrageous act in these circles. Rohan's response? His lackeys beat Voltaire brutally as he left the duc de Sully's *hôtel* in the Place Royale. When Voltaire returned inside, none of the privileged guests made an effort to help him, and he was the one who had to flee to England. His courtier patroness at the time, Mme de Prie, dropped him and pronounced that he was right in fact, but as to "form, he was wrong."[49]

Du Châtelet's pleasure in the playful and apparently asexual nature of her relationship with Voltaire could reflect her reservations as well—in particular, her unfortunate experience with the comte Louis Vincent de Goesbriand. This military man, who was the same age as her husband, probably sought her out at the Villars-Brancas' soon after her return to Paris in 1728. In this affair, Du Châtelet not only accepted the attentions of the wrong kind of man, but also, by her behavior at the end of the affair, created the dreaded *le bruit* (noise), a public scene so inappropriate that news of it doubtless reached her husband and her scandal-wary relatives. As Du Châtelet learned, the punishment for such *gaucherie* was ridicule, to become the subject of that week's gossip, whether at the Café Procope, in the anterooms of Versailles, or at the gaming tables of the most prestigious *salons* in Paris.[50]

Du Châtelet was not the first or the only woman to force public notice of her extramarital liaison because of errors of judgment. The *nouvelliste* Dubuisson's readers laughed at the wife who had an affair with her husband's secretary, for "she had had the imprudence" to leave evidence in writing: pages of letters were discovered after her sudden death. Another made the unfortunate mistake of imagining that she could juggle two lovers at once, an earnest young nobleman and the grand master of *galanterie* and seduction (according to all his contemporaries), the duc de Richelieu. The memoir by Maurepas, Cardinal Fleury's adviser, is the principal source for the closing scene of Du Châtelet's affair with the comte de Goesbriand. The aging Maurepas remembered that the young marquise, "desperate at seeing herself abandoned by the marquis de Guébriant [sic], whom she idolized," wrote him a farewell letter. She wanted to die, she explained in her note, because "he did not live for her." Refused entry by her Swiss guards, he pushed them aside, "flies to her *appartement*" to find her lying down, asleep from a "dose of opium great enough to kill." He saved her, but still rejected her despite "this proof of love." The young marquise then "consoles herself with many others."[51]

The real story? Du Châtelet, imagining herself discarded, probably in favor of another young woman, was certainly capable of a scene such as Maurepas recounted. Did Goesbriand rush back to save her? Or did he just read the note and walk to his sedan chair laughing and already forming in his mind how he would transform the events into an amusing anecdote? The latter seems likely, the story gaining details as it passed from café to *salon* to *nouvelliste*. Goesbriand never rose above the rank of captain, and he died with so many debts that his creditors stepped in and sold the family possessions. His disgrace, however, went relatively unnoticed. In contrast, the wits never forgot Du Châtelet's poisoned "pills." In 1748, decades after the event, the duc de Luynes included in his diary the verses of an insulting song about Du Châtelet that was then circulating at court. It mocked her participation in the amateur theatricals at Lunéville, her social pretensions, her aged appearance, and her insolent behavior, and it ended: "And for monsieur de Guébriant [sic], / She took some pills."[52]

Two of Du Châtelet's writings suggest that this public ridicule had taught her to regret passionate attachments played on such a public stage. Her reading in Montaigne would have given her the traditional images of women's susceptibility to passion, "the natural violence of their desire." She did not repeat these truisms in her version of some of the "remarks" in Mandeville's *Fable,* but she drew on them, as perhaps Mandeville had. In the section on the ways in which society counters this female susceptibility, Du Châtelet faithfully translated the value of "shame" in maintaining a young woman's chastity. Any man who wanted to seduce a woman knew that it was her fear of shame, not her modesty and love of virtue, that had to be conquered. In fact, her image of a shamed man's feelings was far more powerful than the original in English: "He dare not lift his head, his eyes covered with a cloud remain attached to the earth, no injury can move it, his being is heavy to him, and he would like to hide from himself and from others." Du Châtelet's *Discours sur le bonheur* offers another insight. Here, as in her version of Mandeville's *Fable,* she wrote of "mépris,"—contempt, disdain. Du Châtelet believed that "no one on earth could feel disdain without feeling despair." "It is worse torture," she explained, than any the authorities could inflict, "because it lasts longer and is never accompanied by hope."[53]

How, then, did Voltaire overcome her reluctance? No letters between them have been found, despite two contemporary accounts of multiple bound volumes.[54] So how did Du Châtelet decide on an action even more melodramatic than the end of her affair with Goesbriand: to abandon her life in Paris and to join the bourgeois playwright in his latest exile? Contemporaries offer no answers, but in April 1734 a series of events must have irrevocably changed Du Châtelet's perspective. The duc de Richelieu had contracted a marriage with a daughter of the Guise family, a great step up in this world of lineages, for it meant alliance to a family only steps away from the throne. The Guises, like the Du Châtelets, came from Lorraine, and Du Châtelet and her husband probably would have been together at the wedding. Richelieu was then commander of the Army of the Rhine, in which her husband had just been promoted to brigadier in February. Perhaps the two noblemen made the journey together from their encampment in Lorraine to the Guise family château, Montjeu, in Burgundy. Voltaire, long a companion of the duc's when he ventured away from court or his military duties to enjoy the *salons* and cafés of Paris, probably came as part of Du Châtelet's entourage. All seemed particularly auspicious. Du Châtelet described the lovely young wife-to-be, Elisabeth Sophie de Lorraine, as charming, with a "strong mind" and a heart "capable of great affection & gratitude." The duchesse's contemporaries agreed in their praise of this gentle, generous woman who against all convention loved her husband. She became almost legendary in a court and Parisian circles that thrived on other qualities.[55]

Then news reached the guests at Montjeu that Voltaire's *Lettres philosophiques* had appeared with a London imprint; within a few weeks, a French edition had been printed in Rouen. Any book published in France had to have a royal *approbation,* but the Rouen edition had no evidence of this official sanction. The representatives of the royal government acted appropriately. On May 3, 1734, Germain Louis Chauvelin, the *garde des sceaux,* issued the order to arrest Voltaire. The author feigned surprise and innocence, but for almost a year, since June 1733, he had been writing to friends such as Thieriot and Cideville of his plans for this collection of irreverent encyclopedialike short essays in the form of letters, and of his fear of reprisals. Chauvelin himself, in July, had warned Voltaire of the consequences of publication. Voltaire had corrected the English proofs nonetheless, and Thieriot arranged for the London edition. Supposedly, Du Châtelet and Cideville had prevailed upon him to delay publication in France, even after the shorter English version appeared in August 1733. He wrote to his friends that he planned to go into exile if necessary, and compared himself first to Calvin and then, in another letter, to Ovid. He was clear in these letters that he understood that his veiled mockery of the established church, his apparent acceptance of Locke's speculation that an omnipotent God could have given the power of thought to all matter, and his own pointed admiration of the religious tolerance of Protestant sects like the Quakers, would lead to his condemnation as "impious."[56]

A few days after the book appeared in France, Du Châtelet heard from Maupertuis about the response in Paris. His letter terrified her; she wondered if Voltaire should go even farther away. An order from Maurepas to enforce the *lettre de cachet* (order to arrest) had been presented to her by the local intendant of Burgundy when he could not find Voltaire. She described what might be Voltaire's fate to Sade, envisioning "my best friend with horrible health in prison, where he will surely die of sadness, if illness doesn't kill him." As Voltaire moved from place to place to avoid arrest, he now imagined himself as St. Augustine forced to retract his writings, and asked would it be his book or he himself that would be burned. Melodramatic in its own way, the royal court, the *parlement* of Paris, chose the book over the author, issuing a ritual condemnation of the writings "as scandalous to religion, morality and the respect due to the authorities." The climax of this government-orchestrated drama occurred at 11 a.m. on the tenth of June: the royal executioner ceremonially tore up and then burned the book in the courtyard of the palace where the Paris *parlement* met. More practically, Hérault, Paris's lieutenant of police, confiscated all the copies he and his men could find. The Rouen publisher who had dared to publish without the royal approval required of every book, even the most orthodox, was arrested. Of course, the book circulated anyway, in pirated editions. Voltaire enlarged the collection of letters and republished it outside of France; the elite bought it from their Dutch and Swiss booksellers.

Voltaire's and Du Châtelet's letters to their friends document not only her role during these months but also the changes in her feelings. With the active help of her husband, she became Voltaire's most ardent if not his most influential protector. She herself approached Maurepas, a relative of her mother's and the son of a significant patron to her father. Still, Voltaire's "affairs go every day from bad to worse," she wrote to Sade. In the end, it was the influence of the young duchesse de Richelieu that calmed "l'orage," "the storm," as Du Châtelet came to describe the incidents. The duchesse presented Voltaire's carefully composed letter of apology with his official denial of any involvement in the publication of the unapproved book. Chauvelin, the *garde des sceaux,* awarded the marquis and the marquise Du Châtelet the "official authorization to sequester" Voltaire, an eighteenth-century version of "house arrest."[57] Exiled from Paris and the court, Voltaire had permission to stay at Cirey, the Du Châtelet family estate in Champagne. The modest château was only a few hours' ride to the borders of Lorraine, the quasi-independent duchy that could be a refuge should Voltaire need more distance from the royal authorities. The local mail coach could take him even farther away, to the more permissive cities of Brussels and Amsterdam.

Voltaire wrote to Cideville and La Condamine of how loyal Du Châtelet had been and of her efforts on his behalf. "She renders good offices to her friends with the same vivacity that she learned the languages of mathematics; and when she has rendered all the services imaginable, she believes she has done nothing." He continued describing her with remarkable acumen: "Just as with her mind and its insights, she believes that she knows nothing and is unaware that she has a mind." Du Châtelet evidently enjoyed the intensity of feelings, the anxiety, the intrigue of secret addresses and hiding places just as much as Voltaire. She imagined "fleeing with him." In the same letter to Sade in which she had feared for the errant poet's death, she declared that being with Voltaire "was the happiness of her life; his safety her tranquillity." In late June, she reported to Maupertuis that Voltaire was in better spirits, and that she could now return to her mathematics. She announced that she planned to leave Montjeu for Paris on the twentieth of June.[58]

Du Châtelet apparently thought she could just return to Paris and resume her accustomed activities. However, she quickly discovered that she missed being with Voltaire and worried about what might happen to him. She explained to Sade in July 1734: "I am not accustomed to living without him, nor to the thought of losing him without recourse. That would poison all the sweetness of my life." Du Châtelet began to write of going back to

Cirey at the beginning of September. There would have been her obligations as a *châtelaine* of the estates, and the need to arrange the accommodations for her guest, but other factors came into play. Ordinarily in the fall she would have followed the court to Fontainebleau, but that year she chose not to. Even Paris, though still amusing, had lost much of its charm. She explained to the abbé de Sade that her young son had been ill, that this had kept her busy. One night the little boy died, probably the last Sunday in August. Then, the next week, Maupertuis, without mentioning it to her beforehand, took Clairaut to Basel to meet his mentor, Johann Bernoulli.[59] After the death of her son, with no opportunity to continue her mathematics lessons, and her husband on campaign, Du Châtelet decided to go to Cirey. She must have instructed her servants to gather together what she considered necessary to her and Voltaire's comfort. At the beginning of October, she set off by coach for the journey to Champagne. Voltaire described to a neighbor Du Châtelet's arrival in a "kind of cart" with "two hundred boxes."

Despite what was still lacking—*fauteuils,* hangings for the beds, horses for the carriage—they settled into a routine that pleased them both. Voltaire's affection for the young noblewoman was obvious: "In the midst of this disorder, Madame Du Châtelet laughs and is charming." The marquise brought energy, intelligence, and excitement. She joined in Voltaire's plans to transform the old brick-and-limestone château into an elegant, if modest, refuge. The wars of the fifteenth and sixteenth centuries had not been kind to the village or its "castle." Much had been burned or destroyed by artillery in 1642 by Cardinal Richelieu—great-uncle to their friend the duc—as part of his leveling of all potential noble strongholds for his king, Louis XIII. Voltaire's letters suggest the haze of love. He enjoyed watching her change the plans for the extension and the gardens: windows became doors, chimney breasts turned into places for stairs, linden trees were planted (though he wanted elms).[60]

That fall of 1734, they each wrote to Maupertuis in Basel, giving him an account of their first two months living together. Both mentioned the workmen who had been engaged and the repairs being made. Du Châtelet described herself as becoming accustomed to the "profound solitude." She divided her time, she explained to her absent mentor, "between the masons and m. Lock[e]." She, like Voltaire, now referred to Cirey as "my hermitage." She wrote of her "sweet hope" that in the future, when he, Maupertuis, had spent more time in Paris, had "gained all that one can of the world," and had become disgusted with it, they would spend "des années philosophiques"— years pursuing their philosophical studies—here in the country.[61]

In his letter to Maupertuis, Voltaire referred to Du Châtelet as "the most beautiful soul in the world." The soul was considered the source of all feeling in the eighteenth century. Certainly, he continued to use his best tools to flatter her: quatrains, odes, more epistles done in the classical styles of Virgil, Horace, Catullus, and Ovid that he replicated with such facility to flatter and delight. He teased her about busying herself with algebra when he wanted to speak to her of love: "Mais hélas, A + D − B / N'est pas = à je vous aime." ("But, alas, A + D − B / Doesn't = I love you"). Did their relationship become sexual? Yes, even though she wrote to Maupertuis that Voltaire was ill, a "hypochondriac," always afraid for his health. To succumb physically would have seemed part of the more significant intellectual seduction during these fall months. She could speak to him of Locke, of mathematics, of his plays; never had she known this kind of companionship. Probably at his suggestion, she began her study and translation of Mandeville's Fable, perhaps to perfect her English and to understand the Dutchman's moral views. In the end, she altered the original dramatically. She omitted the verses that gave the book its name, The Fable of the Bees or the Grumbling Hive, compressed an accompanying essay on the "origins of moral virtue," and completed only the first eleven of twenty-two "Remarks" meant to elucidate couplets from the opening poem. Some of the ideas of Mandeville that she favored became part of Voltaire's writing. He continued to work on his Traité de métaphysique. At the St. Petersburg National Library, in the Collection of Occidental Manuscripts, there is a copy of his Traité that she must have read at this time. Her effort to correct some of his ideas, particularly on human liberty, or free will, are clearly evident.[62] They continued to revise his tragedy Alzire, and he showed her early drafts of the dedication to her that he planned to include with the published version.

Despite her projects, her mention of the pastoral idyll, of "mon Académie," and the prospect of a life with a circle of intellectual friends, Du Châtelet still had not decided that Cirey would be her permanent residence. Her letter to Maupertuis inviting him to share in the philosophical life was also full of the news of Paris from just before she left and expressed her desire to have them all reunited in December for dinner and midnight mass. She kept to her plan. Once in Paris again, she returned to the round of courtier's activities, to her lessons in mathematics. That winter of 1734–35, Voltaire's close friends, such as Formont and Thieriot, met and recommended her to one another. Formont wrote of a dinner they both attended, of another to come.[63] Voltaire also assumed his time at Cirey would be only another temporary exile. He hoped that the religious message of *Alzire* would silence accusations of his apostasy and please the *dévots,* the very devout group in the queen's circle at court and in the *parlement* of Paris, even before its first presentation. Thus, he reasoned, his friends would be able to prevail upon the royal ministers to rescind the *lettre de cachet.* On March 2, 1735, Chauvelin and Fleury agreed that the Rouen publisher Jore was more at fault than the author, and granted Voltaire the right to return to Paris as long as he did nothing "similar to that which had caused the former complaints against him." The minister and the *garde des sceaux* did not, however, revoke the *lettre de cachet,* the order for his arrest; they simply chose to ignore it for the time being.

Voltaire had arrived in the capital by the twentieth of March but he immediately placed himself in danger again. While at Cirey, he had begun *La Pucelle,* irreverent verses about Jeanne d'Arc. Du Châtelet, like his intimate friends, enjoyed the scatalogical humor, but public mockery of Jeanne d'Arc invited a government response. Cantos of *La Pucelle* began to make the rounds of the *salons,* eventually finding their way into the reports of the *nouvellistes* and, more important, of the police. Within six weeks condemned by the royal officials as a "public nuisance," Voltaire had to flee again, first to the court of Lorraine under the protection of the duchesse de Richelieu. At the end of June, as the result of another series of negotiations, again with the active intervention of the marquis Du Châtelet, Voltaire returned to Cirey.[64] The marquis's acceptance of responsibility for Voltaire indicated his tacit approval of his wife's association with the popular but foolish playwright.

Voltaire's extended stay at their country estate in Champagne and Du Châtelet's visits there could be seen as a generous arrangement for his protection, a fact of which both the marquis and his wife could be proud. The question of sexual intimacy, of an inappropriate adultery, could be masked, and scandal thus avoided. Ironically, one source of scandal, the disparity in rank, could discourage such thoughts. Du Châtelet was Voltaire's muse, a prodigy "of knowledge and *esprit* [wit]." He was, in a sense, part of her entourage, her poet and playwright, her mentor. So Voltaire was described by the *nouvelliste* Bouhier, August 6, 1735: "It is true, Mr., that Voltaire is at present in Champagne. He is in the following of the marquise Du Châtelet, he scarcely leaves, and he is building on one of her lands." It is likely that Voltaire's reputation for a lack of sexual prowess also made Du Châtelet's companionship with him more acceptable than it otherwise might have been. For example, contemporaries knew that Mme de Fontaine-Martel took men of the Republic of Letters into her household in the Palais Royal, but she preferred those who had no interest in women. She was reputed to have thrown out Voltaire's friend Thieriot when he became infatuated with a star of the Opéra. Voltaire was supposedly the perfect guest, because he was presumed "to be impotent."[65]

In 1735 and throughout the years of his association with Du Châtelet and her husband, Voltaire took on his share of the household expenses and of the costs of the renovations and additions to the château. Voltaire's wealth certainly could also have been a mitigating factor. Once it was decided that Voltaire would go to live at Cirey, Dubuisson reported that the poet had loaned the marquis Du Châtelet between twenty-five and thirty thousand livres "pour le lui faire trouver bien," "to make him find it good," a phrase suggesting both that Voltaire was giving money for the use of the house and that he was ensuring the marquis's approval of the arrangement. Voltaire loaned many noblemen money in order to elicit their protection. Dubuisson wrote in June 1735 that the duc de Richelieu owed a hundred thousand livres to the playwright, a complicated debt resolved piecemeal over decades. Men of Voltaire's rank routinely did this. Fontenelle, another prominent bourgeois man of letters, commonly made loans, living off the *rente* (a fixed payment), or making what constituted outright gifts, indefinite loans with no interest.[66]

What was unusual in these arrangements between Voltaire and the *noblesse d'épée* was the extent of Voltaire's resources. He was arguably the richest playwright of the first half of the eighteenth century in France. For five acts, he received one-ninth of the receipts after all the expenses and fixed charges, such as the king's 15 percent of all gross receipts, had been paid. Voltaire's plays at the Comédie française, beginning with *Oedipe* in 1718, routinely brought him thirty-five to fifty-two hundred livres during a run of performances, rarely less than six thousand livres per season. As well as the production, the publication of a play earned Voltaire money, as did the frequent editions of all of his writings. The English translation of his verse epic *La Henriade* netted him thirty thousand livres. All Voltaire scholars agree, however, that the real basis of his fortune was the financial coup that he, La Condamine, and a group of their friends engineered with the royal lottery of 1729. Voltaire then invested his share of the twelve million livres they won in a variety of very profitable enterprises and created a complicated financial web that in some years gave him an income rivaling that of the wealthiest nobility, up to eighty thousand livres. From the 1740s on, much of Voltaire's income came from royal contracts. He acquired a share in a business that provisioned part of the French army at a considerable profit. Most lucrative of all were the investments Voltaire made in the "Barbary trade," the triangle shipping from North Africa to Cadiz, Spain, to the Spanish viceroyalties of Mexico and Peru. In an accounting of 1749, Longchamps, his valet, reported the interest on this investment as 32 to 33 percent, giving Voltaire assets in the millions of livres.[67]

The Decision: June 1735

Du Châtelet wrote to Maupertuis that he would have to go back to the "world" a number of times before he would be prepared to join her and Voltaire at Cirey. This seems to have been advice derived from her own experience of the last year and a half. The process of moving from one life to another was an intermittent theme in her letters from as early as the winter of 1733. They show that, though she never gave up her love of anecdote, of gossip—about appointments, benefices, royal-family squabbles, arranged noble marriages, a new opera production—increasingly these frivolous entertainments, which she now referred to as the world of "princesses and pompons," made her feel tired and constrained. In December 1733, almost seven months after her association with Voltaire began, Du Châtelet confided to Sade: "I give myself up to the world without liking it very much. Imperceptible chains make entire days pass often without one being aware that one has lived." Her life was "disordered." In May 1734, after Voltaire's troubles with the government over the *Lettres philosophiques* had begun, she wrote to Sade that even their circle of friends now disgusted her: "so false, so unjust, so full of prejudices, so tyrannical." She lived among "envious vipers," the "punishment for being alive and young." Better, she continued, to be fifty years old and to be far from Paris with Voltaire, with Mme de Richelieu, and with him.[68]

Du Châtelet wrote four long stream-of-consciousness–like letters to the duc de Richelieu from May 21, 1735, to the day she left Paris for Cirey, the fifteenth of June. "Mes bavardages," "my conversations," she called them, jumping from one subject to another, from the "brouhahas of the world" to the "sweetnesses of love."[69] Here can be read the gradual rejection of the one life and the gathering of justifications for embracing the other. On May 21, she wrote the duc from Chantilly, a château used by Louis XV for hunting, of Mme Villars-Brancas's attentions, but also suggested the courtier's insincerity and willfulness: "the pleasantries of people that I please today and whom, I will perhaps displease tomorrow." On that particular afternoon, bored with the court after only eight days, she had left her friends to walk in the woods. She wrote to the duc by the "soft murmur of a fountain, like a heroine in a novel." The language she chose reflects this simile: "I lose my life far from all that I love. . . . In twenty-four hours [Paris] became a desert." She wrote of life as "insupportable" because he and the duchesse were not there. Only in Champagne did the feeling of boredom leave her. For the first time, she acknowledged Voltaire as more than her affectionate companion. She had "tasted the happiness of living in the country with my lover," and tentatively announced that she might return sometime toward the end of June.

The next day, Sunday, she began to sort through the potential problems to be overcome. How her husband might view this decision preoccupied her, especially with talk of peace and thus his likely return to Paris and to Cirey. She presumed that Richelieu would see him, since the duc was his commander. She formulated a strategy: Richelieu was to tell her husband of her plans, "to boast of her trip, of her courage, and the good effect it will have in society." She continued, "Just speak to him of Voltaire, but with interest and affection, and above all try to insinuate that it would be crazy to be jealous of a wife with whom one is content, that one esteems, and who conducts herself well." She assumed the marquis, who respected Richelieu, would accept his counsel.

From her next letter to the duc—over a week later, on May 30—it is evident that Richelieu did not approve of her plan and had not told her husband. Du Châtelet acknowledged, "My situation is thorny enough, but love changes all the thorns to flowers, as it will the mountains of Cirey, the earthly paradise." If one loved passionately, one should live in the country. She edged toward the decision, imagining "the pleasure to pass all the moments of my life with the one I love." She hoped to leave Paris on June twentieth. The more she reflected on Voltaire's situation and her own, the more "I believe the course of action I am taking necessary." She laid out the nature of this necessity. She focused on the anguish Voltaire's behavior had caused her. She must find a way to protect him and to give herself peace. Voltaire's imagination, she believed, continually created trouble: "I would lose him sooner or later in Paris, or at the least pass my life in fear of losing him or of having reason to complain about him." She saw no way to control him, or to protect him from the government's persecution, if she stayed in the city; only in the country did she believe she could be effective. Voltaire was, in her eyes, so brilliant and rational on the one hand and so blind on the other. Hard as it might have been for the duc to believe, she insisted, "I love Voltaire enough to sacrifice all that I could find pleasurable and agreeable in Paris for the happiness of living with him without dangers, and the pleasure of tearing him away in spite of himself from his imprudences and his destiny."[70]

Two more weeks passed. On June 15, in the last letter of this sequence, she acknowledged Richelieu's dire predictions should she take this course of action: "There is heroism in it, or perhaps folly for me, to bury myself entirely at Cirey: however," she continued, "the choice has been made." She would leave for Cirey in four hours. She felt that she must explain her decision: "I feel that I am not eloquent; but the longing to communicate my ideas to you, as confused as they are, silences my pride." Du Châtelet then interwove the gossip of the court—for example, another marquise's flirtatious message for him—with the justifications for her unorthodox behavior and the firmness of her resolve. She continued with an image that tells much about her husband's feelings for her: "I believe myself mistress enough to destroy the suspicions of my husband more than to stop V.'s imagination. . . . At Cirey, I can at least hope that love will thicken the veil that should, for his [the marquis's] happiness and ours, cover my husband's eyes." And, once again, she counted on the duc to use "his eloquence" with M. Du Châtelet.

The duc's fears, in addition to those concerning her husband, must also have been for Voltaire. Was this young woman serious, or just pleased to act the lover? Voltaire had publicly expressed his doubts in his epistle "A Madame la Marquise Du Châtelet sur sa liaison avec Maupertuis." In response, Du Châtelet displayed the righteousness of the innocent. "You are wrong," she assured Richelieu, "my head is turned, and his worries and distrust distress me. I know that this makes the torment of his life; it would be better . . . if this corrupted mine as well." "There is a great deal of difference," she continued, "between jealousy and the fear of not being loved enough; . . . one can stand the one, when one feels it unmerited; but one cannot refrain from being touched and afflicted by the other." These doubts on Voltaire's part, "of not being loved enough," became the final justification. Jealousy, she explained, "is an annoying feeling, and the other a delicate worry against which there are fewer weapons and fewer remedies, outside of going to be happy at Cirey."

The remedy for all these ills now seemed simple: she would go to Cirey to be with the poet, to enjoy his companionship and love, to protect him from himself, and to prove how much he was loved. With this gesture she could serve her passions as well. "I do not believe," Du Châtelet told Richelieu in this last letter before her departure, "that I was born to be unhappy." Deciding on a clear course of action was a solution in and of itself. She later described these sentiments in her *Discours,* confidently insisting on one's ability to make one's own happiness, to make one's passions work for, not against one. She presented her prescription: "The first of all is to be very decided on what one wants to be and on what one wants to do. . . . It is the condition without which there is no happiness at all." Time had now become precious—hence, the urgency of her departure.[71]

In her June 15 letter to Richelieu, at the end of a paragraph filled with more anecdotes of the court, Du Châtelet mentioned that she had spent two hours walking with Fontenelle in the Tuileries Gardens. This promenade may have come about as a chance encounter, or it may have been the result of a flattering invitation from the grand old man of the Republic of Letters for an afternoon outing and conversation on a spring day. It was not, however, an accident that Du Châtelet wrote with such certainty after she had returned to her rooms. In some way, this promenade in the June sunshine with the old friend of her father and mother brought her to the final realization that she must join Voltaire at Cirey. They talked, and somehow—as she gathered together the justifications for her unorthodox choice—the potential disapproval of her husband and her family, and the possible ridicule from contemporaries, fell away. What did they discuss? What could he have said?

Bernard le Bovier de Fontenelle was seventy-eight. Du Châtelet probably slowed her pace to accommodate the aging secretary of the Académie
des sciences. The air would have been warm; by mid-June in Paris, the sun
regained most of its strength, and the leaves on the linden trees had the soft
green of new growth. They paused to greet acquaintances, or perhaps they
were so engrossed in conversation that they never noticed the passersby.
Fontenelle could not approve of Du Châtelet's enthusiasms; he believed
that women should "conceal the knowledge acquired by their minds as much
as the natural sentiments of their hearts." "Science" for them, he would explain should she ask, was "to observe to the point of scrupulousness the external proprieties of ignorance." Despite these views, however, he enjoyed
discussing her mathematics lessons with her. He himself at one time gave
lessons to the *honnêtes femmes* (noblewomen) of the *salons*.[72] Perhaps she had
become, in both their views, the fictional marquise of the book that made
his fame and much of his fortune, the *Entretiens* (*Conversations*). Maupertuis
had introduced her to Newton's universe. Perhaps she offered the younger
mathematician's hypothesis that Newton's attraction was as probable an explanation for the movement within the universe as Descartes's swirling
masses of particles, his *tourbillons*.

What of her dilemma would Du Châtelet have revealed? Fontenelle did
not like Voltaire, even though the younger man had courted him with verses
and flattery since the 1720s.[73] Perhaps Du Châtelet presented him with a
simple query: how does one know the right course of action? All of Fontenelle's life demonstrated his ability to make such choices rationally and
dispassionately. Though of her father's generation, by 1735 "*le roi* Fontenelle,"
as contemporaries called him, was probably the most famous French *savant*
of those decades. As Président Hénault described it, he was master "in every
genre." From a bourgeois family in Normandy, he was a model to the ambitious, the self-made, and self-defined man.[74] The success of Fontenelle's
Entretiens, its endless editions both in French and in other languages, explained only part of his success and the admiration he inspired. From his
twenties, he devoted himself to perfecting what he and his contemporaries
called "the art of pleasing," "of being agreeable." Others used the words "*fin
et rare*" (refined and pure), to convey his crystal-clear intellect, subtle, lively,
and sensitive, but never quick, always weighing and reflecting without emotion. He considered laughing a noisy, intrusive act, and preferred a slight

smile and the appropriate *bon mot*. His only moment of apparent irrationality, according to Du Châtelet's cousin Créqui, came at strawberry season, but even then there was an appropriately rational explanation: it was to this fruit that he attributed his longevity. He died one month short of his hundredth birthday.[75]

Du Châtelet also would have known of Fontenelle's unusual influence in setting the priorities and images of French science over the half-century when he held office as perpetual secretary of the Académie royale des sciences. His significant contributions to the Académie included all the measures he instituted to publicize its activities and its members. He established the twice-yearly public meetings, the publication of the best papers read at the two weekly private sessions, and the *éloge,* a gracefully composed extended obituary of a member. Du Châtelet in her own writings paid tribute to Fontenelle as an example of "un esprit superieur" and to the "immortality" his writings had gained for the Académie and himself.[76]

On that afternoon in the Tuileries Gardens, in his characteristic manner, Fontenelle perhaps paused, listened, and offered no comment until she had finished. Then he offered a suggestion from his treatise on happiness: one must weigh the hopes against the fears involved in a decision. He explained, in his mathematical way, "It is only a question of calculating, and wisdom always holds the counters [*les jetons*] in her hand." Like the counters used in a shop to add up the bill, or in a game of *trictrac* to indicate the points won, so the *jetons* could tip the balance in favor of one decision or another. The side with the most counters indicated wisdom's choice. Du Châtelet returned to her rooms and gave orders to her servants for the household's departure for Cirey that night. She wrote that one last letter to the duc de Richelieu to explain her "métaphysique d'amour," the reasons for her choice all counted and weighed to justify the decision to live at Cirey with her lover.[77]

Fontenelle's formula for happiness became a guiding principle of her life. One can hear the calculations in subsequent quandaries of like importance, when once again she found herself lost in "the sea of uncertainty." In fact, his phrases became so integral to her thinking that she later presented the wisdom of the *jetons* as her own maxim. In the late 1740s, when she had the time and occasion to finish her own *Discours* on happiness, she would repeat it word for word.

PART II

JULY 1735—MARCH 1741

CHAPTER THREE

"Mon Académie": *Châtelaine* of Cirey

From June of 1735 until October 1741, the young marquise Du Châtelet made only sporadic trips to Paris, and then it was more for family business than to enjoy "frivolous things." Instead, in Champagne and then in Brussels, Du Châtelet reveled in the discovery that she was "a thinking creature," adored and encouraged by Voltaire, the man she loved and revered. With her ambitious program of study during these years, she claimed the use of her intellect and spirit, the education that had been denied to her as a female by custom and circumstance, but that she now saw as "the rights of humanity and most of all those of the mind," as she would write in her translator's preface to Mandeville's *Fable*.[1] Initially, Du Châtelet set herself the role of companion and helpmate to Voltaire—"removing the thorns," as she pictured it, "that slow the true geniuses in their course." She read literature, philosophy, and science. She continued her own study of mathematics. With each project, her preference for the sciences became more evident, as did her unusual gifts. As she herself described the phenomenon in her version of Mandeville's *Fable,* it "sometimes happens that work and study force genius to declare itself."[2] This "genius" led her beyond her collaboration with Voltaire to the formulation of her own questions and the writing of her own answers.

When a *nouvelliste* described Voltaire as part of "the entourage of the marquise Du Châtelet," he gave the public an acceptable explanation well within the bounds of propriety for her unorthodox decision to make a life with him. This public acceptance must have helped to allay Du Châtelet's fears about her husband's reaction. Florent-Claude Du Châtelet-Lomont could endorse the image of the muse and her poet and the reality of this expanded household. Though he was rarely in residence at Cirey until the peace of November 1738, he neither turned away from his wife nor gave any sign of disapproval of her association with the sometimes notorious playwright. No "veil" seems to have been needed. He raised no objection to Voltaire's suggestions of a *précepteur* for his son, or to the dedicatory prose epistle that Voltaire wrote to his wife for the published version of *Alzire,* the play they had been working on together in Paris.[3] When not on campaign, he became his wife's and Voltaire's most trusted messenger, whether it was with a new manuscript for a publisher, corrections of a play, borrowed books being returned, or contracts and moneys for Voltaire's man of business in Paris. Du Châtelet included his greetings along with those of "m. de V." when she wrote to friends, telling them how much her husband wished to see them. To Maupertuis she sent, on the marquis's behalf, "a thousand compliments" and his admiration. Florent-Claude aided her in creating and sustaining her networks of friendships through his own letters and with his trips to Paris, and to Lunéville. He visited with courtiers and ministers and with men of letters such as Thieriot and Algarotti, in addition to Maupertuis. He might insist that she attend a wedding at the court of Lorraine; Du Châtelet, in turn, could ask him to bring Johann Bernoulli's son to join the household in Brussels as her own mathematics tutor.[4]

From the marquis's perspective, having his wife, the *châtelaine* of Cirey, in attendance at his feudal residence, the lands that formed the basis of his titles and rank, had other advantages. It meant a family presence on his estates. Each January when not on campaign, he returned to Cirey to deal with the business of rents, lumber sales, moneys from the forges. Now with her husband's *procuration* (power of attorney), she could deal with these affairs, so important to the family's financial well-being. In addition, with Cirey as their principal residence, when he did perform his duties to these and the other lands he had inherited on his father's death in 1732, it would be only a long day's ride—thirteen hours—to the court of Lorraine, rather than the week or so it had been from Semur or from Paris. The queen of France's father, King Stanislas of Poland, became duc of Lorraine in 1738, so new ties had to be created; the Du Châtelets' claims to special status as one of the four first families would have to be reaffirmed.

Florent-Claude not only allowed the poet to remain on the estate, but also took responsibility for his protection. Both the marquise and Mme de Graffigny, her husband's distant relative, referred in their letters of the late 1730s and the 1740s to his trips to Paris and Versailles on Voltaire's behalf. Du Châtelet herself counted on his effectiveness; in January 1737, she wrote to d'Argental, in the midst of the hysteria about Voltaire's images of Adam and Eve in his poem "Le Mondain" ("The Sophisticate"), that she was waiting for the right moment to enlist her husband's aid with Chauvelin, the *garde des sceaux,* for she did not "want to use his credit [*crédit*]" unnecessarily. Similarly, when Voltaire suffered the worst of new attacks in the press from a former friend, the abbé Desfontaines, Graffigny reported that the marquis himself went to Versailles and met with Cardinal Fleury. Du Châtelet explained to d'Argental that her husband would speak "with firmness and affection" on the poet's behalf.[5]

The marquis spent the winter of 1738–39 at Cirey. He acted the proper host while his wife and Voltaire kept to their rooms. Mme de Graffigny reported to her Lunéville correspondent, Devaux, that the military man spoke little and was boring if he spoke at length, yet he had been the one to seek her out. On some nights he might have retired from the galas over which Du Châtelet and Voltaire presided, but on others he played a willing part in the entertainments they organized. Du Châtelet and Voltaire could count on him to enlist visitors to participate in their plays and operas—he convinced Léopold Desmarest to join them for a marathon forty-eight hours of performances in February 1739.[6]

The Duties of a *Châtelaine*

The adjustment, however, away from what Maupertuis called "la cour et la ville" was neither easy nor simple. Voltaire described the refuge in Champagne as a "desert" when writing of his initial impression in May 1734, to his friend the comte d'Argental. Visitors noticed the distance and the isolation right away. The Venetian Francesco Algarotti, making his grand tour of Northern Europe, seemed amazed to find himself in countryside like this, with the château an "oasis." Du Châtelet called it "my Carthusian monastery"—the Carthusians were known for the desolate, lonely places they chose for their life of prayer. Voltaire understood what it was like for his lover. He wrote d'Argental that she was "someone who has done everything for me, who, for me, left Paris, all her friends, and all of the charms of life." Decades later, in his memoirs, he once again acknowledged her sacrifice: to "bury herself in a dilapidated house on the frontiers of Champagne and Lorraine."[7]

Voltaire's niece Mlle Mignot (soon to be Mme Denis) identified the initial problem, especially for a noblewomen in love with Paris. Though Mignot enjoyed the company, she found the "frightening solitude" and the fact that the château was four leagues from "all habitation" reason enough not to linger. Wolf packs still lived in the forests. Weather and circumstance played havoc with travel. One November, Du Châtelet left Paris on a Monday afternoon and arrived at the château at ten o'clock at night a week later—a journey that usually took only three to four days. On another occasion, when she and Voltaire made the journey together, the axle of the carriage broke. Their principal servant, Longchamps, left the coachman and two other attendants to deal with the horses while he walked half a league to the nearest village to find the men and materials needed to make repairs.[8]

Then as now, Paris was the hub of the kingdom, with major roads, paved and maintained by the king, leading out in the four directions from the city. More than 215 kilometers from Paris was Bar-sur-Aube, the ancient site of the comtes of Champagne and the nearest town to Cirey. It was a stop on the eastern post road to Lorraine and to Switzerland, and thus there was regular service for those who did not have their own *carrosse*. Du Châtelet always sent careful instructions to her visitors. The "poste," as she referred to the public coach, left every Saturday at 6 a.m. in summer and 6:30 in the winter from the rue de Braque in front of the convent of La Merci, across from the Hôtel de Soubise. When the *poste* halted in the dusty square by the castle walls of Bar-sur-Aube, most passengers stepped down to find their own refreshment while the coachman arranged the change of horses before going on. This was the route followed by Maupertuis when he visited Du Châtelet and Voltaire on his way to see the Bernoullis in Basel, and by Président Hénault on his way to take the waters at the spa of Plombières. There was no public transportation for the twenty kilometers from Bar-sur-Aube to Cirey.[9] Once she was in residence, Du Châtelet usually sent the phaeton, a light two-horse carriage. Mme de Graffigny arrived one snowy winter night at 2 a.m., cold, hungry, and exhausted, having missed the sight of the hillsides for wheat and maize, the vineyards that produced the "wine of Champagne" that Voltaire so liked, and the long stretches of forest, for the area was famous not only for its iron and champagne but also for its lumber and charcoal. Dirt tracks connected the villages and the estate's small foundries and forges. The village of Cirey-sur-Blaise came up quickly, and there on the left were the gates to the château. The Blaise River, which gave the area its name, ran along behind the château on its way to the Marne. Twenty or so small houses lined the road then, as they do now, as it continues on to Arnancourt and Doulevant.

Over the previous century, the marquis's father and grandfather had rebuilt the keep, the central part of the old château, and probably many of the surrounding barns and outbuildings. They had made practical choices in the reconstruction. The keep, a more or less square building of three stories, had been constructed in the local limestone and in orange-red bricks from the tile works on the estate. Each year, 21,500 bricks or tiles made from the local reddish clay were owed to the *seigneur,* lord of the manor, thus providing cheap, convenient building materials.[10] The exterior use of the combination of white and red was reminiscent of the buildings in the Place Royale, where Du Châtelet grew up. The orange-red brick was also part of the interior vaulting, striking against the white stucco of the walls. By the time Du Châtelet, Voltaire, and the marquis finished their renovations, it had become a modest but elegant château with one additional wing on the ground floor, new rows of fruit trees, and manicured gardens. Initially, however, for Du Châtelet, a young woman used to the luxuries and comforts of a Paris *hôtel* done in the latest styles and fabrics, the place must have seemed virtually uninhabitable.[11] Until Voltaire arrived, it had not been lived in for at least a decade. The duc de Richelieu, one of their first important visitors, in November 1735, stayed only a few days, perhaps because of the workmen and the relatively primitive conditions.

When Du Châtelet came back to Cirey in the summer of 1735 with the idea of living in the countryside for four years, the renovations and additions were well under way. The planning and the construction were a joint project, with Voltaire contributing forty thousand livres and the marquis paying for the rest. Voltaire systematically numbered the instructions to his man of business, abbé Bonaventure Moussinot; the letters for 1737 and 1738 tell of furniture ordered and plans to buy property nearby, but they also suggest that he had committed too much and had begun to worry about costs. In late November 1736, he counted on an outstanding loan of fifty thousand livres to the duc de Richelieu. Nevertheless, he paid taxes for the marquis and advanced modest sums to Du Châtelet throughout their time together. Voltaire probably engaged the architects, Dufort and Champenois, soon after he took up permanent residence in 1734. Two colored drawings that now hang in the second-floor hallway of the château give an idea of their plans. One can identify the central building, of old brick and white limestone. Additions create a square courtyard that in turn opens to a series of manicured gardens stretching to the front of the picture, perhaps an original architect's renderings. Only one of these wings was completed.[12]

The two drawings do not show the marquis's improvements. As the *seigneur* of Cirey, he undertook work on the château as part of a larger project both for his household and for the villagers. The records for the property suggest that the marquis was particularly active in 1737–38 and again in 1740–41, years when he could take time from his duties with the king's army. He had augmented his forest land in 1738–39 and enlisted a local man to create a plan for developing the forests specifically for his use. He built the village a new courtroom, the communal flour mill, and a meeting hall; he contributed to the costs of the village stone bridge and its wells. The marquis would have been perceived as generous. It was in 1748 that he purchased land from a neighbor to extend the château garden area in order to accommodate an *orangerie*, an eighteenth-century greenhouse, to provide winter flowers when the family was in residence, and an ice house where large blocks could be stored for cooling drinks in the heat of summer.

Du Châtelet and Voltaire concentrated their energies on the ground floor, where he had his suite, and on the floor above, where she had hers. From the winter of 1734 until the spring of 1736, masons, plasterers, painters, all the workmen that Voltaire claimed he had to prod and keep accounts on for "Minerva," worked in the rooms and corridors. Du Châtelet was involved in every aspect of the renovations, except when she had to go to Paris and left Voltaire as both "architect and landscape gardener," as he described himself. She was working miracles inside the house, he wrote to their neighbor and a relative of the marquis, the comtesse de La Neuville: "She found the secret of furnishing Cirey with nothing." According to Voltaire, Du Châtelet was up each morning before the workmen to inspect what they had done and to plan that day's instructions. Voltaire wished to commission François Boucher to paint a series of tableaux based on *La Henriade,* but it proved too expensive. For her boudoir, Du Châtelet purchased wall panels cut to fit particular spaces depicting the *Five Senses* and scenes from La Fontaine fables, all by Watteau. She gave over the rest of the interior decorations to the student of a fairly well-known Parisian artist, arranging for him to come and live at the château for three years. The ceiling of the "appartement des bains" was probably one of his projects.[13]

Both Du Châtelet and Voltaire believed in bathing—another way in which they went against custom. Even their learned contemporaries believed that bathwater made the body porous and thus open to miasmas that could enter through the skin.[14] At Cirey, the couple created an entirely separate *appartement des bains,* with its own antechamber, chamber, and *cabinet de toilette.* Mme de Graffigny, who visited in the winter of 1738–39, described it as "like a pretty snuffbox, all of it perfect." The bathing room itself was tiled and had a marble floor, a small fireplace where the water for the copper *baignoire,* or small bathing tub, could be heated, and lacquer tables covered with "amusing books." The carved paneling in the adjoining *cabinet* was celadon, a pale green, with paintings, engravings, and the art student's decorations for the ceiling. There a little sofa, and small *fauteuils* that were all carved wood painted in gold, waited for a day such as the Monday when Graffigny had the "vapors," dosed herself with opium, and sat quietly in this pleasant room while Voltaire read to her from *La Pucelle.* On another occasion, when Desmarest, Graffigny's lover from Lorraine, had joined them, the bathing room became the site for an afternoon's entertainment. The hostess bathed, discreetly clad in her *chemise de bain,* while Voltaire read the sections on "equality" and "pleasure" from his "Discours en vers sur l'homme" ("Epistle in Verse on Man"), followed by his "Défense du mondain" ("Defense of the Sophisticate"). Her bath completed, they stayed on in this suite. The chambermaids served them refreshments as afternoon turned into evening and then the small hours of the next morning. One highlight was the appearance of Du Châtelet's eleven-year-old son, dressed as Cupid in preparation for a local carnival to celebrate Mardi Gras.[15]

Not surprisingly, there were other plans that were never completed. The marquis wanted to move the chapel; Voltaire designed another wing to balance that on the left as one faced the central keep; Du Châtelet was to have a library off of her bedroom, but in early 1739 only the mirror-and-glass door leading from her bedchamber was in place. She probably left the basement as she found it. This was a series of large rooms for work and storage where the servants prepared the food, cleaned and mended clothes, dealt with all of the business of the household, and spent their time when they were not at their chores upstairs. Nor did she renovate the older suites of rooms on the upper floor of the château, where the marquis and visitors like Mme de Graffigny and the neighbor Mme de Champbonin stayed. Graffigny had an antechamber, as large as the one downstairs in Voltaire's ground-floor *appartement,* and a pretty decorated table with drawers and a mirror for her toilette. Otherwise she found the accommodations old, dusty, and inadequate. The drafts were so bad that on Christmas Eve they blew out the candles.[16]

৵৵৶

Just as in Semur, Du Châtelet would have been responsible for all the details of their daily lives. How many would have been in the immediate household of the château? Du Châtelet came with her own *femme de chambre* to deal with her clothes, to dress her, and to do her hair. Other members of her family also had servants. There was her son's *précepteur,* her daughter's *gouvernante.* Voltaire had one servant, ideally what he called a "valet de chambre copiste," a valet who could write a clear hand and read aloud tolerably well in French and in Latin. Voltaire also had at least two other "lackeys." One accosted a kitchen maid, who responded by hitting him on the head with an earthenware pot. There would have been a cook and kitchen staff, laundresses and other daily help from the surrounding villages, and the outdoor staff, associated with the gardens and the stables. Since Du Châtelet's projects needed a copyist as well, they enlisted Mme de Champbonin's son to help. When, in the late 1730s, Du Châtelet worked up to twenty hours a day on the *Institutions de physique,* she had him sleep in her rooms so that she could call upon him at any time of the day or night. This was no insult: he could make as much as sixty livres a month at the job.[17]

Du Châtelet, not unlike other prominent noblewomen, assumed that relatives and close friends would visit for long periods of time, thereby becoming part of the family, and their servants part of the household. Graffigny brought her *femme de chambre.* Du Châtelet's younger brother, the abbé de Breteuil, stayed for a week at a time at Cirey, probably a lively retreat from his duties in the service of the Archbishop of Sens. Though Graffigny reported that he spoke only of Paris, he was an easy, friendly addition. Louis Gabriel, the *bailli* de Froullay, a cousin and another favorite of Du Châtelet, made at least one visit. Her husband's cousin Marc-Antoine Du Châtelet, marquis de Trichâteau, retired from military life to Cirey and, in return for making Florent-Claude his heir, expected to be cared for and have his affairs attended to, an arrangement reported matter-of-factly by the *nouvelliste* Dubuisson to his correspondent. Graffigny described Trichâteau's pleasure in music and also his silence. He was physically fragile, with gout, stomach problems, and epilepsy. One Saturday, she wrote for him after he had suffered one of his seizures. He shared his library with them all; some of his books—for example, one on the negotiations for the Peace of Ryswick—were among those taken by Voltaire after Du Châtelet's death.[18]

The comtesse de La Neuville, whose husband's estate was in the vicinity, occasionally visited and became a recipient of Voltaire's flirtatious letters. Anne-Antoinette-Françoise Paulin, Mme de Champbonin, was six years Du Châtelet's senior and was married to another local *seigneur,* also a regimental officer. For about four years, she lived at Cirey more or less all the time. A distant relative of Voltaire's, she became his constant admirer, reading anything he gave her, engaging in theatricals with him and Du Châtelet, traveling to Paris for them. Mme de Graffigny called Champbonin "gros chat," fat cat, meant with affection, since Champbonin was a bit heavy but likable. Voltaire described her as "helpful, active and capable" and complimented her "good heart." Du Châtelet accepted Champbonin's services and encouragement of her own projects, and found her an especially useful member of the entourage, for she could cajole and charm Voltaire out of his bad tempers and sulks.[19] There are brief references in Du Châtelet's and Voltaire's letters to Mlle de Thil, Du Châtelet's friend from Semur. She never married, but she enjoyed revenues from properties in Burgundy sufficient for a comfortable living in Paris, and enough to allow her to join Du Châtelet at Cirey and later at Lunéville. Voltaire made a point of including de Thil in his list of people to receive new editions of his works. She used her connections in Rome to help him gain Pope Benedict XIV's tacit approval of his play *Mahomet.*[20]

The move to the Du Châtelet family estate meant that, in her husband's absence, the marquise had to oversee the fulfillment of their tenants' manorial obligations, as well as the other business of their lands. All of this would have been new to her. Perhaps, in the first months, the marquis instructed her in his letters. The intendant for the estate and the affairs of the château, Simon-Martin de La Bonardière, a local man from the more prosperous

ranks, saw to the actual supervision of their properties and tenants. In the
absence of the marquis, he would report to the marquise. In fact, La Bonardière was more like a member of the household than an employee. One day
in January, Graffigny played *trictrac* with him.[21]

By the eighteenth century, everything about the lands and rights of the
barony of Cirey, as it was called, had become complicated. First of all, the
properties were not contiguous. The estates, some as far away as Normandy, on the northwest coast of France, and Franche-Comté, in the east,
consisted of a hodgepodge of villages, forests, vineyards, and buildings like
mills and forges, each with its separate combination of rights in lands,
money, goods, and labor. By the 1730s, when Du Châtelet had to oversee
their holdings, all but a few of the customary labor services and goods owed
in kind by the estate tenants had been transmuted into money payments.
For example, traditional labor services on the lands held by the marquis for
his own cultivation, the *corvées* of French manorialism, three days a year at
Cirey at the times of the wine and wheat harvests, could be waived and
forgotten for five sous. The system seems circular at best: the peasant paid
to be exempt, the Du Châtelets' agent took the money and then paid someone, in all likelihood someone from the same village, to perform the tasks,
and arranged to buy the produce, previously owed in kind, from another
village family. Then there were the special rights of the *seigneur* that could
be particularly onerous depending on how they were exercised: the exclusive right to sell wine between May 3 and June 11 (St. Croix's Day to
St. Barnabé's Day)—a not inconsiderable right, since the region supplied
15 percent of the champagne drunk in Paris.[22]

Neither Du Châtelet nor the intendant expected to handle the collection
of these seigneurial payments in money, kind, and service. The marquis and
marquise "farmed out," as the term went in French, those responsibilities.
In 1740, Pierre Chretien negotiated a nine-year lease on the lands of Cirey
and the seigneurial rights of the adjoining villages. In 1744, when he had
failed to pay the agreed-upon rents, Du Châtelet, acting for her husband,
instituted the successful proceedings that lost Chretien the lease and the
lumber he had cut from their forests, and regained ten of the fourteen thousand livres that he owed them. Between 1743 and 1748, she must have negotiated a number of other nine-year leases for properties in Normandy, as
well as in Champagne. They found someone particularly trustworthy for

the Cirey lands in 1747. The realities of life in the countryside are represented by the different amounts Nicolas Perin owed them for the use of
their lands, forests, and forges: only sixty-five hundred livres per year in
wartime, seventeen thousand when there was peace. Twice during her time
at Cirey, enemy troops threatened Lorraine, whose borders were only a
long day's ride away from the château.[23]

Du Châtelet would also have looked to the "bailli," Nicolas Varin. A man
of some substance by birth, licensed in law, Varin had risen in the service of
the Du Châtelet family. He presided in the new courtroom built by the
marquis, and, assisted by his sergeant, clerk, and prosecutor, all local men
like himself, kept the peace, dealt with criminals, and acted as game war-
den. Du Châtelet probably learned more about some aspects of the estate
than others. For example, the iron ore in the soil could have netted good
money. The marquis authorized reconstruction of foundries, forges, and
furnaces, most notably at Le Fourneau, on the way from Cirey to Arnancourt. One January, she supervised the installation of a new *maître de forge*
and made visits to inspect the management of their woods.[24]

Du Châtelet also read contemporary essays on economic subjects. However, once she had begun her own studies and writings in natural philosophy, she found her responsibilities as a *châtelaine* a hindrance. About six
weeks after completing her essay on fire for the Académie des sciences competition, she wrote to Maupertuis: "Life is so short and so filled with duties
and useless details, when one has a family and a house"—"*the pointlessnesses
of life*," she called them. She had underlined those words for emphasis. Not
unlike other women, she saw this as part of the difficulty of her sex. "If I had
been a man," again underlined, "*I could be at Mont Valérien with you.*"[25] Her
life at Cirey created this conflict, but also made possible the time and the
means for her to begin to realize her intellectual goals.

"Paradise on Earth"

In May 1735, Du Châtelet coined the phrase *le paradis terrestre,* the paradise
on earth, to describe the life she imagined for herself and Voltaire at Cirey.
Once there, she delighted in the excitement of reading, talking with Voltaire, collaborating on his projects, entertaining the visiting members of the
Republic of Letters with whom she and Voltaire corresponded. Du Châtelet

issued invitations eagerly. In October, only months after she had arrived, she wrote to Francesco Algarotti that she hoped he might decide "to spend the winter philosophizing with us. I have a very pretty library. Voltaire's is all anecdotes, and mine is all philosophy." She added that she was learning Italian in preparation for his arrival. Her calling Cirey "mon Académie" was an obvious reference not only to Socrates and Plato, but also to the royal institutions whose members could not conceive of a woman as an intellectual peer. She had already written to Maupertuis, comparing Cirey to his Mont Valérien and then to the academy founded by Queen Christina of Sweden after her abdication. Maupertuis became her Descartes, to be lured to the mountains of Champagne.[26]

In fact, with her husband's blessing, and Voltaire's financial help and approval, she did create her own "Académie," where she could entertain the learned men of philosophy and science—"les Emiliens," as Voltaire called them. Algarotti planned and wrote much of his *Newtonianismo per le dame* (*Newton for the Ladies*) during his extended stay at Cirey and inspired Du Châtelet and Voltaire's *Eléments de la philosophie de Newton*. The abbé Du Resnel, translator of Pope's *Essay on Man*, stopped by on his way to visit his order. Two of France's most prominent *géomètres* stayed with them: Maupertuis came for four days in January 1739, and in March returned with Johann Bernoulli II, son of the great mathematician. Claude Adrien Helvétius, then a protégé of Voltaire, came at his invitation. Du Châtelet reported to d'Argental that the young man was "a lovely soul, a child full of honor and affection" for Voltaire. Père François Jacquier, a coeditor of the Geneva edition of the *Principia* (1739–42), described by his fellow visitor Charles Jean François Hénault as the "great mathematician and professor of philosophy," was among their celebrated visitors in the 1740s.[27]

In June 1736, when Du Châtelet had been in these unusual circumstances almost a year, she wrote to Algarotti, "My kingdom of Cirey is not of this world." In a very real sense, she was correct. As a woman, she could not attend the obvious places of learning, the *collège,* the Académie. Even the informal gatherings of Maupertuis's friends and protégés were intended to be exclusively male. In addition, a marquise could not travel alone. And travel was, as Jordan explained, an essential aspect of one's education for membership in the Republic of Letters, the means to "know the learned with whose works you were already familiar." She envied Algarotti's trip to

England after he had left Cirey. She described the English as "this philosophical people" with "their free and manly ways of thinking and of expressing themselves." There he would find "the country of virtues," of John
Locke, "of people who think." Algarotti's letters telling of his encounters
"turned her desire into a passion." "I torture myself," she wrote him in January 1737, searching for a pretext to make the voyage. It was never to be,
and she never met Algarotti's and Voltaire's friend (from his time in exile)
Lord Hervey. Unable to take advantage of these alternatives open only to
men, she founded "une colonie" and assembled her own learned company.
Her pleasure in "our little republic of Cirey" never waned. Du Châtelet told
Algarotti in 1738 that she loved it "more than ever," "the country of philosophy and of reason." In 1741, on her return to Cirey from Brussels, she reported to d'Argental, "We are finally, my dear friend, at Cirey, which we
love so much, and where I would gladly pass my life." Visitors, the *gens qui
pensent,* were equally entranced. Cirey was, according to Voltaire, the "delicious retreat," the ideal of one of his favorite Roman authors, Horace, where
the *philosophe* could escape the tumult of politics, a "little province inhabited
by philosophy, the graces, liberty and study." For Maupertuis, it was "a
universal Académie of sciences and wit." Devaux suggested to Graffigny
that she had happened upon the "Plombière of the spirit," if such a thing
could exist.[28]

When visitors left, it did not mean that Du Châtelet's Académie had
disbanded, or that her tutelage came to an end. At first Du Châtelet wrote
to maintain her courtier networks and to keep up with the news of Paris
society. The duc de Richelieu received long gossip-filled letters meant to
indicate to him that her move to the country was in fact the right choice,
and to make sure that he would not forget her or her charge—to speak
to her husband. Over the next months, however, and into the next few
years—1736, 1737, and 1738—and then in the 1740s, Du Châtelet's extant
letters reflect the changes in her activities. Her correspondents included
members of the Republic of Letters: Maupertuis, Algarotti, Maupertuis's
mentor Johann Bernoulli, the English mathematician James Jurin, the Roman physicist père Jacquier. There was sometimes news of Voltaire, greetings from him and from her husband, a thank-you for a book, but usually the
topics related to her writing, a question about a point of mathematics, or of
physics. This was what one of her modern commentators has called her

"lettre laboratoire," as if she conducted experiments via letter. She maintained her ties with these men as assiduously as she did with the courtiers who made possible the advancement of her family. She consulted with them, made clear her disagreements—later footnoting their works in her writings— and sent them her own publications.[29]

Du Châtelet could count on a letter's leaving Wassy, the nearest postal stop to Cirey, at noon on Monday, Wednesday, and Saturday, and arriving in Paris within a week. When she wished a letter to arrive more quickly, she hired a courier. Her letters all look very much the same, written on glossy stationery with a hand-painted border, folded in half or in quarters; one last fold turned the letter into its own envelope. Du Châtelet used a whole series of abbreviations: *vs* for *vous* (you), *me* for *madame*—and rarely wrote out suffixes such as the *-ment* of *seulement* (only). Her big handwriting on the front indicated the simplest of addresses: *"M. Maupertuis à Basle en Suisse."* She sealed her letters with dark-orange wax and the image of her crest, or with the portrait seal of Voltaire that she had ordered made.[30]

The postal system had its flaws. Sometimes Du Châtelet repeated her news or her inquiries, probably because she had not received answers and assumed the original had gone astray. Packages disappeared, or took an inordinately long time to arrive either in Paris or in Cirey. For example, in January 1737, she sent some venison from the estate to their friend d'Argental, and by the time it arrived, three weeks later, she assumed that it must have been rotten. This perhaps explains why she often sent gifts and letters with her husband or with guests when they left Cirey for Paris (the next venison went with Mme de Champbonin). Algarotti had a number of letters to deliver once he reached the capital. He forgot or did not care about one for a publisher, and Du Châtelet scolded and teased him: "In truth, I could complain very seriously to you. One can be negligent in trade, but it is not permitted to be so in essential things; and surely that which was confided to you is among that number."[31]

Sometimes Du Châtelet's correspondence reveals the course of a project— for example, the gradual evolution of her views on *forces vives* for the last chapter of her *Institutions de physique*. Initially, however, the letters to her learned friends and acquaintances have something even more exciting to reveal: her discovery of all that had been denied her, not out of malice, but by custom. Here was a young woman reading what she had missed of a clas-

sical *collège* education, and at the same time acquiring knowledge never offered to young men by Jesuit instructors. She was exuberant, puzzled,
delighted, pedantic, as her interests took her into so many areas in such a
short time. Voltaire had brought some of his library. Both of them counted
on relatives and friends, or Voltaire's man of business, Moussinot, to buy
what they needed or borrow from the Bibliothèque du roi. Du Châtelet's
husband brought her one of Newton's books when he returned from a trip
to Paris.[32]

Those from the booksellers probably arrived bound but with just a paper
cover. The first task was to add in the corrections from the sheet of errata.
One can only estimate how many books there were. When Voltaire's library was sold to Catherine the Great after his death, it numbered more
than seven thousand volumes. Many of them were books that he and Du
Châtelet had shared.[33] Her reading from this period falls across many categories. There were Latin authors, read sometimes in the original and sometimes in translation: Petronius, Virgil, Cicero, Juvenal, Ovid, Horace,
Lucretius. There were sixteenth- and seventeenth-century authors, such as
La Fontaine, Mme Lambert, Montaigne, Bossuet, the Italian poet Ariosto.
Voltaire introduced her to many English writers: Lord Rochester, Alexander Pope (his *Essay on Man* and *Essay on Criticism*), James Thomson (*The Seasons*), Joseph Addison. These she enjoyed, but she found the biography of
the French general Turenne (by an Englishman) that was the talk of Paris in
1735 very boring. She had her favorite French poets, some of whom she had
included in her copybooks, such as J. B. L. Gresset and Moncrif. Like others
in the Republic of Letters, she also followed numerous periodicals: the gazettes of Amsterdam and Utrecht, and the official government news sheet,
the *Gazette de France*. Some gave her information about new publications:
abbé Prevost's *Pour et contre* gave particular attention to English authors and
titles; she would eventually write for the *Journal des savants,* and the *Journal
de Trévoux* and *Mercure de France* later reviewed her own writings.

Du Châtelet never stopped working with the mathematics books, such
as Euclid and Guisnée, the text recommended by Maupertuis. Increasingly,
however, she referred only to works of what the English called "natural
philosophy"—the study of the natural world, from first causes to the mechanics of motion, a combination of what would now be called metaphysics,
philosophy, and physics. She wrote to Maupertuis, "We have become *phi-*

losophes completely." She read or reread some standard philosophical reference works of her day, such as abbé Pluche's *Le Spectacle de la nature* and Bayle's skeptic's dictionary. Although she made light of her efforts in one letter —"and I, I neutonize more or less"—she studied not only Newton on optics, mechanics, and universal attraction, but also Galileo, Descartes, Cassini, and Halley.[34] She referred to the public lecturers in physics, such as the Dutchman Petrus van Musschenbroek, Privat de Molières, Gamaches, and the British physicist John Keill. By early 1738, she had begun to be fascinated by the controversy over the formula for motion, the confusion between momentum and what today we call kinetic energy, and widened her reading of those who proposed answers. The metaphysical aspects of natural philosophy took her further and further away from Voltaire's more pragmatic approach. First, certainly at his suggestion, she returned to John Locke's *Essay Concerning Human Understanding* and the published interchange between the two natural philosophers Gottfried Wilhelm Leibniz and Samuel Clarke on the nature and workings of the universe; then she turned to Leibniz's own articles from the learned journal the *Acta Eruditorum*. Frederick of Prussia sent them French translations of writings by Christian Wolff, a former student and follower of Leibniz intent on systematizing his mentor's thoughts on metaphysics and physics.

Du Châtelet's eagerness to read and study, coupled with Voltaire's enthusiasm for his own and their shared activities, added another dimension to guests' experience of this paradise on earth. Unlike hosts of other country sojourns, filled with card games, flirtations, hunting, and walks in the gardens, Du Châtelet and Voltaire made little effort to provide entertainment for their guests at Cirey, who instead followed the routine established by the marquise and the playwright for their own work and pleasure. Both assumed that visitors would also want to spend most of their day reading: reading in their rooms, reading together, reading aloud. This could intimidate the less well-prepared intellectuals, such as Mme de Graffigny, who purposely studied Locke's *Essay on Human Understanding* (in the Coste French translation) in preparation for her visit. After her arrival, Du Châtelet and Voltaire gave her more to read: Du Châtelet's translator's preface for Mandeville's *Fable;* Voltaire's *Eléments de la philosophie de Newton,* and both of the essays on fire that they had submitted to the Académie des sciences for the 1738 competition. Du Châtelet seems to have been circumspect in the sharing of her writings, in contrast to Voltaire, who gave everyone his works to read. On his visit, Algarotti received the play *La Mort de César*. Reading naturally led to another art of the Republic of Letters. Algarotti wrote that he had found at Cirey "the beautiful habits of conversation" that he hoped to transpose into his *Newtonianismo per le dame*. A "tone of playfulness and of gentility," a sense of fun but with a particular refinement and wit, as a late-morning *café* interlude with Voltaire was described by Mme de Graffigny.[35]

However, learned discussions, as Voltaire explained to Thieriot, could not take place "without the wine of Champagne and excellent food, because we are very voluptuous *philosophes*." This letter suggested the images Voltaire would develop in his poem "Le Mondain": Cirey as a contemporary, and by comparison much-improved, Eden, a luxurious abode with good company, fine food, and champagne corks popping to the ceiling. The Biblical Eden had only its dirty-fingernailed, ragged Adam and Eve. Voltaire's hedonistic image of the luxurious life of the *honnête homme*—"the earthly paradise is where I am"—described the reality and the ideal for the men of the Republic of Letters.[36]

A day in the winter of 1738–39 might begin for Du Châtelet in the bedchamber of her suite of rooms. She had ordered it painted pale yellow with blue accents on the wainscoting. She followed the same color scheme for the furniture and upholstery, and even the small decorated doghouse for the black puppy, Dear Love, that Mlle Quinault of the Comédie française had given to them in the fall of 1736. Perhaps Du Châtelet took her first refreshment of the day in the adjacent boudoir, with its white-taffeta-covered armchairs. With the panels by Watteau, this room, according to Graffigny, was even more decorated than her bedchamber, perhaps because it was where she worked. The amber desk, Graffigny explained to Devaux, had been a gift from Frederick of Prussia. Du Châtelet herself had written verses to inscribe here: "Leisure, sweet study. / Few books, no bores, / A friend in the solitude / That's my lot: a happy one." Was it here that she had the pendulum wall clock that she referred to so often in her *Institutions de physique*?[37]

At ten-thirty or eleven, Du Châtelet and her guests joined Voltaire for *café* in the long *galerie*. While Mme de Graffigny was visiting that winter, most of the public gatherings took place here or in Voltaire's suite of rooms on the ground floor. There would have been the same stone and brick-ceilinged main hall that exists today, and just behind the château's interior stone stairs up to the next floors was the door to his *appartement*. Voltaire had created this new suite for himself: an antechamber, a bedchamber, and the long *galerie,* the extension that made the planned north wing of the château. Voltaire had purchased new furniture for himself, including a lacquered desk in the chinoiserie style that he and Du Châtelet admired. She probably supervised the placement of mirrors, the choice of India papers, and the crimson coverings on the walls. Meissen porcelains on the tables and the portrait of Frederick of Prussia added to the decoration.[38]

All who visited found the *galerie* impressive: more than thirty feet long, paneled in varnished wood, with its own tiled stove to keep it as "warm as springtime." A door on one side, opening to the garden, and windows on the other, looking to the meadow and the river below, brought the countryside to immediate view. There were statues of Hercules and Venus set between the windows, and a portrait of Mme Du Châtelet hung on the wall. Two armoires held his books and his collection of scientific instruments—his "machines de physique," as Graffigny called them. Perhaps his valet moved the canaries and the parrot with the black collar into this long room to give them the advantage of the morning sunlight. Voltaire had arranged to have them delivered to Cirey by courier the year before, in 1737. Now their singing and squawking would punctuate the readings and discussions. Ironically, considering Voltaire's controversial religious views, the chapel also opened off of his bedroom. In one of her letters, Graffigny presented the odd image of Voltaire reclining in his bed, protected from the draft by a screen, while others sat at the door listening to the chaplain, François Berthel, say mass on Christmas evening. Voltaire recited the litany along with everyone else.

One waited in one's room to be summoned by a servant for the morning interlude in Voltaire's *galerie,* which always lasted an hour and a half. Usually Du Châtelet or Voltaire read aloud. Mme de Graffigny told of a Tuesday morning spent with the French translation of Algarotti's dialogues on Newton. The translator was an adherent of Descartes and therefore made changes freely—much to the amusement of *les Emiliens*. On Thursday, Du Châtelet read the geometric calculations of an "English dreamer" who, based on the distance from Jupiter to the sun and the amount of sunlight the eye's pupil can receive, had determined that the inhabitants of that planet must be as large as King Og of the Old Testament. The group found "diverting the folly of a man who took so much time and work to learn something so useless." When she looked at the book herself, Graffigny was "astonished" to discover that it was in Latin, and that her hostess had not only been translating into French as she read, but was also making the calculations that completed the description of the different parts of the giant's body.[39]

Such scenes could have a more serious side as well, for reading aloud was also an integral part of learning in the eighteenth century. Du Châtelet and Voltaire worked their way through Dom Augustin Calmet's multivolume study of the Bible in this way, taking turns reading and marking the text. Graffigny and Champbonin dabbled in the same book on one of their long afternoons together. Exceptional visitors, such as Algarotti, received tacit permission to make their own contributions to the gatherings. Voltaire wrote to Thieriot praising the "young man . . . who makes verses like Aristo [sic], and who knows his Loke [sic] and Newton." Du Châtelet found him exciting and stimulating, even though she often misspelled his name. She described him in a subsequent letter of introduction, probably to her relative the comte de Froullay, who was then ambassador to Venice, as a "young Venetian, . . . unique for this insatiable thirst to see and know that characterizes men of genius. He merits this title at the age of twenty-two."[40]

Dismissed from *café*, the guests again had to fend for themselves. Some afternoons Du Châtelet went for a ride on her mare Hirondelle (Swallow), with one of their male visitors, such as her brother, or Graffigny's lover Desmarest. She took female guests for a tour of the seigneury in the phaeton she had brought on her first extended trip to Cirey, in the fall of 1734. Graffigny was never enthusiastic about these outings. The horses, obviously those from the farm, not only resembled elephants, according to Voltaire, but also, according to Graffigny, were uncontrollable. Visitors who were hungry could join the marquis, Champbonin, and Du Châtelet's son for something to eat at noon. There would also be a dinner for the boy and his *précepteur* later in the afternoon, while Du Châtelet and Voltaire might simply go to their rooms and not emerge again. When working intensely on a project, Du Châtelet followed this rigorous routine, having only the lightest refreshment in her *appartement*, remaining at her desk, tables, and papers until early the next morning.[41]

The marquise presided over the occasional evenings when guests enjoyed a late supper with their hosts. Beginning at 9 p.m., these breaks from study and writing usually continued into the early hours of the morning. The marquis left after the table had been cleared or, if the meal was taken in the *galerie,* after they had finished eating. Champbonin retired about eleven. For those who remained, there would be the quick, lively conversations, interchanges laced with wordplay, quotations from Racine or the Latin classics, all the accoutrements of eighteenth-century French wit. The stories of these late-night suppers, of the challenging as well as entertaining atmosphere created by two brilliant minds and Du Châtelet's unflagging energy, became part of the legend of Cirey that circulated in Paris in the correspondence of the *nouvellistes* and among the *gens qui pensent.* Du Châtelet probably ordered an elegant table set, the silver displayed, the crest on the forks, spoons, and knives carefully shown, and the best dinner service in use. She and Voltaire dressed for these occasions, she in full court attire *à la française,* with a bodice embroidered in gold thread, wide skirts, lace trailing out of the sleeves, her hair powdered and perfumed. Voltaire perhaps sported the diamond garter and shoe buckles that he had ordered from Moussinot in November 1736. He was vain enough to wear his powdered wig even for the morning conversations over coffee, and had a special pomade "of cucumbers" that he ordered from Paris to keep its curls in place. At supper, the servants presented all the dishes at once, with the expectation that guests would find something that pleased them. Reports indicate that the food was very good. The guests enjoyed an array of Rhine wines and champagnes from the region, wine from Alicante brought by Maupertuis, another sent by Frederick of Prussia from Hungary. Then delicacies such as lemons, oranges, *marrons glacés,* and other candies from the Café Procope, and coffee that Moussinot supplied from Paris. "L'eau de Barbados" was a cordial Du Châtelet had flavored with lemon and orange peel. The peaches her cook bought from a local estate.[42]

According to Graffigny, Voltaire often set the tone of the evening, alternately sulking, agreeing to be cajoled, convulsing the party with his tales, reciting his poetry, or narrating scenes from his newest play. One Tuesday evening in December 1738, Du Châtelet was not feeling well. She and Voltaire argued, speaking in English, to the intense annoyance of Mme de Graffigny, who reported the night's events to her Lorraine correspondent, Devaux, the next morning. Voltaire then announced that he had colic, left the table, and refused to read the expected scene from *Mérope.* A typical night's drama? Apparently. Du Châtelet asked Graffigny and Champbonin to seek him out, and he returned with the ladies in the best of humors and read as promised. Even though he was creating the verses almost as he went along, his listeners never stopped crying. Du Châtelet described the play to d'Argental as a combination of the *Cid,* a play of Corneille, and another popular drama. "The beauty of the verses," she continued, "once joined with the force of the situation," would make it "a masterpiece." Other evenings, Graffigny reported, Du Châtelet's younger brother, the abbé de Breteuil, kept them laughing with his stories of Paris and of Versailles; one night, it was the stupidities of the ugly, awkward wife of the new Spanish ambassador. On one occasion, Du Châtelet teased Voltaire, much to the delight of the group. He wished to read an epistle he had written to her, but she repeated each line as he read it, and nothing would convince her to stop. Sometimes they took advantage of the instruments in the *galerie:* they looked at liqueurs through the microscope, watched Voltaire's abortive efforts at a magic-lantern demonstration. Du Châtelet might sing for the guests, in a voice that all report to have been wonderful. When Maupertuis visited, the topic for the whole evening was mathematics.[43]

The liveliest times for guests came when Du Châtelet and Voltaire decided to abandon their routines altogether and devote their energies to performing plays that he had written, or a favorite opera. Long winter evenings seemed to require new diversions, and the cold weather made the attic where the little theater had been built habitable. This is one of the few parts of the château believed to be as it was in Du Châtelet's time. One comes up the stairs and through a small door into an open-timbered room, which leads into the theater itself. The current owners have restored it carefully to reflect what it might have been in the 1730s, when the variously assembled troupe of *Emiliens* did their productions. The walls and ceiling have been plastered and whitewashed. One's attention goes immediately to the small proscenium stage, framed by the illusion of red-orange–and–white marble facing. A skein of painted intertwined red, white, and pale-pink wildflowers and dark-green leaves makes the decoration across the top of the stage, on either side of a coat of arms. A simple piece of canvas has been transformed into a blue-and-gold tasseled curtain that can be raised and lowered to indicate the beginning and end of an act or scene. The last players left the country-kitchen set frescoed on the back wall: a big fireplace with a long hook for hanging pots, and the handle of a spit for cooking meat, similar to the larger version of the same in the château basement; a small container for salt in the shape of a slipper, hanging inside the fireplace, as if waiting to be used for seasoning; a high, small shelf of plates; a pendulum clock; a cabinet on the wall; a window looking out on trees—all are painted so artfully that they still suggest dimension. The characters would have made their entrances and exits from a door at stage left. The boxed area along the front of the stage for the candles or small lanterns that would have served as footlights remains as it must have been when Du Châtelet played her favorite roles, and Voltaire demonstrated his dancing abilities.[44]

There could not have been room for more than three or four actors at once, although this would have suited Voltaire's plays. The problem for the eager producers, Du Châtelet and Voltaire, would have been how best to use the family members, neighbors, and guests. Sometimes there was probably no one left to watch. There were the imaginary abbé and the woman in the painted trompe-l'oeil of a loge high on the wall to the right of the stage, but the low wooden benches made by a local carpenter, with simple caned seats woven from rushes gathered along the banks of the Blaise River, must often have stood empty. When the abbé de Breteuil visited in December 1738, they chose to perform one of Du Châtelet's favorites, *Le Petit Boursoufle*. This was a comedy, Du Châtelet explained to a friend, Voltaire "had made for us and only us." Champbonin joined in the project, making printed and decorated announcements of the play with Graffigny, who also took a part, as the governess to the heroine, played by Du Châtelet's twelve-year-old daughter. Gabrielle-Pauline came from her convent school in Joinville, having learned her lines during the four-league coach ride.[45]

Du Châtelet did not usually give up the leading female role. *Le Petit Boursoufle* is the story of a frivolous country daughter, Mlle de la Cochonnière, who wants to marry as soon as possible in order to move to Paris. There she imagines she will have "a great magnificent house, diamonds, six tall lackeys, and opera every day, all night gambling, and all the young men in love with me and all the women jealous," a refrain she repeats in abbreviated form throughout the comedy, while her father and two suitors sort out who will be her husband, though she clearly prefers the man with the title and the money. Voltaire laced the dialogue with sexual innuendo and offered many opportunities for embellishment by an enthusiastic performer such as

Du Châtelet, especially in the scenes between the prospective bride and her governess.[46]

In February 1739, the marquis prevailed upon Desmarest to come from Lunéville, and his visit occasioned a seemingly endless series of performances that stopped only when he and Graffigny left for Paris. The son of a successful composer, he had a creditable voice and proved more than up to the task, learning the parts, going sleepless, and performing "44 acts in 48 hours." Echoing other visitors, he wrote, "Never have I passed more agreeable days than those of my sojourn at Cirey." The day he arrived, Du Châtelet sang a whole opera after supper. Delighted to have another talented singer in residence, she monopolized Desmarest's time for the next four days and nights. (Not surprisingly, Graffigny reported in her letter to Devaux that she was not feeling well.) The marathon began on Monday with the comedy *L'Enfant prodigue* (The Prodigal Son), an unnamed three-act play, and scenes from *Zaïre,* a story set in the time of the Crusades and one of Voltaire's most successful tragedies. The intendant for the estate, La Bonardière, was called in to take a role in *L'Enfant prodigue.* They did not sit down to supper on Monday until one the next morning. Still full of energy, with supper over at two-thirty, Du Châtelet suggested more opera. She and Desmarest sang and laughed together at the château's harpsichord until seven, when she finally allowed him to go to bed—only to wake him at ten for more arias. Tuesday, it was a lyric tragedy from 1728, *Tarsis et Zélie,* for two hours, and then Du Châtelet took him out riding for a trip to the forge, where she explained everything about its workings. They returned at four, in time for a repeat of *L'Enfant prodigue* until six, then two acts of an opera until seven, and, at nine, the prodigal again, and finally *Le Petit Boursoufle.* There were numerous repetitions of this comedy, three at least. Somewhere in these days, they also made time for two comedies by authors other than Voltaire.[47]

Wednesday's audiences, if there were any left, had more scenes from *Zaïre.* By this time, the little theater would be littered with bits of ribbon, discarded laces and hats, pages of comedies and tragedies, loose sheets of music, on the cane benches, in corners of the attic, on the stairs where they had fallen as the actors rushed to prepare for the next play or opera. For this, their last production, Du Châtelet took the title role of the pure and principled slave girl; Voltaire played Orosmane, the sultan of Jerusalem, who loves her and stabs her out of jealousy; and the marquis was Nérestan, Zaïre's brother. Du Châtelet's eleven-year-old son and Desmarest filled out minor roles, and Graffigny was cast as Fatima, the maid companion to the heroine. Graffigny recorded all of this faithfully in one of her long letters to Devaux. Voltaire never learned his lines, but it did not matter. Du Châtelet apparently read and spoke hers indifferently; the marquis stammered through. Their son did his best but had to be prompted word for word. They continued until 6 p.m., when Voltaire told the women to dress "à la Turque." In their excitement, the principal actresses spent three hours outfitting themselves in the new stylish mode. The performance began again at nine, followed by another short play, and then an elaborate supper, even though it was Ash Wednesday, traditionally a day for restraint. Though Graffigny gave her criticisms, Desmarest, in his own letter to the same correspondent, used Du Châtelet and Voltaire's phrase to describe the whirlwind experience: this was "paradise on earth."

~❧~

For Du Châtelet, another obvious pleasure of this paradise was that she and Voltaire were very much in love. The excitement and exuberance in their letters from 1735 to 1737, their first two years at Cirey, suggest they were enjoying each other's company in all possible ways. *Nouvellistes* in Paris reported their disagreements and speculated about their sex life. Stories circulated from the capital to the provinces and back, when guests added their descriptions of life at Cirey. Did Du Châtelet and Voltaire enjoy each other sexually? Yes, certainly. In her *Discours sur le bonheur,* she explicitly referred to "jouissance," or "sexual pleasure," when she wrote of their love. Though Voltaire could write in his "Discours en vers" that "all mortals owe their existence to pleasure," "the spark" of a look, and a "purified ardor," he probably was not a particularly accomplished lover. The letters to his next woman partner and companion, his niece Mme Denis, complimenting her "cute ass [cul]," suggest a basic approach to intercourse. Then, too, Voltaire was so often ill. Cramps and diarrhea could be set off by an article by one of his enemies in a Paris journal, adverse criticism of one of his writings, too many hours working. Chronic problems with his digestion and his intestines were a constant of their lives, exacerbated in an age when harsh emetics like saltpeter, elixirs made from quinine, willow bark, other herbs and syrups, enemas, and bleeding were the only remedies. Voltaire might have to spend days entertaining, reading, and writing from his bed, sometimes from his *chaise de commodité.* When his troubles led to longer bouts of pain and fever, Du Châtelet dosed him with *gouttes d'Angleterre,* an opium derivative, and then sat with him, read to him—Cicero's *Tusculanes,* Pope's fourth "Epistle on Happiness," or Moncrif's reworking of the *Mille et une nuits (Thousand and One Nights)*—copied verses for him, and wrote the letters to his friends and to his man of business.[48]

For Du Châtelet and Voltaire, however, the physical was only a small part of their attraction for each other. In his letters about her to his friends Cideville, Formont, and Thieriot, Du Châtelet was his "amiable nymph," his "bright nymph," the "deiesse of Cirey." As early as July 1736, the *nouvelliste* Dubuisson had acquired verses that Voltaire wrote to "Sylvie," the traditional heroine of pastoral verses that presented images of their country idyll. Voltaire began with an idea that Du Châtelet would later borrow and adapt in her own musings on love for her *Discours sur le bonheur:* that one must love, for without loving it was sad to be a man. One must have the "sweet society" of the friend who listens, whom one consulted, who could release a tumultuous soul from its anxieties and make its pleasures greater. At night, "one holds the tender object that one's heart adores, to caress her, to sleep in her arms. And in the morning it begins again."[49] Du Châtelet knew that her own allure was both physical and intellectual. As he had during his courtship of her, Voltaire showered her with odes, epistles comparing her to Dido, to Aspasia (Pericles' mistress); he took Love as his master and Ovid as his teacher. "Listen to his lessons," "allow yourself to be brought to the country of desires. I will teach you his mysteries; happy, if you would learn his pleasures from me." Past loves were worth nothing when compared with "a glance from your eyes." "Your mind has strength and charms! / God! Your heart is adorable and tender! / And what pleasures I taste between your arms! / So very fortunate, I love that which I admire." "I adore you, my dear Uranie."[50]

This reference to "Uranie," the muse of geometry and astronomy, indicates another way in which he flattered her. He wrote of her intellect, sometimes mocking her seriousness—as "Emilia Neutonia"—sometimes awestruck by her wit and her genius, words he used frequently in his descriptions of her talents and accomplishments. She could play the coquette, but she had a mind worthy of Horace (whom Voltaire liked to quote). Her soul was "a cloth that she had embroidered in a thousand ways." This combination of beauty and genius, of lover and *philosophe* in a female body, never ceased to amaze Voltaire and his friends. He bragged that Du Châtelet was "unique"; she went through Pope's *Essay on Man* with greater facility than he, and algebra as if it were a novel. She was a woman led by the lights of reason who, he told his English friend Sir Everard Fawkener, had "retired from the bubbles and the stunning noise of Paris to cultivate in the country the great and amiable genius she is born with." In another letter to Fawkener, Voltaire gave her the highest praise: she was a "lady whom I look upon as a man."[51]

Du Châtelet never expressed any regret over her passion or the unorthodox choices she had made to satisfy it. In their first months together, she wrote to the duc de Richelieu that when he came to visit he would "see the phenomenon, two people who have passed three months tête-à-tête, and who only love each other more." She herself was amazed: "If someone had told me two years ago that I would be leading the life I lead now by choice, I would have been astonished; my heart had no idea of happiness." In Voltaire she had found "the only person who [has] ever been able to fill my heart and my mind." He was for her the quintessential example of genius, "the most honorable man in the world," her lover, her mentor, her companion in the full range of interests and activities of a remarkable new life.[52]

"Storms in Paradise"

Du Châtelet discovered, however, that life with Voltaire could also mean worrisome difficulties and annoying distractions. His sulks, his tempers, and his jealousy tested her love. In the intimacy of their morning *café* together, he knocked a favorite cup from her hand with an angry, impatient gesture. Voltaire's jealousy had posed problems from the first months of 1734, when he was at Cirey and she still in Paris. His letters to the comtesse de La Neuville referred derisively to "my wife" and to being cuckolded. He wrote teasing verses to Richelieu about taking every woman in sight, but leaving the one that he adored. In 1735, Voltaire sent verses to Du Châtelet "on her liaison with Maupertuis." The lines reflected the bourgeois poet's uncertainty: that she had chosen the study of the stars with Maupertuis over the attentions of the author of *La Henriade*. He feared that "the sublime Maupertuis will eclipse my bagatelles." He posed as neither angry nor surprised that she must be in love with the search for eternal truths, "but these truths, what are they? / And what is their use and their price?" However much she might unveil the most hidden parts of nature, he warned, "without the secret of being happy, / What will it then have taught her?"[53] In these years, it was her love of study that distracted her, not other men's attentions, but still Voltaire showed annoyance. Longchamps reported his master's rage one evening when Du Châtelet spent hours closeted with Clairaut. They were working on mathematics and simply had forgotten him and the supper waiting to be served.

In explaining to the duc de Richelieu why she had to move to Cirey to be with Voltaire, she listed his insecurity about being worthy of her love, and also the dangers in which he continually placed himself. She believed that only by living with him in the country could she "stop Voltaire's imagination," "tear him away in spite of himself from his imprudences and his destiny." In these letters to the duc de Richelieu that May and June 1735, she acknowledged that failure meant she would lose her lover, and he would be forced to leave France forever.[54] Contemporaries reported her angry outbursts, but most occurred as a result of her fierce loyalty and protectiveness, her efforts to keep Voltaire from the provocative acts and gestures that had twice sent him to the Bastille, and periodically into exile, even before he began to court her. The *lettre de cachet* issued in 1734 because of his *Lettres philosophiques* remained in effect throughout their years together. At any time, the king and his ministers could enforce it and imprison him once again. Although Du Châtelet suspected the difficulties if she could not "bridle his imagination," she had no idea of the vigilance, persistence, and time it would take to constrain such a prolific writer so eager to share his new creations and to win public acclaim. Almost every year while they were at Cirey, from 1735 until 1739, brought "orages [storms]," as she referred to them, that became a new source of anxiety for her, some new danger threatening his freedom.

For example, on December 1, 1736, the *nouvelliste* Dubuisson reported that verses of the new poem "Le Mondain" could be heard in Paris. Voltaire had already had to leave the city in the spring of 1735, because of government disapproval of his cantos on Jeanne d'Arc. That response paled in the face of the furor over the images of a disheveled Adam and Eve and their

Eden. Louis XV's principal minister, Cardinal Fleury, responded to the complaints of the *dévots* who assumed Voltaire was an atheist. This time the poet had to flee the country for his "heresies," his blatant disrespect for Christian dogma. Du Châtelet herself took him to the mail coach at Bar-sur-Aube for the journey to Holland. But though he was safe, she worried that his health would suffer in the cold and damp of Amsterdam and Leiden. Then he talked of meeting with Frederick of Prussia. This raised new fears: that Voltaire's flirtation with the twenty-four-year-old prince and talk of a prolonged stay at a rival court would so anger the king that he would forbid Voltaire's return to France altogether.[55]

Voltaire had acknowledged all that Du Châtelet had done for him in the past. During the furor over *La Pucelle*—the most recent "persecution," as he called it—he announced to Thieriot that "the manner [in which] she served me would attach me to her for ever, if the singular lights of her mind, and this superiority that she has over all women had not already enchained me." To some extent, part of the difficulty must have been Voltaire's sense of being held back by her, restrained, unable to write and make public whatever he chose. Du Châtelet complained to d'Argental in January 1737 that Voltaire now dismissed her warnings. He told her, "All my letters are sermons," "I am afraid of my own shadow, and that I don't see things as they are." Perhaps Voltaire could maintain circumspect, careful behavior for only so long. Certainly the freedom of Cirey must have highlighted the conflict. In 1736, he had written some verses to Formont describing it as a place of "the true pleasures," liberty and reason, where lived "all those damned by the holy roman Church," like himself. "The prejudices have been banished from it; / Happiness is our domain."[56] Du Châtelet had encouraged him in these feelings with her love, with her collaboration on his projects, and with her obvious enjoyment of even his most dangerous writings, such as *La Pucelle* and his *Traité de métaphysique*.

Once assured of her husband's approval, Du Châtelet naïvely failed to see the other danger to herself from interweaving her life with Voltaire's. Her cousin François-Victor le Tonnelier de Breteuil, the titular head of the family, did not approve of the poet or of her patronage. As a former government minister and part of the queen's circle of devout Catholics, he abhorred her association with this man, who must have appeared to him as little more than a bourgeois outlaw and iconoclast. He watched for opportunities to use his influence against Voltaire. Du Châtelet had further alienated her cousin by supporting the claims of her father's illegitimate daughter. The old family disgrace melded with the new *cause célèbre*. From François-Victor's perspective, it was like father, like daughter. It took Du Châtelet many months to understand these connections. She knew, however, from the beginning of her association with Voltaire, that a delicate balance had to be kept between what she wished to do for her happiness and how her unorthodox actions appeared to others of her *état*. She did not wish to jeopardize the position that she had inherited from her parents and that she planned to sustain and augment for her children. In the eyes of the public, the illusion had to be maintained: that she and her husband, the marquise and marquis Du Châtelet, acted as protectors of France's greatest poet, but nothing more.

From their first months together in Cirey, each time Voltaire threatened this balance, Du Châtelet was surprisingly forgiving. Not only did he declare their loving association in his writings, but he also, inadvertently, pulled her into his rivalries with other poets and journalists. He repeatedly brought her unwelcome publicity, fears of retribution from her cousin, and ridicule from the wits of the court and the *salons*. He wrote an epistle to Algarotti just after his visit to Cirey, with a last stanza lauding "the star Emilie" and mentioning Cirey specifically, thus leaving in the minds of the gossips no doubt about the identity of the woman to whom he referred. Eager as always to share the new poem, Voltaire sent it to Thieriot, who, perhaps out of jealousy of his friend's intense enjoyment of this new female lover, passed it on to the abbé Desfontaines, editor of the journal *Observations sur les écrits modernes*. Despite the ill will between Voltaire and Desfontaines, the abbé did ask Voltaire's permission to publish the verses, but paid no attention when it was refused. The November 19, 1735, issue gave the public Voltaire's indiscreet tribute. The poet was quick to protest "that the name of madame Du Châtelet should be given over shamefully to the malignity of a pamphleteer," but this did not stop him from future misjudgments that left Du Châtelet equally open to ridicule and disdain.[57]

In that instance, Du Châtelet raged against "this pirate of literature" and blamed Thieriot. But throughout 1736, she continued to miss or ignore the ways in which Voltaire's own actions generated these crises and precipitated threats to her reputation. *Alzire* posed its own problems when first presented at the Comédie française in January. The heroine's monologue in

favor of suicide made an obvious challenge to Catholic doctrine. The published version of *Alzire* included a long dedication to Du Châtelet, which,
even though approved by her husband, only brought her relationship with
Voltaire into the public spotlight once again. His extravagant praise of her
"genius" seemed ridiculous to those who knew her only from her days in
Paris. Next, Voltaire was so pleased with his "Ode sur le fanatisme" ("Ode
on Fanaticism") that he sent it not only to his trusted friends, such as Cideville and Formont, but also to the young Prince Frederick of Prussia, who
inevitably shared it with his courtiers and any number of correspondents.
The topic—an overt condemnation of the *dévots* as "nourished on superstition," coupled with praise for atheists, "estimable" because of their morals—
was guaranteed to anger the censors. From Du Châtelet's perspective, the
poem posed other dangers as well: Voltaire had dedicated it to "Emilie" and
addressed her in the intimate *tu* form throughout. Even so, she directed her
invective against the persecutors, "the inquisition that reigns in France in
literature."[58]

Only at the end of 1736, with Voltaire in exile in Holland, did Du Châtelet realize that she had enemies as well. Initially, Du Châtelet assumed that
she, her husband, Voltaire's close friend the marquis d'Argental, and the
duchesse de Richelieu could intervene with the cardinal, and with Chauvelin, the *garde des sceaux,* to calm each storm. She also hoped that d'Argental
could prevail upon Voltaire not to keep answering the likes of Desfontaines,
"for the reason that one never fights against one's lackeys." "Command him
in general," she wrote to d'Argental after the poet had been gone for almost
two weeks, "that he writes too much and that his letters hurt him," because
people just wanted to read them aloud in cafés. And anyway, she kept telling Voltaire, "the greatest vengeance one can take against the people who
hate us is to be happy."[59]

Her cousin Chevalier Louis Gabriel de Froullay, always referred to as
the *bailli* in her letters, would, she hoped, speak most effectively on Voltaire's behalf. He had more of that precious court commodity, *crédit,* with
the *garde des sceaux* than even the duchesse de Richelieu. He did act for Voltaire, but, more important, it was he, as she told d'Argental, who had
warned her "to be on my guard," to beware that "*it is only public words* that
could attract noise, one must fear it [the public], respect it, and not give it
anything to talk about." At first she could not imagine who might use these

"public words" against her. Who would talk? It could not be someone connected to Voltaire: "the public spends its life talking about him." When she
realized that it must be François-Victor de Breteuil, she was horrified by "an
action so black." In 1735, he had already tried to obtain an "interdiction"
against Voltaire that would have prevented his plays from being performed.
Now he hoped to use the unsavory "noise" about Voltaire to force his separation from Du Châtelet and to take revenge for her support of her half-
sister's claims. He tried to enlist her own mother to write to the marquis.
She worried that the "Epître sur la philosophie de Newton," which Voltaire
planned as another magnificent dedication to her, would only make matters
worse. With so much talk, so much attention brought to his wife, Florent-
Claude could not countenance Voltaire's return to the household from
his refuge in Holland. Though she felt assured of "the kindnesses of M. du
[Châtelet]," his honor would demand that he bow to convention in response
to such notoriety.[60]

By this late-December day in 1736, her letter to d'Argental reflected the
pressure of events, the lack of news from Voltaire, her distance from Paris
and from those who could help them. Her tone was desperate. She agreed
to wait for approval from d'Argental before taking any action, but "my life,
my place in society, my reputation, my happiness—all is in your hands."
Both she and Voltaire found great comfort in their friendship with the man
she referred to as "my angel," "the one who consoles me and my savior." In
her fright, she pleaded, "calm me, answer me, and have pity on my state. I
only open my heart to you, and only you should truly instruct me." She
continued: "Your prudence will drive all, I have a blind confidence." The
problem was that d'Argental could neither reassure her about Voltaire's
health nor predict any better than she what Voltaire might do next. She
joked, "An insurance company is necessary for us to have a restful sleep."[61]

With the new year, in January 1737, she speculated that some of the
troubles might dissipate, with both his book on Newton and the comedy
L'Enfant prodigue coming out in the same year, but Voltaire had also given
new evidence of his "imprudence." His "La Défense du mondain" had begun
to circulate in the *salons* of Paris. Contemporaries also thought he had written a letter mocking the lieutenant general of Paris's police. He threatened
to send his chapter on the "metaphysics of Newton" to Frederick of Prussia.
In these final pages of his *Eléments de la philosophie de Newton*, Voltaire as-

serted that all matter might be endowed with the ability to think, the very speculation that had occasioned much of the original furor in 1734. Out of "stupid vanity," wrote Du Châtelet to d'Argental, Voltaire risked having this chapter, "a thousand times more dangerous and surely more punishable than la Pucelle," made public by the unpredictable young Frederick, "of whom neither the heart nor the mind are yet formed, whom a sickness could make devout." Even worse, all that she and her supporters had been able to gain from the *garde des sceaux* was an assurance that the government would not act against Voltaire without warning them. She felt herself "a person lost," for she believed that the poet would return to France to be with her, but return to what kind of life? She confided with a touch of melodrama, yet aware of the realities of their situation, "I prefer to die of sadness than to cost him a false step." She never wanted him "leading for me the life of a criminal in his own country," nor did she want to give him "counsel that he could repent for having followed." She concluded, "I love him more free and happy in Holland."[62]

In these months, Du Châtelet realized that she could not "hold his imagination in check." Justifiably vain about his talents, Voltaire enjoyed the power of his words, the vengeance of a satirical "ode" or a damning public letter. He published books without the appropriate censor's approval, actively worked to produce others outside of France, and let those around him believe that he might simply leave and accept favors at the Prussian court. He continued to criticize the intolerance of the Christian religion, to mock religious officials, to assert the odd bit of heresy, all the while insisting that he was neither impious nor disrespectful of the king's authority. There was the childlike excitement about secret mail addresses, and disguise. In January 1737, Du Châtelet marveled at his placing announcements in the Dutch gazettes, thus revealing where he was and making his incognito "useless and ridiculous."[63] He always assumed that he could make his way out of trouble. He sued one publisher, or turned in another to the police, for making his works public without his apparent permission. He bribed when he could, bought out whole editions to avoid government action. He published anonymously, he disavowed his works, and, when all else failed, he fled.

Near the end of January, Du Châtelet gave herself up to despair. She accepted that there would be no "tranquillity in my life." Instead, she saw herself in an impossible situation, "in combat against him [but] for him, without saving him, trembling for him, or bemoaning his faults, and his absence." Events had taken the awful turn she had predicted earlier, in June 1735, only then she had believed her moving to Cirey would prevent it. No amount of her care, however, had stopped him from placing himself in danger. Still, she found "my destiny more dear than a happier one." How, then, to live with these realities? She assumed, as she explained to d'Argental on the thirtieth of January, that Voltaire was now lost to them. "But who could save him in spite of himself?" she asked. She continued, "I have nothing to reproach myself with; but it is a sad consolation: I was not born to be happy." This recalled her letter to the duc de Richelieu a year and a half before, but then she had assumed the opposite, that happiness could be hers. Now she wrote d'Argental and asked him to tell Voltaire how sick she was, to return to prevent her death from "the violence" of her own imagination.[64]

⤜⧽⤛

This stormy mixing of their destinies changed the atmosphere at Cirey. When Voltaire did return, in March 1737, Du Châtelet locked up his most dangerous writings. She opened his mail in hopes of avoiding imprudent responses on his part. She burned incoming letters that she thought would upset him and endanger his health or occasion an angry public response. The summer day when Voltaire tried to give cantos of *La Pucelle* and *Traité de métaphysique* to their visitor, Frederick's courtier Keyserlingk, she grabbed it from the German's hand. When the prince insisted ever more vehemently on reading Voltaire's philosophical works, she convinced Voltaire to send an essay called "Liberty." They both probably enjoyed the joke of it all, should Frederick pass the essay around—it was actually written by Du Châtelet.[65]

In 1738, although she kept the blasphemous last chapter of the *Eléments* secret, she could not prevent Voltaire from continuing his feud with Desfontaines. The abbé took his revenge in December with the *Voltairomanie,* a vicious dissection of Voltaire's major works that sold two thousand copies in the first two weeks. So upsetting to them was Desfontaines's critique that when they heard about it each tried to hide it from the other. Du Châtelet, outraged at the attack and Desfontaines's ingratitude to Voltaire, decided to write the necessary answer herself. Thus, she explained to d'Argental, she could satisfy Voltaire's honor, yet still keep from him the news of this latest affront. She flattered herself that she would be "more moderate than he, if not as witty." She also reasoned that if she answered then Voltaire could not. In her short response, written, she imagined, in "the greatest incognito," she made no secret of her disgust, identifying Desfontaines by name as "this monster . . . [whose] extirpation would be very necessary." She then calmly, methodically, point by numbered point, explained the injuries Voltaire had suffered.[66]

Mme de Graffigny had arrived at Cirey for the start of her winter visit on Thursday, December 4, 1738, just ten days before Desfontaines's attack appeared. She was unaware of the tensions between Du Châtelet and Voltaire, and knew nothing of this new storm in paradise. Instead, she delighted in the first gracious attentions of her hosts on her arrival at two in the morning, and hoped to adapt to their odd routines. Her portraits show a pleasing oval face. At forty-three, she chose to dress in somewhat dowdy fashion, with lace to cover her chest between the bodice of her dress and her neck, and a gauze bonnet to cover her hair. A widow with limited resources, she worried about visiting such an elegant household without "une robe honnête," an outfit worthy of Cirey. Reassured by Du Châtelet's repeated invitations, given "always with the same attentiveness" and "full of love," as Graffigny put it, she agreed to spend the winter with them, and then go to Paris in April to stay with the duchesse de Richelieu, another Lorraine connection.[67]

Despite her worries about her appearance, and numerous difficulties about horses and how a woman with little means might travel from one invitation to another, Graffigny left what she considered a boring situation for one that she imagined would be very exciting. Her correspondent Devaux idolized Voltaire, and she would be able to give him daily descriptions of the great man's activities and accounts of his current writing projects. On her third day, with books from her hosts piled on the tables in her bedchamber, she wrote that she had "this desire to appear intelligent." She established "a rule" for herself, not to look at anything having to do with "mathematics and physics," because it was just "too difficult." She had expected to be in awe of Voltaire, but the marquise's brilliance astonished her. When she compared the two dissertations on fire that had been submitted to the Académie, Du Châtelet's was of "a neatness, a precision, and an admirable rationality" and far superior to his. "Ah, what a woman," she wrote, who could translate, do calculation in her head, write a treatise on fire. Though Graffigny felt diminished in comparison, "it is very true," she concluded, "that when women involve themselves in writing they surpass men." Much in the spirit of Du Châtelet's own musings in her preface to Mandeville's *Fable,* she wondered, "How many centuries must pass to create a woman like this?" She declared, "Our sex should raise altars to her."[68]

Her adulation of Du Châtelet existed alongside her obvious desire to be thought well of by Voltaire. Graffigny began to imagine him as particularly attentive and approving of her knowledge of his plays—she had a remarkable aural memory and could recite whole scenes. She appreciated his poetic gifts and believed herself more in tune with the poet's needs, whereas Du Châtelet appeared to be forcing him to do physics instead. A simple question from Du Châtelet, asking if the older woman had children, reduced both Graffigny and Voltaire to tears. Graffigny had lost five infants within months of their births. Du Châtelet, with her own memories, remained quiet. In a sense, Graffigny sought to ally herself with both Champbonin and Voltaire, perhaps because they were in a situation similar to hers in terms of birth. Always a member of the lesser nobility, and not of France but of Lorraine, without sufficient means to present herself with distinction, Graffigny must have been reminded every day in small ways of her inferior *état.* The expectation by someone like Du Châtelet that Graffigny would understand and accept her "place" would have been evident without words.

The letters to Devaux—her "Bibles," as she called them, with obvious reference to their length—seem to have been the center of her life at this time: her connection to the world she had known and to the ones she now had to negotiate. She filled every corner of the pages, gave coded, symbolic, and often insulting names to those she described, showed little discretion in what she told of their lives, and did not always consider how very dangerous her interchanges could be. Part of her task, as she defined it at Cirey, was to copy, repeat, and send the writings of its inhabitants to her friends. She copied from Du Châtelet's translation of Mandeville's *Fable,* and sections of Voltaire's writings on the reign of Louis XIV. Graffigny did realize that *La Pucelle* was dangerous. After describing two cantos in her letter of December 18, 1738, including the last two verses of one of them, she acknowledged that this must be a secret between them, and that, by her protectiveness of Voltaire, Du Châtelet "saves him from many follies."

The story of the household drama over a subsequent letter has become a staple of Du Châtelet and Voltaire biographies. As was her custom, Du Châtelet, fearful that Voltaire would learn of Desfontaines's most recent attack, opened all incoming mail. She read Devaux's letter in which he wrote appreciatively, "The canto of Jeanne is charming." Voltaire must have recited more verses—perhaps canto number seven, on Dorothée—for this pure, unhappy, persecuted heroine of one of the numerous subplots gave Graffigny one of her nicknames for Du Châtelet.[69]

Voltaire came into Graffigny's rooms and announced that one hundred copies of "Jeanne" were circulating in Lunéville. By her own account, Graffigny understood his inference and suggested any number of other friends who could have been responsible for this terrible threat to his safety. The couple had proof, Voltaire explained, that Devaux was the source.

Du Châtelet appeared in the next hour. Her tirade, recounted by Graffigny, reflects her frustration with the months of vigilance, and her new fears about a possible response from Voltaire to Desfontaines's attack. Now all her precautions seemed futile because of this little widow's desire to appear important: "You are the most unworthy of creatures," Du Châtelet shouted, "a monster that I brought into my home—not for affection, because I never had any for you, but because you did not know where to go." Drawing on every bit of her social superiority, Du Châtelet continued: "And you have the infamy to betray me, to assassinate me, to steal from my desk a work to copy." The vehemence of Du Châtelet's rage occasioned Voltaire's solicitude. The marquis hoped to bring peace. He proposed that Graffigny prove her innocence by asking Devaux to return her letter. The life of the château returned to a stiff normality while Graffigny waited for it, most of the time in her rooms. When the letter arrived, she showed it to no one. Instead, Graffigny threw the key pages into the fire, exclaiming to Champbonin, the single witness, "that she was not their dupe." Did she mean by this that she was not subject to their bidding? Or did she simply wish to destroy the evidence of her indiscreet behavior? At the marquis's urging, Desmarest arrived from Lunéville a few days later. Perhaps Florent-Claude hoped he could shift attention from Graffigny's unfortunate situation. That was indeed the effect. In the subsequent days and nights of theatricals, all but Graffigny forgot the ill feelings. For, though she had filled pages with stories of the activities and personalities during her six weeks at Cirey, in their extant letters neither Du Châtelet nor Voltaire mentioned her presence, not even her indiscretions. They had other matters that seemed far more important to write about.[70]

Collaboration on the *Traité de métaphysique*

Du Châtelet wrote of her fears for Voltaire's safety to d'Argental, but to others she described her reading, the questions it raised, and her rich and varied collaboration with Voltaire. Undoubtedly, these opportunities and the wonders of watching Voltaire work explain why she stayed with him despite the anxieties that plagued her about his safety and her reputation. In the eyes of his contemporaries, the tragedies from this period, *Alzire, Mérope,* and *Mahomet,* rivaled those of Racine. There were also *L'Enfant prodigue* (the comedy that Du Châtelet dubbed "the orphan" because initially it was billed with the author as anonymous), *La Mort de César, Zulime,* and two versions of *Boursoufle.* She marveled at his ability to write anywhere. When Voltaire had to flee in December 1736, she suggested to d'Argental, "Perhaps in the mail coach he will make a tragedy." She had seen the plan for a comedy, and she continued, "You know how it is with him, one study does not exclude another," for in this period he also revised his *Traité de métaphysique,* wrote his prize entry on the nature of fire for the Académie des sciences, finished the *Eléments de la philosophie de Newton,* and produced numerous verses such as "Le Mondain" and "La Défense du mondain," five of the six "Discours en vers sur l'homme," and the infamous epic *La Pucelle,* to name only the best known. In the winter of 1738–39, Graffigny reported to Devaux that Voltaire alone kept four copyists busy.[71]

Although on occasion Voltaire joked with correspondents that "one can scarcely write less; but the supper, Newton & Emilie carry me away," he usually described her as key to his tasks. Du Châtelet read, translated, wrote précis of books she researched for him, critiqued and edited his prose, plays, and verse. He explained to Thieriot, "When Emilie is ill, I have no imagination." In the rewriting of "his children," as he called his plays, she was "worth all the parterre," able to predict the popular response long before the Comédie française mounted the production. Voltaire acknowledged Du Châtelet's role in the creation of *Alzire* in its dedication to her: "Everything that I can say, is that I composed it in your house and under your eyes." Here he also gave his readers their first glimpse of her unorthodox course of study.

She was an example for other women, as Queen Caroline of England, Christina of Sweden, and the duchesse du Maine had been models for her. She had brought honor to the world of letters as they brought honor to their princely realms. He complimented the way she had hidden her learning—advice she perhaps took from Fontenelle—but now she must continue to study, and not to blush at the praise of her merit: "A mind embellished, is only beauty enhanced."[72]

Du Châtelet's own interests lay elsewhere, in "philosophy" in its most inclusive, eighteenth-century meaning. She wrote to Algarotti that Voltaire "[is] my guide . . . in the country of philosophy and reason." He had given her a preliminary draft of his *Traité de métaphysique* even before she moved to Cirey. From Locke they took a concept that to them seemed a simple truth, the primacy of the senses—"the doors by which all ideas enter into our understanding," as it was phrased in chapter III of the *Traité*. How men acted on these sensory perceptions posed other questions. Her own work in mathematics and reading about the universe intertwined metaphysics, the study of first causes and the nature of being; morality, the rules of conduct permitted and practiced in a society; and *la physique,* physics, the laws governing the natural world. In the eighteenth century, the three kinds of knowledge could not be separated. If the motion of objects is governed by immutable laws, why would these not apply to human motion or action? If the body is matter, would it not be affected in the same way as other matter? How, then, could man have free will? The nature of the body, of man's free will, led in turn to consideration of the nature of the God who created both these laws and all matter. To deal with questions about the nature of the deity—both God the father and Jesus, his son—and the origins of Christian morality, they began reading a well-known multivolume commentary on the Bible by a local cleric, Dom Augustin Calmet. They wrote answers, passed drafts back and forth, and in the end had a revised version of the *Traité.*[73]

As part of this study, Voltaire introduced Du Châtelet to the English moral philosophers and what they both identified as a distinct exemplary English morality. He would have acquired Bernard Mandeville's *Fable of the Bees* during his exile in England. It had gone through multiple editions and had made Mandeville, a Dutch physician (from a Huguenot family) who had lived in London from the end of the 1690s, both rich and notorious. It was at this point that Du Châtelet decided to make a free translation of portions of this controversial book, because, as she explained in her translator's preface, she believed Mandeville to be.the "English Montaigne," the author of the "best book of ethics ever written, that is to say the one that most leads men to the true source of their feelings." According to Voltaire in one of his letters to Thieriot, she had finished her translation by late October 1736. In the end, in her self-defined role as the "entrepreneur" of Mandeville's text, she altered the original so extensively that it became very much her own creation, and more French than English in tone and content. She told her readers that she found literal translations "dry" and preferred "lively turns of phrase and animated expressions that render the force and grace of the original." Like translators of the previous generation, such as Anne Dacier, author of the French versions of the *Iliad* and the *Odyssey,* and Pierre Coste, whose edition of Locke she had read, she felt no compunction about simplifying the language or omitting sections she deemed unnecessary, "dangerous," or "untrue." An earlier draft of her preface gave her goals: "simplicity, clarity and brevity."[74]

Many of the most significant changes that Du Châtelet made are easy to identify, because, unlike previous translators, when Du Châtelet wanted to insert "my own reflections on the material I was working on," she set them off with quotation marks. Usually translators, like authors who quoted at length, made no such acknowledgment. It was these views of her own, particularly on the origins of human society and of vice and virtue, that she also added to chapters VII and VIII of Voltaire's *Traité.* Despite such care with her first project as a *philosophe,* she did not publish her *Fable,* probably because its unorthodoxy would have brought too much attention both to herself and to Voltaire (the subsequent literal translation of 1740 was immediately banned). It circulated in manuscript, however, among the traffic in clandestine texts. When shown part of the translation in the winter of 1738–39, Mme de Graffigny copied out for Devaux a few of the "boldest" parts, as Du Châtelet would have described them, from chapter I, where it is argued that good comes from evil "as naturally as chickens come from eggs." Graffigny referred to these pages as "the secret of secrets," thus presumably more dangerous than Voltaire's "secret" *La Pucelle.*[75]

The principal "dangers" lay in the key paradox of Mandeville's *Fable.* What guides human nature? he asked. His answer: vices. Du Châtelet translated this sentiment, thus apparently giving her approval to this blasphemy that private vice, man's willingness "to gratify any of his Appetites," makes public virtue and the prosperity of the nation. For example, the profligate's loss of his fortune creates work for all in the luxury trades. But Du Châtelet could not wholeheartedly endorse this negative picture of human nature and the primacy of passions over reason as the sole motivating force throughout all ranks of society. To both accept and reject Mandeville's view led her into a series of contradictions and her own eclectic views.[76] In her system of "la morale," she insisted that man might be governed by good intentions, not just "involuntary effects, like hunger and thirst." Her readers would have found such good intentions—innate, God-given, "universal moral ideas"—familiar: *not to do to others what you would not want done to you.*" This statement of the Golden Rule led Du Châtelet to a simple definition of "vice" and "virtue": "Men have agreed to call all action prejudicial to society *vice,* and to give the name of *virtue* to all those which the reasonable ambition to be just makes happen." Without even noting her obvious disagreement with Mandeville, she then translated his discussion of the use by those most astute in that society of "self-interest [*amour propre*]," "pride," and their opposites, dishonor and shame, to create civilization.[77]

The power of "pride" and "shame" depended on man's ability to choose his behavior. Mandeville paid no attention to this classic religious paradox; he assumed man's "free will." "Liberty," as Du Châtelet and Voltaire called it in chapter VII of the *Traité,* in theory differentiated men from beasts, but raised its own questions. How could man control the passions resulting from his senses? How to act freely in the presence of an omniscient God who knew all that would happen? Some of Du Châtelet's additions remain in the *Traité,* but her fullest answer can be found in an essay entitled "De la liberté," among Voltaire's St. Petersburg papers. She began her essay with her definition of free will: *"Liberty, I call, the power to think of a thing, or not to think of it, to move or not to move, in conformance with the choice of one's own mind."*[78]

Du Châtelet's systematic discussion of liberty was part of a larger work and intended, as her definition suggests, to follow a section on movement. For the physics of the natural laws of motion in the universe raised the metaphysical question how man could move of his own volition. Voltaire chose to avoid these subjects. He wrote to Frederick of Prussia in October 1737, "All of metaphysics in my opinion consists of two things, the first that which all men of good sense can know, the second that which they could never know." He acknowledged in his "Discours en vers sur l'homme" that Du Châtelet, "my muse," was very different: she "sang the truth." For Du Châtelet, to know the "truth" meant working through such apparent contradictions. She reasoned that God's liberty is infinite; he gave "a little portion of liberty [to man] just as he gave a little portion of intelligence." This was a "weak and limited power to carry out certain movements, and to implement some thoughts," but it was liberty nonetheless.[79] Her final resolution came with her own synthesis of reading in philosophy, metaphysics, theology, and physics and would be presented in works she completed over the next ten years: her *Institutions de physique, Examens de la Bible,* and *Discours sur le bonheur.*

Co-author of the *Eléments de la philosophie de Newton*

Du Châtelet's biographers, when describing her writings, have always assumed that she worked on projects sequentially, but, like Voltaire, she did not. This makes their next collaboration more difficult to describe. Their letters suggest a clear sequence from Algarotti's six-week visit in the fall of 1735 until the first printing, in March 1737, of the book *Eléments de la philosophie de Newton,* but this was only one of many of their projects, both shared and individual. In that period, she read Newton's *Principia* and Pemberton's commentary, while she made notes from dom Calmet, transformed Mandeville's *Fable* for her French audience, and made additions to Voltaire's *Traité*—perhaps all in the same week, or even the same day.

Algarotti arrived at Cirey with the beginnings of a book he planned on Newton's *Opticks* and its relationship to the theory of attraction. Meant for the general reader, the explanation was to be in the form of dialogues modeled on Fontenelle's *Entretiens sur la pluralité des mondes.* Despite his youth, Algarotti was already a recognized scholar in Italy. Optics had been his special interest when he studied in Bologna, and he had published a defense of Newton's view of light as particles carrying color, against the views of his mentors, who followed Aristotle in believing that the object itself held the color. From there he went to Rome and, with the resources of his wealthy businessman father, began his grand tour of the learned *physiciens, géomètres,* and *philosophes* of Europe. One introduction led to another, and it was Maupertuis who recommended him to Du Châtelet. The engraving that Algarotti placed at the beginning of the first edition of his book *Il Newtonianismo per le donne* shows a clearly recognizable marquise Du Châtelet and her equally recognizable companion, the young Algarotti. The château in the background might as well be Cirey. The engraving suggests strolls in the gardens, walks along the banks of the Blaise, or rides through the countryside in the phaeton. Algarotti saw his weeks at Cirey as the model of taste and the good life of the social elite, qualities he hoped to capture in his dialogues.[80]

"*Mi caro cignio di Padova* [My dear swan of Padua]," Voltaire called him, with obvious affection and clear reference to Algarotti's physique. He honored Algarotti by allowing him to read chapters of "la luce," the light, as he and Du Châtelet referred to the project, aloud to *les Emiliens*. At some point, Voltaire decided that he, too, should write more extensively on Newton. Du Châtelet's evident enthusiasm perhaps suggested to Voltaire that the young Venetian was usurping his mentor role. But, more important, if the Venetian was bringing Newton to the Italians, could he not then do the same for the French, and thus contribute to the acceptance of the great man's theories? There was Coste's translation of the *Opticks* into French, there were the Latin and English editions of Newton's *Principia* and his *System of the World*; there was Maupertuis's essay, the *Astres,* comparing Descartes's *tourbillons* to Newton's attraction. However, no one in France had yet undertaken an explanation as inclusive or as engaging as Fontenelle had done for the seventeenth-century Frenchman's theories. Like Fontenelle, Voltaire had written essays and plays. He had dabbled in physics and philosophy with his *Lettres philosophiques,* and now, with a serious work on Newton, he would place himself in a position to rival "le roi," the grand old *philosophe.*[81]

By July 1736, they were deeply immersed in the project. Du Châtelet had already reported to a friend that she had turned to Newton's own writings. Beginning in April, Voltaire sent requests to Moussinot and another Paris connection for Newton's works as well as those of the men who argued for and against his theories on light and attraction. Voltaire had set aside his history of Louis XIV's reign and described the new project as "a little work that will place everyone in a state to understand this philosopher [Newton], of whom the world speaks & still knows so little." During that spring, summer, and fall together, he and Du Châtelet read widely in physics, astronomy, and the mathematics of motion. They consulted others over questions on refraction and *forces vives*. By December 1736, she reported to Maupertuis, now far away in Lapland, that there was a draft of "an introduction to the philosophy of mr. Newton." She enclosed the dedicatory verses Voltaire had written to her.[82]

In many ways, this was as daring an endeavor as their collaboration on the *Traité,* but, as she wrote to Maupertuis, Du Châtelet was eager to help "my companion of solitude" in the effort to bring the "truths" of the great Newton to the French.[83] The project involved two of Newton's works, the *Opticks* and the *Principia.* The *Opticks* had initially been discredited when Academicians could not replicate the experiments described in it. By 1720, however, Newton's observations and explanations of many of the phenomena of light and vision had found supporters. The same could not be said for his theory of universal attraction. It remained for most members of the Académie des sciences an incomplete, unproved, and thus unacceptable set of hypotheses: that the gravity that operated on earth had its equivalent in the universe. Although, as Maupertuis had so artfully demonstrated, astronomical observations fitted Newton's explanation for planetary motion better than Descartes's, Newton's still lacked a causal explanation. This was the issue that divided members like Maupertuis and Clairaut from Fontenelle and Bernoulli, however admiring they all might be of Newton's mathematics. And it was the issue that Du Châtelet had to deal with in collaboration with Voltaire in his *Eléments* and alone in her *Institutions de physique.*

The older Scholastic descriptions of the working of the universe—those that Copernicus and Galileo had argued against—assumed that one formulated a natural law and its explanation and then searched for the observations to confirm it. That system of reasoning had been defeated at great cost by the adherents of Descartes. He became the authority because he offered a material, rational, causal explanation for the workings of the cosmos. And though this mechanical explanation could not incorporate all of the observations assembled by astronomers like Kepler, it offered a unified system that explained the actions of all matter on earth and in the universe in simple, comprehensible terms. All matter was particles; all particles were perpetually in motion. This motion, initiated by the Creator, meant the impact of one particle on another in a universe filled to the brim with particles; there was no space between them. These impacts accounted for all observable shapes and interactions. Descartes's moving particles, a natural philosophy called "materialism," explained all known phenomena, everything from color (the result of the impact of light particles on the particles of bodies) to the orbits of the planets and their satellites.[84]

Thus, in the *Eléments,* in order to prove the validity of Newton's ideas, Du Châtelet and Voltaire had to disprove the previous authority. This meant arguing with Descartes over more than just his explanation for planetary movement. His views on refraction, vision, and the effects of lenses included in *Dioptrics* had to be compared with Newton's, all couched in the terms of angles and lines, and the constituent relationships that one could describe with the Frenchman's analytic geometry. By the beginning of August, Voltaire's letters show his disenchantment. To Mlle Quinault, eager for a new play for the Comédie française, he confided, "There is in this world a devil of Newton, who finds precisely how much the sun weighs, and which colors light is composed of. This strange man turns my head." Voltaire made errors in arithmetic when doing simple accounts, and so he found the mathematics daunting. To another friend, he admitted he could not even think of two rhymes of verse because it was just "angles, a's and b's, planets and comets": "I am straining my brain with Newton." To the Academician Henri Pitot, he wondered if he could continue: "I have health too frail to apply myself to mathematics. I cannot work more than an hour a day without much suffering."[85] Not surprisingly, he finished the dedicatory "Epître" to Du Châtelet first and with more enthusiasm.

In contrast, Du Châtelet thrived on the tasks, and on the arduous regimen of days and nights of study and writing. Her comments on Newton's works have not survived, but there are six pages of notes on three other books mixed in with her papers in St. Petersburg. The questions she sought to answer reflect all the projects that she and Voltaire shared in these years. Chapter VI of the *Traité* could have occasioned her note citing Descartes's famous conclusion from his *Discours sur la méthode,* "I think, therefore I am," and its corollary that thought requires no body, extension, or position in space. From there she went on to question the definition of "time" and discuss her uncertainty about how one can know anything outside of oneself. Were these notes made the same night? She then turned to the French translation of Descartes's *Principes de la philosophie,* the source for the next set of notes, going from one chapter to another and then back. The page numbers cited progress from 55 to 34 and then to 74, then 91–92, and, like her scribbled comments, relate to disparate questions: her doubts about Descartes's distinctions between length and color, her disagreement with his way of differentiating between modes and substances. She commented briefly on his views of motion and concluded with her own images of the relativity of movement: that she moves does not mean that the *fauteuil* in which she sits has moved—a commonsense bit of reasoning from observation that she would use in her *Institutions de physique*. She filled two pages with information on the motion of planetary bodies and random statistics about the relative weight of air and water (which became part of her critique of the Bible) from volume 2 of Noël Regnault's *L'Origine ancienne de la physique nouvelle*. She copied a riddle that she perhaps thought would amuse her son in their lessons: what is always old and always new? Answer: the tides. The last page of notes? A few details from Fontenelle's *Eloge,* his tribute to Isaac Newton.[86]

Voltaire incorporated notes like these, her finished paragraphs and pages, into the *Eléments*. To Du Châtelet, this free collaboration with Voltaire seemed appropriate not because she was a woman or unlettered, but because, as the novice, she deferred to his genius, and because the co-opting of others' work was common practice in this era. Voltaire copied the order of his chapters for his *Eléments* from Algarotti's dialogues, just as he took the ideas of others for his plays. "Originality" was in how one used the available material, not necessarily in its novelty. The section on "color" in the *Eléments* is very similar to an essay Du Châtelet sent to Johann Bernoulli and to the chemist Du Fay. The description of comets and their behavior that he added to the second edition (1741) is strikingly similar to the one she ultimately included in her own description of the universe in her commentary for her translation of the *Principia*.[87]

Du Châtelet's other contributions were less obvious but no less significant. Voltaire wrote of the universe in the rich imagery of the poet. He brought the moon to life. In contrast, chapters on particularly abstract mathematical or scientific topics, such as Du Châtelet would have contributed, were written in a clear, straightforward style. These chapters ended with neat paragraphs that not only summarized them but also suggested what was to come next—a common device in her *Institutions*. To help readers follow a surprising statement such as that "visible things" were just "colored light" and that the other properties "we only sense over time and by experience," Du Châtelet chose an analogy taken from everyday experience, a rhetorical device she employed in all of her own writings. One such analogy came from childhood: "We learn to see," she explained, "precisely as we learn to speak and to read. The difference is that the art of seeing is much easier, & that Nature is equally our teacher [maître] in all."[88]

Voltaire dedicated the Eléments de la philosophie de Newton to "Madame la Marquise Du Ch**" and made it plain that she was his co-author. He began with obvious reference to Algarotti, and, if one wished to make the connection, to Fontenelle: "Here is neither a [coquettish] marquise, nor an imaginary philosophy." Instead, as he explained in the preface, he offered to the public, to her glory and that of her sex, "the solid study that you have made of many new truths and the fruit of respectable work." His effort to present these truths with "order and clarity" would enable those who wished it "to enjoy your researches without pain." Their roles had been reversed. By analogy, he explained what she had done. He imagined a minister of state who "forms an idea," the result of operations "that he himself cannot do; other eyes saw for him, other hands worked, and put it in a state" faithful to his intention. "All men of wit will be a bit in the situation of this minister."[89]

When in the course of these collaborations did Du Châtelet realize just how capable and intelligent she was? Translating Mandeville's Fable had amused and challenged her. Then the work on the Eléments with Voltaire, and the gradual narrowing of her reading, indicated her rejection of "literature" for "science." A letter to Maupertuis mentioning her translation of Mandeville's "Remark" on luxury had more questions about forces vives than about the morals of the wealthy. Once again, however, Du Châtelet left no directions to answer the biographer's next question: why did she decide to leave her mentors to their projects and to write original works of natural philosophy? As she explained in her translator's preface, the enemy was "irresolution that produced false steps for one [person] and confused ideas for another." Many failed, she noted, for "lack of courage."[90] A learned woman always invited ridicule. By the summer of 1737, Du Châtelet had found the requisite courage and resolution.

Voltaire described the fundamental choices of her life in his dedication to her of the play *Alzire:* "Born for the arts of pleasing, [she] prefers the truth." In the course of their collaboration, she had discovered that she did not agree with Voltaire on key points of his *Eléments,* or with his conclusions from the experiments on fire that they had conducted together. And though she was "used to acceding to him in everything," these were not matters of opinion, but truths that she could not allow to stand uncontested.[91] Du Châtelet's response? She reordered her work and her household to make time to formulate her own accounts of these scientific phenomena.

CHAPTER FOUR

An Independent Reputation:
Géomètre and *Physicien*

Du Châtelet's change from helpmate to published author in her own right began as a consequence of Voltaire's decision to enter the Académie royale des sciences' 1738 prize competition. As was the custom, a topic had been set: the nature and propagation of fire. Submissions were due in September 1737. In the late spring and early summer, Du Châtelet stood with the aspiring *physicien* at the iron forge near the château, watching the melting and cooling of substances as part of their experiments to understand the relationship between heat and fire. In the *galerie,* she supervised the boiling and the measuring of the temperatures of liquids. To her amazement, Voltaire stubbornly refused to accept that their results did not confirm Newton's hypothesis: that fire was matter and thus subject to the force of gravity. Visitors had seen them argue, but no one ever reported the kind of profound disagreements that must have been voiced with each new set of experiments.

What arguments did Du Châtelet use to challenge Voltaire? From her perspective, his obstinacy betrayed the essence of what they had sought to understand and describe in their collaborations: the reasoned, informed search for "the truth" about the origins of society, the rules of human behavior, and now the laws of nature and the workings of the universe. Du Châtelet's conviction that Voltaire was in error prompted the most unorthodox decision in a life already filled with unorthodoxy: she would write and submit her own essay. European women had studied together with fathers, husbands, and brothers; they had long assisted men in their experiments, their observations, and their writing. But no woman had ever made her own submission to the Académie royale des sciences. Only with her own entry, however, could Du Châtelet ensure that the "true" results of their experiments and the conclusions to which these led were presented. The decision would give her her first taste of "la gloire," what she identified in her *Discours sur le bonheur* as the fame that eluded women because of their exclusion from the usual routes to prominence.[1]

Experiments with Fire

In the course of 1736, still intent on "removing the thorns" in Voltaire's path, Du Châtelet had made notes from Newton's *Opticks* and continued her study of the *Principia*.[2] Did she continue with her reading when Voltaire fled to Holland in December because of his poem "Le Mondain"? Apparently unaffected by his new circumstances, Voltaire kept on with the *Eléments de la philosophie de Newton* and had sent proofs to her within a few weeks of his arrival. While in Leiden, Voltaire became an enthusiastic adherent of what Newton called "experimental philosophy." He met Petrus van Musschenbroek, one of Holland's most distinguished Newtonian *physiciens*, famous for his natural philosophy texts filled with experiments. Voltaire also attended the demonstration lectures of Willem Jacob 'sGravesande, another follower of Newton.[3] He was enthralled by the possibility of doing his own experiments. When he returned to Cirey in March 1737, he instructed Moussinot to purchase more scientific equipment from abbé Nollet, Paris's premier instrument-maker. Nollet's 1738 catalogue included more than 345 items divided into eight categories. By the time Voltaire had finished, he had spent close to ten thousand livres and must have had one of the most complete collections of physics equipment in Europe for the day. After receiving a pendulum apparatus, Voltaire commented to Moussinot, "We are in a century where one cannot be learned without money."[4] While working through Newton's *Opticks*, Du Châtelet and Voltaire certainly had a set of prisms, and a set of lenses as well. Perhaps Algarotti helped them with their first efforts to create the separation of white light into colors and then their recombination. Longchamps later mentioned rooftop observations of the night sky, perhaps with the reflecting telescope that arrived from Paris in the same package with a new pair of slippers for Voltaire. Pitot, the Academician who reviewed the *Eléments* for publication, supervised other purchases—an air pump, a Copernican globe, and a burning glass—and perhaps he also chose the microscope. Du Châtelet took evident delight in the transformation of the *galerie* where they set up the apparatus. She reported to Maupertuis in December 1737 that he "would find a good enough *cabinet de physique*," with telescopes and mathematics instruments, and only then mentioned more typical entertainments: the view of the mountains, their theatrical productions.[5]

Though Voltaire must have viewed the *Eléments* as largely done by the time most of the instruments arrived, his investment did make possible another scientific project. He had asked Moussinot to inquire about the Académie des sciences' current prize competition. The *Mercure de France* and the *Gazette de France* had announced the topic, the nature and propagation of fire, in April 1736. Annoyed that membership in the Académie française, the literary royal society, still eluded him, Voltaire perhaps imagined that, with a second scientific publication, he, like Fontenelle, could cross over: become a member of one royal academy, then of the other.[6]

Du Châtelet and Voltaire embarked on the project together. Having studied the behavior of light for the *Eléments,* they could see that fire, a source of light and heat, offered possible analogies. Newton had suggested as much in his queries at the end of the *Opticks:* the similarity between the interactions of particles of matter activated by heat could be compared to those activated by light. But what was fire? An element in the Aristotelian sense of a constituent property of bodies? Separate matter like other bodies, as Newton argued? Or some medium in between, as Descartes asserted? What caused it? How did it function? In an effort to answer these questions, Du Châtelet and Voltaire consulted, in addition to Newton and Descartes, the writings of chemists such as Hermann Boerhaave, who saw fire both as particles and an element. Du Châtelet's markers with her scrawls in pencil, the notes to herself—in one instance a geometric figure—remain where she left them in Boerhaave's two-volume 1733 *Elementa chemiae (Elements of Chemistry).* She wanted to remember his experiments on combustion, alcohol, oil and sulphur, the "elasticity" of air, and freezing. Voltaire, eager to use his essay to present yet more arguments for attraction, to prove Newton's view that fire consisted of particles—but particles governed by attraction and gravity like other matter—marked passages in Musschenbroek's 1734 *Elementa physicae (Elements of Physics)* where the Dutchman claimed to have proved this supposition with his experiments.[7]

Reading completed, Voltaire and Du Châtelet must have gathered their papers, pens, and ink, or perhaps just simple graphite pencils, and called for the phaeton to take them to the iron forge only a few miles from the château. The marquis must have given permission for the two *physiciens* to interrupt the work at the forges and use the materials produced on his lands for their experiments. The temporary loss of time, lumber, and income from the usual sales of the output of the forges, charcoal burners, and cut timber would have been noticeable, given that Voltaire heated a thousand pounds of iron for just one experiment.[8] Du Châtelet and Voltaire must also have disrupted the household, for staff from the château would have been enlisted to help carry out and record the results of the ambitious list of experiments they had made. At the forge, they melted and weighed metals, thus replicating Musschenbroek's experiments with the same phenomena. They presumed that they could reason backward, in a sense: like Musschenbroek, they would discern the "nature of fire" by observing and measuring its effects as heat. Similarly, experiments with a burning glass, or *verre ardente*, by focusing the light of the sun and igniting matter, might help to explain the "propagation of fire." Voltaire had instructed Moussinot to acquire a number of lenses just for this purpose.

Such assumptions and procedures characterized experimental philosophy in their era. In French, the word *expérience* carries two meanings, both "experiment" and "experience." Even with the best instruction, experiment remained an uncertain enterprise. In April 1736, Du Châtelet complained to Algarotti of a defective *chambre obscure,* or camera obscura, a rectangular black box with holes at both ends and a slot for inserting different lenses. With it one studied the effects of light passing through concave and convex crafted pieces of glass. The resulting images were projected onto a wall or sheet of paper. Du Châtelet spared no sarcasm in her description of her correspondence with the camera's famous maker: one had already been returned, but "the abbé Nollet has sent me a *chambre obscure,* more obscure than ever." He insisted that it had worked well when Algarotti chose it for her in Paris. She concluded, "It must be that the sun in Cirey is not favorable for it."[9] However, even simple re-creation of another person's experiment, replicating what others had observed through the experience of the senses, often presented difficulties. Given these realities, the Dutch *physicien* 'sGravesande used experiments to establish "regularity" in the results and thus the "probability" of his explanation. For others, even this assumed too much, and the artificial, contrived, and constructed machinery of experimentation seemed far away from the "realm of sensible reality." Maupertuis was reluctant to use the microscope until after 1750.[10]

From their two essays, it is possible to discern the evolution of the dis-agreement between Du Châtelet and Voltaire. It must have been very hot those summer days at the forge on the estate, even though both would have dressed in lighter fabrics to accommodate the time of year. Du Châtelet, still corseted with multiple petticoats, probably also experienced the heat of the fire created by the ironworkers at the big bellows as it heaved and pulled the air to strengthen the flames. She watched hundreds of pounds of iron ore melt in the crucibles and then cool. She would have seen the soot fly into the ironmaster's face, and into the faces of the boys who assisted him. Their dull-colored wool breeches and homemade linen shirts became grimy and sweat-stained as they worked. Du Châtelet carefully noted that the ex-periments produced disparate results. The melted iron weighed the same when it cooled and retained its essential nature. Lead, in contrast, became a powder and weighed more. They wondered, Why this effect on lead and not on iron? This process, now known as calcination, remained a mystery to them. The question of fire's essential nature remained open. How could it have weight like matter in one instance, and not in another? They agreed that their pyrometer measurements of the iron ore confirmed Réaumur's 1726 Académie *Mémoire;* they could testify to the fact that it expanded and then contracted again. Otherwise, these experiments with iron proved not Musschenbroek's conclusions but those of Boerhaave, the Dutch author whose work Du Châtelet had marked so carefully. The weight of the ore never changed; fire added nothing, subtracted nothing. Thus, fire did not have weight, an essential property of matter.

They persevered at the forge and back in the *galerie* of Voltaire's suite at the château. With a simple heating lamp, a balance, and a boxed set of weights purchased from abbé Nollet, they melted and boiled all kinds of substances over a spirit lamp, weighed them before and then after, even those that turned into the powdery dust calx. Newton in the *Opticks* sug-gested experimenting with substances such as quicklime, oil of cloves, salt water, and nitrates. Sometimes nothing happened; sometimes, as in the case of antimony, as reported by Homberg, another authority they consulted, the weight increased. They had neither "regularity" nor "probability."[11]

When did Du Châtelet first voice her doubts about Voltaire's insistence on the meaning of these experiments? After the first melting and cooling of iron ore left the weight unchanged? After the experiments at the château?

Perhaps because of Du Châtelet's objections, Voltaire asked Moussinot to question one of the Académie's chemists, and then two well-known pharmacists. When did Du Châtelet begin to show frustration with Voltaire's failings as an experimenter? Even those procedures he did succeed in completing allowed no conclusions of significance. For example, he used the Réaumur thermometer in order to study, as Boerhaave had, the effects of mixing hot and cold substances, but Réaumur used purified alcohol (*esprit de vin*) as the medium of measurement. This boiled at eighty degrees Celsius, and so the glass tube exploded when Voltaire put it in hot oil. After this experience, Voltaire wrote to Moussinot to send Daniel Fahrenheit's thermometer, which, filled with mercury, could withstand temperatures above 212 degrees Fahrenheit, the boiling point of water. However, like the air pump that he requested to replicate other experiments, it did not arrive before he had to submit his essay.[12]

Voltaire had embarked on his experiments with the thermometer for the second part of the competition essay, their exploration of the origins of fire and its propagation. At first, Voltaire was confused about even the meaning of the question and had Moussinot seek out Fontenelle for an explanation. Trading again on the marquis's good will, Voltaire had the branches from all the trees in a nursery cut into pieces, had them arranged on an iron plaque, and, with his pendulum calibrated in seconds, measured how long it took for the wood to burn to cinders. He observed that a pile of vegetables did not take the same amount of time. A fire in a cleared section of the marquis's forest burned at different rates depending on whether or not there was a wind. By mid-July, frustrated by his problems with experiments, he wrote to Moussinot to hire a chemist for him who would come to Cirey after having purchased instruments in Paris.[13]

Du Châtelet's letters from 1737 never mention the disasters with the thermometers or the search for a skilled assistant. However, even before Voltaire finished the final draft of his submission for the Académie prize, she must have turned away from him and his insistence that fire had weight, was subject to gravity, and, as Newton asserted, was "matter." Their disagreement was fundamental. None of their experiments, least of all those Voltaire had conducted, convinced her that fire had any weight or demonstrated any behavior similar to that of matter that could be attributed to the fire itself. In the experiments at the forge, she, like many of the authorities they had consulted, could see that both the increase and the decrease in the weight of the metals could be explained by the material itself that was being heated or burned; fire could remain a constant.

Realizing the importance of these discoveries must have convinced Du Châtelet to write her own *Dissertation sur la nature et la propagation du feu,* both to counter Voltaire's mistaken opinions and to present what she knew to be the correct answers to the Académie's questions. She later confided to Mme de Graffigny that she had made the decision at the last minute, for she began to write only two weeks before the submission deadline. In the past, she had once acknowledged the boldness of her thoughts and actions. In her preface to Mandeville's *Fable,* she had asked her readers, "before making this judgment," to examine "if they are accurate . . . [and] true." Similarly, she explained in her modest disclaimer at the end of her essay on fire, "I hope that my love for the truth will stand for me in place of eloquence, & that the sincere desire that I have to contribute to knowledge will gain forgiveness for my faults."[14] For Du Châtelet, the pursuit of "truth" justified her audacious foray into the debates between the most prominent natural philosophers of her day.

The essay she submitted, number six of fourteen entries, differed from Voltaire's not only in content but also in her evident enthusiasm both for experiment and further speculation. She wrote it so quickly that one can hear her voice as she formulated what she wanted to say and marshaled the evidence. Her essay, in accordance with the implied specifications of the Académie's questions, fell into two parts. Like Voltaire, she drew from her summaries of works they had read together, the current draft of his *Eléments,* and the results of the recent experiments they had done. She found numerous ways to assert what she assumed any reasonable person must conclude: "from all of these experiments, that Fire has no weight, or that, if it does, it is impossible for us ever to perceive it [with our senses]."

She never missed an opportunity to argue against Newton's hypothesis that fire, light, and matter consisted of the same material. Instead, she affirmed Boerhaave's conclusion that fire had its own particular essence, with light and heat as its "modes," or manifestations. In this, she not only turned away from Newton, but also accepted a hypothesis of Voltaire's nemesis Descartes. She suggested that their experiments confirmed Descartes's definition of fire. As she later explained in a letter to Maupertuis, "Fire has no weight, and—as has been demonstrated for space—it might very well be neither spirit nor matter." That this "subtle matter," "of an in-between nature," could not be discerned did not trouble her. More comfortable with this kind of speculation than Voltaire, she happily included whimsical queries, such as: if the rays of the sun are yellow, would those of other suns project red or green, or some other color?[15]

Where Voltaire seemed increasingly bored with the subject and the reporting of experimental results and conclusions, Du Châtelet delighted in what she observed. Even a simple optical experiment—looking through a pinhole made in a card that captured "all between the horizon and us" and that blended "the prodigious quantity of rays that pass through the pinhole" without confusing anything in view—"surprises the imagination." In another section, she noted, "In examining the effects of fire on bodies, one goes from miracles to miracles." As she saw, for example, when a stone and iron made a spark, "Fire the most violent could be produced in a moment by the percussion of two bodies the coldest in appearance." She also suggested other avenues of investigation, possible causes and ramifications. They agreed on the probable causal connection between fire and electricity, but where Voltaire made only a simple statement, Du Châtelet offered ten proofs and suggested questions for an "ingenious *philosophe*" to explore: if a heated object generated more electricity through friction, was this similar to the interaction between an object and fire?[16] Voltaire ended his essay abruptly, simply announcing that he had nothing more to say.[17] Du Châtelet, in contrast, expanded the second part of her *Dissertation* to report her own experiments and the resulting speculations.

Graffigny reported that the marquise liked to work after the household had retired. One visitor's account to a friend of his arrival at the château in the middle of the night described the scene as "like a fairy tale," with its dark corridors, and Du Châtelet studying by the light of twenty candles.[18] On such a night in August 1737, she might have asked for a simple meal of bread, cheese, and fruit, and then left the empty plate, except for a few crumbs and the knife, on the small table beside her desk. Standing, she could have gone to the mantel and moved one candlestick close to the other, then separated them. As she recorded in her *Dissertation*, the two flames brought so close together did not join, as Voltaire reported, but avoided each other. She called out and woke her *femme de chambre*, asleep on a cot in the antechamber. She wanted the glass covers brought for a "very simple experiment, & [one] that I have often repeated." She draped her napkin over the top of the open glass cover, then reached for her plate and repeated the experiment. The candle gradually went out, but as it did, the flame remained conical in shape and always tended upward. Thus, she could report further confirmation that fire was the very opposite of gravity. Fire, she wrote, was in "a perpetual antagonism" with the force of gravity, preventing it from compressing and thus destroying all in the universe. Her analysis echoed today's descriptions of energy: fire was in everything, always moving, and therefore the cause of the elasticity of matter, its ability to change in shape and kind. Without fire's manifestation in the mode of light, "this breath of life that God has scattered on his work, Nature would languish at rest & the Universe could not subsist a moment as it is."[19]

Du Châtelet confided to Graffigny the secret of how she kept awake for so many consecutive nights: she put her hands in ice water, walked about the room slapping them on her arms, and then returned to writing.[20] Du Châtelet probably had the ice for other reasons as well, for both she and Voltaire mentioned in their essays Daniel Fahrenheit's experiments with freezing water. Du Châtelet and other *physiciens* interpreted this as an indirect way to study fire's nature and propagation—by its absence. Voltaire gave a sentence to the idea, while Du Châtelet added two chapters in part II of her essay, on the "cooling of bodies" and "the causes of water freezing." She cited the observations of others: reports of the Academy of Florence about giant five-hundred-pound blocks of ice, of grottoes where water froze in summer and melted in winter, chemists' measurements of temperature in different seasons, of bodies under pressure and not, an Académie *Mémoire* by Dortous de Mairan on ice. These authorities, however, offered nothing conclusive.

She also conceived of an eclectic series of very simple experiments of her own to explore the cooling that she saw as a result of fire's "abandoning the bodies."[21] Although she made no specific reference to Newton, like him, Du Châtelet accepted that similar causes would produce similar effects, and that the fixed qualities of bodies demonstrated by experiment could be considered "universal" qualities of all matter. To some extent, she also reasoned according to Descartes's method: using experiments to test an unverifiable but altogether reasonable hypothesis. She believed, for example, that fire communicated its heat equally in all things, so, like a Cartesian, she heated water to two different temperatures with a "burning lamp," and then mixed them together. She discovered that they would come to have a new temperature, half of the difference between the original temperatures of the two. More in the spirit of a Newtonian, she took melted wax from her candle, designated it as "vegetable matter," and dropped it into cold water. She generalized from the result she observed: the congealing of the wax, like the cold of the air, united the nutritive matter of plants, while the heat of a summer day separated and dispersed them, just as the flame melted the wax.[22] In the end, the fantastical answer she formulated to explain freezing came from observation, process of elimination, and reasoned analogy. It tells as much about eighteenth-century science as it does about Du Châtelet's approach to experimental philosophy.

On another August night, though it was hot, she must have instructed the servants to bring her crushed ice. She knew from the authorities she had read, or from her own experience in the cold Cirey winters, that frozen water would expand and could break a vase. She replicated the process. She surrounded a water-filled vase with ice mixed with salt and nitrates. As predicted, the water froze. Du Châtelet had already assumed that all bodies had particles of fire in them, which must somehow be gone when a body is frozen, but she could not accept that their absence alone explained the transformation of the water. Just as in combustion, when a body bursts into flame, she must have come to believe that something had to be added. It is easy to imagine her taking up her quill pen and listing hypothetical factors, each of which she rejected. Wind alone could not be the cause of freezing, for a bellows blown on a thermometer, perhaps at the forge with Voltaire, did not change its temperature. What could it be? She must have returned to the original experiment with the water frozen in the vase. Of course, salt and nitrates. They existed in abundance in certain parts of the world, especially the warm areas, but how, then, would they come to be thousands of miles away, in cold climates with no obvious deposits of these refrigerating agents? By process of elimination, she reasoned that the wind carried them throughout the world. When they met the cold air, these particles would fall and become the means of creating the ice and snow of the pole. The hot air of the other regions kept the particles high in the air and thus unable to unite with water. Her own experience offered the final confirmation. It was for this reason, she wrote, her phrasing reflecting her excitement, that the ponds at Cirey froze only in the winter.[23]

When Du Châtelet made her decision to write her own entry, she took only her husband into her confidence, perhaps to be sure of his approval. He kept the secret so well that he did not even tell Maupertuis when they met in Paris.[24] As she knew, only anonymity would make submission by a woman at all possible, and spare her from the condemnation of her work before it had even been read. Her essay had the style and the authority of the other thirteen entries; her explanations of phenomena might be contested, but they could not be dismissed. Du Châtelet appreciated the significance of her accomplishment. In the inventory of her papers, the notaries had listed the receipt for her submission dated August 23, 1737, and signed by the perpetual secretary of the Académie, Fontenelle, whom she had known since she was a child.[25]

Publication in the Republic of Letters

Du Châtelet and Voltaire had to wait until April 1738 for Fontenelle to announce the winner of the Académie competition at the public meeting held the week after Easter. In those eight months, Algarotti's *Newtonianismo per le dame* was published in Venice, an unauthorized and incomplete Amsterdam edition of Voltaire's *Eléments* appeared in March, and Du Châtelet took over her son's education. Each of these events played a role in her next "bold" decision, as she described it: to write her own account not of just one phenomenon, like fire, but of the entire workings of the universe. While Voltaire produced revisions for the *Eléments* and worked on a variety of literary projects, Du Châtelet persevered in her mathematical studies and now boasted a shelf-full of texts. Algebra and analytic geometry continued to fill her time until the fall of 1739, when she began to work on integral calculus—first with Maupertuis, in his brief visit to Cirey, and then with Samuel König, the Swiss *géomètre* whom she hired as her tutor at the recommendation of Maupertuis. Du Châtelet built her own library of physics texts as well. She later told Maupertuis that she knew the *Opticks* "almost by heart." Now she instructed Prault, Voltaire's Paris printer and bookseller, to buy her her own copy of Newton's *Principia* and to have it covered in Russian leather with gold tooling. Particularly interested in the concept of *forces vives,* she wanted a collection of the *Mémoires* of the Académie, and told Prault to buy them even though they cost six hundred livres, twice the yearly salary of her son's *précepteur.* She also gave him a blanket request for Royal Society *Transactions* "and all the books of *physique* that you will find come your way."[26]

Du Châtelet and Voltaire had waited eagerly for the appearance of Algarotti's book: Voltaire because of the probable similarities to his *Eléments,* Du Châtelet because of the Venetian's promise to dedicate the book to her. She wrote of learning more Italian and of "training myself in the art of translation," with the idea that she might do a French version for him. However, she soon discovered that she had not understood Algarotti's intentions at all. Du Châtelet learned that he had dedicated his book to Fontenelle, an odd gesture given the Academician's lifelong opposition to Newton's planetary system. By May 1738, she had seen the Italian edition, and then the French translation. In the end, only the Italian version published early in 1737 used her image, but neither its engraved frontispiece nor the portrayal of the marquise in the Italian and French texts bore any resemblance to the sketch she had permitted Algarotti to take away, or to the draft she remembered and believed herself to have participated in developing.[27]

There could be no denying Algarotti's references to his time at Cirey: five days spent in conversation at a château "that served as a retreat for us," set high on a hill with the river flowing below. The marquise he created could follow his descriptions, knew something of mathematics, was quick and bright, emphatic and aggressive in her eagerness for knowledge of the causes of the phenomena he described—and easily recognizable to Du Châtelet's contemporaries in the Republic of Letters. In addition, however, Algarotti's marquise was petulant, childish, easily bored, and sometimes uncomprehending.

Du Châtelet explained to Maupertuis that, in the draft Algarotti had read aloud at Cirey, the elegant young pair had joked about light, but not so frequently about love. She probably saw it then as part of the pleasure of conversation between women and men, signifying sexual possibilities that need not be acted upon. However, Algarotti had transformed this *badinage,* as it was called, into dialogues that denigrated her intelligence and mocked her social superiority in relation to her charming mentor. In one dialogue, Algarotti interlaced every aspect of the explanations of the nature of color, the

workings of the microscope, a lens, and a mirror with flirtation and potentially erotic situations. The mutability of colors occasioned a reference to
the fickleness of lovers. Algarotti had amused his readers with an analogy to
one of Newton's most important algebraic formulas. This, and the pages of
calculations demonstrating that "the devotion of a lover decreases in relation
to the square of the time and the cube of the distance," so annoyed Du Châtelet that she mentioned it in her letters to friends on three occasions.[28]

Voltaire rose to Du Châtelet's defense immediately and wrote to Thieriot that she knew more than Algarotti and "had corrected things in his book."
He called all the flirtatious games "useless wit." Yet Voltaire also fueled the
potential ridicule with his own words and actions. In letters to Algarotti and
Thieriot, he coined playful nicknames such as "Emilia Neutonia" and "My
lady Emily Newton" that brought smiles at cafés and salons and were repeated in letters to the provinces.[29] When the Eléments de la philosophie de
Newton appeared in April 1738, though Voltaire credited her in the dedication as his co-author, he gave his readers an even more difficult image for
Du Châtelet to counter. Voltaire, like Algarotti, supervised the engraving
of his frontispiece. He is portrayed as Virgil crowned with laurel leaves,
seated at a table, intent on his manuscript, with mathematical instruments
strewn about the floor. She is his goddess, a robust female figure also in classical dress, but with one breast bare, floating above him held aloft by numerous putti. She looks up and to her left, to the great Newton, a figure in the
clouds. A shaft of light, the symbol of the Englishman's divinely inspired reason, passes through the great man, to be caught and reflected downward by the
mirror in the woman's arms to illuminate the writer and his papers below.[30]

Voltaire certainly assumed that he was flattering Du Châtelet with this
image of his "Minerva of France," as he described her in the "Epître à la
marquise Du Chastellet," which also appeared at the beginning of the Eléments. It had been circulating among his friends in Paris and Berlin since the
fall of 1736 and was published in one of the Paris weeklies in 1737. Using the
familiar "tu" form, it began: "You call me to you, vast and powerful
genius, / Minerva of France, immortal Emilie, / Disciple of Newton, and of
truth, / You penetrate my senses with the fires of your pure light." As a result of her inspiration, the author had left the theater, braved his enemies,
and turned to "la philosophie" and the wonders of Newton's universe. He
praised her again in the last two stanzas, for her rejection of youthful de-

lights in order to follow Newton on this arduous path, "an immense laby-rinth," and for her beauty, which was beyond any eulogy, beyond his art of description.[31] Du Châtelet ultimately answered these fanciful and subtly demeaning images with her own unique frontispiece to her own book.

❧

To take Du Châtelet at her word, the idea of writing an account of natural philosophy originated with the lessons she had prepared for her ten-year-old son, Florent-Louis. As she explained to Frederick of Prussia in late April 1740, during the final printing of the *Institutions de physique:* "This book was destined . . . for the education of my only son, whom I love with extreme tenderness." She believed she could give the boy "no greater proof than try-ing to render him a little less ignorant than we usually are in our youth." She wanted him to "learn the basics of physics," and, having no such complete study in French "appropriate for his age," she had been "obliged to compose one."[32] Du Châtelet never intended to take on her son's tutelage, but she had no other choice after her son's *précepteur* had proved so inadequate. Some of the chapters of her *Institutions,* particularly those on Newton's me-chanics, could easily have been drawn from morning and afternoon outings together.

Did they go into the garden at Cirey to watch the flight of the ball she described throwing in the air? He had studied the mathematics involved in this demonstration, the conic sections and the properties of a parabola, in the last lessons Clairaut had prepared for his geometry text. Many of the decorative illustrations at the beginnings of the *Institutions*'s chapters show a young boy at games and activities demonstrating one or another law of motion: lacrosse, billiards, balancing on a seesaw, shuttlecock, riding, shoot-ing a gun. Perhaps Du Châtelet permitted him to do other kinds of experi-ments. Did she summon his valet and instruct him to bring the young *seigneur* a bowl of soapy water and a straw? The artist Chardin painted a boy of just this age blowing bubbles, thus illustrating experiment number 4 of New-ton's *Opticks.* The thin film of the bubble not only produced a spectrum, but also served as a contemporary analogy for light itself, a substance in neither the rays nor the body through which it passed. Scattered references suggest other lessons, reading aloud from texts that constituted her own "little course of study," as she modestly described it. From her comments, she had obviously told her son of Descartes, Galileo, Huygens, Leibniz, and Newton, and had him study Kepler's second law in Voltaire's *Eléments*. At the end of the preface, she described her pedagogical ideal: to remove any "shadows," "to enable you to see the truths in which I wish to instruct you." In an earlier draft she had written "truths which I want to engrave on your soul," indicating the intensity of her feelings.[33]

The final book, as she explained in her preface, covered a "vast terrain," far more extensive than her hours with her son, or anything either she or Voltaire had attempted before. The title of the *Institutions de physique* has customarily been translated as the *Institutions of Physics;* more accurately, it should be *Foundations of Physics*.[34] This was, in fact, what she formulated and presented to her readers: "foundations," in its most literal sense, from a consideration of how one can know anything, to the origins of the universe and the role of the divine. Only after establishing these underlying premises did she turn to the more usual topics of guides to physics, the nature of the material world all around us—definitions of "matter"—and the rules determining its movements.

With this broader sweep of concerns, Du Châtelet formulated a "unified theory," a goal that physicists still find elusive today, the study not only of how things happen in the universe, but also of why they happen in that particular way. She reasoned this original synthesis across what are now the separate disciplines—metaphysics, philosophy, and physics—and combined and reconciled authors considered by her contemporaries to be in opposition to one another. And she did so in an age when her mentor Maupertuis speculated about such a project but, like other Academicians, published on more limited questions, with demonstrable mathematical or experimental answers. Even a natural philosopher as renowned as Newton only suggested how important such a synthesis was to him, but never felt that he could offer the public a single causal explanation for the workings of nature within a divinely ordered universe.[35]

⚜

Du Châtelet's correspondence suggests that she considered and then constructed the first acceptable draft of the *Institutions* over most of a year, not in the days and weeks of her prize submission on fire. Even so, she worked with the same energy and concentration. By the end of the summer of 1738, she had turned lessons for her son, notes for her *Eléments* and her study on the Bible, comments on Voltaire's *Traité de métaphysique,* parts of her essay on fire, and thoughts from new sources and on new controversies, into a book, which she submitted to Henri Pitot, the Academician Voltaire often consulted. She had asked Pitot to judge the work for the royal government, to see whether or not it could be published. Pitot described the *Institutions* as having "presented the principles of philosophy of Mr. Leibnits [sic] & that of Mr. Newton . . . with much clarity," and signed the "approbation," the necessary government approval, on September 18, 1738. Right away, Du Châtelet had the manuscript brought to Prault, Voltaire's Paris printer and their bookseller, to begin typesetting the proofs.

In the past, Du Châtelet had circulated her writings—her version of Mandeville's *Fable,* a short essay on color—among friends and other learned members of the Republic of Letters. What caused her to change her customary practice and to publish? According to Du Châtelet, a woman friend, perhaps Mlle de Thil or Mme de Champbonin, encouraged her.[36] The laughter of courtiers and of members of the Paris *salons* at Algarotti's portrayal of his eager marquise, and the panegyrics of Voltaire's "Epître" for the *Eléments,* necessitated a response, though it could just as well have silenced her. In the course of 1738, however, any concerns about potential ridicule must have faded to insignificance, when Du Châtelet received recognition for her views of physics, despite her disagreements with eminent English and continental *physiciens* and chemists. This came first from a learned journal that accepted a review she had written, and then from the Académie des sciences, which published her *Dissertation* on fire, even though it was not one of the three winners of the competition.

In September 1738, Du Châtelet's review of the *Eléments,* presented in the form of a letter, appeared in the prestigious *Journal des savants,* the major French government publication specializing in "Philosophy, Science, and the Arts." The very fact of inclusion placed the author among the *savants* by definition. Both Clairaut and the abbé Du Resnel were on the review board. Du Resnel had been a visitor to Cirey, and Du Châtelet had corresponded with him about his translation of Pope. Even so, Du Châtelet submitted her critique anonymously. As she explained to Maupertuis when she sent him a copy, "I do not want this little work to pass as mine, for good reasons."[37] One reason certainly was the fact that she was a woman. Hers must have been among the few such reviews, if not the first, ever published by the journal. Commonly, however, male authors also kept their identity secret, both to retain their credibility and to avoid making enemies. In such matters, the Republic of Letters could become a very small world. Du Châtelet's association with Voltaire would also have discredited her views and opened her to yet more ridicule as effectively as the fact of her sex. Du Châtelet had a third reason for wishing to keep her name secret, at least for the present: her *Institutions*. The editors gave no clear explanation for the inclusion of her anonymous contribution, only that it had been received and "we believed that it would be viewed with pleasure."[38]

Du Châtelet, as custom dictated, began her review with praise. She noted the omissions and faults of the Amsterdam edition and drew attention to Voltaire's newly published "clarifications." She described the *Eléments* as the French equivalent of Englishman Henry Pemberton's guide to the *Principia*, in that it avoided the calculations and algebra that had made Newton's ideas seem such a mystery. Du Châtelet's polite disclaimer as a reviewer, another customary gesture, appeared just before she embarked on less favorable comments: "I flatter myself that M. de V. will pardon these criticisms; they are some light spots that I believed noticeable on a painting by Raphael." After remarking on inconsistencies and on instances where he could have developed one idea more and another less, she moved on to the main point she wished to make, a refutation which Voltaire had neglected to include. She particularly wanted to argue against those who, like the Swiss *géomètre* Johann Bernoulli, accepted attraction but still favored Descartes's impulsion as its cause. "All *Philosophes*" today accepted "the impossibility of an exterior force acting equally on all bodies at the same time." So, in Descartes's particle-filled universe, how could "a ray of light come in a straight line from the Sun to us with such rapidity, [when] it encountered 300,000 leagues of matter to disarrange and in the very diverse directions claimed by the vortices?" Not that she believed that Newton and his supporters offered any better explanation. Like Voltaire in his *Eléments*, she quoted Newton's "General Scholium," but rejected the inconclusive phrases. Thus, she opposed aspects of both Newtonian and Cartesian descriptions of the universe.[39]

Du Châtelet had shown herself to be equally contentious and eclectic in her *Dissertation* on fire, but in theory only the judges of the Académie would have seen her essay. She had told Voltaire of her daring submission only after the outcome of the competition had been announced and neither had won. She "did not want," as she explained to Maupertuis in June 1738, "to blush in his eyes over an enterprise that I feared would displease him."[40] Instead, Voltaire ignored their disagreements and enthusiastically campaigned for publication of her *Dissertation,* her "chef d'oeuvre," as he described it to Frederick of Prussia, as well as his own. It was not without precedent in the Académie's history to publish nonwinners. It had been done in 1727 and would be done again for the 1747 and 1753 competitions. Publication by the Académie, Voltaire reasoned, would be a way to vitiate some of his embarrassment over the hybrid Dutch edition of the *Eléments,* and to show his expertise. Voltaire explained to Pitot that, since they disagreed, it would be obvious that Du Châtelet had done her own work.[41] He left the reverse unsaid, that, since they disagreed, he also must have formulated his own, despite her reputation as a mathematician and a reader of Newton's very difficult texts, and his acknowledgment of her as his coauthor.

However, the Académie had never published a dissertation by a woman. In this case, the dual novelty of the situation prevailed. The editors, in the explanation to their readers, noted that both essays demonstrated "much knowledge of the good works of physics and were filled with many well-explained facts and points of view." The marquis had perhaps encouraged his wife to risk the potential notoriety; he spoke with pride of her authorship on one of his visits to the court at Lunéville. Du Châtelet accepted the honor, but with appropriate modesty, and again insisted on anonymity. Still, she knew that the Académie attributions, as finally agreed upon—of "Piece No. 6" "by a young Lady of high rank" and "Piece No. 7" "by one of our premier Poets"—would leave no mysteries in the minds of the *gens qui pensent.*[42]

Institutions de Physique

Du Châtelet's *Dissertation* on fire appeared just as she began supervising the printing of her *Institutions de physique*. Reviews of her essay in the *Mémoires de Trévoux* and in Desfontaines's *Observations* followed in the first half of 1739, and though all favored the three Cartesian winners, the very fact of being treated as an authority encouraged her to act with greater confidence. She still made modest disclaimers to Cideville about her "audacity," and that she had done it only in "imitation" of Voltaire, but she used the *Dissertation* to introduce herself to Europe's most important *géomètres* and *physiciens*. Maupertuis sent it to others at her request. In his letter to the English mathematician James Jurin, he echoed and enhanced the Académie description of Du Châtelet: "A young woman of the first condition who honors our sciences by the taste she has for them." He also enclosed Voltaire's essay, but it was to hers that he referred when he continued: "Perhaps [it] may surprise you that it did not win."[43] She sent her essay to Frederick of Prussia and in a teasing way claimed "la physique" as her special territory, not Voltaire's. She then bluntly corrected a scientific point the prince had made with citations and references to the *Transactions* of London's Royal Academy. In December 1739, a *nouvelliste* reported that, at a learned gathering at the Sorbonne, one of the participants, speaking in favor of Newton, referred to her essay. An important Dutch publisher wrote to Voltaire admiringly of the "great proofs of her ability & her genius"; she "must be regarded as the marvel of the century."[44]

Then, in the winter of 1738–39, she stopped the printing of her *Institutions,* now about half completed, and began to rethink the project altogether. In particular, she must have decided to expand her discussion of the underlying premises for all knowledge and the fundamental causes of phenomena in the universe. Only in this way could she supply the metaphysical underpinnings that would answer Newton's European critics. That winter, she also realized, as a result of reading about *forces vives* in Leibniz and in the French translations of Christian Wolff's writings from Frederick of Prussia, as well as from her conversations with Maupertuis when he visited Cirey in January 1739, that, to do justice to these new "truths," she must return to her study of mathematics.[45]

As in the past, Du Châtelet worked despite family obligations. She and the marquis planned to move the household, including Voltaire and her children, to Brussels. Her husband's inheritance rights to the property from his Trichâteau cousin had been contested in the Belgian court. Initially, she hoped that Maupertuis's friend Johann Bernoulli II (son of the eminent Swiss *géomètre*) would be her "guide" in learning "le calcul" (integral calculus), but she had to be content with another young scholar they found for her. In February 1739, Du Châtelet announced to Frederick that she was leaving "*la physique* for mathematics," and that a former student of the elder Bernoulli and Christian Wolff had been engaged "to conduct me in the immense labyrinth where nature loses its way." "Mathematics," she explained "is the key to all the doors & I am going to work to acquire it."[46]

Once established in Brussels, copying problems on her slate like a young mathematics student, she found Samuel König's lessons "disorienting." She confessed to Maupertuis in late June, after six weeks of working with König, that, even though she rose every morning at six, "he set a pace for classes that I can barely follow." She had not finished "algorithms" and feared it might be "too late for me to learn so many difficult things." She continued, "I am sometimes ready to abandon it all," even though mathematics was for her "the only [science] that I love and . . . . the only [true] science if one does not want to abuse the term."[47] Early on, she had admitted to König that the study of mathematics formed part of her larger project, the *Institutions de physique*. This admission proved fortuitous, because, having studied at the University of Marburg under Wolff, who in turn was a follower of Leibniz, König could help her decipher the metaphysical writings of the two men, the one more obscure than the other. As she later explained to Bernoulli II, she asked König to read her whole book for errors and, once she had authorized the printing to resume in September 1739, to help her go through Wolff's massive texts and to summarize key parts of the chapters that she needed for her revisions, as she had done with Newton's works for Voltaire. In this way, she could include, as she explained to Frederick, "the *métaphysique* of mr de Leibnitz [sic], who I confess is the only one who satisfied me, though some doubts still remain." The result would be, she told the German prince in a less respectful tone, "an entire philosophy, to the taste of mr. Wolff, but with a French sauce."[48]

Du Châtelet assumed that she could remain the anonymous author of the *Institutions*. At the Bibliothèque Nationale, there are as many as three drafts for different sections of the preface, where she first enunciated her self-defined role, and all indicate how carefully she masked her gender. She presented herself as a parent—contemporaries would assume a father—who would guide and who, in the favored image of her generation, "removes the thorns that could wound [her son's] delicate hands."[49] Even the frontispiece, showing a figure in a loose, flowing, heavy silk dressing gown, hair casually tied back, ascending a cloudlike stairway, could suggest a man or a woman author. The muses of Botany, Grammar, Mechanics, Astronomy, and Chemistry watch the scene from below. The viewer follows the central figure's intent gaze up to a nude woman, a goddess with long hair, standing above the clouds in her temple. This is "truth."[50]

The frontispiece of the *Institutions* thus illustrated Du Châtelet's underlying purpose, for "truth" remained her goal. Although the author ascends above the clouds alone, Du Châtelet did not fail to acknowledge the debt she owed to "les grands Hommes," the great Men, as she called them, referring in her preface to Newton's image of "standing on the shoulders of giants." The putti of her frontispiece hold three cameos at the center top of the engraving, portraits of Descartes, Newton, and Leibniz, *philosophes* often portrayed by their adherents as irreconcilable. Du Châtelet decried these "sectarians," men like Voltaire, who were absolute supporters of one set of explanations. She continued: "When it concerns a book of *Physique*, one must ask if it is good, & not if the author is English, German, or French." Her *Institutions* would, in fact, represent an original synthesis of the hypotheses of Newton the Englishman, Leibniz the German, and Descartes the Frenchman.[51]

◈

In her review of the *Eléments,* Du Châtelet had agreed with other critics about Voltaire's extreme criticism of Descartes. Although she wished to distance herself from the Cartesian theory of vortices and "subtle matter," in her preface to the *Institutions* Du Châtelet made it clear how profoundly Descartes had influenced the subsequent construction of "science," in its meaning of "certain" knowledge. With his three "masterpieces of wisdom," *La Dioptrique (Dioptrics), La Géométrie (Geometry), Discours sur la méthode (Discourse on Method)*, he caused "a revolution in the sciences." If Descartes was wrong on some points of physics, she explained, this was no criticism, for "it is because he was a man & it is not given to a single man, or a single century, to know all."[52] The significance of Descartes's *Méthode* for her, and for all the scientists who came after, even into modern times, lay in the new authority Descartes gave to a "man of common sense," proceeding according to an agreed-upon method, by self-evident "rules of reasoning." Newton took his authority in this way; so now would the marquise.[53] The organization Du Châtelet chose for the *Institutions* also reflected Descartes's way of reasoning and these premises. Whether intentionally or not, Du Châtelet's *Institutions* in its final form echoed Descartes's *Principes de la philosophie,* the book for which he had constructed his "method." In chapter I, on "Knowledge," she described the rules of reasoning that would govern the entire text. Then, because she readily accepted that "many truths of Physics, Metaphysics, Geometry are intertwined," she went on to the metaphysical questions: the concept of "God" and his role in the universe, descriptions of the essential constituent parts of God's creation known as "Space," "Time," and "Matter." Only then did she turn to "Physics," the natural laws governing matter, and Newtonian mechanics.

Du Châtelet found her rules of reasoning in an unlikely source, the writings of Gottfried Wilhelm von Leibniz, and the disciple who endeavored to systematize his thinking, Christian Wolff—unlikely because she first knew of Leibniz as an opponent of Newton's concept of attraction. In 1711, in a letter published in the *Mémoires de Trévoux,* Leibniz had been the first to label attraction as a return to "occult" explanations. Lacking a mechanical component, attraction seemed an indiscernible "quality" of matter that sounded like miracles and spiritual agency, and that was just as "unscientific" as the explanations of the thirteenth-century Scholastics. In the summer of 1736, Frederick of Prussia had sent to Voltaire French translations of Wolff made for him by one of his closest intimates at court. Neither Voltaire nor Du Châtelet gave much time to the selections. This did not deter Frederick. His courtier baron Keyserlingk bought the "second part of the Métaphysic [sic] of m. Wolff." The third arrived in mid-October 1737. Du Châtelet first came to appreciate Leibniz through both his own writings and the explanations and variations made by his student Wolff when she began to question the law of motion formulated by the Academician Jean-Jacques Dortous de Mairan. She had almost sabotaged publication of her *Dissertation* on fire when, against all Académie policy, she requested that the original submission be changed for the printed edition. She insisted that Leibniz's law concerning force, not that formulated by Mairan, be included. Her exploration of other ideas of Wolff, and her appreciation of "the great richness of Leibniz," coincided with her decision late in 1738 to stop the printing of the *Institutions.*[54]

Chapter I of the *Institutions* presented the results of her reading and rethinking, her rules of reasoning, a hybrid of Leibniz and Wolff. These underlying principles established what made one statement "certain" and another only "probable" or false. Like Wolff, she made the first of these rules Descartes's principle of contradiction: that nothing can be and not be at the same time, true and untrue at the same time. Using the language of mathematics, she reasoned, "This Axiom is the foundation of all certainty in human knowledge." Otherwise, she explained, "there would no longer be any truth even in numbers, & each thing could be, or not, according to everyone's fancy, so 2 and 2 could be 4 or 6 equally, & even both at the same time." Although she believed this rule to be "self-evident," the imagination could still deceive. One could fall into error. Corroboration had to come from mathematics, or from demonstration by experience or observation.[55] And, she continued, all truths could not be established by this one principle alone. The rule of contradiction was sufficient for "necessary truths"—those truths determined in only one way. But what of other truths, whose existence could be shown in any number of ways, and none was more necessary than another? For these "contingent truths" she turned to Leibniz and his first premise, the principle of sufficient reason. For all actions, for all that exists, she argued, there must be a reason for this to exist and not that, for this to happen and not that. She believed this principle to be obvious: "All men follow it naturally; because no one decides for one thing rather than another, without a sufficient reason which makes him see that this thing is preferable to the other."[56]

With these two principles, she eliminated unpredictability and chance from her world. For all scientists into the twentieth century, this was of paramount importance. For Du Châtelet, the world without these two principles was only dreams, or nightmares. "I dream that I am in my room, occupied with writing; all at once my chair changes into a winged horse, & I find myself in an instant a hundred leagues from the place I was in, & with people who were dead for a long time." In the world of "chimeras," all "would be equally possible." The principles of contradiction and sufficient reason "bridled the imagination." Together they banished the infinity of possibilities, the worlds of probability, and gave the certainty of reasoned causes and effects. The principle of sufficient reason proved key to her reasoning throughout the *Institutions:* "a compass capable of guiding us in the moving sands of this science" and "the Touchstone which distinguishes truth from error."[57]

Leibniz's axiom of the principle of sufficient reason had two corollaries: the principle of indiscernibles and the law of continuity. Du Châtelet took time to explicate them because both would be significant in subsequent chapters, as she went on to explain why this universe existed and not another. Sufficient reason told us that there could be nothing identical in the universe. Everything from what we can see under the microscope to what we can view through the telescope is shown to be discernible, unique. And it must be so; otherwise, all would be interchangeable with no effect. Leibniz's law of continuity also banished unpredictability. All change came in stages, one state holding the reason for the next one. If these states did not follow one from another, then what necessitated this change and not another? Common sense suggested proof: one could not go along a road from one town to another without passing through all the towns in between. Geometry offered the example of a concave line which could not become convex without passing through a series of points in between. According to Du Châtelet, when this continuity was not evident, the error lay in our reasoning, for nature never violated this law in her world. Sufficient reason allowed infinite diversity, but with each particle in a particular place for a particular reason.

Du Châtelet, now armed with these fundamental principles and their corollaries, proceeded to the rational construction of the constituent parts of the universe: God, space, time, and matter. Every aspect of this construction was controversial, if for no other reason than the very secular manner in which she defined the nature and role of the Creator. Though by different routes, Descartes and Leibniz had gone from the simplest idea of an individual's own existence to the knowledge of God's existence. Du Châtelet did so as well in chapter II of the *Institutions:* "Something exists, since I exist." This something must be an eternal "supreme Being." This Being must be its own cause, or there would be an endless chain of causes—or its reverse, a contradiction in terms, nothingness as a cause of something. Similarly, the other attributes of this deity must be self-evident, clear, and distinct, "immutable," "unique," "simple" (in the sense of having no constituent parts). To imagine the alternatives led, she continued, as any person of reason would know, to "absurdities," to contradictions and impossibilities. Du Châtelet's learned contemporaries in eighteenth-century France would have found this sequence of thought and her conclusions familiar.[58]

Less familiar would have been Du Châtelet's use of her two rules of reasoning and their corollaries to deduce the creation of the world. In answer to the Newtonians, some of whom saw all matter as part of a divine "Sensorium," she insisted that this "Supreme Being" was separate from the world that we perceive. Everything in the universe, all matter, she explained, was "contingent," therefore not necessary, and so it could not be of the same substance as the deity. This contingency represented the infinite choices available to the Creator. There could be many "histories of a possible World that only lacks actualization." For example, Alexander the Great could have turned against the West instead of the Persians. The Creator could have made the universe six million years earlier or later. But this is not senseless probability, for sufficient reason governs these choices. This Being could simultaneously imagine all possibilities, consider them, and choose that which pleased him most to make actual or real. An "intelligent" Being, she added, in contrast to a capricious, vengeful deity, would make no other choice. Thus, she offered her readers a clear and distinct explanation for all the possible worlds that could exist, and sufficient reason for this particular one. This meant no limitation on God's power: "He has been the absolute master of his choice . . . for to follow the choice of one's own will, this is to be free." In fact, God had chosen to create this world to communicate to us a part of his infinite perfection.[59]

Inevitably in the study of the Supreme Being, Du Châtelet understood that one would come to that which one did not understand; if one did not, then one would become God. So she did not ignore the inherent contradiction in the Christian image of a perfect God of infinite goodness in whose world evil existed.[60] As with our inability to discern a law of nature, so it was with the existence of evil: the fault lay in our perception, not in the creation, in our focus on the particular event, not on its relationship to other events in every other place and time. One must think of how the human eye sees, she wrote, and the way in which one loses sight of the whole when looking at an entity under the microscope. It was the overall that was perfect, she reasoned, and to achieve this perfection, the Supreme Being "has accorded to each thing in particular, as much essential perfection as it can receive." The inevitable evils he had in his wisdom directed to the greatest good. In the conclusion, she referred her readers to Leibniz's *Théodicée* and gave her own version of his now famous hypothesis: "This world here, is then the best of worlds possible, the one where the most variety with the most order reigns, & where the most effects are the products of the simplest Laws."[61]

With but a few references to the word "God," Du Châtelet had done what should have been impossible in eighteenth-century Catholic France: she had created a deity, a story of the creation and of the overall workings of the universe, without any reference to established religious doctrines, religious texts, or their authorities, and she had eliminated any role for this "Supreme Being" other than that of "First Cause." He created the constituent particles of the universe, set them in motion, and after that had no need to act in the world. Matter set in motion combined to create all other matter. Du Châtelet compared "this great automaton of the universe" to a watch, and the Creator to its inventor, who brought it from possibility to actuality but then ceased to be necessary to explain how the watch worked or to make the time pass. By the law of continuity, "the present is born from the past & will give birth to what follows"; and if one adds natural laws, "all mechanical changes follow from the arrangement of the parts, & the rules of movement, & that which does not follow by these principles does not exist."[62]

Her readers would have known that she had rejected the Newtonian assumption that God had to intervene perpetually in his creation to perform "miracles," as his critics described it. On the one hand, such a God negated her image of his necessary perfection, and, on the other, it raised the chimera of unpredictability. No law, not even Newton's, would be fixed if always subject to "the will of God." Thus, there could be no certain knowledge, no science, of the workings of the universe. More than 150 years later, Albert Einstein's general theory of relativity would hinge on these principles that Du Châtelet set out so carefully.

⤳⁂⤳

Such arguments about God's role, and his relationship to his creation, led Du Châtelet in chapters III, V, and VI to deduce a description of the essential nature of that creation: its most basic components and their existence in space and time. In these chapters, her willingness to take ideas from different authorities and combine them into her own synthesis was particularly marked, as was her relentless rejection of those ideas she thought "absurdities." One can recognize Locke, Leibniz and Wolff, Newton and Descartes, and her mentors Maupertuis and Clairaut in the concepts she put forward, the logic of her explanation, the examples she gave. For instance, in describing the most basic characteristics of all "beings," she took from Locke, Descartes, and Leibniz and Wolff. All "beings" had their "essence," the essential invariable properties that defined them and their "attributes." These attributes, as Du Châtelet accepted from Locke, had the variable properties that followed in turn from the essential nature of each particular "being."[63]

No experiments demonstrated this "truth," but Du Châtelet could borrow a proof offered by Descartes taken from geometry, a proof simple enough for even a boy of ten or eleven, and thus, by implication, for all of her readers. The "essence" of a triangle lay in its three-sided nature; all else was variable. The angles, the length of the sides, the overall shape of the figure could change, but its essential nature had to remain: a three-sided closed figure with three angles. Adding a fourth side would create a new "being" entirely, whereas adding a fourth line dividing the figure would not. This choice, to use geometry as the defining example, highlighted another important underlying premise of the *Institutions:* the primacy of mathematics as the universal language of philosophy, as a way of proving even the most abstract metaphysical hypotheses. Where in previous ages the learned turned to faith as the final answer, and even in her own time to "the will of God," Du Châtelet saw the authority of geometry to be self-evident and, borrowing Plato's phrase, the Creator as "the eternal Géomètre." Addressing her son in the preface, she explained that geometry "is the key to all discoveries; & if there are still many unexplained things in Physics, it is [because] one has not applied Geometry enough to the search."[64]

When Du Châtelet turned to the subject of "Space," though she never mentioned Voltaire by name, her disagreements with him and his uncritical acceptance of Newton almost leap off the pages. The argument over space had to do with attraction. The Newtonians questioned how it could operate against the resistance of a Cartesian universe filled with matter. They offered "light" as their principal example and hypothesized that space might be a void. Yet all knew that "nature abhorred a vacuum." Leibniz reasoned that space must be filled, or there would be no limit to the extension of any body—and how, argued Newton's opponents, could the force of attraction work across a void with no particles to transmit its effects? Du Châtelet had puzzled over these contradictions. It was yet another measure of her "boldness" that she offered a clear and simple solution to the apparent impossibility. She presented an idealization of space that sounds very modern. Like her contemporaries, whether adherents of Descartes, Newton, or Leibniz, she left the world of the real for the abstract. In the abstract, she reasoned, space must have certain qualities in order to satisfy that which we observe; it must be immutable, eternal, uniform, penetrable. What of the problem of resistance? Is this, then, a void? Du Châtelet concluded that both groups had approached the answer. In this imagined space, there might be, she hypothesized, matter so fine, moving so fast—her contemporaries knew that she was thinking of "light"—that it eliminated the effects of resistance.[65]

Even more characteristic of the modern ways in which her mind worked, having altered the model of space and answered the objections to attraction, she negated the need for any such explanations by turning again to abstraction. She wrote that to understand "space" and "time" one needed only to see them in the abstract, as representations of how bodies coexist. In fact, she believed this was the truest way to describe these two aspects of the universe. Du Châtelet made the analogy to numbers: space was to coexisting things as numbers were to numbered things. One thing required no number, just as one thing required no space. Only a "multitude of things" made numbers necessary; similarly, only a "multitude of things" required the idea of space. She described time in the same way. In its most basic aspect it, too, was only spatial; it was nothing more than the order of things in succession. Du Châtelet accepted that our understanding of time had been easily confused. We imagined it as separate from ourselves and from things, and we attributed properties to it. But, she pointed out, time was nothing more than a way of conceptualizing the relationship of bodies in successive states, a relationship that could be represented geometrically, as "the uniform movement of a point which describes a straight line." As with space, if bodies did not exist in a continuous succession, there would be no time, no sense of a need to mark the passage of things from one state to another. To put it another way, she wrote, "Successive existence makes Time."[66]

Like "all peoples," she continued, we sought ways to measure this perceived movement. We had chosen the sun as our measurement for a day and a year. For hours, on clock faces, "the twenty-fourth part of the circumference of the circle makes one." Even so, she continued, some movement was so rapid it could not be perceived at all; similarly, very slow movement, such as that of the moon or the planets, could only be measured over a long period of time. What we saw, what we took our notion of time from, then, was in fact "mediocre movement." Du Châtelet also considered why we did not use our own internal sense of the passage of time as its measure—that is, why we did not depend on the succession of our own thoughts rather than an external mechanism such as Christiaan Huygens's pendulum, accurate and consistent as it might be. Once again, she had a simple answer: because we must be able to agree on this measurement. We all know, she wrote, that the speed with which ideas succeed one another varies from person to person. Some, she knew from her own experience, think faster than others.[67]

The last basic concept of the universe, "Matter," was no less controversial than that of the nature of God, space, and time. In chapters VII through X—"On the Elements of Matter," "On the Nature of Bodies," "On Divisibility and Distinctiveness," and "On the Shape and Porosity of Bodies"—Du Châtelet placed herself squarely with the continental *philosophes*—"the majority of learned Europe," as she pointed out—who favored the explanations of Leibniz and Wolff. Actually, as she explained, most *philosophes* agreed on the broad definition of "Matter" as "a uniform and similar mass without disagreement or difference in its constituent parts." After that the arguments led all the way to discussions of the freedom of God's will. Initially, Du Châtelet suggested matter had three levels: the substance that we perceive with our senses; atoms; and a smaller unit also, like atoms, imperceptible to the senses. She concluded, however, that, given our experience with the microscope, which gave results that "astonish the imagination," we could not know how many levels there might be. Therefore, she described matter as indefinitely divisible, each level consisting of smaller but no less distinct entities. Having looked at a drop of blood, she saw entities within entities.[68] So, she reasoned, there must be a hierarchy to these levels, from the most homogeneous combinations at the bottom to the more complex. Following Leibniz, she identified the most basic constituent parts that combined to make more and more complex substances as "monads."

Perhaps to avoid the adverse associations that Voltaire had been touting in his scientific writings, she subsequently referred to these basic entities as "êtres simples," or "simple [most basic] beings." The inherent nature of all matter came from the qualities and combinations of these *êtres simples*. She freely acknowledged, as Leibniz had, that one could "neither see, nor touch, nor represent in our imagination by any sense image" these entities, but still one could conceive of them. In the end, her method of reasoning here was very characteristic of her approach. She argued, on the one hand, that their existence could not be proved to be impossible, but then she gave examples of how that which we could not sense was possible. A stone thrown into the water far from a boat would make ripples that would extend for miles, and would eventually touch the boat, but that might not be perceived by anyone. A child in the womb could not distinguish one impression from another, since the least movement by the mother would shake the whole body.[69] As she had reasoned in her *Dissertation* on fire, and as Newton had done in his defense of attraction, she argued for the necessary existence of *êtres simples* because of the effects that could be perceived, as it were, backward. As modern scientists argue today, when all other methods fail, one must reason the essence of beings from the perceivable effects, or movements, caused by their particular set of qualities.

Combining bits of Aristotle with "the system of Leibniz" as explained by Wolff, she hypothesized the qualities of the *êtres simples*, the true substances, the essential entities in the universe. They were indivisible, for otherwise they would not be the basic unit; there would be something yet more basic. They could have no extension, or they would be divisible. In a few words, she placed herself in opposition to both Descartes and Newton, who accepted "extension," the fact of taking space, as an essential property of all matter, including its constituent parts. These *êtres simples* must be durable, or they could not make anything else, and modifiable, because they could combine in an indefinite number of ways. In what seemed to some of her contemporaries to be a dangerous return to Aristotle's idea of the "inherent nature of a substance," she stated that the *êtres simples* contained all the characteristics of the more complex entities which they would constitute. Much like the modern concept of DNA, their essential properties determined why an object became this way and not that.[70]

Du Châtelet broke with Descartes and Newton in describing another quality of the *êtres simples*. Descartes's world of impulsion and Newton's world of attraction left objects passive, to be acted upon by forces outside of themselves. She followed Leibniz, who presented a world of perpetual

change in which objects themselves had force, what scientists now call "kinetic energy" and she called "forces vives," from the Latin for "living forces."
This force, and therefore the inherent potential for motion, necessarily was
internal, an intrinsic part of the nature of *êtres simples*.[71] The significance of
these forces for and against motion at the most basic level of matter was so
important because motion meant change, and change in turn defined not
only the form, the attributes, and the possible actions of the *êtres simples* but
also all of the more "complex beings [*êtres composés*]" that would be created
by their union.

What of the forces that acted in the larger world of our senses? Those,
Leibniz called "derivative," in that they were the result of the basic, or
"primitive," forces in all the component parts of the moving object. Thus,
Du Châtelet could assert along with Descartes that all in the universe could
and did have a mechanical explanation, even attraction. This was Du Châtelet's genius: she adapted from Leibniz a concept about the nature of beings
that gave a more convincing mechanical explanation than anything Newton
himself had suggested. Like Descartes, she gave a mechanical explanation
rooted in metaphysics, but one that did not contradict or require distortion
of the laws of the universe created out of observations of the movement of
its parts. Her synthesis sounds remarkably like the modern concept of
"energy."[72]

᷒᷒

The second half of the *Institutions* has always been presumed to be a clear,
neatly argued explanation of Newton's laws of motion and how they operated on earth—what Du Châtelet's contemporaries called "rational mechanics." And so it is at first reading, but there was much more here as well.
In fact, in her day, chapters XI through XXI, on the laws of motion and the
forces of gravity and attraction, were as controversial as, and represented a
synthesis similar in complexity to, her descriptions of the constituent parts
of the universe. Once again, she chose one concept from one authority and
joined it with the speculations of another. She rejected Descartes's *tourbillons* and parts of Newton's *Principia*. She accepted some of Leibniz's and
Newton's laws. In the course of these chapters, she wrote with increasing
authority. Controversies became old errors corrected by new explanations,

with, in many instances, references not to the writings of members of Europe's royal academies but to her own previous chapters.

Du Châtelet defined "simple" and "complex" motion in chapters XI and XII. "Complex motion" meant that more than one force acted on a body at the same time. Du Châtelet showed the way in which these motions could be described geometrically and then transformed into algebraic equations, such as: speed multiplied by time equals distance. She presented Newton's laws of motion, but, once again, like Leibniz, she imagined a body as potentially active, with its own innate *forces vives*. This meant that when a body moved it had to overcome obstacles; similarly, when it stopped, obstacles had "consumed" its force "in whole or in part."[73] That many rejected the existence of this force because it was imperceptible to the senses prompted her to offer the image of the boat, an illustrative example familiar to Newton's readers and used by his commentators. In her freehand drawing in the manuscript, an object is thrown horizontally on the boat. Many forces act upon it, but only two are apparent to the one who threw the object: the force of the throw and that of gravity. In fact, many forces affect the speed and trajectory of the thrown object, and these cannot be perceived by the senses alone: there is the motion of the boat, of the river, of the earth turning on its axis, of the earth moving in its orbit about the sun.[74]

As she had in previous chapters, Du Châtelet proceeded from the incomplete proof of observation to the more certain proof of mathematics. She broke motion, the result of forces, into parts that could be described in geometric figures, a skill she had learned from Clairaut. Du Châtelet realized, however, that such transformations of observed movement into geometric figures and algebraic equations were also flawed, and thus highlighted the current limitations of the sciences in general. "For, to reduce Physical effects to Mathematical calculations, one is always obliged to suppose many things," and to ignore such phenomena as changes in temperature, air resistance, and friction. The calculations must be premised on "ideal," and thus unreal, circumstances. Like modern mathematicians, Du Châtelet believed it more valid to think of all of these representations, whether experimental or mathematical, not as "absolutes" but as relational, or relative, and to express them as proportions.[75]

Having introduced this Leibnizian way of thinking in her earlier chapters on space and time, Du Châtelet made it a recurrent device in the second half of the *Institutions,* whether in discussions of movement or of other aspects of *la physique.* She corrected Newton's second law, dismissing his specific ratios, and instead describing the changes in motion caused by an external force as proportional. There was "relative" and "absolute" place, the one the reality, the other an ideal. One could see two things in place only in relation to each other. Similarly, motion of a body was only in relation to another, which might or might not be at rest, such as a dead fish moving with the current of the river. Mass never could be measured accurately, given the porosity of bodies. So mass must always be expressed relatively, the mass of one body in relation to the mass of another. Even the measurement of force itself could only be known comparatively, by increases and decreases in relation to the object it acted upon. This was, as she concluded in chapter XX, "because all of our knowledge is only comparative."[76]

Such reasoning Du Châtelet confidently categorized as "hypothetical." Unlike many of her contemporaries, especially the most ardent followers of Newton, she did not feel "disgust," as she described it, for the use of hypothesis. Du Châtelet, much like modern scientists, saw the creation of hypotheses and their testing as necessary to *la physique,* as the key method by which any truths, however imperfect or incomplete, about the natural world could be arrived at. So significant to her was this method of reasoning that she devoted a whole chapter to its proper use.[77] Du Châtelet acknowledged the dangers inherent in "hypothesis," the creation of "fictions," which led to centuries of superstition and error, as in the time of the Scholastics. However, she explained, there were good and bad hypotheses. Du Châtelet assumed that the formulation of sound hypotheses and their acceptance as scientific "truth" came about because one followed clear rules of reasoning, guidelines for the choices one had to make. For example, the law of sufficient reason governed the evaluation of one universal truth against another. Finally, she explained, much as a modern experimental scientist would, that hypotheses were nothing more than "probable propositions with more or less degree of certainty according to how many or how few of the circumstances accompanying the Phenomenon can be satisfied and explained by them." One contradictory observation or experiment was enough to reject the hypothesis all or in part. One confirmation, however, was not enough to confirm it all, only to encourage more testing of its validity. Each noncontradictory result would add to the probability of the hypothesis, and ul-

The marquise Du Châtelet in her twenties by F.-B. Lépicié

(By courtesy of Mme Thierry)

Baron Louis-Nicolas de
Breteuil and his eldest son,
René-Alexandre
*(From the collection of the Château de
Breteuil)*

Gabrielle Anne de Froullay
*(From the collection of the Château de
Breteuil)*

The Place Royale (Place des Vosges) with the equestrian statue of Louis XIII
(J. P. Zinsser)

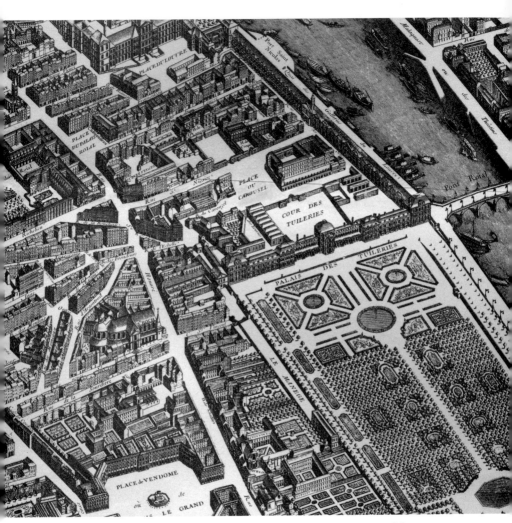

Paris, Plan de Turgot, 1739, showing the rue Traversière and the area of the city most frequented by the marquise Du Châtelet and her friends

Maupertuis in 1739, after his return from the Lapland expedition for the Académie des sciences

(©The Royal Society)

Voltaire as a young man
(From Special Collections, Miami University)

VUE·DU·CHATEAU·DE·CIREY·
SUIVANT·COMME·IL·DOIT·ÊTRE·
QUAND·IL·SERA·FINY·1742

Plan for Cirey
(From the collection of the Château de Cirey)

Views of the Château de Cirey showing Du Châtelet's suite on the second floor in the old wing (*above*) and the entrance to a new wing with its decorative doorway (*below*)
(M. E. Goldby)

Frontispiece for the first edition of Du Châtelet's *Institutions de physique*

(From the collection of R. K. Smeltzer)

INSTITUTIONS
PHYSIQUES
DE MADAME LA MARQUISE
DU CHASTELLET
adreſſées à Mr. ſon Fils.

Nouvelle Edition, corrigée & augmentée,
conſiderablement par l'Auteur.

TOME PREMIER.

A AMSTERDAM,
AUX DEPENS DE LA COMPAGNIE,
M DCC XLII.

Title page of the second edition of Du Châtelet's *Institutions de physique*

(From the collection of R. K. Smeltzer)

The marquise Du Châtelet, c. 1741. Marianne Loir.
(From the collection of the Château de Breteuil, Choiseul near Chevreuse)

Headpieces for chapters of the
Institutions de physique
(All from the collection of R. K. Smeltzer)

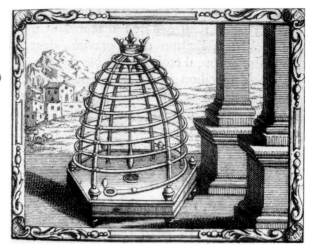

Chapter XIV
(on the phenomena of gravity)

Chapter XIX (on the movement of projectiles)

Illustrative figure of the
boat and a thrown object,
fig. 81, Plate 11, to
accompany Chapter XXI
(on the force of bodies)

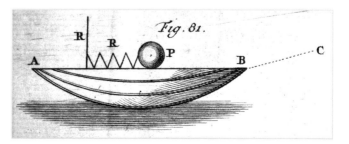

Cochin. Performance of *La Princesse de Navarre* at Versailles, 1745
(The Metropolitan Museum of Art. New York. The Elisha Whittelsey Collection,
The Elisha Whittelsey Fund. 1960 [60.622.1])

The marquise Du Châtelet, c. 1745. French school, eighteenth century

(From the collection of the Château de Breteuil)

Jean-François de Saint-Lambert
(The Pierpont Morgan Library, New York)

Letter from the marquise
Du Châtelet to Saint-Lambert,
July 1748
(The Pierpont Morgan Library, New York)

View of the gardens, Palace of Lunéville

(J. P. Zinsser)

PRINCIPES
MATHÉMATIQUES
DE LA
PHILOSOPHIE NATURELLE,

Par feue Madame la Marquife DU CHASTELLET.

TOME PREMIER.

A PARIS,

Chez { DESAINT & SAILLANT, rue S. Jean de Beauvais,
LAMBERT, Imprimeur - Libraire, rue & à côté
de la Comédie Françoife, au Parnaffe.

M. D. C C L I X.

AVEC APPROBATION ET PRIVILÉGE DU ROI.

Title page of Du Châtelet's *Principes mathématiques*
(From the collection of R. K. Smeltzer)

timately, Du Châtelet continued, we would arrive at a point where its "certitude," and even its "truth," was so probable that we could not refuse our assent.

Such was the case, for example, with Copernicus' system of the world. As Du Châtelet explained, "There must be a beginning to all research, & this beginning must almost always be tentative, very imperfect & often without success." Even so, she concluded, "these efforts that one makes to find the truth are always glorious, even when they are without fruit."[78] Just as the work of astronomers demonstrated the interrelationship between hypothesis and experiment, suppositions checked against observation, so, too, did the laws of mechanics. She gave the example of Huygens's and Newton's experiments to explain how gravity acts on bodies. Their work passed easily from hypothesis to mathematical formulation to observation and demonstration, and back again.[79]

Of all the controversial parts of Du Châtelet's magisterial synthesis, only her last chapter, XXI, on *forces vives,* occasioned an overt attack on her and her ideas. The controversy over *forces vives* began long before Du Châtelet was born. In Descartes's and Newton's world, there was but one kind of force, the modern concept of "momentum," and one formula to measure it: mv. This force was canceled out or dissipated in the collisions of bodies. Leibniz's 1686 article for the *Acta Eruditorum* ascribed a dynamic quality to matter and hypothesized an alternative kind of force in operation in the universe that was not lost; this had a different formula, mv^2. It did not occur to the seventeenth-century *physiciens* that both formulas had validity. Each side believed in its formulation and no other. (Today the first describes momentum, mass times velocity, and the second kinetic energy, $\frac{1}{2}mv^2$.)

The 1720s saw the height of the argument in the English, French, and Dutch learned journals. In 1722, two articles in the *Journal littéraire* described 'sGravesande's version of an experiment with copper and ceramic balls—bodies of different masses—falling into a clay-filled tray. He compared the depressions they made as a way of quantifying the "force" of the collision of one body with another and confirming Leibniz's concept. Bernoulli, Maupertuis's mentor, became an adherent of Leibniz's views and argued on his behalf, as did Wolff. Though Bernoulli presented his argument in favor of *forces vives* in successive Académie prize competitions on the laws of motion, Dortous de Mairan's 1728 *Discours* on the "Estimation and the Measure of Motor Forces of Bodies," supporting $f = mv$ as the only formulation, became the final word in France until Du Châtelet chose to reopen the controversy.[80]

Du Châtelet's correspondence with Maupertuis from February 1738 to March 1739 shows how she puzzled over various aspects of the controversy. Initially, she gratefully accepted the clarifications of "Sir Isaac Maupertuis," as she and Voltaire called him, and humbly presented her own suggestions. As early as May 1738, however, her tone changed. She numbered her queries in her impatience to have his thoughts on specific points, especially when she disagreed with him. Questions about hard bodies, Newton's experiments with resisting and nonresisting fluids, and the indissolubility of particles filled her thoughts; she "racked her brain" over contradictions. When Maupertuis failed to answer her letters, she returned to her reading. She would begin his 1734 *Mémoire* (on attraction) "tomorrow." Leibniz gave her some answers; others she formulated on her own. "J'ai une idée dans la tête," she wrote—"I have an idea in my head." Gradually, she drew away from Maupertuis's tutelage. Her essay on fire appeared with her public disavowal of Mairan's and Newton's formula and her adherence to the continental description of force enunciated by Leibniz and Johann Bernoulli.[81] Even Maupertuis, who agreed with Bernoulli and acknowledged in their correspondence, as would Clairaut in his, that he favored the mv^2 formula, hedged on the issue in his published essays, and, much to Bernoulli's disappointment, had never taken up the issue in the Académie itself. Ironically, it was Du Châtelet, a woman and by all contemporary definitions an amateur, who took up the challenge and did battle over the issue for the eminent, aging *géomètre*.

❧

From the first pages of the preface to her *Institutions,* Du Châtelet had questioned and rejected the conclusions of the "grands Hommes," not just Aristotle and Descartes, but also Galileo, Newton, and lesser-known authorities such as Mariotte, Frenicle, and Keill. Contemporaries knew of her disagreement with Voltaire. Only in her concluding chapter XXI, however, did she write at such length, and isolate the authority she was answering in such an unforgiving way. Du Châtelet had mentioned the formula $f = mv^2$ in previous chapters as a given. As she noted emphatically at the beginning of XXI: "Nothing appears more evident than this proposition, & if one would deny it, I no longer know what would remain certain in human knowledge, nor sure what principle one could build on in Philosophy; it would be much better, it seems to me, to renounce all research." Thus, she made clear that all rational *géomètres* and *physiciens* must accept Leibniz's and Bernoulli's formulation.

Du Châtelet gave Leibniz's rationale for the concept of *forces vives:* a moving body accumulated force, and thus the formula describing this movement must include the squaring of the speed. She offered gravity as an analogy: *forces vives* worked like an "infinite spring" putting greater and greater pressure on a body. Du Châtelet then moved on to consider the arguments posed against Leibniz and Bernoulli. Because it was accepted as the definitive statement on the subject, Du Châtelet chose the 1728 *Discours* by Dortous de Mairan to refute, a particularly brave decision since he had just been selected as Fontenelle's successor as perpetual secretary of the Académie. She also chose it, she explained to her son and thus her readers with an equally brave note of sarcasm, because, despite the implausibility of its points, despite its inherent contradictions, Mairan's *Discours* was the most ingenious argument against *forces vives*—the most that could be said in a bad cause.[82]

Du Châtelet identified four main points made by the adherents of $f = mv$: experiments, the role of time, the difficulty posed by "hard bodies," and the dissipation of force in the universe. She had, in the course of the *Institutions,* mentioned experiments that had gone wrong or that had to be dismissed. She noted that "*forces vives* is perhaps the only point of Physics on which one still disputes while agreeing on the experiments that prove it." That interpretations of the same observations could differ so completely may explain some of the ambivalence she expressed about experimentation at different points in the *Institutions.* Here, however, she attributed the disagreement to willfulness. In particular, Mairan's supporters rejected all of the very clear results of experiments made on the depressions of bodies in soft materials, such as those by 'sGravesande.[83]

Her own reading in Leibniz gave her the answer to the second objection, which she described as the most common "confusion" about *mv.* Adherents said that time was the unmarked measure of the equation, and time doubled if the force doubled, so there was no need to square the speed to indicate the force. But time had nothing to do with it, Du Châtelet explained, as she turned to an analogy with ironic overtones for her privileged readers: we measure a rich man's wealth in the same way regardless of how long it takes him to give it away. Another analogy showed how this faulty observation about time could be refuted by "very simple reasoning, & [reasoning] that all the world makes naturally when the occasion presents itself." One man walks a league in an hour, another two leagues in two hours. Their speed (v) remains the same. But what of a third man who walks two leagues in one hour? He must walk with more force to achieve the greater speed. Thus his speed must be squared, not merely doubled, if one wished to know the amount of force or, as would be said today, "energy" he had to expend. Once again she subtly mocked her adversary: every courier "senses" this; when he covered the same route in less time, he expected to be paid more for his efforts.[84]

Du Châtelet's letters to Maupertuis showed her own struggle to resolve the third objection to *forces vives,* represented by the collision of two "hard bodies." In experiments, colliding objects of the same mass came to a complete standstill. Where, then, were the *forces vives?* Nothing shattered, so one could not say that the force was dispersed. Nothing moved, so one could not say it had been transferred from one body to another. In May 1738, she wrote in despair of ideas "that cannot be untangled." By the end of the month, however, with Bernoulli's essays of 1724 and 1726 to draw from, she had formulated the explanation she gave to her readers. "One sees easily," she now wrote. The bodies stopped; they no longer moved, but not because they had no force. The hard bodies had consumed their force in the effort to overcome their mutual impenetrability; instead of creating movement, the forces acted as counterforces to each other. There was no movement, but there was still force.[85]

The fourth objection, and one particularly identified with Newton and his adherents, concerned the dissipation or conservation of force (energy) in the universe. This issue had occasioned the argument between Leibniz and Newton, and it was with Newton's followers that she argued explicitly. She could not accept the metaphysical connotations of his hypothesis in the last query of the *Opticks,* that, given the loss of force in the universe because of the infinite number of impacts, "our System will sometimes need to be corrected by its Author." In Newton's world, the Creator had to replenish the force periodically and in perpetuity. From Du Châtelet's perspective, accepting this image of the Supreme Being and his "continual miracles" undermined any claim to certain knowledge of the workings of nature's laws. As she had argued in chapter II, there could be no "science" in a universe subject to unpredictable intervention by a deity, however benevolent and reasonable. In contrast, in Leibniz's world of *forces vives,* there was no need for God to intervene, for the German *philosophe* believed that this force was conserved in the universe. In fact, Du Châtelet explained to Maupertuis, "all things being equal," the conservation of force "would be more worthy of the eternal *géomètre.*"[86]

Challenges and Victory

Throughout the last year and a half of the writing of the *Institutions,* from May of 1739, Du Châtelet was in Brussels, dividing her time between the legal dispute over her husband's inheritance and her course of study and writing. She also traveled back to Paris, to the court at Fontainebleau to see to family affairs, or to act once again on Voltaire's behalf. On her return to Paris in the middle of August 1739, Du Châtelet brought her new tutor, Samuel König, and his younger brother, more to allow him to enjoy the excitements of Paris than because she thought that she would have time to continue their work together. She treated him generously, housing him and his brother with her mother and then in rooms she rented for them; arranging for them to see the fireworks display at Versailles; and introducing them to her circle—at a dinner at the duchesse de Richelieu's *hôtel,* for example.[87]

Despite her difficulties with the pace of his lessons, König, initially, had seemed perfect for her needs. Du Châtelet was flattered to hear that he had refused an offer from the prince of Orange in order to join her household. From the first, however, "Mme Du Châtelet's Swiss," as Graffigny called him, seemed unhappy with his new position. Despite his erudition, he remained only a paid member of the marquise's staff who could be dismissed at her will. While in Paris that fall of 1739, König indicated that he did not want to return to Brussels. Though Du Châtelet had already written to Bernoulli II with the idea that he might replace the discontented *géomètre,* she found König's request "unreasonable" and his "conduct" incomprehensible. She described him as a "lackey and a badly raised one," the kind of domestic one would "chase . . . away as unworthy of your service, if you had not beat him to death." In contrast to the way she spoke of König, she flattered Bernoulli II with her best courtier's skills, promised him money, a servant, and the possibility of "a place at the Académie." Maupertuis initially encouraged Bernoulli II to take the post and then did not, probably because he feared Du Châtelet might view his friend as she viewed König. In the end, Maupertuis counseled him, "Blame [your refusal] on your health or on M. your father." Bernoulli II did just that, and eventually Du Châtelet turned to other subjects in their correspondence.[88]

König made good use of his time in Paris to speak against Du Châtelet and, as if in revenge, to cast doubt on her authorship of the Institutions. Nouvellistes reported his account: "that this work was nothing else but the lessons he had given to her." The story, as Maupertuis wrote to the elder Bernoulli on December 28, 1739, "ran through the city," but not without some understanding of other aspects of the relationship. The wits dubbed König the "Valet de Chambre Géomètre," the "Mathematician Valet." This must have caused him to redouble his efforts to discredit her. He spread images of the marquise offering vast sums of money, in tears, on her knees begging for his help.[89]

In February 1740, Du Châtelet found herself the subject of this gossip, without a tutor, and briefly estranged from Maupertuis because of his part in the final negotiation with the younger Bernoulli. König's accusations of her ill treatment, and his assertion that all she had done was worthless and that she had copied from another book he had written, disheartened her. In addition, König's stories, even if outrageous and untrue, had destroyed the incognito she had maintained so carefully for two years. This anonymity, she explained to the elder Bernoulli in June 1740, would have enabled her to "enjoy the pleasure of seeing myself judged without running any risk if the judgment were unfavorable." She had considered abandoning the project, but after all "le bruit," she realized it would be worse not to publish it; by then it was already half printed. The manuscript preserved at the Bibliothèque Nationale shows the extent of her final efforts: pages of printer's proofs, corrections and whole sections in her hand, others by copyists also covered with her corrections. Additions are indicated by her symbols, including the hangman's scaffold for a whole new paragraph, asterisks for a phrase or sentence. Where the text became too crowded with overwriting, the margins were filled with yet more changes.[90]

~ॐ~

Du Châtelet proudly sent the first copies of the *Institutions de physique* to Frederick of Prussia, to Maupertuis, and to many of the most important *philosophes, physiciens,* and *géomètres* of Europe's Republic of Letters. The *Journal des savants* had a copy in time to publish the first of a two-part review in its December 1740 issue.[91] That the review was positive could only have reassured her and justified the risks she had taken. Du Châtelet learned that her defense of *forces vives* had been attacked only after her return to Brussels. Jean-Jacques Dortous de Mairan's short pamphlet was his first public act as the newly elected perpetual secretary of the Académie royale des sciences. This official response, even more than the review in the *Journal des savants,* represented an unusual honor for someone outside the Académie. Just the fact of such a pamphlet addressed to Du Châtelet by such an opponent brought validation that she, as a woman, never could have achieved purely by dint of her publications.

Du Châtelet's challenge took Mairan by surprise. She sent him a copy of the *Institutions* just as she left Paris for Brussels late in December 1740, only weeks before he was to assume his official responsibilities in the new year. As he first perused the *Institutions,* he must have been pleased by the compliments for his work on time and astonished by her advocacy of so many of Leibniz's ideas. Then he would have come to the final chapter and the pages of overt attack on him, his famous *Discours* of 1728, and his views of *forces vives.* Mairan saw himself, once again, as the one who must defend French science and Descartes. A small, portly man in his sixties whom Graffigny described as "modesty itself," he had not sought his new post and would resign as soon as his three-year term was completed. Even so, he felt that as the Académie's official spokesman he must answer her attack. This marquise had overstepped the boundaries of polite disputation. She had brought "their different manner of thinking about Forces Vives" before the "Tribunal" of the public. He showed himself ready to accept its judgment.[92]

In fact, he would have done better to ignore the *Institutions de physique* and to jest at her expense within the safe confines of the Académie. According to the marquise de Créqui's memoirs, he had been encouraged to do just that, rather than to draw the *épée* against "this poor Emilie!" His hostess feared that he would be mocked for such an action, an *épée* against a fan. His response, given in his most courtly style, was widely reported: "I implore you to observe that it would not be an *épée:* a compass suffices. . . . That is quite enough to check the strikes of a fan." He chose this course of action partly, as the anecdote illustrated, because answering her appeared an easy task, like Fontenelle's *Entretiens* come to life.[93]

Mairan had his answer printed as a "letter" and ready for distribution on March 4, 1741. The first name the reader saw was his, followed by reference to his new office: "Lettre de m. de Mairan, secrétaire perpetuel de l'Académie royale des sciences." He identified her by her title: "madame la marquise Du Chastellet." With these social and professional distinctions established, he spent the first section of the pamphlet drawing on stereotypical images of the female—for example, highlighting how easily she changed her mind. She had once agreed with him and then did not. Cirey had become a "school" for the ideas of Leibniz where she had been seduced, where "Forces Vives were enthroned next to Monads." Continuing in the same imperious tone, he accused her of not understanding the mathematics, of misquoting him, of substituting her own words and thoughts for his. Thus, she had claimed to refute his argument "a bit cavalierly." He wondered how a woman of such discernment could be so wrong. All she need do, he suggested in the phrasing of Fontenelle's instructions to his female readers, was return to his original *Discours* and "Read, I implore you, Madame, & reread, you will see that it is nothing but [what I have said.]."[94]

In the second part of his letter, Mairan instructed this errant young noblewoman in the methods of correct thinking. He chided her for disagreeing with authorities such as Newton. He offered to do the experiments with her and warned her that "there certainly is someone here who is wrong, . . . & whose reasoning, applauded today by a number of *Savants,* will furnish the future race with another example of the feebleness of the human mind." Lest she take offense at the obvious insult, he concluded: "I flatter myself, Madame, that you will regard all of these reflections as a proof that I attach great importance to your knowledge & your good mind, which would not know how to permit you to resist the truth when presented to you without clouds."[95]

Mairan had seriously underestimated and miscast his adversary. Rather than quietly accept his gallantly delivered reproaches like the marquise in Fontenelle's *Entretiens,* Du Châtelet argued back in the same style and published her own response. She took apart his letter, paragraph by paragraph, and answered in the same ironic, deprecating tone that characterized his attack. Inadvertently, Mairan gave her the opportunity not only to prove that she understood the complicated issues of the *forces-vives* controversy, and thus to confirm her authorship of the *Institutions,* but also to demonstrate her facility with the ironies and subtle insults that formed part of the rhetorical skills of a member of the Republic of Letters. She wrote to her most trusted friends, in theory to consult them, but the letters actually show her excitement and her outrage, rather than any doubts about her views or her course of action. "I am very honored to have such an adversary," she confided to d'Argental in her letter of March 22, when her "Réponse" was probably already being typeset. She confessed that, in such an enterprise, *"It is even beautiful to fall,"* and, she continued, "I hope that I will not fall." Now reconciled with Maupertuis, she bragged to him that she had completed the thirty-seven-page response in three weeks, and that now no one could dispute her authorship of the *Institutions.* Du Châtelet had it brought to the Brussels printer by the twenty-sixth of March. Her husband delivered a copy to Mairan in Paris during the next week. Five hundred copies went by post to members of the Académie and to others in the Republic of Letters. In her cover letter, she addressed Mairan respectfully, but as an equal: "However the public decides, I hold myself honored always to dispute against a person of your merit."[96]

Two months after she had completed and sent her response, Du Châtelet admitted to Maupertuis that she had felt "all the ridicule of the secretary's letter," but this only seems to have encouraged her to return the same in kind. As she explained to her former mentor, it was not she who had interjected "the personal in a purely literary dispute."[97] As Mairan had established his authority on his title page, so Du Châtelet did with her pointed use of capitalization: *RESPONSE OF MADAME LA MARQUISE DU CHASTELET to the Letter That M. de Mairan, Perpetual Secretary of the Royal Academy of Sciences, Wrote to her February 18, 1741, on the Question of Forces Vives.* Like Mairan, she divided her letter in two parts: in the first she dealt with what she called his "reproaches"; in the second she answered his attack on her case for *forces vives.* Except for the sections detailing experiments and mathematical solutions, every paragraph exuded sarcasm and implied insult, particularly noticeable because Du Châtelet chose to answer Mairan's letter sentence by sentence, point by point. She was methodical, meticulous, and relentless. She feigned confusion at his logic, mocked his calculations, and corrected him on "an error in which I do not want to leave you." Since he accused her of truncating and disfiguring his memoir, she created what she referred to as a "gloss," parallel columns of text with her quotation on one side, his original on the other. She turned the secretary's effort to scold her for disagreeing with the English mathematician James Jurin into praise for Jurin: "His response, if he made one, will be filled with politeness, & that wisdom that characterizes all that he does." This was in obvious contrast to Mairan's efforts.[98]

Du Châtelet's tone was sharpest, her ironies were most obvious, when she discussed each of their arguments for and against *forces vives.* In a letter to Maupertuis, she referred to Mairan's ideas as "a ridiculous way of estimating the force of a body." Here she simply stated, "You have reasoned badly in your memoir of 1728," and "The conclusions that you have drawn were always false, because that which implies contradiction can never become true." She acknowledged that a more ample refutation would have been possible, "if I had wanted to bore my readers."[99] Du Châtelet took most to heart Mairan's accusation that she had not read and understood his memoir. In her *Réponse* she repeatedly played on this point, always to Mairan's disadvantage. She accused him in turn: "You have not read, or at the least you have not read *well,* pages 431 & 432 of the *Institutions*." Du Châtelet's last reference to his reproach was the most devastating. As she wrote to d'Argental, she "wanted to pierce him to the soul." Mairan had implored her to reread his memoir so many times that "I fear that in the end you persuaded me: I have then just reread again, for the third time, so that I would be very assured of having read it, but I confess that I found not one thing there that you had given me hope of."[100]

❧

By the middle of April, Du Châtelet's answer to Mairan had been received and read by the most influential of the *gens du monde.* The secretary must have realized that his gesture, to play Fontenelle to a young marquise, had not succeeded. Even in Brussels, Du Châtelet could write to Maupertuis of the news from Paris: "His has succeeded very badly, it has had three-quarters of the success of mine." Mairan was, she acknowledged to d'Argental at the beginning of May, "in a cruel situation." She understood that "his silence is an acknowledgment that he is wrong, and his response would only show his weakness." He now had no acceptable course of action: "It will be very bad if he does not answer, but, having nothing good to say, it would be still worse to respond." If the secretary wished to continue the dialogue, others dissuaded him.[101]

Mairan had assessed correctly the potential effectiveness of Du Châtelet's presentation of Leibniz's, Wolff's, and Bernoulli's hypotheses. It was not only the educated of the *salons* who found the *Institutions* convincing but also, over the course of the next few years, many in the Republic of Letters. As the duchesse d'Aiguillon wrote to Maupertuis, who was newly installed in Berlin as the director of Frederick of Prussia's Academy: "I have read a dozen chapters of it, but I am enchanted with it more than I can say, above all with the part concerning metaphysics." She particularly complimented the style; this alone made it a "masterpiece," for "nothing is so clear, so well written." Many Academicians openly praised the *Institutions* right away. Buffon, a friend of Du Châtelet's from the Royal Botanical Gardens and from dinners at the duchesse de Richelieu's *hôtel,* praised the "clarity, order, neatness, precision of the words and the ideas," even though he did not agree with the German metaphysics. Clairaut concurred: "I am charmed to know it [Leibniz's metaphysics] and I believe that no one had made me understand it as well as you." He continued, "It also gave great pleasure, not as the first work to open a new field, but in placing before our eyes the most satisfying truths of physics in a beautiful order and in an agreeable manner."[102]

By her own efforts and willingness to act counter to every tradition of her sex and circumstances, Du Châtelet had won a well-deserved victory. She could not help expressing satisfaction to her friends. How sad it was that Mairan "had imputed to me things so easy to destroy." She was not the secretary of the Académie, she could not have the last word, "but I am right, and that is worth all the titles."[103] What would Du Châtelet choose to do with this "fame" and her new status in the Republic of Letters? Although she returned to the unfinished Biblical commentary she had begun at Cirey, ambitious goals for her family and for Voltaire necessitated her attendance at court, at Fontainebleau and Versailles. How could she fulfill these obligations as well as those to herself as a newly recognized member of the Republic of Letters? By living as if there were more than twenty-four hours in each day.

PART III

APRIL 1741—SEPTEMBER 1749

CHAPTER FIVE

Philosophe and Courtier:
"Uranie" and Breteuil Du Châtelet

In April 1741, Du Châtelet and Voltaire traveled to Lille to see a production of his new play, *Mahomet;* it was also an opportunity for him to visit with his favorite niece. They probably made the return journey to the *hôtel* on the rue de la Grosse Tour in Brussels at night: Du Châtelet insisted that the daylight was too precious to waste. One could always sleep, she pointed out if ever Voltaire protested. Perhaps, true to her prediction, he dozed off, his head falling against the side of the coach, and Du Châtelet could reflect on the events of the past year. Both her mother and her closest ally in the efforts to protect Voltaire from the king's ministers, the gentle, young duchesse de Richelieu, had died the previous August. She had finished her *Institutions de physique* and dealt with the ridiculous charges from König. She could smile to herself thinking of the marquis personally delivering her answer to Mairan. News had already filtered back across the frontier from Paris of positive reactions to her audacious decision to make a public response. Cideville wrote to Voltaire of signs of "a complete victory" and planned to "sing of her triumph with all my strengths."[1]

Time now to focus on "the eternal lawsuit," as that foolish Graffigny had dubbed the challenge to the bequest of his Flemish properties from the marquis's cousin Marc-Antoine Du Châtelet, marquis de Trichâteau. Voltaire had complimented her efforts in a letter to Frederick of Prussia, calling the legal documents she had submitted as forceful as her *Dissertation* on fire. The move to Brussels, she knew, had been unavoidable. Only there could she and the marquis assert his claims successfully. The visit to the properties at Beringhem, about ten leagues from Brussels, with a rundown château, brought disappointment, but the marquis now hoped to sell the lands and titles for one million livres. For Du Châtelet, however, Trichâteau's death in April 1740, in the early stages of the court case, complicated matters even further, leaving a "mess to clean up." Some days she thought of it as "a sea where I still see no bottom and no shore."[2]

Du Châtelet might pull aside the curtain at the window of the *carrosse* (large coach). The night outside would seem as fathomless as the case. Still, it was her duty, in particular to her children; this was their patrimony. She knew all responsibility would fall to her again, as the marquis, after this trip to Paris, would rejoin the army for the summer campaign against the new Hapsburg empress. In January of 1739 Voltaire had predicted that the litigation would take two years; she could foresee two more at least. Even so, she must have vowed to herself to continue with her studies and her writing. Rising early in the morning, she could continue the routine established when she completed her *Institutions.* Did she let the curtain fall and lean back to rest until the next change of horses? The valet would have ridden ahead to see to the arrangements.[3]

Challenges of New Varieties: 1741–42

At the beginning of their time in Brussels, in 1739, Du Châtelet and Voltaire had more or less re-created their Cirey routine: "We take our *café au lait* the day after a good supper party," as he described it to Mme de Champbonin. The marquise had her lessons with König, revised another chapter of her *Institutions;* Voltaire worked on his plays *Zulime* and *Mahomet* and numerous other projects. Now, in 1741, Du Châtelet devoted even more of her energies to "mon procès"—"my lawsuit"—as she called it. She had already done her best to identify the "very useful acquaintances to make." Her entourage had stopped at Hénault's father-in-law's estate on their way to Brussels in the summer of 1739. The princesse de Chimay, a daughter of the Lorraine family of Beauvau-Craon, had watched the fireworks that Voltaire organized when they first arrived, a successful event despite the damage done to the third floor of their rented *hôtel.* Du Châtelet had visited the city's notables, attended balls, card-playing evenings, and theatricals. She had learned Flemish, taken steps to become a citizen, joined the city's most elite congregation, and once participated in the confraternity's rituals in honor of the Virgin on the first of May.[4]

Moments of intense activity and apparent victories followed by long periods of little progress characterized this time in Brussels. Du Châtelet supervised the writing of petitions, hired agents to collect witnesses, *rapporteurs* to act as spokemen, prosecutors and lawyers accredited to the different courts. That year, 1741, their opponent, the marquis d'Hoensbroeck found endless ways to contest and to delay resolution. In May, she sought d'Argental's opinion of the case she had formulated; he was councilor to a Parisian court. She listed her opponent's accusations and her responses. Was Trichâteau competent at the time he made the gift and then signed his will? There had been a notary and witnesses. Could the notary and witnesses have been bribed, or convinced to swear he was not an imbecile? Du Châtelet proposed to *"demand proof of this falsity"* (the emphasis is hers). "What," she asked, "would one answer [to that]?" Following the line of defense to establish the validity of the bequest, in January and February 1742 she was in Cirey, gaining testimony from those who had witnessed the old cousin's will.[5] Voltaire reported to their friends how hard she worked on her family's behalf: any victory came because of her "courage, wit and fatigue." "If success depends [on] . . . her travail, she will be very rich, but," Voltaire continued, "sadly all of this depends on people who haven't as much intelligence as she." In September 1742, with no apparent end in sight, she reported to d'Argental, "I am here in the horrors of the procedure, working much and scarcely advancing." Then an "incident" would encourage her once again.[6]

A month later, in October, Du Châtelet despaired that she might have to "pass my life going from Paris to Brussels, which would be sad and expensive." She viewed the country as snowy and cold, and so distant from Paris. As Voltaire remarked, she found there "few people with whom she could speak of philosophy." From this point on, she decided to supervise the case from Paris or Cirey. When the English came to occupy Brussels in June 1743, much of the life of the privileged could go on as if there were no battles and no enemies, and Du Châtelet could still enter and leave the city. She chose, however, to sublet the *hôtel* to an English colonel and returned only when necessary, and for as briefly as possible. For example, she found a new *rapporteur* when the one she had employed had a stroke; she enlisted Christian Wolff's assistance when she needed a formal opinion on the legal meaning of *Leibzucht,* a key term in the suit. When matters were decided is not clear. The records indicate only that the marquis d'Hoensbroeck contracted a substantial sum for right to the lands—not the one million livres the marquis had hoped for, but more than two hundred thousand livres, and fifty thousand more than the original offer.[7]

Other difficulties made Brussels an unpleasant place for Du Châtelet in 1741 and 1742. Voltaire had decided that he was no longer capable of sexual activity. He had not meant, however, that this should diminish their affection for each other or their life of companionship. Yet, as Du Châtelet would write later, in her Discours sur le bonheur, his decision was very difficult for her to accept. Then there were the ever more obvious differences in their views about the universe and what constituted the "certain knowledge" of the sciences. Once Voltaire realized that Du Châtelet found Leibniz and Wolff's metaphysics a convincing answer to the problems of causes and the lack of a mechanical explanation for attraction, he became adamant in his rejection of what he viewed as anathema to Newton's system. Just as, in 1738, when Voltaire had seen himself arrayed against those who favored Descartes at the expense of Newton, now he perceived a similar dichotomy, his revered Newton challenged by the ideas of Leibniz. So Du Châtelet fell victim to his black-and-white view.[8]

Those months present a disconcerting image: Du Châtelet and Voltaire lived together with her household, including her children, in the hôtel in Brussels, each composing and revising books and discours, traveling back and forth to Paris, no longer arguing over café, now only disputing each other's views in published works presented to the gens qui pensent. Voltaire criticized and mocked her freely in his letters as "the illustrious neuto-leibnitzienne." He identified the whole of the Institutions as about Leibniz, despite Du Châtelet's very obvious synthesis of many philosophes' views and her sections on Newtonian mechanics. "If Leibnitz still lived," he wrote to Helvétius, "he would die of joy to see himself so explained or of shame to see himself surpassed in clarity, in method, and in elegance." Although he defended her against König's charges that she had merely copied the work of others, he agreed with Mairan that she had been seduced by "the religion of monads." Voltaire deplored that "a French woman such as madame Du Châtelet made her mind serve to embroider these spider webs."[9]

Du Châtelet, in contrast, accepted these challenges, even the most venomous and denigrating, with remarkable restraint. She wrote to d'Argental in March 1741, after Voltaire had published four different attacks on her views, that she understood that there could be no "greater contrast in philosophical sentiments nor greater uniformity in others," and resigned herself to realities. Even so, Voltaire's first attack must have seemed a betrayal. In the course of 1740, he had rewritten the *Traité de métaphysique*, which they had puzzled over together, and transformed it into a clearly directed refutation of specific chapters of her book: her discussions of God, matter, space, and Leibniz's laws of motion. The changes from their original *Traité* in the now titled *La Métaphysique de Newton* would have read starkly to her. The God of Voltaire's chapter I decided all in accordance with Samuel Clarke's ideas on Newton, as expressed in his published interchange with Leibniz. This God knew nothing of the limits of "sufficient reason," required a void, and "put [all] back in order" when the dissipation of "force" in the universe required his intervention. Voltaire made the concept of monads sound absurd and revolting: "Would you then advance that a drop of urine could be an infinity of *monads,* and that each of them had ideas, however obscure, of the entire universe . . . ?" He taunted her: "I call on your conscience, don't you sense how much such a system is pure imagination . . . ?"[10]

Throughout 1741, Voltaire was indefatigable in his defense of Newton and now of Mairan as well. His next sally, an essay on *forces vives* titled *Doutes sur la mésure des forces motrices* (Doubts on the Measurement of *forces vives*) for the Académie des sciences, represented not only a clear challenge to chapter XXI of her *Institutions,* but also a vigorous gesture in support of the new perpetual secretary. Though Voltaire and Mairan had met many years before, the poet had been cultivating Mairan's mentoring and friendship in earnest only since 1736. Perhaps Voltaire had joined the fray hoping to improve upon the mixed reception to his own *Eléments de la philosophie de Newton;* when reviewers praised his accomplishment it was more for its exceptionality as the "worthy enterprise" of a "poet" than for its merit. Voltaire also prepared a negative review of the *Institutions* for the *Mercure de France,* the same journal that had published his contentious review of her *Dissertation sur le feu.* It appeared in the June issue, after both Du Châtelet and Mairan's *Lettres* had been circulating for at least a month. He gave extravagant praise to her preface and her chapters on Newton's mechanics, and then, with veiled sarcasm, quotations out of context, and purposeful misreadings of her text, he made the patronizing suggestion that she could not possibly believe what Leibniz had written and Wolff had then commented upon.[11]

Voltaire's final attack on Du Châtelet and her supposedly exclusive adherence to Leibniz came in the second edition of his *Eléments de la philosophie de Newton,* which appeared later in 1741. Voltaire made significant changes and additions and included as the first section of the book the *Métaphysique de Newton* that had already been published separately. Most cutting of all, however, was the new dedication. Here Voltaire ignored her genius and underlined his traditional image of her as a woman. The marquise had proved that "constant application, which is perhaps the gift of the most rare *esprit*," could bring understanding of philosophy without sacrificing "the duties of *la vie civile*." She had ceased to be his companion and mentor. He alone, as the follower of the philosopher Samuel Clarke, presented "the opinions that you accept, and those that you combat."[12]

Recognition as a *Philosophe:* "Uranie"

In the end, these attacks from the man she loved and respected had little if any effect on the public argument. Du Châtelet emerged from the battle of the "compass" and the "fan" a clear, if not explicitly acknowledged, victor. To the Republic of Letters, a respected member of the *gens des lettres* and keeper of one of the king's most prestigious institutions had been challenged not once but twice by a woman of the *haute noblesse*. These challenges had been not the frivolous repartee of a flirtatious courtier but, as described by the reviewer of the *Institutions* for the *Mémoires de Trévoux,* a serious presentation of a position on a relatively arcane point of physics, and one endorsed by many important *philosophes* on the Continent. Despite the reviewer's obvious disagreement with the Leibnizian / Wolffian system and the formula for *forces vives,* the reviewer acknowledged Du Châtelet's skills as a defender in the interchange with Mairan and continually praised "the anonymous author" as "a person of *esprit* [intelligence], knowledgeable about modern opinions, which are rendered in a style with much finesse & lively imagination." It was in this "colloquial, instructional tone, graceful, intelligible & moreover noble & full of decorum," that the author, "always ingenious," presented "the system little known" in France. The *Institutions* was "in a word . . . a good compendium of modern physics." Neither here nor in the review in the *Journal des savants* was her sex or her *état* mentioned. She was a peer with work to be critiqued, not patronized for its exceptionality. The second part of a review from the March issue of the *Journal des savants* praised the *Institutions* and made favorable comments about the formula for force, mv^2. As the reviewer concluded, the author had explained ideas and given mathematical demonstrations on a "path . . . so different that few readers had the courage to follow." She, however, "had not been afraid; great passions," the reviewer suggested, "surmount great obstacles."[13]

Mairan remained silent. He had changed his view of "literary battles" and now asserted that he had "neither the desire nor the necessary talents to play with the Public." Du Châtelet guessed that "the honor of the Académie had become part of his defeat, and one judged it not appropriate to allow him to continue the dispute." She commented to Maupertuis that the lack of learned support suggested that "it was more comfortable to impose silence than to speak to his [Mairan's] liking." Maupertuis, newly returned to Paris and thus able to survey the battlefield in person, took particular pleasure in the predicament of the old Academician, who was a former adversary of his as well. Maupertuis wrote to Algarotti: "M. De Mairan . . . wrote a work against her, to which she responded by another in which she was right in the content and the form, and where she treated Mairan with all types of superiority." Echoing Du Châtelet's own characterization, he continued, "There is nothing so ridiculous as this adventure for a secretary of the Académie."[14]

When the members of the Académie did respond, it was indirectly and anonymously, in the form of two reviews of the interchange in the *Mémoires de Trévoux*. Mairan's *Lettre,* as expected, was praised. The review of Du Châtelet's *Résponse* was less inclusive, with long quotations from only the second part of her essay, which, when taken out of context, appeared difficult to follow and unconvincing. Even so, the reviewer did not condescend. He identified her as an "illustrious" "savant Auteur," though one of a minority among the learned, the "partisans of *forces vives*." Du Châtelet was lauded for her "diligence" in responding so quickly and so thoroughly, and for the literary aspects of her answer. "Madame la marquise Du Châtelet leaves nothing without a reply, opposing reasoning for reasoning, stroke of wit for stroke of wit, politeness for politeness." In fact, she had mastered a particularly ingenious part of the French language and culture: "irony." She, like Mairan, had demonstrated this skill with the "finesse" that the ancients had never achieved.[15]

Probably about this time, in the early 1740s, Du Châtelet commissioned another portrait, choosing a popular artist of her day named Marianne Loir. The marquise has dressed in the more comfortable, free-flowing style of the *robe à l'anglaise* instead of the formed and fitted courtier's *robe à la française*. Du Châtelet sits very straight in a brocade *fauteuil* with her left elbow resting on the table beside her. Her feet appear firmly planted, as if she were ready to stand up and rush to other, more immediate tasks. The yards of deep-blue fabric make the skirt appear to flow across her legs. The bodice, in contrast, is stiff. The wide sleeves are the same blue velvet, trimmed in layers of lace and large satin bows. The long black martin fur piece from her previous portrait edges the bodice; the palatine, as it was called, falls from both shoulders across her skirt, to disappear off the canvas. A small rectangular diamond (or paste) brooch is pinned to the ribbon at her throat. It is the only jewelry ever worn in her portraits. Du Châtelet has turned her head to the right and offers her slight smile to the viewer.

Symbols abound in this portrait. A string of crystal beads is carelessly displayed on the table to indicate their lesser importance in her life. An open book, loose pages of manuscript, and an orrery (an adjustable representation of the solar system) on the table beside the beads, and shelves of massive outsized tomes forming the backdrop, indicate the more important interests and activities of this woman. Du Châtelet holds a white carnation in her left hand to signify "passion"—appropriately, on the side of the heart. In her right hand, traditionally the side of reason, she holds a compass, the mathematician's symbol. There were traditions in eighteenth-century French portraiture about the positioning of the compass. Holding the points straight up signified abstractions; down meant the measurement of the earth and matter. In this portrait, Du Châtelet holds the points horizontally, neither up nor down, an indication of her skill with both kinds of mathematics. Those who knew of her exchange with Mairan might even see a subtle reminder that she could fight with this instrument—not the fan he had expected.[16]

⁓❦⁓

Despite or perhaps because of her victory over Mairan, Du Châtelet found the relative silence annoying. She saw her encounter as "a pleasant anecdote that I don't want anyone to forget." This explains her reason for deciding to prepare a second edition of the *Institutions* and to publish with it the only serious opposition to her ideas, her interchange with Mairan. When she then moved on to revise her *Dissertation* on fire, she included the two *Lettres* once again. By the end of June 1741, she wrote to Maupertuis that she had completed the revisions of the *Institutions*.[17] She had a number of the engravings at the beginnings of the chapters redone so that they appeared less cluttered and more effectively highlighted the activities being illustrated in the foreground. Her name appeared as the author; her portrait, based on the Loir but without the mixture of allegorical symbols, as the frontispiece. It shows her facing the reader, with her compass, other mathematical instruments, and a globe on the table beside her. In addition, Du Châtelet had instructed her publisher to reset many pages of the book to accommodate her changes. She conformed the endings of adjectives and participles throughout the text to reflect her female sex. She found words, phrases, paragraphs to clarify, to amend, to delete, on almost every page. In all respects she made the book more effective.

On the disputed points, she wrote with new clarity and authority. Concepts that she disagreed with were now "absolutely false." She adhered to Leibniz's concept of "sufficient reason" even more emphatically. Her image of a God of choice and reason was her way of answering Voltaire's critiques in his *Métaphysique de Newton*. Similarly, she reworded parts of the chapters on space and time, but only to express her views more directly and forcefully. There was no void; the continuity of bodies throughout the cosmos was a reality. She still believed in monads; like Leibniz, she saw "force" everywhere in a universe whose constituent parts were always in motion. To be at rest meant to be stopped by resistances; movement was a body's natural state. Du Châtelet took similar care with the revised edition of her *Dissertation* on fire, not published until 1744, several years later. She made the same kinds of stylistic changes and eliminated digressions. The essay now read more like other Académie submissions, the tone drier, less discursive. The paragraphs of humble apology, the sentences in praise of different authorities were gone. The "great Philosophers" became "some Philosophers." Du Châtelet clearly had now joined their ranks and presented her own views as uncontested. In fact, for the next decade, any *philosophe* or *géomètre* writing on *forces vives* dealt with her arguments in one way or another. More immediately, when, having returned to Paris from Brussels, she decided to attend the opening of the Académie des sciences after its fall recess, she could report to Bernoulli II, "I flatter myself that I embarrassed it." This would have been the first time that Mairan and many of the Academicians had seen her since she had first challenged him in her *Institutions de physique*.[18]

~~~

Du Châtelet's new status as a member of the learned elite resulted first from the publication of her writings, and then from her correspondence with other *philosophes, géomètres,* and *physiciens*. Letters were commonly the means by which the learned exchanged information, tested hypotheses, and earned the favor of mutual esteem. Like the men of this circle, Du Châtelet sent her books as gifts, exchanged portraits, asked for opinions and corrections. In the course of the first months of 1741, she arranged for copies of the *Institutions* to go to Maupertuis, through him to Leonhard Euler, and to other continental *physiciens* and *géomètres*, and to their friends, such as the sons of Johann Bernoulli. All awkwardness about the abortive attempt to bring Bernoulli II into her household had dissipated. She reported to the Basel *savant* about the end of her interchange with Mairan. The secretary had not answered her, and therefore, citing Corneille's *Le Cid*, she noted that "the combat ended for lack of combatants." In the years to come, there would be her polite congratulations on his marriage, on the birth of a child, purchase of a pendulum clock for her, the loan of his father's copy of the *Principia*. Du Châtelet exchanged news of common friends, especially Maupertuis and his "honorable though not very lucrative" marriage to one of the Prussian queen's ladies-in-waiting.[19]

Through the younger Bernoulli, she acquired new correspondents, like the Swiss mathematician Gabriel Cramer; Frédéric Moula, a mathematician in Neuchâtel; and père François Jacquier, a few years her junior and corresponding secretary of the Academy of Rome. She reported to Jacquier on Buffon's demonstration and praised his *Mémoire* proposing the use of multiple *miroirs ardents* to create fire at great distances as "well written and very instructive." Le Monnier considered her so much a part of this circle of "natural philosophers" that he sent her his translation of John Keill's lessons on astronomy before its formal publication. Des Champs, in his "avertissement" to the reader for his French translation of an abridged course in Wolff's philosophy, admitted that only after he finished did he see "a book, of which one cannot say enough good; it is the *Institutions de physique* of Madame la Marquise Du Châtelet."[20]

When in Paris, Du Châtelet saw Clairaut often. He also passed on news of others, including Jacquier's complaint that she had not written. Clairaut, of all her correspondents, actually asked questions of her and sent corrections for the *Institutions*, "quibbles as he called them," along with his praise. All was done in the spirit of a dialogue, not lessons. Du Châtelet was in the midst of her revisions and wrote impatiently, asking him to clarify his comments on a few of the mathematical calculations and explanations in her description of the experiments concerning attraction. As for the controversial chapter XXI, he was in total agreement with her. He assured her in the same letter that he also "entirely" concurred with her about James Jurin's article. "I am even astonished that a man of such wit could give such reasons." He could only explain it by "the spirit of partisanship."[21]

Du Châtelet's first contact with Jurin, the eminent English mathematician, had come through Maupertuis. In 1738, he had arranged for Algarotti to take a copy of her *Dissertation sur la nature du feu* to Jurin on his trip to London. Du Châtelet herself sent him her response to Mairan's criticism in February 1741. That summer, Jurin complimented her in a letter to Voltaire, noting that she "has found the secret of making Mr Leibnitz himself speak clearly, of rendering [him] intelligible to others, whatever you conceive yourself. . . ." Jurin had already responded to Du Châtelet's critique of his hypothetical boat in chapter XXI. As she explained to Wolff, this "scientific letter" from "a man of merit" deserved a thoughtful response. She consulted Maupertuis, as well as Clairaut, Wolff, and Cramer, on how best to formulate her answer. The final version ran to five pages and gave the reasoning and the mathematics in great detail. Du Châtelet sent it to Jurin with the second edition of the *Institutions*.[22]

Père Jacquier supervised the Italian translation of the *Institutions,* including Mairan's letter and her response (1743), and of her letter answering Jurin. He encouraged her next project, the translation of and commentary on Newton's *Principia,* and he arranged for her election to the Bologna Academy of Sciences.[23] Du Châtelet chose "Uranie," Voltaire's poetic name for her, as the honorific for this prestigious Italian learned group, and looked forward one day to "assisting at the meetings and profiting from the wisdom of the *savants* who are its members." Perhaps because she knew that the Newtonian Laura Bassi was also a member, and a lecturer at the University of Bologna, Du Châtelet noted what an "encouragement" this was for "persons of my sex" "to engage in and cultivate the Sciences from which prejudice had up to the present appeared to exclude them." Bassi used the *Institutions* in her classes, and into the 1750s Du Châtelet appeared in Italian books as the example of the learned woman. The editors of the *Journal universel* noted the unusual honor of Du Châtelet's election with accolades for the learned woman who had developed her own thoughts and "even entered into dispute with the most famous *Philosophes* of this era." Du Châtelet kept the official letter of recognition from Bologna among her most important papers.[24]

Ironically, in the German states Du Châtelet became famous for making Leibniz clearer than he had been in his native language. She sent the *Institutions* to Christian Wolff, whose writings had so influenced her, and continued to correspond with him. Wolff initially had difficulty believing her "a solidly learned lady." Soon, however, he accepted her as "a phenomenon." A friend read chapters of the *Institutions* in Berlin and described it to him as "very nice and very clear on your metaphysics." If the rest read as well, "it will render much service to the truth and to philosophy." She asked Wolff to recommend a *géomètre* for her son, and to send the German translation of her answer to Mairan, so that her boy might perfect his German reading his mother's prose. Wolff in turn wrote to her and to his friend about his pleasure with the *Institutions* and "the clarity with which she can talk about the subtlest things." He saw her as the mediator for his philosophy in France. It was probably by Wolff's arrangement that the second edition was translated into German and published in 1743.[25]

Du Châtelet's reputation in the German states was also enhanced by her inclusion in the fourth volume of the *Bilder-Sal heutiges Tages lebender und durch Gelahrheit berühmter Schrifft-Steller* (Portrait Gallery of Contemporary Authors Famous for Their Learning) (Augsburg, 1745). She was one of four women among a total of one hundred scholars believed to represent the best of Europe's *savants*. Bernoulli acted as the agent for the editor; Voltaire contributed a short account of her life. Du Châtelet sent reprints of her books to be described in the entry. Fearing that it might be too short, she listed some of her correspondents—Wolff, Euler, Maupertuis, Clairaut, Jurin, Jacquier, Musschenbroek—and offered information about the illustrious careers of her son and daughter. The publishers of the *Bilder-Sal* made it a point not to mention marriages and children, but they did incorporate her other additions. The introductory section on learned women placed her in a tradition stretching back to Plato's mentors Diotima and Aspasia. By comparison, Du Châtelet brought victory to the moderns over the ancients: "Our age can offer no more remarkable example to counterbalance the fame of Antiquity" than the marquise. The entry ended with stanzas from an ode written to her by the translator of her *Réponse* to Mairan, Louise Gottsched: "Woman! you who serve your country better than a thousand men."[26]

The *Examens de la Bible*

The image from Louise Gottsched's ode was a military one. Gottsched wrote during what history books remember as the War of Austrian Succession. Bits of military information dot the *Institutions,* for, in the midst of her intellectual activities, Du Châtelet had other preoccupations. In addition to the seemingly endless *procès* that dragged on year after year, she was continually concerned for her husband's safety and his advancement in the king's service. To her fell the principal responsibility for their children's future as well. With all that Du Châtelet was doing in the years represented just by these publications, from 1740 to 1744, it seems she had found a way to multiply the number of hours in her days. Her Paris inventory included a black Moroccan-leather writing case, with a small silver inkstand and powderer. She must have used them on her days of journeying between the sites of her varied activities and responsibilities.[27]

In August 1741, France's decision to challenge Maria Theresa's claim to the Hapsburg throne necessitated the marquis Du Châtelet-Lomont's return to his regiment, to serve with the Army of the Meuse and then of the Rhine. From then until the signing of the Treaty of Aix-la-Chapelle in October 1748, he participated in all of the major campaigns fought along the Rhine, in Alsace, east into the German states, and northwest into Flanders, then part of the Hapsburg Empire. To list the marquis's battles is to give a brief history of this war. He fought at Dettingen in June 1743, and at the sieges of Wissembourg and Fribourg in 1744. The marquis was at the great French victory of Fontenoy with the king and the dauphin in May 1745. In 1746, he fought with Maurice de Saxe's victorious army in the taking of

Flanders from the English, at the Battle of Raucoux, and at the sieges of towns that would become famous again in the wars of the twentieth century: Mons, Charleroi, and Namur.[28]

Du Châtelet must have received letters from her husband, and in August 1743 she passed a letter of his on to the minister for war, the comte d'Argenson. The battles rarely interfered with communications, or even with the freedom of individuals to pass through battle lines from one territory to another, as Du Châtelet and Voltaire did to see her son when he was suspected of having smallpox. Still in Brussels in the fall of 1742, she had seen Hessians and Hanoverians arriving in strength, and arrangements being made for the king of England's entourage. She assumed there would be a siege of Dunkerque. Du Châtelet understood that war in the 1740s meant combat for an officer, having lost a cousin who died a few days after his leg was shot off by a cannon. She was relieved when, in August 1744, she had news of her husband and the retreat "in good order" with the Army of the Rhine. She explained to Cideville that he had had no choice but to withdraw and his conduct did him "honor." She then learned that the marquis and her son, just turned seventeen, were together, safely wintering with their troops at Bingen, at the juncture of the Rhine and the Nahe rivers. The marquis himself left an account of one of these engagements, which he believed entitled him to France's highest military order, the Croix de Saint-Louis: seven pages dictated to a secretary, or recorded by a copyist. In the marquis's file at the Château de Vincennes is the royal authorization, in the large, clear hand of Louis XV: "bon pour le m. duchastelet lomont."[29]

Perhaps it was the injustices inherent in war, the apparent randomness of death, the questions about a Creator's purpose, that caused Du Châtelet to leave the projected volume II of the *Institutions* and to return during these years, 1742–44, to the notes that she and Voltaire had made about the Bible. These had been one of their projects while they had enjoyed their morning *café* in the *galerie* at Cirey. Anger and exasperation with Voltaire's efforts to counter her synthesis of Leibniz and Newton must also have played a part. She decided that Voltaire's version of Newton's God and the role of random divine intervention must be discredited. Their research and the records of their discussions offered two ways to do this. The New Testament Jesus could be shown to be an impostor—human, not divine—and thus, his miracles a sham; with the discrediting of the prophesied Messiah, the Old Testament deity then demonstrated nothing more than the horror and the absurdity of a God acting without reason.[30]

The notes and texts that Du Châtelet returned to had been part of her and Voltaire's larger inquiry into God's nature, his role in the universe, and the origins of morality, and included ideas from clandestine French texts and works by the English deists. At some point Du Châtelet had undertaken her own translation and précis of Thomas Woolston's *Six Discourses on the Miracles of Our Saviour* (1727–29). She also knew of a seventeenth-century anonymous tract, *Les Trois Imposteurs* (The Three Impostors), which asserted that Moses, Jesus, and Mohammed were all frauds. For their reading of the Latin Vulgate, they also had the most complete and authoritative French Biblical commentary of their day, the multivolume work by the Augustinian church scholar Dom Augustin Calmet, which could not have been a better source for the project. To defend the dogma of the Catholic faith, its rituals and its institutions, Calmet had gone through the Bible sentence by sentence, giving information about all the possible readings and interpretations. He believed that he thus answered all objections, resolved all contradictions, and reaffirmed the truth and efficacy of God's revelation as enshrined in Catholic Christianity. For Du Châtelet and Voltaire, however, this careful accounting of doubts and "misreadings" of the Old and New Testaments could be evaluated from a less accepting, more skeptical perspective, and the apologist's comments discounted or dismissed altogether.[31]

The neatest and most concise part of Du Châtelet's *Examens de la Bible* is the commentary on the New Testament, where she systematically explained away the miraculous and thus disproved the divinity of Jesus. She began the commentary with the problem she and Voltaire must have discussed. The "authenticity" of the books had to be established, but it was impossible, she explained, to see how the choice of what was "canonical" and what was "apocryphal" had been made. She knew from Calmet that there had been many evangelists in the first years of the church. How were these four gospels selected from the thirty-nine which had been recorded?[32] Calmet accepted that these were considered the "most reasonable and most respected." Du Châtelet proceeded to show just how unreasonable and silly they could be. John, for example, began with "Platonic gibberish on the 'word' that I strongly doubt anyone understands."[33]

Du Châtelet took the Gospel according to Matthew as the primary text.

With her knowledge of Woolston's critique, the miracles of the New Testament gave her ample opportunity to point out the flaws, contradictions, and practical "absurdities" (a favorite word of Du Châtelet's) in the evangelists' accounts. The new medical knowledge explained some, chicanery explained others. Miraculous returns to life must be a charade, in one case concocted by Jesus, Lazarus, and his daughter. Matthew's story of devils changing themselves into two thousand pigs that then had to be slaughtered was outrageous. Even if such a transformation had occurred, how could the owners recover from the loss of so much livestock? She noted with great care every discrepancy among the versions of the Apostles and every instance in which Jesus' life and actions did not fit the prophecies. In the end, she concluded that Jesus was a cowardly, crazy impostor, "a pious fraud."[34]

No wonder, Du Châtelet reasoned, that the Jews did not recognize him as their Messiah. He broke their laws and hid the miracles that might have justified his behavior. He could not answer the questions of the rabbis, and he cleverly avoided those of the Apostles with parables that no one understood. Much of the time he appeared to be a crazy person, "un fou," a carpenter with four fishermen as disciples. She noted that, "without the women who always followed him, his affection for John would have lost him his reputation." Surely the Jews should not be blamed for their unwillingness to believe "this fable of the christ."[35] From Du Châtelet's perspective, the miracle of Jesus' rising from the dead offered no proof. That no witnesses saw the actual rising made the rest of the account suspect. She reasoned that a deity who could walk through walls would not need an angel to move the stone at the entrance to his tomb. Also, she noted sarcastically, it was "pleasing" to observe that "the son of God was just crucified publicly in this world, [but] that he resurrects incognito."[36]

Du Châtelet turned to Woolston to explain this "absurd" series of events. The Apostles feared that the prophecies would not come true, that Jesus might never come alive on the third day. They, not the soldiers they accused, accomplished "la belle finesse." They stole the body, then claimed that their Messiah had risen from the dead. Du Châtelet contended that all this happened before the third day of the prophecy, and that "no one saw it who did not have an interest in seeing it." This apparent miracle was the ultimate fraud, the clever ruse of a group of self-seeking men, not the fulfillment of a prophecy.

Jesus and his followers the evangelists, Du Châtelet concluded, had only invented the miracles to fulfill the prophecies of the Old Testament. The contradictions, the missing pieces in the stories, the appeal to allegorical rather than literal meaning, for her "rendered all the history of Jesus' miracles suspect." Thus, one must doubt any claim to his being the Messiah of the prophets, the son of God.[37] These conclusions took her back to the prophecies and the books of the Old Testament.

Du Châtelet wrote about this part of the Bible with a sense of outrage at the inconsistencies, cruelties, and "absurdities." She offered references to the certain knowledge of the sciences: "Every discovery that men have made in physics and in astronomy has made evident a new absurdity in this story of the creation," everything from the moon's inability to give off light— something that even children know—to a serpent's preference for fruits and plants like other animals—not dirt, as described in Genesis. "The rainbow that Noah and his sons saw can be explained by Newton's *Opticks*"; the flood, by her own calculations, was physically impossible because "it would require at least 8 times more water than the ocean contained" and the clouds could provide. When the waters receded, people would die from infection if they had tried to live on the muddy land and the bad air given off by the silt. The plagues sent by God to frighten and punish the Egyptians drew similar criticism. By her count, "no one ought to be left in Egypt" after so many devastating occurrences.[38] Her knowledge of the human body revealed other errors. She wrote, obviously from her own experience, that God's pronouncement that the vaginal bleeding after giving birth to a girl lasted longer than for a boy "is certainly false."[39]

Initially, as she worked her way through the notes for the Old Testament, she commented extensively, but then, as one prophet followed another, she turned to an almost formulaic pattern—Joel, for example, becoming "the Seigneur's prophet of the day."[40] Her critiques of the prophecies themselves were merciless. Some of these pronouncements were so vague as to be applicable to anyone: "Louis 14 [sic] and King James are predicted much more clearly than J.C." (her usual way of referring to Jesus). In Isaiah, one was "forced to abandon the literal [meaning] and then one sees in the verses all that one wants." With this kind of metaphorical imagining, she suggested, "it could be Mohammed."[41]

Du Châtelet's *Examens* also rejected the Old Testament as a guide to moral behavior, further undermining any claims for its divine origin. To her, each successive leader and king seemed more cruel and "revolting" than the last.[42] In the midst of describing Saul's cruelties and the horror of Joshua's actions, Du Châtelet explained that they were done "in the name of Holy Scripture"; if they were done in the name of God, then that God must also be accountable for "these abominations." This image of the deity formed the essence of Du Châtelet's answer to Voltaire. This bizarre God made promises that he did not keep. He gave his favors without rhyme or reason: Lot and his drunken, incestuous daughters "offered a pretty family to save by preference." The story of Job could be made into an entertaining *conte* (tale), but she saw it as a "bad joke between God and Satan" that cost the lives of Job's "poor children," a tragedy inflicted by a God who demanded obedience and then punished his loyal believer to show his power and to win a wager. Later in her commentary, she noted simply, that "the God of the Jews was more powerful for doing evil than for doing good."[43] This God of the Old Testament could not be the God she saw in the rational, predictable universe of her *Institutions*.

What did Du Châtelet plan to do with this monumental exegesis, which ran to more than seven hundred pages? She certainly did not mean to publish it. Neither she nor Voltaire wanted that kind of notoriety in 1743 or 1744, among their most active years as courtiers. It is not even clear if Voltaire ever read it. Only the barest references suggest that he did, and even these could be from the notes they created together, not from Du Châtelet's final text.[44] It did circulate, however, in the Republic of Letters. Three extant manuscripts have been identified. At the end of the eighteenth century, when Nicolas-Sylvestre Bergier embarked on his apologia for the Catholic church, Du Châtelet's *Examens de la Bible* was one of the sources that he felt must be answered. This is yet more proof of her status in the Republic of Letters.[45]

A Courtier at Versailles and Fontainebleau

On a frosty morning in October 1740, Du Châtelet and the marquis were both at Fontainebleau, in attendance at the court. Usually they made their visits separately. While Du Châtelet was at Cirey, and then in Brussels, the marquis traveled from Champagne or from Lorraine to Paris, and then to

the royal palaces. He was the one who created the relationship with the new
duc de Lorraine, the queen's father, King Stanislas of Poland, and thus sus-
tained the Du Châtelet networks at Lunéville. In turn, when her husband
was away on campaign in the 1740s, the principal responsibility not only to
continue the advancement of his career, but also to provide for their daughter and their son, fell to her. She accepted this task of working "for the
grandeur of their line" as a source of pleasure. As she explained in her *Discours* on happiness, arranging for one's children was a reason why one delighted in the future.[46]

Courtiers commonly referred to the world they frequented as "ce pays-
ci," "this country," a space functioning like a country within a country, or,
more aptly, endless small sovereignties deriving their importance from the
carefully constructed grandeur and authority of the royal center, the king.
Louis XIV had created his galaxy of sun, planets, and the hierarchy of satellites in the last decades of his reign, with himself, to use a metaphor he actively touted, as *le roi-soleil* (the sun king). His great-grandson Louis XV
only came back to Versailles in his teens, but he wanted his court to function
just as it had in the time of the "Grand Monarch." A number of his and the
queen's favorite courtiers, such as the duc de Richelieu and Charles Philippe
d'Albret, the duc de Luynes, accepted responsibility when memories of
royal rituals and orders of precedence did not agree. So intricate and detailed were these rules that even an experienced courtier like the duchesse
de Luynes, *dame d'honneur* (first lady-in-waiting) to Her Majesty, made mis-
takes. Her own husband protested when she requested permission to leave
Fontainebleau—*prit congé* (took leave), as it was called—from the queen
before asking the king.[47]

One could join *ce pays-ci* at many levels of intimacy. Most distant would
be those who had only their friends or the news sheets for information. In
the years when Du Châtelet could not be at court or in Paris, she, her husband, and Voltaire depended on their correspondence to maintain their networks of information and potential favor. They read the *Gazette de France,*
where most news of the king appeared under the entries for Versailles:
lands assigned, appointments made. For example, the August 15, 1744, issue had much news of the war against England and Prussia, the numbers of
the wounded, and the names of those promoted, including the marquis Du
Châtelet to the rank of lieutenant general. In January 1745, with Voltaire in

the last stages of preparing the opera ballet to celebrate the marriage of the dauphin, she could peruse the list of the nobles designated to escort the young infanta and her household from the Spanish border to Versailles.[48]

On those ritual occasions when the king returned to Versailles from a military campaign, as many as two thousand people of every *état* could gather in the parks to see him and to greet him. The great gardens and parks created by Louis XIV's designer, Le Nôtre, were always open to the public, and anyone could attend the big fireworks displays and *fêtes* staged for ceremonial occasions and for the visits of foreign royalty. When she first moved to Paris in early 1739, Mme de Graffigny, like an eighteenth-century tourist, was accustomed to going to Versailles with her friends. They stayed in the town, went to the gardens, walked in the maze, and stood with others in the great public rooms of the palace, hoping to catch glimpses of the royal family. They might be seen at mass in the royal chapel, or in their public *appartements* on the days when the king and queen sat in review on their thrones, and then dined *en grand couvert,* attended by their courtiers, immediate family, and innumerable servants. Approximately three hundred people worked to create the display of the king eating his main meal of the day. Even for the monarch to have a drink of water, a series of courtiers and valets took a glass, filled it, had it tasted, and then passed it to one and then another of the men who had the right to participate in the completion of this simple task.[49] At public events, three to four thousand eager courtiers might fill the rooms along the central core of Versailles: the queen's antechamber, the *salon de la paix* (Hall of Peace), the *grande galerie* (Hall of Mirrors), and the *salon de la guerre* (Hall of War).

Up to twenty-five thousand people may have been officially involved with the court on a daily basis, according to some estimates. Foreign visitors were shocked by the mixing of ranks, and found it hard to tell the nobility from the servants. All these individuals benefited from being at the court, even if they never came near the king or queen. One might have the right of *bouche de la cour,* to eat at the king's kitchens—across the street, on the north side of the palace. All who attended the courtiers, and especially those who served the royal family, expected commissions on anything they bought for the court, and the proceeds from anything that had been discarded. Courtiers' servants sold leftover food at stalls outside the gates of the palace and thus fed many in the town. Two noble officeholders for the king's *grand couvert* argued over the partially empty wine bottles, a potential windfall of thirty thousand livres. Du Châtelet and other nobles made sure that these offices and the numbers of those with privileges never diminished in the course of Louis XV's reign. Functions disappeared, like the need for a captain to take responsibility for mules when no mules remained in the stables, but the titles, with their pensions and privileges, remained.[50]

The highest level of this country apart, where Du Châtelet and her husband exerted their efforts, despite its grandeur and ceremony, was a small world in which the marquise de Créqui, Du Châtelet's Froullay cousin, could name the fifteen to twenty great families. In Lorraine, the Du Châtelets in theory held this status. In France, however, even though the family could trace its ancestry back to the eleventh century, its members fell to the next level, and changes in regulations and procedures sometimes required new validation of their birthrights and the unbroken line of succession. In 1749, the marquis still owed a bit more than 890 livres for a new genealogy that had been required, perhaps because of the reorganizations of the military. Most prized of all was a post that carried the right of *entrée,* direct "access" to the royal family, which was literally the right to be in the king's presence. Failing this, like Du Châtelet in the first months of her return to the courtier's life, one sought *entrée* to officials or nobles who enjoyed this access, and thus the possibility of other connections that would bring the desired honors, offices, and pensions.[51]

"La vie civile," as Voltaire called it, demanded assiduous attention from those who wished to enjoy its bounty. Du Châtelet and her husband built their *crédit* in the traditional manner. In addition, she also enjoyed a number of valuable family connections. As was expected, sons of the different branches of the Du Châtelet family had risen in the king's infantry and cavalry. The marquis's cousin François-Bernardin served as commander of the hunt at Vincennes, married Richelieu's sister, and later became the governor of the Fortress of Vincennes. In April 1744, the king appointed François-Bernardin's daughter to the household for the new dauphine. Two members of Du Châtelet's mother's family, the Froullays, also of the *noblesse d'épée,* proved to be important advocates and supporters. Both she and Créqui wrote with respect of their uncle the *bailli* de Froullay, who from 1732 represented the ancient chivalric Order of Malta in France and held a number of minor but useful appointments from Louis XV that gave him access to the king and queen. On a Tuesday at the beginning of November 1745, he was part of the queen's evening of a *dîner* and then cards, thirty-two tables of *cavagnole* in her *appartements* at Fontainebleau. The king sent Froullay and his brother Charles François on several diplomatic missions. Du Châtelet also had many connections to the royal administration, to those among the most important of the king's advisers. The Lefèvre de Caumartins, her mother's cousins, served the king as councilors of state. The titular head of the Breteuil family, François-Victor le Tonnelier de Breteuil, became a minister in 1741.[52] Undeterred by his sudden death from a stroke in January 1743, Du Châtelet turned then to the cultivation of her ties with the marquis d'Argenson's brother, Marc-Pierre, comte d'Argenson, who was appointed his successor as secretary for war that same afternoon.

Vying for the *bons du roi,* favors in the gift of the king, created a tenuous, volatile world in *ce pays-ci.* A death, a marriage, a quarrel or disagreement that sent a courtier away from Versailles created *le bruit,* the word used to describe the rushing sound of rumor. Excitement was generated by the possibility of a vacancy, the opportunity for advancement: death in war meant a regiment for a new colonel; death in childbirth meant a widower and a potential new family alliance; a misplaced remark and loss of favor freed an *appartement* at Versailles. To take advantage of these shifts and turns required Du Châtelet's vigilance and more or less constant attendance on those whose *crédit* she depended upon. In addition to the carefully maintained fact of one's presence—for example, waiting with as many as sixty other petitioners in the antechamber to a minister like Breteuil or d'Argenson—Du Châtelet wrote letters, sent appropriate celebratory verses by Voltaire, and cultivated the currency of the snuffbox.

New Year's Day meant the king's distribution of offices and appointments. It was also the occasion for courtiers to write to their sponsors and to give small gifts. A number of Du Châtelet's letters to Frederick of Prussia offering New Year's greetings and respect have survived among his papers. In the 1740s, the snuffbox seems to have been the preferred gift. Louis XV bought thirty for his new young daughter-in-law, the dauphine, from the Parisian *bijoutier* Hébert, whom Du Châtelet also patronized. Du Châtelet kept part of her own collection in a walnut box. Their fanciful shapes and exotic materials give yet another glimpse of Du Châtelet's courtier's world:

an ivory one was carved in the shape of an onion; a square tortoiseshell box was lined in *vermeil*.[53]

Success for the Family: Breteuil Du Châtelet

From the late 1730s on, the immediate goal of Du Châtelet and her husband was the advancement of his career. The marquis's service in the wars of the 1740s, coupled with their connections and family ties, explains his steady rise from maréchal de camp in 1738 to one of eleven of the king's lieutenant generals in 1745. His appointment to the Ordre Militaire de Saint-Louis in June 1743 was also a particularly coveted honor, reserved by the king for those who, whether of high birth or not, had served him with distinction in war.[54] Du Châtelet's next priority was her children. Her daughter, Gabrielle-Pauline, turned sixteen in 1742, and Du Châtelet must have used her father's and mother's families' diplomatic ties to the Italian courts to negotiate the advantageous marriage of her daughter to the duc de Montenaro-Carafa, a member of the Neapolitan papal aristocracy. Though Voltaire, in a letter to one of his young followers, mocked this young relative of a previous pope for his big nose and sunken chest—ironically, not unlike Voltaire's own physique—Du Châtelet was pleased with herself, her cleverly negotiated system of dowry payments, and the opportunity she had created for her daughter. Her letters gave news of the young woman's progress to her new home. Married in April 1743, she traveled to Naples by way of Rome. Du Châtelet reported to Cideville on July 28, 1743, that her daughter had found the trip "very agreeable" and that "it seems to me that she begins to be consoled," presumably adjusting to the dramatic changes in her life and the demands of her new status within the Italian aristocracy. Jacquier met her in Naples, and Du Châtelet would write to him of the young woman's pregnancy, and in 1747 of her successes, including her appointment as a lady-in-waiting to the queen of Naples, the highest honor available to a noblewoman, and one that Gabrielle-Pauline had "desired very much."[55]

By the end of 1743, Du Châtelet had turned her attention to her son, Florent-Louis. Although she had insisted on a relatively unorthodox education for him in mathematics, physics, and philosophy, she knew that he would follow the military career dictated by his Lorraine heritage and his lineage. His entrance into the Royal Musketeers in June 1740 signaled the auspicious beginning of his career. A family could do no better, for service in this special corps meant the continuation of his education at royal expense, as well as easy admission to the ranks of officers in the king's army and to the most prestigious of the royal regiments. From twelve to sixteen, the young boy learned the skills deemed necessary for an officer: some engineering information and dressage, to name only two. As early as January 1743, Du Châtelet noted to Cideville that she was working on "the establishment of my son." A letter later that year mentioning five hundred livres for her husband to arrange "l'équipage" for their son probably indicated approval for his appointment to one of the king's regiments, first as a lieutenant and an aide-de-camp to his father. At nineteen, as a result of her efforts, he had his own infantry command. Key to this success was Du Châtelet's ability to generate capital at crucial moments; the price of the regiment of Quercy was thirty thousand livres.[56]

Du Châtelet's letters tell nothing of aspirations for herself. Perhaps just after her marriage, or now, in the early 1740s, when she again spent most of her time in Paris and at the court, Du Châtelet was formally presented to the king and the queen. Any number of the members of her and her husband's families—Froullays, Breteuils, Du Châtelets, and collateral relatives—had been granted this honor and enjoyed the privileges it brought, principally to be part of the ritual day and entertainments of Their Majesties.[57] The right to be presented lay in the gift of the king. The ceremony began at Versailles the night before, when Du Châtelet would have made ceremonial visits to the queen's *dames d'honneur,* to the king's daughters, to the princesses of the Blood (Bourbon relatives), and to the king's sisters-in-law. The actual presentation day was set by the king, always a Sunday, and it was exhausting for the favored courtier. Probably Du Châtelet would have dressed at her *hôtel* in Paris—perhaps she chose the green brocade *habit de cour,* with its gold and silk embroidery. She would have traveled to Versailles in the green-velvet-upholstered coach—the *berline* with the family crest painted on the door, her liveried servants in attendance. Only after she had arrived at the palace would she have ordered her *femme de chambre* to attach the *bas de robe,* the long train, the length of which was determined by her rank.

At her height of five feet six, Du Châtelet would have made an elegant presence. With her sponsor, she would have had to walk in her heavy gown, the train laid out behind her, through most of the rooms on the queen's side of the palace, through the *salle des gardes* and the antechamber to the royal Grand Cabinet. Du Châtelet made the deep bow of the *révérence* at the door, again midway to the queen, and then, a third time, in front of Her Majesty. The queen rose to receive her official gestures of homage. The queen then sat down again to indicate the end of the ceremony. The worst part remained: the marquise would have to make three more *révérences* as she backed out of the queen's presence, kicking the train—well over fifteen meters of fabric—out of the way with her right foot. The chances of falling, or at the least losing one's mule (the backless shoe favored at court), were great. Having completed this ritual with the queen, Du Châtelet and her sponsor would present themselves to the king at his quarters across the *cour de marbe* (Marble Courtyard), on the opposite side of the palace.[58]

At the beginning of October 1745, Du Châtelet had told the queen she hoped to enjoy the "bontés de la Reine" (the kindnesses of the queen), to accompany her from Versailles to Fontainebleau in one of the royal *carrosses,* probably as part of the exercise of her new rights. Du Châtelet, however, arrived from Paris only fifteen minutes before the queen was to leave. This did not presage well for her inauguration into the rituals of the queen's life. Her Majesty left the palace immediately after mass and took her place in the first *carrosse* with the duchesse de Luynes and three of her other ladies. Over-anxious, nervous, distracted, oblivious, her motives unclear, Du Châtelet rushed to the second *carrosse,* stepped up, sat down, and then looked out and asked the other three women, waiting in astonishment, to come in as well. Whether it was the order of precedence or the apparent impudence of her invitation to those above her in *état* is not clear. "Shocked," the three women left her to herself and went to the third *carrosse*. Who might ride where and in what order was as significant as any other set of rituals at the court. The duc de Richelieu always rode in the king's second *carrosse*. "A little embarrassed," according to the duc de Luynes, whose wife must have told him the story, Du Châtelet stepped out of the *carrosse* and assumed she should join the other women. A servant, instructed by the others, informed her there was no room. Not to be defeated, Du Châtelet simply returned to the empty *carrosse* and made the journey alone.[59]

Although the story of this "tracasserie," Du Châtelet's error in protocol, had reached the Paris *nouvellistes* and gossips by the end of the next week, the duc de Luynes, who was the court's unofficial expert on protocol, excused Du Châtelet's unfortunate faux pas. In an uncharacteristically sympathetic manner, Luynes offered an explanation for Du Châtelet's "hauteur," her prideful action. On the one hand, she was "filled with the grandeur of the house of Du Châtelet and the prerogatives that she believed were its due." On the other, he acknowledged her amazing accomplishments. "One could not have more *esprit*, nor more *science*; she has a thorough knowledge of even the most abstract *sciences*, and has composed a book that was published." He concluded: "She is so lively that she sometimes is absentminded." The duc's wife and the queen seem to have been similarly understanding. The next day, Richelieu, having learned of "her adventure," as he described it, spoke on her behalf. He asked the duchesse de Luynes to make Du Châtelet's "excuses" to the queen, and to indicate his own disapproval of his friend's conduct. Du Châtelet also went to see this most important woman of the queen's household. Nothing was left for the gossips: "The excuses were well received by the queen, and there was no more to this affair." All the fun of the scandal was forgotten when, on Saturday, November 20, the queen went to Choisy, and Du Châtelet did not ride alone, but in the second *carrosse* with the usual royal attendants. Others would know of this honor, for a list was issued a few days before indicating who would be allowed to accompany Her Majesty to this or another of the smaller residences frequented by the king in his passion for hunting. Thus, despite her missteps, Du Châtelet had become part of the group invited to attend the queen.

In the 1740s, the queen, Marie Leszczyńska of Poland, had her own fairly rigid routine—subject, of course, to her ceremonial duties and to abrupt changes at the pleasure of the king, who might summon her to eat *en grand couvert*, or to follow him to Marly or Choisy. This had not always been the case. Louis XV had been quite taken with his Polish bride, the finalist in a field of seventeen possible wives, in the first years of their marriage. Married in 1725, Maria Leszczyńska presented him with ten children in the next twelve years. Only one son survived, but there were numerous daughters. From 1738, when, according to the gossips, the king ceased to come to her bed, they led more separate lives. Maria Leszczyńska enjoyed her children and visited her daughters at the convent of Fontevrault, where they had been sent for their education. And she spent time in her own *appartements*, where she busied herself with needlework, a game of *piquet,* or listening to a history or book of piety read aloud. She usually had with her her most intimate attendants, her particular favorites: Marie Brûlart, duchesse de Luynes, and her husband, the duc; the duchesse de Villars, daughter of the supervisor of Versailles; Président Hénault, her chamberlain; her *lecteur,* or "reader," the playwright Moncrif.[60]

The queen, as the center of the court party, *les dévots,* was known for her religious devotions. To be in attendance would mean mass at least once and sometimes twice a day, and there were more observances on holy days and important devotional days or religious fêtes. As part of her Holy Week Easter ritual, on April 15, 1745, the queen heard the sermon, received absolution, and then washed the feet of twelve young girls, chosen for their poverty. The queen's piety was tempered by her love of music, a taste she shared with her son, the dauphin, and indulged with concerts once or twice a week in the *salon de la paix,* a large room between her *chambre à coucher* (bedchamber) and the *grande galerie,* the Hall of Mirrors. The duc de Luynes described one such evening: two hours of chamber music with five musicians, strings, harpsichord, and a German flute, and selections from different operas performed by two of Paris's best opera singers.[61]

As part of the queen's broader circle, Du Châtelet joined these larger gatherings and would usually attend the other entertainments scheduled at Versailles. The Comédie française, the Comédie italienne, and the royal opera company from the Académie royale de musique performed Tuesdays, Wednesdays, or Thursdays. The theater at Versailles, a relatively small stage with seating for only a portion of the thousands of courtiers, had been constructed off the *cour des princes* (Princes' Courtyard), to the left side of the queen's wing of the palace. The companies also acted at Fontainebleau when the royal couple was in attendance there. The *premier gentilhomme,* one of the four nobles in immediate attendance to the king, not only supervised the theaters in Paris, giving his consent for productions and sometimes helping to gain money from the king for a particular production, but also chose what would be played at court. Louis XV enjoyed the theater. Between 1740 and 1750, there were 626 performances for the court, twice as many each year as in his great-grandfather's day. Despite the king's lingering discomfort with and distrust of Voltaire, and the active disapproval of some of the queen's circle, the Comédie française did perform eleven of his plays at court over the decade, some of them—*Oedipe, Alzire, Zaïre*—four or five times, with *Mérope* the sentimental favorite at seven performances.[62]

Advancing Voltaire's Career and Winning the Prize

In addition to seeking favors for the advancement of her husband and children, Du Châtelet wanted to use the *crédit* available to her to protect Voltaire as she had in the past, and to secure new honors and position for him. She felt, as he did, that one of the great injustices had been the omission of France's "greatest poet" from the ranks of the Académie française. Year after year, audiences and readers anticipated his new plays and new editions of his works, and yet he had not been elected to the august body founded by Louis XIV to honor the nation's most renowned and learned men of letters. The chosen were those who could marshal the right support from existing members, from the literary and social elite of Paris—for example, those who attended the *salon* of Mme Lambert, and after her death that of Mme Du Deffand or Mme de Tencin—and from the ministers who advised the king. Voltaire's gift for notoriety and controversy worked against him in each of those venues. To his friends and noble patrons, his ability to sabotage their best efforts must have seemed almost deliberate. Mme de Graffigny wrote Devaux of an interchange between Voltaire and Du Châtelet when she visited Cirey in the winter of 1738–39. He had told a story of an abbé making a fool of himself in front of the king. Mocking this man, whom he dubbed the "king's fool," he asked Du Châtelet if she was in need of a fool. "No, my friend," she replied, "the post is not vacant."[63]

✥

Du Châtelet's efforts to protect Voltaire from the potential consequences of his own actions had taken many forms over the years. She had kept him away from Paris. With the 1734 *lettre de cachet* always available to the ministers, Cirey was a refuge in all senses of the word, as was Brussels. The pious advisers to the queen made a clear case against him as an atheist. This influenced Louis XV. Nor did the king see Voltaire's flirtation with Frederick of Prussia and their first meeting in 1740 in a positive light. After he became king, the young Frederick's military victories and diplomatic machinations in the War of Austrian Succession, including a separate peace with Maria

Theresa, only raised more questions about Voltaire's loyalty—not just to the church but also to the crown.

Du Châtelet saw no good in the courtship between the elder poet-mentor and his young Apollo, as Voltaire addressed Frederick. Voltaire enjoyed the excitement of flirting with his royal admirer, who appreciated his talents and courted the elder Frenchman, hoping he would join the collection of learned *philosophes* assembled at Berlin, including Maupertuis and Algarotti. Du Châtelet was certainly jealous and fearful that Voltaire would leave her for the reflected glory of his student prince. In the fall of 1740, when Voltaire went to The Hague, she had gone to Fontainebleau and argued on the poet's behalf, only to have her efforts undermined once again by his imprudent decision to meet with Frederick. In her letter to the duc de Richelieu, she proudly announced that she had in three weeks "regained all that [Voltaire] had tried to lose for the last ten years." She had argued successfully for him, resolved the most difficult aspect of his situation, and procured for him "an honorable return to his country." "The benevolence of the minister," she continued, had "reopened for him the route to the académies." How did he thank her for so much zeal and attachment? By leaving for Berlin. "I have been cruelly paid for all that I did at Fontainebleau," she concluded.[64]

Voltaire's own efforts early in the 1740s to prove his orthodoxy and his loyalty, far from eliciting favor, raised new doubts about his character and occasioned new displeasure with his activities. He believed that his play *Mahomet* would be interpreted as a condemnation of the tyrant of Islam, and thus a demonstration of his Christian faith. To those who watched the first performance by the Comédie française on August 9, 1742, however, it was not the portrayal of Mohammed that struck them, but the appeals to the deity by the young heroine and her brother. Some interpreted this as Deism, a faith lacking the intervention of the established rituals and institutions of France's official religion. Du Châtelet was with Voltaire when the lieutenant of police delivered the government ultimatum that *Mahomet* must be withdrawn from the stage, and with the least *bruit,* if the playwright did not wish to suffer the consequences of the ever-present *lettre de cachet.* Voltaire's subsequent efforts to make it appear that Pope Benedict XIV approved of the play had little effect.[65]

In addition, the published version of *Mahomet* that appeared only a few months later included a gushing dedication to Frederick of Prussia: "My heart, deeply penetrated with the sense of your majesty's goodness, knows no grief but that which arises from my incapacity of being always with you." Voltaire tried to turn a second meeting with Frederick, in 1743, into proof of his loyalty to Louis XV by presenting himself to the government ministers as a potential spy. He made no secret of his goals, writing on December 30, 1743, that he awaited the king's orders and that these "secret liaisons" in which he had been engaged would, he hoped, "perhaps place me in a state of demonstrating my zeal for the service of his majesty." On his return to France, as further evidence of his loyalty, Voltaire made it known that he had refused a pension of twelve thousand livres, a house, and the opportunity to eat with the dowager queen of Prussia.[66] Such apparent sacrifice, however, meant little to Louis XV, his ministers, or his courtiers, who saw their privileged society as the center of civilization.

~❧~

Du Châtelet had written to her close friend and relative, Louis François Armand Du Plessis, duc de Richelieu, of her annoyance in connection with Voltaire's first trip to Prussia, because the duc and the duchesse had been among Voltaire's most influential and effective advocates. Throughout the 1730s, the duchesse in particular had calmed the appropriate minister's rage and stilled the periodic storms. Du Châtelet, in turn, attended her as she passed through the traditional events of a marriage, including her pregnancies and the births of her son and daughter, and visited with her in 1739, when the tuberculosis that would ultimately kill the duchesse became more aggressive.

After the duchesse's death in August 1740, Du Châtelet continued to count on the duc to aid her with each project on behalf of her family and Voltaire. Her faith could not have been better placed. Richelieu thrived as a courtier. His reputation for seduction and his ability to produce willing sexual partners, coupled with his love of hunting, had made him a good companion to Louis XV and won him the king's friendship. In addition, he became a trusted military commander, rising to the coveted rank of maréchal. Du Châtelet's husband, and then her son, served with Richelieu in the German campaigns during the War of Austrian Succession. One government minister described Richelieu as fearless in battle: "He scorns death as a gambler scorns ruin, loving the risks and trusting himself only to fortune." Maurepas could continue to denigrate him as succeeding only "par le canal des femmes"—through women's channels—with the obviously smutty double meaning as both vagina and intermediary. Still, Richelieu collected one lucrative, important royal appointment after another. In February 1744, he outmaneuvered the disgruntled courtier; Richelieu, not Maurepas, became one of the four first *gentilshommes de la chambre du roi*, the highest ceremonial post for a man at court. So favored was Richelieu that he always had an *appartement* at Versailles. In the 1740s, he lived on the floor above the king's public rooms, on the corridor that was reserved for the succession of royal mistresses. He had numbers 56 and 57. Mme le Normant d'Etioles, the most accomplished of Louis XV's *maîtresses-en-titre*, with whom Richelieu enjoyed a polite but chilly relationship, had her *appartement* at numbers 61 and 62, just a few doors away.[67]

As one of the four *gentilshommes de la chambre du roi*, he had constant direct access to the king from the time His Majesty woke up until he retired. His duties included handing the monarch his *épée* and his hat, and answering royal requests throughout the long day of ceremonies and activities. He frequently participated in the dinners in the king's private quarters, and on occasion a *petit couvert* for the selected few. So important was his post that those seeking influence gave the duc money toward its cost: the *salonnière* Mme de Tencin contributed forty thousand livres. The duc became one of what Voltaire referred to in his instructions to his man of business as "my illustrious debtors." The poet might write at length and hint at lawsuits, but he could only close in the ritual language emblematic of the difference in their *états*: "I console myself with a bit of philosophy and above all with the hope that your kindness to me continues." Richelieu found a way to show that "kindness" almost immediately after assuming his post as *premier gentilhomme*. One of his duties in 1744 entailed responsibility for all of the entertainments at court. The dauphin was to be married, and Louis XV wanted the festivities to rival those of his great-grandfather. In fact, this would be the first elaborate celebration of his reign. Richelieu chose Voltaire to write the celebratory opera for the event. Jean-Philippe Rameau, the playwright's sometime collaborator, was to provide the music.[68]

By April 1744, Du Châtelet and Voltaire had returned to Cirey so that both could work. Initially, the marquis was with them, but by the last week in April, he was called back to the war. Both Du Châtelet and Voltaire claimed to friends that they had recaptured much of what they had known at Cirey in the first years of their time together. Du Châtelet confided to d'Argental, "I am finally at this charming Cirey, which is more charming than ever." She could report, "Your friend appears to be enchanted to be here."[69] Voltaire had already written of his pleasure at the prospect of a return to Cirey. In that spring and summer of 1744, the small château and its "delicious solitude" did not disappoint him. He called it "a jewel" and arranged for a mason to carve verses at the entrance to his *galerie,* praising this refuge from society, exalting in its profound peace and the happiness it gave. Hénault, who stopped on his way to and from taking the waters at Plombières, described their pleasures: "The one makes verses in his corner and the other triangles." Du Châtelet wrote to d'Argental of her pleasure in showing this well-connected courtier "ma maison" (my house), and particularly noted his astonishment at all they enjoyed in so remote a corner of France. They cried together when Voltaire read act III of his libretto for *La Princesse de Navarre* to them.[70] However, neither Hénault nor Du Châtelet refrained from suggesting changes and corrections.

Voltaire had the usual problems with copyists, and Du Châtelet must have made demands on their time as well. She was then finishing her new edition of her *Dissertation* on fire, and perhaps also her *Examens de la Bible.* In addition, the physicist-mathematician père Jacquier, editor of the new annotated Latin edition of Newton's *Principia,* paid an extended visit from May to July, giving Du Châtelet an opportunity to consult him about a possible next project: a translation of this monumental work of mathematics and physics into French. Though her work went well, Voltaire, needing the approval of Rameau and Richelieu over his commission for the dauphin's wedding, ran into problems. As in the past with Voltaire's artistic difficulties, Du Châtelet and he counted on their friend the comte d'Argental to act as intermediary. Voltaire described *La Princesse de Navarre* to d'Argental as a "new genre," a "comédie-ballet," in which, instead of continuous musical accompaniment, the orchestral parts were interlaced between the "speeches of the actors." He hoped that his friend would explain to Richelieu that "the great symphonic constructions" natural for an event of this sort were not appropriate on this occasion.

Given the purpose of the opera, Rameau's ego, and Richelieu's mandate from the king, Voltaire's changes in the form did not find favor. By the second week in July, Du Châtelet feared for his health and devoted all her time to him. She assured d'Argental that she would have Voltaire do all of the corrections, but asked him not to express any discontent with Voltaire's work at this time. "His health," she explained, "is in a frightful state, he has made himself distressed, worried himself, forced himself to work, given himself fever, and now he is in a terrible languor." He did not eat or sleep. But this crisis passed, and rehearsals began in September. Most important, Richelieu saw the final draft before leaving to supervise the ritual procession of the dauphine from the Franco-Spanish border north to Versailles, and he was "content." Historians estimate the production costs at six hundred thousand livres. Mlle Camargo, the star of the Paris ballet, was one of forty dancers; 220 others sang and played small parts. As the date of the performance approached, from February 18, 1745, on, all of the court musicians were engaged in the rehearsals. In the end, Voltaire won his royal favor. It was reported that the king was also "very content."[71]

Du Châtelet would have been an eager if distant participant in all that went on the day of the wedding and the opera, February 23. The king had already announced the most important arrangements for the life of the new dauphine. Most opportunely, Du Châtelet's friends the elder duchesse de Brancas and the duchesse de Lauraguais had been named her principal attendants. The young Spanish princess, Marie-Thérèse-Raphaële, arrived on the twenty-first for a sequence of ritual introductions to the king, to the dauphin, to the royal family, and to the court at large. On the twenty-third at one o'clock, the nineteen-year-old was dressed in silver brocade decorated with pearls. She joined the dauphin—at sixteen, three years her junior—resplendent in his coat of cloth of gold and diamonds, in the procession following the queen, *mesdames* (the king's daughters), and the princes of the Blood. They marched from the *Grande Galerie* through the king's *appartements,* where he joined them, down the broad Stairway of the Ambassadors to the chapel on the ground floor. There, in the presence of the principal officers and participants in the everyday rituals of the court, the couple knelt at the altar. Cardinal de Rohan blessed the ring for the dauphine and gave the nuptial benediction. After mass, the court procession made its way back into the main part of the palace. Voltaire and Rameau's opera began at seven that evening. For the event, Du Châtelet would have worn her richest, most elegant *habit de cour*—perhaps the "robe à la Toscanne" with its gold background on the finest Italian silk, valued at 250 livres, and the three-hundred-thousand-livre diamond collar and ten-thousand-livre earrings that belonged to her husband's family and thus were hers to wear on such an occasion.[72]

No part of the Riding School arena, which Richelieu had converted into the theater, or *salle de spectacle,* would have been recognizable. At one end was the stage, with its three arcades to create perspective, and seating for sixty musicians. Two levels of loges had been constructed along both sides, and a long rectangular space of sixty-three meters for use as the parterre. Stucco decoration had been sculpted on the fronts of the twenty loges for the royal family and their attendants, on the Ionic columns with their garlands of leaves, over the proscenium arch, and on the stage itself. Glass chandeliers hung from the ceiling, which was painted in trompe l'oeil, a vast sky of clouds and figures, as if these divinities, too, had come to watch. No surface was left ungilded or undecorated. The "opéra-ballet" could only seem a pale reflection. And so Voltaire complained: the size of the stage dwarfed the actors, and the huge vault of the space and the loudness of the instruments meant that no one heard his libretto.

Much of the expense of the theater arose from Richelieu's biggest challenge, as he explained to the duc de Luynes: how to convert the theater into a ballroom in just twenty-four hours for the *bal paré,* the next major event of the festivities. Du Châtelet would have attended this as well. Like the other members of the court, she would have received her invitation from the duc de Richelieu, by "order of the king," for five o'clock in the afternoon of February 24. Each day brought new entertainments. On February 25, there was a *souper au grand couvert,* and then a *bal masqué* at midnight. To attend, one only needed a mask, and almost fifteen hundred people crowded into the king's *appartements:* the Halls of Hercules, Mars, Mercury, and Apollo, the *grandes salles* stretching one after another along the north wing of the palace. Three buffets with wine and food had been set up in the *galerie* surrounding the Stairway of the Ambassadors. What contemporaries remembered, however, was not the music, the food, or the guests, but the candles. All the rooms in the royal section of the palace had been lit for the occasion. The celebration stretched on intermittently into April. As the weeks passed, Du Châtelet's enthusiasm for it seems to have waned. She wrote to Bernoulli's son from Versailles that she had not yet seen La Condamine, who had finally returned to Paris from his equatorial expedition to verify Newton's hypothesis about the shape of the earth, "because the marriage festivities of monsieur the dauphin have scarcely permitted me to leave here."[73]

Mme de Graffigny conveyed the gossip of Versailles to Devaux: the sixteen-year-old dauphin doted on his bride, called her "'my wife'" in public, and "caresses her like a bourgeois." There was news of Louis XV as well. In his thirties, he was still considered handsome, healthy, and vigorous, a presence when he walked among his courtiers or received them on ceremonial occasions. Everyone knew that a new woman, Mme d'Etioles, had been the object of his attention at the *bal masqué* and had attended the theater with him as well. Graffigny had not yet heard, however, of Voltaire's next piece of good fortune, yet more bounty from his association with the duc de Richelieu. Like the playwright Racine before him, he had been named historiographer of France, with a yearly pension of two thousand livres postdated to the previous January.[74] Du Châtelet certainly influenced this appointment, for it guaranteed that her companion could now regularly participate in events at court. If Voltaire performed this literary role well, he would increase his chances of finally winning one of the honored *fauteuils*, literally one of the forty armchairs reserved for the members of the Académie française. Yet a third chance to shine came within weeks.

Richelieu sent instructions for Voltaire to compose a poem commemorating the king's victory against the English at the Battle of Fontenoy on May 11. This gave Voltaire the immediate opportunity he needed to publicize his skills and his new post. Because Richelieu played a key role in the winning strategy at Fontenoy, Voltaire could, while glorifying the role of his sovereign, also glorify that of his generous patron. In forty successive editions, the poem "La Bataille de Fontenoy" grew from its original hundred verses to 350. Maurepas finally called a halt to the display with the fortieth edition, remarking that the constant changing gave the poem "the faults of an old ecstasy." Louis XV rewarded his poet-historiographer with the battle's commemorative medal, valued at fifteen thousand livres. Voltaire responded with plans for a history of the king's wars. Louis XV could not have helped being impressed by Voltaire's research at the offices of the *bureaux de la guerre*, with French ministers and officers, and even with members of the English command. In addition, Richelieu gave Voltaire and Rameau another commission: for a "comédie-ballet" to celebrate the success of this war. They called it *Le Temple de la gloire* (The Temple of Glory). Presented at Versailles November 27, it was a disaster. At the *souper* (late night supper) after the performance, Louis XV spoke briefly to Rameau but ignored Voltaire. "Trajan," as Voltaire now called the king, was bored. Voltaire had no part in the festivities for the next grand celebration at Versailles, in February 1747.[75]

This did not, however, mean the end of Voltaire's life as a courtier. Jeanne-Antoinette Poisson, Mme le Normant d'Etioles, the royal mistress first brought to public attention at the *bal masqué* in honor of the dauphine's marriage, seemed to offer the prospect of new access to royal favor. Though from a bourgeois family, she had been schooled for her role and proved a brilliant student. At the height of her powers, she was, as one courtier noted, "a woman any man would have wanted as a mistress." Her portraits illustrate the physical traits he admired—the oval face, the "magnificent complexion, superb hands and arms"—but her sweet expressions and formal poses give no hint of the part of her face that seemed most important to the nobleman: her "eyes which were pretty if on the smallish side, yet which possessed a fieriness, an intelligence and a brilliance that I have never seen in any other woman." Within weeks of the dauphin's marriage, Graffigny knew that the twenty-four-year-old was officially separating from her husband and could report to Devaux the nicknames the lovers used: "Chat Roi [King Cat]" and "Belle Minette [Pretty Pussy]." The king arranged the purchase of the property that authorized her to assume the title of "marquise de Pompadour" soon after. Despite the enmity of the dauphin and the most devout of the queen's party, Pompadour was formally presented at court and became Louis XV's official *maîtresse-en-titre*. She ingratiated herself with Maria Leszczyńska who, according to Luynes, often remarked, "Since there is a mistress, she liked madame de Pompadour better than any other."[76]

Du Châtelet and Pompadour shared the friendship of members of the *haute noblesse* who surrounded the king in his private quarters. Du Châtelet also watched rehearsals, if not the finished performances of Les Petits Cabinets, so named because of the intimacy of the gatherings, the theatrical troupe formed as a means to amuse the king. Wednesday at 5:45 p.m. did not conflict with any other entertainments, and so became the usual time for their performances. No tragedies were staged, only the lightest operas and comedies, with the royal favorite usually taking the ingenue role.[77]

Though the king's general distaste for Voltaire meant that Pompadour rarely suggested his plays, she certainly facilitated his appointment to a new ceremonial post despite his lack of noble birth—*gentilhomme ordinaire de la chambre du roi*. It carried no duties, but it gave him that most coveted of privileges, the right of *entrée* to the king. Voltaire heard in April 1745 that it would soon be his. The real prize, however, would not be this court appointment but recognition as a member of the Académie française. Men had been admitted on much less in the way of publications than even *La Henriade*, Voltaire's youthful achievement. As the comparisons of his plays to those of Corneille and Racine multiplied, the neglect of his candidacy became ever more glaring. Beginning in 1731, over fifteen years, Du Châtelet and Voltaire watched Maupertuis, Bernis, Du Resnel, Moncrif, Marivaux, and even Dortous de Mairan each gain one of the forty *fauteuils*. Du Châtelet used her influence when she could. For the vacancy in 1742 that eventually went to Marivaux, she enlisted the support of Richelieu and Cardinal Fleury, though they, too, were then political rivals and thus unlikely to support the same candidate. Mme de Tencin, the *salonnière*, wrote to Richelieu on the inappropriateness of the "vivacity that she [Du Châtelet] had put into this affair." Tencin opposed Voltaire because of his reputation as an atheist. The Academician Mirepoix, one of the dauphin's former *précepteurs*, opposed him on similar grounds in 1743, when Fleury's death created another opening. With so many opportunities lost, whether the result of conscious choice or merely new circumstances, Du Châtelet and Voltaire changed their tactics. They would seek not only the support of many more members of the Académie and the advisers to the king, but also the acquiescence of Voltaire's most determined enemies. Like the wisest strategists, they realized that they must not only elicit approval but also quiet all opposition.[78]

༄ঙ৯৯

To seek allies and to silence enemies meant courting the influential in Paris as well as at Versailles. Du Châtelet and Voltaire had the *hôtel* she had leased for them in the best of neighborhoods, in the parish of Saint-Roch, on the rue Traversière. Proximity to the rue Saint-Honoré meant an easy journey by sedan chair to the Place Vendôme, where Président Hénault, part of the queen's circle, owned no. 7. Mme de Tencin favored her guests with *entrée* to her *salon* in her suite of rooms at the convent of the Filles de la Conception, at no. 382, rue Neuve Saint-Honoré. The campaign to quiet opposition meant cultivating the two legendary *salonnières* in Paris who had often worked to block Voltaire's nomination for the Académie française. Claudine Alexandrine Guérin de Tencin, now in her sixties, had been the most active in her opposition to Voltaire. In her eyes, his fate had been determined by his 1734 *Lettres philosophiques*. She made no secret of her distaste for his impiety, despite the irreligious acts of her own youth, including escape from a convent, numerous affairs, and an illegitimate son (who was raised by his father, given the name d'Alembert, and grew up to be a mathematician and editor of the *Encyclopédie*).[79] By the time Du Châtelet and Voltaire returned from Brussels, her brother, the abbé Tencin, had risen to the rank of cardinal in the church, and together they presided over a *salon* that had acquired a reputation as the most learned in Paris.

Although some of Du Châtelet's biographers have placed her at the afternoon and evening gatherings, her participation would have been occasional at best. Tencin, like her *salonnière* predecessor Mme Lambert, wished to be the center of what she called "ma ménagerie." Three members of the Republic of Letters who had regularly attended Lambert's *salon* came to her *dîners* on Tuesday afternoons: Fontenelle, Marivaux, and Dortous de Mairan. She chose four others, two of them also members of the Académie française. Her "seven sages"—"mes bêtes," "mes chiens," as she also called them—gave her *salon* its esteemed aura. Although she treated them like servants or worse with these nicknames ("my beasts," "my dogs"), and with her New Year's gift of two *aulnes* of velvet for making *culottes* (loose trousers), they enjoyed her biting, vicious jibes, her intellectual puzzles, her requirement of continual *bons mots,* and the favors she worked to acquire for them. Her most famous maxim placed her clearly above the men of letters she entertained and challenged: "The great error of men of wit is to not believe that men are as stupid as they are." If "stupid" was her usual insult for a man, "ugly" she reserved for women. Du Châtelet seems to have been immune from Tencin's jibes. When Voltaire had visited Frederick of Prussia for an extended period in the fall of 1743, the younger woman spent time with Tencin. The acerbic *salonnière* wrote to Richelieu with uncharacteristic charity for Du Châtelet: "She is crazy, but she isn't bad."[80] Had Tencin chosen to support Voltaire, it would have made a significant difference. In the end, her silence had the same effect.

Though Voltaire had a long history of association with the marquise Du Deffand, the other *salonnière* with a particular interest in the Académie française, he finally approached her only indirectly, through the men who attended her *salon*. Marie de Vichy-Chamrond lived separately from her noble military husband for most of her marriage, and it was through her long-term though not exclusive liaison with Hénault that she was introduced to the court of the duchesse du Maine at Sceaux. She also visited other important families well connected with the court, including the duchesse de Luynes, who was her aunt. In 1739, she established herself in the rue de Beaune, and there entertained Hénault and others of his circle. Sunday was her designated afternoon and evening. She prided herself on mixing what she considered "cultivated aristocrats" and the *gens des lettres,* so she entertained many from among Du Châtelet's and Voltaire's regular companions, both women and men. Hénault described the evolution of her gatherings: "Soon there was assembled there the best and most brilliant company; and all subjugated to her."[81]

Though Du Deffand accepted both Du Châtelet and Voltaire into her circle, they also fell victim to her scorn. Her portrait of Du Châtelet was one of many vicious images resulting from the popular game she enjoyed: making quick descriptions of contemporaries. The aging *salonnière* chose to highlight Du Châtelet's masculine physical and mental qualities—her height, for example—and also to mock her feminine enjoyment of dressing well. She ridiculed Du Châtelet's acting and singing, declaring she only performed to become "a princess." Du Châtelet's laugh, her teeth, her facial expressions—all were cited as negatives. The woman did geometry just to appear superior to other women, as if singularity gave this status. In addition, she spoke Latin only in front of those who could not understand it. Du Deffand even questioned her authorship of the *Institutions*.

From the fall of 1745, Voltaire solicited promises of votes from members of the Académie. After Du Châtelet's admission to the queen's evenings, she had the opportunity to help in the execution of another key aspect of their strategy, the need for Marie Leszczyńska's tacit acceptance. For, though the queen played no direct role in the process of nomination and selection, her piety and that of some of her ladies made her a powerful, if discreet, opponent. Allies had to be secured among her circle, starting with those who already appreciated Voltaire's skills as a playwright and Du

Châtelet's energy and intelligence. Hénault, as the queen's *chancelier,* certainly had influence with her. She enjoyed his company and conversation so much that she sought him out at her own gatherings and when she went to those of others. At *souper* in the duchesse de Luynes's *appartement,* she even left her daughters and the courtiers at their card games to enjoy another three-quarters of an hour with him.[82]

Du Châtelet also attended these late-night activities in the quarters of the duchesse de Luynes, across the prince's courtyard, in the south wing of the palace. She would have taken advantage of such proximity to soften the queen's hostility to Voltaire, particularly after the poet had been so enthusiastic in praising the king with his celebration of the Battle of Fontenoy. The queen's *lecteur,* Moncrif, also could have been helpful to Du Châtelet in this regard. Voltaire actively cultivated the former playwright's support. Their paths continued to cross in Paris, at the theater, the opera, and the *salons* they both attended. In 1743, Voltaire sent him his verses on Fontenoy, asking that Moncrif "tell the queen" how important it was to him to work in the service of "her husband and her son." He closed affectionately with "Aimez-moy. V"—"Love me, V."[83]

On March 19, 1746, the presiding officer of the *parlement* of Dijon died. *Fauteuil* number 12 fell vacant. Although Voltaire admitted to d'Argental that he was ill and felt that he had not been active enough to count on the king's assent, he rallied. He and Du Châtelet spent the next weeks gathering support and neutralizing any remaining opposition. Pompadour could have spoken to her adviser, abbé Bernis, another member of the Académie française. Tencin had no candidate of her own on this occasion, but one of her seven sages gave his support, thus perhaps indicating that others would vote in Voltaire's favor as well. An attack in the Jansenist press against the poet's impiety called up an immediate public response from Voltaire directed to the principal of his *collège,* in which he offered a clear confession of his faith: "I want to live and die tranquilly in the bosom of the catholic, apostolic, roman Church without attacking anyone."[84] This public statement gained the support of the Jesuits at court, including the king's confessor. By the second week in April 1746, Graffigny reported to Devaux that Richelieu had gained the assent of Louis XV. Even Maurepas, perhaps at Du Châtelet's urging, dared not object.

The last letters Voltaire wrote in this campaign were to Moncrif: "I place myself in your hands, and at the feet of St. De Villars [a reference to the duchesse de Villars, a *dévot*]." The queen remained silent, and it was Moncrif who proposed Voltaire's admission. On Wednesday, April 27, 1746, twenty-nine of the forty gathered and voted. Twenty-eight indicated their approval with white balls; only one member voted with the black. On May 9, Voltaire was formally inducted, gave his *éloge* for his predecessor, and at last was received into this hallowed fold by his former teacher, abbé d'Olivet, now the director of the Académie française.[85]

With so much achieved, why was it in 1746 that Du Châtelet began exploring ways to "reunite her family," as she referred to the project, in Lorraine, at the Lunéville court of King Stanislas? Did she guess that it was only a matter of time before Voltaire chafed at the requirements of the courtier's life, and again overstepped the limits of royal indulgence? Had she herself tired of the life of "dissipation," as she referred to it? With the futures of her son, her daughter, and her husband taken care of, did she now set other goals and priorities? Once again, her decisions would confound all contemporary expectations of a woman's capabilities and appropriate actions.

CHAPTER SIX

The Woman of Passions and the Historians: "La Divine Emilie"

Du Châtelet sat for another portrait in the 1740s, when she was an active courtier but still intent on preserving her reputation as a *savant* and a *philosophe*. Rather than the relative informality of the blue velvet dress *à l'anglaise* that she had chosen for the sitting for Marianne Loir, Du Châtelet wore the stiff-bodiced and beribboned finery of the *habit de cour*. The bows and trimmings were of the style now made popular by Mme de Pompadour, Louis XV's gifted new *maîtresse-en-titre*. Long swaths of lace flow from the ends of her bright-colored sleeves, and though the *paniers* of her skirts are not visible, she seems dressed for a courtier's day rather than a mathematician's morning of equations. However, she is posed seated at a table, holding a compass in her right hand. This time the points are down, touching the single large geometric figure on the page of the quarto-sized volume that lies open before her.

There is no room in this image for a tribute to the abstract. Du Châtelet's left arm is bent, her elbow resting on a smaller leather-bound volume. The lightly closed left hand touches her cheek, suggesting that she is tired and would like to lean to the side and rest her head for a moment. As in her other portraits, Du Châtelet looks straight at her viewers, but the expression is different. She could be dreaming; she could have been tracing the arc on the page in front of her; she could be playing with the compass, marching it across the book as if it were a small toy soldier. There is none of the contained energy of the other images she created for her contemporaries and left for her biographers. A number of copies of this portrait exist; the color of her dress changes, but not the expression. One hangs over the mantelpiece in the main salon at Cirey today. Perhaps Voltaire, not Du Châtelet, commissioned it for the château in 1744, when he arranged for the carving over the door to the *galerie*. More likely it was done in late 1745 or early

1746, when, according to Clairaut, she produced the first draft of her translation of Newton's *Principia,* spent countless hours working the family networks of influence at Versailles and Fontainebleau, and had reconciled herself to Voltaire's unexpected changes of heart.

Translating Newton's *Principia*

In the summer of 1744, Du Châtelet had entertained père Jacquier, the young member of the Franciscan *minimes* brought to Rome as part of the modernizing initiatives of the new Pope Benedict XIV. Jacquier had come to visit because of his admiration for her *Institutions.* It probably was he who had arranged for the translation and publication of the second edition in Venice in 1743. He and another friar, Thomas Le Seur, had just finished their new Latin edition of the *Principia* (1739–42). The extensive annotation they included functioned as a continuous commentary on the work, critiquing weak points, bringing others up to date with the latest treatises by subsequent *physiciens* and *géomètres.* While Voltaire labored over his libretto for the dauphin's wedding, Du Châtelet and Jacquier's conversations must have ranged over all the contested points of physics she had been studying and writing about. Did they speak of her plans for a volume II of the *Institutions?* Did Jacquier encourage her in a more ambitious project? She had thought to translate into French John Keill's commentary on Newton. Why not the *Principia* itself?

In France, three types of writing existed on the *Principia:* the vernacular descriptions that avoided most of the mathematics, such as that by Algarotti, Voltaire, and Keill; the very specialized *Mémoires* of the Académie that explored a specific point of the theory of attraction or its mathematics; and Newton's own writings in Latin and in English translation. The translation project would have appealed to Du Châtelet, not only because of the service she might perform for "science," but also because it would prove once and for all her adherence to Newton's theory of attraction, which Voltaire's more recent scientific publications had called into question. This translation, she hoped, "would be useful particularly to the French, for the latin of m. Newton is one of the difficulties."[1] Could she have had another, unspoken goal? This project would certainly demonstrate once again her ability to understand the complexities of the Englishman's ideas and the very difficult Leibnizian and Newtonian mathematics involved in their proof—more evidence that could silence any who still believed König's claims.

Though she kept the project a secret, as she had her other major writings, she left no doubt in the manuscript of her sex or her authorship. Feminine endings when she wrote in her own voice are evident in both the translation and the commentary that she subsequently added. The title pages to her *cahiers* clearly say *"par madame la marquise du chastellet."* There is some irony in the fact that the cover page of the final published version makes no mention of Newton at all: only her name appears, as if she had written the original book itself. How she managed the entire translation in a single year remains a mystery, especially considering that she sacrificed none of her activities as a courtier. She described her progress and her difficulties to Jacquier in November 1745: "I lead the life of the world the most disordered. . . . I pass my days in the antechamber of the minister of war to obtain a regiment for my son." As it was, "I go to bed at 4 and 5 in the morning and I work when I have the time." Obligations to Voltaire probably also filled her hours, for, from the fall of 1745 to the spring of 1746, they were campaigning intensely to gain him membership in the Académie française. She noted to Jacquier that "if I had more time" more could have been done. As soon as she had enough of the translation completed, she gave pages to her publisher, Prault. In December, 1745 she estimated six months for the printing and the engraving of the figures.[2]

Even twenty-first-century physicists and historians of science speak of the difficulty of understanding the *Principia,* let alone translating it. Newton wrote in a somewhat obscure prose style, created a hybrid analytical geometry for the mathematics, and at times, as in Book III—the last section, in which he described how attraction worked in the universe—purposely presented his hypotheses in an elliptical fashion that began with the moons of Jupiter and only later described the system as a whole. A close reading reveals ambiguities in the Latin, data presented so as to mask instances where the theory of attraction could not explain a phenomenon, and faulty logic within propositions. In Du Châtelet's own day, no other continental *physicien* or *géomètre* had undertaken even a partial translation, and many, including Maupertuis, acknowledged that they found the work hard to follow. Newton himself had assumed that most would not read the two first books, with their abstract consideration of idealized demonstrations and mathematical models, unless a specific citation suggested it.[3]

Du Châtelet worked from both the second (1713) and third (1726) editions of Newton's work. One was a red Morocco-bound volume she had purchased; the other she had borrowed from Bernoulli II (it was his father's copy). Du Châtelet's manuscript at the Bibliothèque Nationale reveals the methodical and careful way in which she translated, corrected, and revised. Among the marginal notations she made in the brown-backed twelve-page *cahiers* that she favored were queries about a particular Latin word "not well rendered," "all of this very bad," or about some aspect of the calculations. She noted contradictions and points where Newton himself was not clear, and then resolved and clarified the problem passages. In one instance, she chose the English mathematician Jurin's interpretation of Newton's meaning instead of that of Henry Pemberton, the editor of the third edition of the *Principia*.[4] She wrote over whole paragraphs, particularly in prose sections such as Newton's "Definitions," and the "scholie" (the conclusions at the end of a series of propositions, theorems, and corollaries), in what for her was tiny handwriting. She cut some phrases, simplified others, changed a singular noun to a plural because "it is good" that way. Crosses in the margins and boxes of text indicate additions and changes when there was no more room to overwrite the lines. When all other methods of indicating changes had been exhausted, she wrote the new version on a small bit of paper, on one occasion on the back of a letter, and pasted it on with sealing wax. As in her other writings, the extensive editing makes each version of the text less a literal translation than a clearer and more succinct rendering.

The manuscript also shows how rushed she became toward the end of the project. All of her usual abbreviations are there. Words run together as if she had no time to lift the quill to indicate the breaks between them. She smudged the ink, left a thumbprint on the back of one page. She drew the tables for Halley's comet but never finished filling them in, and must have completed this section on the printer's proofs. Her apparently haphazard system succeeded. When she later sent the translation to the comte d'Argenson, he remarked, "You translate elegantly, neatly, strongly." He had compared it with the English translation and found hers far superior.[5]

Throughout 1745, in the course of her relentless translating, Du Châtelet came upon sections in Newton's *Principia* where his hypotheses and his use of supportive, experimental data did not always give clear corroboration, and a few others where more recent findings threw his reconciliation into doubt. With her commitment to "truth," to certain knowledge, Du Châtelet could not leave these places in his text without comment. Voltaire found any questioning of Newton an attack on the whole planetary system. Yet to make no acknowledgment and to present none of the more recent answers, especially those of continental natural philosophers, invited skepticism and discouraged new adherents. In November 1745, while reporting her progress to Jacquier, she told him she had decided to include some of her own commentary and asked him to send his "calcul intégral" (integral calculus), a guide perhaps brought to Cirey in manuscript that would be useful in this new aspect of her project. Thus, Clairaut, in his *approbation* of December 10, 1745, described her book as a translation "with a mathematical *Commentaire*." Du Châtelet had the *privilège du roi*—royal permission to publish—by March 7, 1746, and assumed that, once difficulties with the illustrative figures had been sorted out, she would have the proofs of the translation by the end of the year. In theory, she could then devote herself exclusively to the new part of her project.[6]

Voltaire's Changes of Heart

However, in the last months of 1745, Du Châtelet put her translation and commentary aside. She explained to Bernoulli II in January 1746: "I am actually very far from all that, and I need great discipline so as not to take time for my actual work from the necessary dissipations of the world." It would be more than a year later before she would again write of the project.[7] Undoubtedly, Du Châtelet had her family's affairs to attend to, as well as Voltaire's aspirations as a courtier, but these commitments had not prevented her projects before. She gave the explanation in the story she told in the last part of her *Discours sur le bonheur,* the essay she had begun at Cirey, and now must have taken up again. She had suffered "terrible shocks." In November 1745, just when she had sent her translation to her publisher, Du Châtelet discovered that Voltaire had regained his sexual appetites and prowess. On a Tuesday evening, the second of November, Graffigny wrote to Devaux: "Yesterday, I learned . . . a little story [*une petite histoire*]." Though Graffigny had all of the details wrong, the essence of the *petite his-*

toire was correct. To Graffigny's delight, "the Monster," as she now referred to Du Châtelet in her letters to Lunéville, had once again opened incoming mail. This time the marquise discovered not the excited, innocent reference to a few stanzas of *La Pucelle,* but evidence of a young woman's passionate love. According to Graffigny, Du Châtelet then searched Voltaire's *appartement* in their rue Traversière *hôtel* and found a whole packet of letters. The story Graffigny heard and passed on left only Du Châtelet as a villain, "regarded successively with contempt and with horror," for publicizing a young woman's misplaced purely Platonic "attraction" for the elder poet.

Graffigny had the woman's name wrong and thought a husband was involved. This was probably part of a story manufactured after the fact to satisfy the *nouvellistes,* should news of the incident begin to circulate. For in all likelihood the letters that Du Châtelet found were from Marie-Louise Denis. Denis had no husband. She was then thirty-three, a widow, and Voltaire's favorite niece. The poet had naïvely assumed that he could keep his secret from Du Châtelet and from the public, and thus avoid the inevitable ridicule and condemnation the incestuous affair would invite. However, once her pain and outrage had subsided, Du Châtelet must have helped him hide the liaison. The stratagem proved successful, for, despite the police, the gossips, and all of the enemies Voltaire had accumulated over the decades of his life, no one discovered the illicit liaison until the 1950s, when an enterprising dealer offered at auction some of Voltaire's own love notes.[8]

Du Châtelet described the sequence of her feelings in her *Discours,* a project that had initially arisen out of conversations with Voltaire and their friend and visitor in the 1740s, Helvétius, who wrote his own essay on the subject. Like Montaigne, Du Châtelet offered experiences from her own life to illustrate the sources of happiness she had identified, such as gambling and the enjoyment of good food. As in her other writings, she wrote in such a way that the reader naturally assumed that the author was a man. Only about halfway through the *Discours* did Du Châtelet mention women specifically. She recommended "study" as a source of happiness for women especially, not only because it afforded women opportunities for "la gloire" denied them in other pursuits reserved to men, but also because it entailed no dependence on others. This reference to independence must have been a response to Voltaire's actions, which she referred to more overtly in the third section of her *Discours.* The changes in tone, style, and manner of addressing the reader are noticeable. Writing in her own voice, in clear, descriptive sentences, she explained: "But I was happy for ten years because of the love of the man who had completely seduced my soul; and these ten years I spent tête-a-tête with him without a single moment of distaste or hint of melancholy." All who knew the identity of the author would know that she was referring to the years of her affair with Voltaire.[9]

Voltaire's choice to break off the sexual aspect of their relationship was described in a poem he sent to Cideville, his old friend from Rouen, in July 1741. He prefaced the central idea with stanzas bemoaning the passage of years and his infirmities; he was then forty-seven. He went on to say that he wanted to share a "painful confidence." With obvious reference to his sexual prowess, he blamed his inability "to love" on his age, what he called the "twilight of my days." He saw this tragedy in terms of himself and its possible consequences: "One dies twice. . . . [You] cease to love and to be loved / It is an insupportable death, / To cease to live is nothing." The poet consoled himself with "l'amitié," the affection that Voltaire often ascribed to his male friends: "Affection comes to my aid: / It is steadier, as tender, and less ardent than love affairs."[10]

From her *Discours,* it is clear that Du Châtelet had found ways to accept Voltaire's decision, preserve her pride, and make the best of this chaste and abstinent friendship. As she explained, if "age and illness had not entirely extinguished his desire, it would perhaps still have been for me." She took comfort in the fact that, though "his heart [was] incapable of love," he still had the most tender feelings for her. Forgotten were the fears that he would leave her forever when, in 1740 and in 1743, he had gone off to Prussia. She had been the reason, as Voltaire had explained not only to Frederick of Prussia but also to many other friends, that he had not stayed in Berlin. He had returned to Brussels, to Paris, always because of his attachment to Du Châtelet; this was his "bargain for life." Du Châtelet's adjustment to the new arrangement seems to have been complete. As she wrote, the "certainty that a return of his inclination & his passion was impossible—I know well that such a return is not in nature—imperceptibly led my heart to the peaceful feeling of deep affection." Du Châtelet's turning to so many intellectual projects in the early 1740s was certainly another consequence of this change in their relationship. She explained: "This sentiment [of affection], together with the passion for study, made me happy enough."[11]

In her *Discours sur le bonheur,* Du Châtelet made her knowledge of the affair between Voltaire and Mme Denis obvious. She had accepted affection without sex: "I was loving for two, I spent all my time with him, & my heart, free from suspicion, delighted in the pleasure of loving and in the illusion of believing myself loved." But with the discovery of Voltaire's new passion, "I have lost this happy state, & this cost me many tears." Despite her pain, Du Châtelet eschewed remorse or recrimination; it was better to give up the cherished feelings. As she explained in her *Discours*: "Terrible shocks are needed to break such chains: the wound to my heart bled for a long time; I had grounds to complain, & I have pardoned all." Du Châtelet never seems to have considered ending their association. They continued to travel together and to share the *hôtel* on the rue Traversière. There remained only the occasional hint of her former feelings. A friend remembered an evening when rereading Voltaire's love letters brought tears to her eyes. At Lunéville, she responded to a frivolous, complimentary verse Voltaire had written about "the doctor Uranie," whose genius could encompass all: verses, books, jewels, pompons, diamonds, optics, algebra, latin, opera, lawsuits, physics. She noted, "You have forgotten, / in this long string" "tender affection." This "I would give for all the rest."[12]

Voltaire's strong attachment to Denis had a history. When her mother, Voltaire's sister, died in 1726, and her father soon after, the famous poet took an interest in both of his nieces, but hoped that the elder, Marie-Louise, would join Du Châtelet's household and "an uncle who loves you tenderly." Even when she refused his suggestion that she marry Mme de Champbonin's son, Voltaire continued to believe that, with enough money to sweeten the prospect, "she would spend part of the year with madame du Chastelet, she would come to Paris with us. . . . Finally I would be her father." When instead his niece chose marriage to Denis, a minor government official, Voltaire still provided the eight thousand livres in *rente* toward the support of the couple. "I only want her happiness," he graciously explained to Thieriot, "[but] I would offer a part of my own to be able to live some times with her."[13]

In the spring of 1745, the frail Voltaire, though sure he was past his sexual prime, could see himself as the darling of the court: his play *La Princesse de Navarre* had been performed with all of the other activities surrounding the dauphin's wedding, and on April 1 it was announced that he had been made the royal historiographer. The lively young widow, who arrived to live for the first time in Paris with her married sister, found herself flattered and courted by her famous uncle. Graffigny described Denis as "a small woman, well enough made, very dark-haired," her skin marked from small-pox, and noted that she had difficulty focusing her eyes in the same direction. After Du Châtelet's death, Voltaire had a pastel done of himself and Denis, in which she appears prettier in a conventional sense than the marquise, any flaws rendered imperceptible.[14] How did they fall into each other's arms? Inadvertently, Denis must have made it easy. Voltaire's notes to her indicate that Denis seemed pleased to fulfill his needs and his fantasies. He was "transported" by one early group of her letters. She was his muse, he "burns to see her every day, at every hour." She had a lovely young body, tending to the plump, to be cosseted and enjoyed, with, according to Voltaire, a particularly appealing "butt [cul]."[15] Then, too, she was not a marquise, not so intelligent or critical. It was no accident that he and Du Châtelet used English, the language of the intellect, for their secret communications. Italian—the "language of love," as Voltaire called it—was the preferred means of writing to Denis.

Perhaps it was in response to these new realities of her life, sometime in 1746, that Du Châtelet began to consider moving "to rejoin" her family in Lunéville, her husband's ancestral court in Lorraine. Voltaire did not object, and followed each part of the odyssey from Versailles and Fontainebleau, to Cirey, to Lorraine. Some of the reasons are obvious, others must be surmised. Lunéville was small: the rituals and personalities perhaps appeared more manageable, leaving more time for her own studies and her writing. Here her husband and her son might acquire offices and advancement more easily, given the family's revered status in the duchy. On each of his visits, Voltaire had been the star of the tiny circle of courtiers, applauded and not patronized. King Stanislas, an indulgent admirer of the poet's antics, also enjoyed the entertainments Voltaire devised, as did his mistress and the center of the court, the marquise de Boufflers. So Du Châtelet could assume that Voltaire would be in a relatively protected environment with much to flatter his vanity. In early October 1746, she started to orchestrate this change in their lives, apparently without much consultation. She wrote to the marquis d'Argenson about a new post for her husband in Lorraine. It could be reasoned that her husband, a loyal officer of the Royal Army, would make an ideal commander in this interim period when Lorraine was ruled by King Stanislas and could help prepare the way for the accession of the territory to France when the Polish monarch died. Du Châtelet proceeded with her plans, making it sound as if it were her husband's wish. He, in fact, knew nothing of her behind-the-scenes efforts on his behalf and was pleased with his current post. The previous fall, he had assumed command of the fortress at Phalsbourg, in northeastern Lorraine.[16]

Du Châtelet's maneuvering and courtier's machinations took time and patience. In answer to Bernoulli II's invitation that she submit an entry on monads to a prize competition of one of the academies, she wrote from Versailles: "I have so little time right now to give to study that I cannot allow myself to be distracted from my present occupation, which absorbs it entirely." Her negotiations with d'Argenson continued into 1748. She reported to him that King Stanislas "would like me to stay in this country at least for part of the year," and "certainly the kindnesses of the king of Poland add very much to the charms of this place for me." In another letter she concluded: "I count very much on your kindnesses toward me." Her importuning ended only with d'Argenson's dismissal, and then her efforts shifted to his successor, Puisieux. She must have already known him or established contacts with him, for it was from him she first heard of the preliminaries of the peace of Aix-la-Chapelle, in May 1748.[17]

᷼᷼᷼

Du Châtelet's instincts about Voltaire's future as a courtier proved correct. All too soon, he once again provoked those upon whose favor he depended. In retrospect, it seems remarkable that Voltaire controlled himself and his habit for provocation as long as he did. Initially, the commissions, appointments, and gifts from the king proved distraction enough. Voltaire wrote on May 1, 1746, to Maupertuis in Berlin to brag of his accomplishments: "Here I am your brother in the Académie française where they elected me in one voice without even the opposition of the Bishop de Mirepoix." This was a stretch of the truth that Maupertuis would probably learn about from less generous members of the Académie. The letter closed with news of another confraternity that had accepted his candidacy, his election to the Bologna Academy.[18]

In December 1746, because of more efforts by Du Châtelet, and also perhaps by Mme de Pompadour, the promised office of a *gentilhomme ordinaire de la chambre du roi* was his. Much to the chagrin of more traditional and pedigreed courtiers, the bourgeois poet and playwright now had the privilege of *entrée:* the right to participate in the daily activities of the monarchs and to approach and speak to the king. A few months earlier, he had acquired the right to a small, cramped set of rooms in the palace of Versailles. Granted, it was in the Gros Pavillon, a multi-storied structure on the other side of the Royal Chapel, not in the more prestigious sections nearer to the royal *appartements.* Voltaire and Du Châtelet complained to little effect of its broken cupboard, damaged shutter, twelve missing pieces of parquet flooring, and a wooden mantel that should have been stone. It was too close to drains and to kitchen chimney smoke. But it was in the palace, and Voltaire's pleasure was evident. Given the opportunity, he closed his letters identifying himself with all of his titles, from "chevalier Gentilhomme ordinaire du Roy," to his membership as "one of the forty" in the Académie française, to royal historian.[19]

Too soon, however, Voltaire's inability to resist the clever quip at someone's expense, especially men of whom he was jealous or whom he disdained for being less talented than himself, reached those that he could not afford to offend. When there was talk that Moncrif, the queen's *lecteur* and a favorite attendant, might succeed him as historiographer of France, Voltaire could not resist a demeaning play on the man's name. Even when Voltaire apparently meant to flatter, he managed to give offense. Some verses composed in praise of Hénault, the queen's favored gallant, began with the wonders of his *soupers;* he was reputed to have the best chef in Paris. Hénault, as the queen's chamberlain, wanted his history of France extolled as his major accomplishment. Voltaire apologized, but his poem had already circulated widely in Paris.[20]

Many Voltaire scholars have assumed that when Jeanne-Antoinette d'Etioles Poisson became Mme de Pompadour, *maîtresse-en-titre* to Louis XV, she would, as a fellow bourgeois and promoter of the Republic of Letters, be Voltaire's natural ally. Indeed, she enjoyed his company in that first year at court, but the presumption of loyalty because of their similar origins shows little understanding of this gifted courtesan. Pompadour did not need anything to remind the court of her lowly *état.* She did appreciate Voltaire's plays, and at sixteen had performed the part of Zaïre in his presence at her future father-in-law's château. However, she chose her favorites because of previous loyalty and service to her, or because these men and women could be counted upon to help her in her principal occupation, which was to amuse and enchant the king. Voltaire had never been a favorite of Louis XV. When her theatrical troupe chose to perform Voltaire's comedy *L'Enfant prodigue,* she had to convince the king just to allow the author to attend.[21]

And, as Voltaire well knew and came to resent, he was not her favorite playwright. She turned instead to Prosper Jolyot de Crébillon, the royal censor, now in his late sixties, who had once been her tutor. Crébillon's court appointments had come decades before, because of the successes of his plays. Elected to the Académie française in 1731, given his court position in 1733, he had produced no more works, but had been zealous in protecting Parisian audiences from what he viewed as dangerous in Voltaire's plays. He and Maurepas had been responsible for the orders that Voltaire close down *Mahomet* in 1742.[22] To Voltaire, this all became a challenge.

When given the opportunity to write "une grande pièce de théâtre" to celebrate the birth of the dauphine's first child, he chose the story of Sémiramis—an odd choice for the occasion, as it told the story of a queen who poisoned her husband, had an incestuous love for her son, and died at the end. Voltaire, in the *dissertation* that accompanied the published version, explained that he had as his main purpose the restoration of French tragedy to its highest form, a drama without a love story. His audiences knew, however, of another obvious motive: *Sémiramis* was one of Crébillon's great successes, from 1717. This was the kind of rivalry that the court and Paris enjoyed. Voltaire had completed act IV when the childbirth went badly, and the young dauphine did not survive. The play was not performed at court or by the Comédie française until 1748. Meanwhile, Crébillon responded to this blatant effort to commandeer his old drama with a return to playwriting, and was rewarded by Pompadour with a small pension and a reading at court, under her auspices, of his new drama, *Catalina.* Voltaire became all but obsessed with the older man and even set to work on his own version.[23]

As Du Châtelet knew, and Pompadour would soon learn, Voltaire was a liability. His habit of composing epistles, quatrains, and couplets could have flattering results, or embarrassing ones. A couplet correcting the royal favorite's misuse of a word was too good not to be repeated all over Paris.

Verses composed in December 1747 meant to flatter, but instead suggested Pompadour's relationship with the king too explicitly: "May your love be eternal," and "Live both of you without enemies: / And both of you keep your conquests." The queen, the dauphin, and the royal family were outraged. This was only months after Voltaire and Du Châtelet had left Fontainebleau quickly because of his whispered suggestion that she could not win at her card game with the queen's companions because she was playing with cheats.[24]

Once again, Du Châtelet understood that Voltaire must be away from Versailles, its temptations and its hazards. Sceaux, sixteen leagues from Paris, had been a refuge in the past—during the Regency, when the duc du Maine was still alive and he and the duchesse celebrated every kind of *fête* for fifty or sixty guests at a time. Both were of the highest *état* in the kingdom: she, Anne Louise Bénédicte de Bourbon-Condé, was the granddaughter of the Grand Condé, one of Louis XIV's greatest generals, and her husband was the Grand Monarch's favorite child by his *maîtresse-en-titre,* Mme de Montespan. When the duc's increasingly disfiguring illness, probably the last stages of syphilis, caused him to retire to his section of the château, the duchesse created her own fantasy world, which she believed rivaled Versailles. She prided herself on having assembled the wittiest, cleverest circle of courtiers, including a number of those who had attended Mme Lambert's *salon* in Paris. Houdar de la Motte, though old and blind, enjoyed fabricating a flirtation. Président Hénault introduced his mistress, Mme Du Deffand, to the circle. Du Maine created an equally entertaining summer refuge at the château of Anet. Just as at Sceaux, the amusements—evenings of verses, maxims, and riddles—and extravagance continued, with operas and plays in which the duchesse played the ingenue, even as she passed age fifty.[25]

By August 1746, however, when Du Châtelet and Voltaire visited Anet at the duchesse's invitation, the duc had been dead for ten years and, as described by the duchesse's dependent and principal confident since her youth, Mme de Staal de Launay, all seemed routine and boring: "We do, we say always the same things: walks, observations on [the games] *vent, cavagnole,* remarks on losses and wins, the measures to hold the doors closed however hot it is, the desolation of those who are suffocating, among whom

I am numbered." Voltaire and Du Châtelet brought the needed unpredict-ability and enthusiasm. Invited for a more extended stay the next summer, Du Châtelet and Voltaire created confusion from the moment of their ar-rival. Oblivious to the problems created for the staff, they appeared at the château at midnight on August 15, 1747, a day early. Du Châtelet then in-sisted on moving from one vacant set of rooms to another. Still, she amused them with her acting in the amateur production that followed. Staal de Lau-nay had to give her grudging praise of the comedienne as the star of *Bour-soufle:* she "had so perfectly executed the extravagance of her role that I was truly pleased."[26]

The *Commentaire* on Newton's "System of the World"

When Du Châtelet insisted on moving from one suite to another, it was because she hoped to work without distraction: reading the proofs of her translation of the *Principia* and drafting her commentary. In fact, she con-fessed to Jacquier that she found going over the proofs "so boring" that she preferred the new aspect of her project. Her initial plan was modest: to provide a summary of Clairaut's Académie *Mémoire* giving the mathematical analysis of the effects of the earth's flattened shape on its orbit and that of the moon, the result of his trip to Lapland with Maupertuis. By September 1746, she could report to Jacquier that she had begun to read his and Le Seur's "perpetual" commentary, but even so she had to admit that her *Com-mentaire* was "scarcely more advanced."[27] With Maupertuis in Berlin, and Clairaut now engaged in his own intense study of the mathematics of three bodies, Du Châtelet counted on Jacquier's expertise. His explanations were essential to the explication of Clairaut's work on the shape of the earth: "The more you send the happier I am." She asked again for his guide to cal-culus, for she had decided that she must expand her commentary further. To give a "true" and correct description of what Newton called "the System of the World," she needed to present the fruits of her readings in the most current astronomical and mathematical studies. There was Clairaut's *Mé-moire,* but also a second Académie *discours:* Daniel Bernoulli's new mathe-matics of the moon's effect on the coming and going of the tides, yet another aspect of the proof of Newton's law of attraction, which she had found re-printed in Jacquier's *Principia*. Finally, she planned to include her own description of the planetary system as a whole, probably based in large part on the notes intended for volume two of the *Institutions*.[28]

In addition to Book III of the *Principia,* Du Châtelet based her "Exposition abrégé"—"Abridged Exposition," as she called the new section of her *Commentaire*—on Newton's 1731 edition of his separate *System of the World,* though she followed what seems a more rational sequence and used simpler, clearer language. She began with a brief history of astronomy from the Babylonians to Kepler and Huygens. Newton then, she explained, had "the advantage of profiting" from each of their works, and thus could go much further. She briefly described all the key aspects of the *Principia*—the "Definitions," the "Laws of Movement," and the subjects of the three Books. After a few paragraphs on Book I, she dismissed Book II as simply the means to "destroy the *tourbillons* of Descartes," and focused on Book III and the "Phenomena" of Newton's universe. This information she presented in seven chapters, starting with a general description of the solar system and covering the secondary planets ("satellites," or moons), the tides, and comets, with numerous references to the appropriate historical texts, Newtonian commentators, and specialized studies.[29]

Du Châtelet's chapter I provides a beautiful, clear description of the universe as perceived in her day. She set down the reasons for assumptions of the spherical shape of the earth and why its shadow always made an arc. The sun must be particles of fire, for its "rays produce the same effect." She explained how ratios were used to calculate the periodic orbits of the planets and their eccentricities—for example, the effects of the sun and the moon on the earth's orbit—and that the resulting variations in the moon's orbit caused "it always [to present] the same side." Her readers learned that, by analogy, one assumed the same laws applied to Mercury and Saturn, though they were too far away to observe.[30]

Although throughout her "Exposition" Du Châtelet periodically referred to propositions and corollaries in Books I and III of the *Principia,* she chose in her chapter II to make explicit the connections between the observational description of Newton's planetary system governed by attraction, and the mathematical and experimental idealizations on which it was based. Here she wished to explain "the path that he [Newton] had followed" to arrive at an explanation for the phenomenon of the "perpetual circulation of planets around the center of their revolution." If one ignored the question of causation and the fact of resistance, the answer lay in analogies from centripetal force, in the mathematics of conics, and in a rule of reasoning that she had accepted in her *Institutions*: "that any other law was impossible in our world such as it is." As she explained, Newton extrapolated from this logical premise to calculate a whole orbit when observations could only be made for a portion of that orbit. In this way he derived the formula for attraction, a ratio in inverse proportion to the square of the distances between the planets. Du Châtelet proudly announced that this essential law of nature arose from "observations & by induction" and by the same means could be applied to other planets and their "satellites."[31]

In chapters III, IV, and V of her "Exposition," she demonstrated the significant role of French Academicians in formulating the three major proofs of attraction, and thus of Newton's hypothetical system of the world. For the first proof, Newton conjectured, using an experimental and mathematical model based on the theory of fluids, that attraction affected the shape of the earth, flattening it at the poles. Maupertuis and Clairaut's expedition to Lapland, and La Condamine's to the equator, provided actual measurements. Clairaut's *Mémoire* of 1742 on the shape of the earth confirmed Newton's hypothesis and corrected his approximations. In addition, as Du Châtelet described, Clairaut had discovered how to determine the shape of the other planets, of which Jupiter had presented particular difficulty. Du Châtelet approached this implicit criticism of Newton graciously. "If he had known the Proposition of M. *Clairaut,* by that I mean, that the added density at the center [of the planet's core] diminishes the flattening, he would have found . . . [the] cause of the Phenomenon that he wanted to explain." Clairaut had solved the problem by supposing Jupiter to be denser at the center than at its surface.[32] Thus, Du Châtelet inserted into the Newtonian system an important corrective, that the earth was not made of a homogeneous substance, as the great Englishman had assumed in his model, nor were the other planets.

The second key proof of Newton's hypothesis about attraction as the law of the universe hinged on the relationship between the earth, the moon, and the sun, what came to be called "the three-body problem." How to calculate the irregularities, or "eccentricities," especially of the earth's and moon's orbits, absorbed the efforts of Europe's best mathematicians throughout the 1740s, including Du Châtelet's mentor Clairaut. The phenomenon of the tides was considered part of this puzzle. So Du Châtelet explained how

Daniel Bernoulli perfected, as she would have said, Newton's system, by accounting for the seemingly endless tidal variations collected by observers from all over the world. Taking into account Clairaut's presumption about the nonhomogeneous nature of the earth's core, he rethought the relative densities of the earth and the moon, and found that the moon must be much denser than Newton had hypothesized—seventy times denser. This led to different proportions for the respective forces of the moon and the sun, producing tides that fit the observations far better than Newton's. Any other variations, Bernoulli explained, arose because of the differences between the ports where the measurements had been taken—the differences in terrain, for example. Du Châtelet found Bernoulli's work so conclusive that there was no need "to research further what is the true cause of the tides; it is known today by *physiciens-géomètres* with all the certainty to which physics is susceptible: nothing more remains at present than to develop this cause, to draw from it all the consequences, & to calculate the effects."[33]

The third proof, Newton's hypothesis on the behavior of "secondary planets" and comets, the subjects of the two last chapters (VI and VII) of her "Exposition," posed the three-body problem on another level of difficulty. Given the complexities of the mathematics, Du Châtelet offered here only the sparest idea of Newton's method, but she noted that "the algebraic method . . . appears to be the only one that could be truly satisfactory in a research of this nature." Du Châtelet turned with evident pleasure to comets, as a phenomenon that had drawn the attention of the greatest *philosophes* over the centuries. Now she could report Newton's discovery: comets also followed the law of attraction, but to describe their parabolic orbits over great distances required endless calculation, what Du Châtelet referred to as "this beautiful astronomical-mathematical problem." When this was completed, however, one could predict the return of a comet for which observational data already existed, and thus prove the Newtonian system once again. Du Châtelet dismissed the comet of 1680 for this purpose. Given the probable length of its orbit, it would not be visible again until the year 2255. With evident excitement, she continued, "But there is another comet whose return is so near [1758–59] that it promises a very agreeable spectacle for the Astronomers of this era: it is the comet that last appeared in 1682."[34] She ended her "Exposition" with this tantalizing statement.

From Versailles to Sceaux to Lunéville

Despite the criticisms of Du Châtelet's and Voltaire's habits as guests, the duchesse du Maine welcomed the couple again in December 1747.[35] Du Châtelet took this opportunity to sing her favorite role in the classic Baroque opera *Issé,* a heroic pastoral by Houdar de la Motte and Destouches. She also sang the lead in *Zélindor,* a new work by Moncrif, and Voltaire could report to the author that she "has sung Zirphé with accuracy, and played her with nobility and with grace." News of Du Châtelet's performances reached the court at Versailles. The duc de Luynes reported, "In these two presentations, Mme Du Châtelet played and sang well." However, the duchesse did not like the crowds of friends and courtiers from Versailles and Paris that the events brought, and now insisted that nothing but plays be produced by her guests. Voltaire accommodated the duchesse by reworking an earlier comedy of his own, once called "La Dévote," now renamed "La Prude," and thus less likely to antagonize the queen's circle of the pious. Perhaps unusually eager for an audience after the confusions over his most recent plays, Voltaire upset the duchesse once again by issuing five hundred invitations to the performance on her behalf. The duc de Luynes included the instructions in his journal: guests were to arrive exactly at six to allow for the expected traffic of noble *carrosses* in the inner courtyard before the performance began at eight. The invitation noted that after six o'clock the gates of the château would be closed.[36]

This series of events in 1747 could only have made Du Châtelet's plan of reuniting her family in Lorraine, at the court of King Stanislas of Poland, seem even more urgent. The portraits of Stanislas reflect the contemporary descriptions of him as a man with an open, smiling gaze who, as he once wrote for his daughter, valued candor and frankness. Known for his compassionate heart, this king hoped "never to praise or blame by prejudice or caprice."[37] He was now in his seventies, a big man and quite portly. Having spent much of the twenty years before coming to Lorraine fighting in wars to defend his title to the Polish throne, after his arrival in Lunéville in April 1737, with his pension of more than a million livres a year from Louis XV, Stanislas gave himself over to the pleasures and rituals of peacetime. He attended mass and wrote serious musings; he also kept a mistress, expected the Jesuits to do his fireworks displays, loved elaborate mechanical creations and practical jokes. The shrieks and antics of the little boy jester to his court, Bébé, a dwarf less than three feet tall, delighted him. Breaking dishes and hiding under women's *paniers* were but a few of the child's most annoying and entertaining activities.

Even with his love of fun, however, Stanislas ran his court, about 450 strong, with an order and regularity that must have seemed strange to Du Châtelet, who was used to the uncertainties of Louis XV's days at Versailles and Fontainebleau. He disliked arguments, and when they occurred among his chosen companions at *dîner,* he had been known to pick at his food— even his favorite Polish cabbage and roasted meat—and then leave his place at table, thus forcing an end to the discussion, since all had to rise and leave with him. A creature of habit, he rose at 5 a.m and met with his advisers— particularly his architect, for he had, on his accession, embarked on building and remodeling sites in his duchy and the gardens of his palace and châteaux. He dined at 11:30 a.m., which left the afternoon for hunting, gambling, plays, an opera, or a concert. At a cost of twenty-five thousand livres a year, he kept an orchestra of more than thirty instruments and seven singers so that he might have music every day. He spent the early evening with his mistress and always retired to his private quarters at 10 p.m. The only dis-locations came with Stanislas's periodic visits to see his daughter, Queen Marie Leszczyńska, at Versailles, and his moves from one of his châteaux to another: from Lunéville to Commercy to Malgrange.

✤

In February 1748, King Stanislas formally invited Du Châtelet and Voltaire to join his court. Thus, the first part of Du Châtelet's strategy fell into place, and just in time, for Voltaire's behavior had now made his position tenuous at both Versailles and Sceaux. Once again she and the playwright took a small, relatively intimate circle of courtiers by storm. Voltaire wrote verses to Mme de Boufflers, "première dame du palais," the official royal mistress, who presided over the evening after the monarch had gone to bed. The verses captured her charming contradictions: "Prudent with an indis-creet air, virtuous, coquettish . . . you please the libertines, you captivate the sages." He noted her youth, her art, even "malice perhaps." Marie-Françoise-Catherine de Beauvau-Craon, marquise de Boufflers, was a daughter of the

most prominent Lorraine family of the previous duc's reign. She characterized herself as "la volupté," the voluptuous one, and enjoyed creating sexual
liaisons and confusions within her circle of companions. First the mistress of
Stanislas's French appointed minister, Antoine-Martin Chaumont de La
Galaizière, and then of the widowed king himself, she reigned as unofficial
consort. Though gossips joked about the pretty, accomplished young woman's being shared by a royal minister, Stanislas indulged Boufflers with a
suite of rooms at Lunéville, particularly enjoyed her ability to write quatrains for him, and later saw to the advancement of her sons.[38]

Du Châtelet arrived at Lunéville that February 1748 with her household
and what must have been cartloads of clothing, dinnerware, linens, books,
and papers. The inventory done just after her death included an old harpsichord that she perhaps had ordered brought from Cirey. As part of the
king's court, Du Châtelet began her day with mass and perhaps a ride in the
park or a royal hunt—she had two riding habits with her. Then she might
assist at the *grand couvert,* at a less formal *dîner,* or join in an entertainment
organized for the whole court at one of the fanciful pavilions that the king
had commissioned for his formal gardens. Du Châtelet and Boufflers, only a
few years apart in age, shared similar delights, and so Du Châtelet had no
difficulty joining her in creating a whirlwind of activities during the afternoons.[39]

Du Châtelet's and also Voltaire's pleasure at the court certainly stemmed
not only from the amusements offered and the king's welcoming generosity
and desire to "make everyone happy," but also from the opportunity to
present dramas, operas, and comedies. Within two weeks of their arrival,
Zaïre was staged. At Lunéville that late winter and spring, then at Commercy in the summer of 1748, they performed Voltaire's *Mérope,* as well as
more lighthearted productions by other playwrights. The court dispersed
while Stanislas visited his daughter at Versailles, but the round of productions began again in the fall. At the end of November, they performed the
play Voltaire had written just for their little troupe, *La Femme qui a raison*
(The Reasonable Wife). The poet reported all this to the d'Argentals and
also wrote of Du Châtelet's greatest triumphs, the many opera roles that she
took on: in *Zélindor* and *Paradis* by Moncrif, *Les Sens* by Roy. Stanislas enjoyed
her *Issé* so much that he insisted on two more performances. Far away, at Versailles, the duc de Luynes heard again of her successes. Knowing Du Châte-

let's pleasure in the opera, Voltaire wondered to the comtesse d'Argental after the third performance "if she will not pass [the rest of] her life here."[40]

At the late-night *soupers* in Boufflers's rooms or those of La Galaizière, the king's adviser, Voltaire became the principal entertainment. He recited new and old verses, read from his *Sémiramis* with all the drama of the actress who had played the part at the Comédie française, read from his new tragedy, *Catalina* (about Cicero in the last days of the Roman Republic), and from *Zadig,* his tale mocking the injustices of the courtiers' world. He amused the group with his parody of Du Châtelet's charms as Issé. Du Châtelet herself sent for Graffigny's *Lettres péruviennes* (*Peruvian Letters*) to be read aloud.[41]

The notes, drafts, and proofs of her *Commentaire* came with her to Lunéville. On Easter Sunday, 1748, Devaux reported to Graffigny that Du Châtelet "did not deign to honor us with her presence." As at Anet and Sceaux, "she stays in her room on the pretext that she has to correct some proofs that must leave by the *poste.*" He had no idea who the publisher was, but he had a clear sense of the content: "a translation of Newton with some commentaries." On a number of these evenings, Voltaire joined Devaux in his room and talked for hours, much to the latter's delight, for he had long admired the poet. Voltaire had written to Champbonin in April 1748, the card game "lansquenet & love occupy this little court." One night, the marquis, Du Châtelet's husband, now in attendance on King Stanislas, joined a hand of *ombre.* His wife may have been there, but generally it was Voltaire that Devaux described to Graffigny at the gaming table. He lost "more than one hundred louis" at *trictrac* on one particular Thursday evening. According to Devaux, "he played like an imbecile." Losing every day put him in a "bad humor." The treat at the end of such evenings, at 3 a.m. on one occasion, was a familiar one: Voltaire read some stanzas of *La Pucelle.* As Jean-François de Saint-Lambert, a longtime friend of Devaux and the protégé of the prince de Beauvau-Craon, described the gatherings, probably after one of their marathon evenings, "We are dying from hunger, from cold, and from laughing."[42]

The Grand Passion of a Lifetime

Voltaire wrote other verses about Du Châtelet at this time. He imagined two jealous gods, Esprit and Amour, with separate interests and separate courts. One day they made peace—a unique occasion, never to be forgotten, "because it produced Emilie."[43] These traits, this combination of "wit" and "love," made her a welcome participant at Lunéville. In turn, however, she was drawn into the world of flirtation and *coquetterie* that were Boufflers's trademark. In her *Discours sur le bonheur,* Du Châtelet had not ruled out the possibility that she might once again be presented with the opportunity to love. Like Voltaire, she was vulnerable to the attentions of a younger lover who was skilled in the gallantries of seduction. That Jean-François de Saint-Lambert, an officer of the king's Gardes and a novice poet, was less sophisticated, less quick to challenge and criticize, had talents in need of nurture, made him as potentially appealing to Du Châtelet as Denis had been to Voltaire.

Du Châtelet and Saint-Lambert must have met before she and Voltaire arrived for their extended stay in Lorraine in the first months of 1748. As on previous occasions at Lunéville, the marquise initially seems to have taken no particular notice of him. Saint-Lambert had been on duty in Nancy, and he and Devaux, his closest friend at the court, were not among the immediate circle with *entrée* to the king. One evening in late February or early March, however, Du Châtelet attended a dinner at La Galaizière's residence. She talked in her habitual enthusiastic manner, and attracted the attention of the younger army officer. At least, that was how she later described the beginning of their affair in one of her letters to him.[44] Saint-Lambert, like Devaux, had been a member of Graffigny's little circle when she had been part of the previous court in Lorraine, and she had tried—unsuccessfully—to promote him as a poet and playwright in Paris during the 1730s. In 1736, Saint-Lambert had sent Voltaire an early part of his long philosophic verses *Les Saisons*—written while he was sick at home—and received in return an encouraging *épître,* the poet's customary gift to such young men. Nothing had come of his efforts.

Saint-Lambert had been no more successful in his military career. He did advance, but not so much by his own successes as by the important patron who favored him. His father had been the lieutenant of grenadiers at the court of Lorraine, a not undignified post. After marrying a woman of the minor nobility, he placed his family in a village that was part of the domain of the princes de Beauvau-Craon and added the distinguished sounding "Saint-" to their name. The young Jean-François attended a Jesuit *collège* where he and Devaux met, but the military was to be his career. In 1740, he became one of the forty members of Stanislas's Gardes de Lorraine, whose colonel was his childhood friend the prince de Beauvau-Craon. Saint-Lambert was never strong physically; his stomach and lung ailments, which today would perhaps be diagnosed as ulcers, tuberculosis, and pleurisy, kept him from active service until 1742, when he fought in Bohemia and then in Italy. He rose to captain and was wounded in October 1744, but without money a further rise in rank proved elusive. His health, now complicated by migraine headaches and trouble with his teeth, continued to plague him. By the fall of 1746, now thirty years old, he was back in Lorraine, still part of the Gardes, but he had time to participate in the evenings with Devaux and the marquise de Boufflers, his patron's sister and now mistress to King Stanislas. In January 1747, Graffigny assumed that he had become one of Boufflers's conquests, expected to write verses like his "Epître à Chloe" and to be attentive and sexually available.[45]

There are no contemporary descriptions of Saint-Lambert from this period, or any explanation for Graffigny's choice of the nickname "Little One" for him. He must, however, have been less imposing than other officers, because of his illnesses if nothing else. In the extant portrait of Saint-Lambert from the city museum in Nancy, he wears a red coat, not the yellow and black of the Gardes de Lorraine, and his body seems compact. He has turned slightly, so that his face is in three-quarter profile. His eyebrows are dark, pronounced; his eyes, brown. Though he is clean-shaven, there is a shadow over his cheeks and chin. He wears a curled and powdered white wig. The artist has portrayed him with the hint of a smile. At the end of August 1748, Du Châtelet wrote to him from Plombières, where she was in attendance on Boufflers: "Your letter is like your conversation: half tender and half detached." This describes his expression exactly.[46]

How would she have appeared to him that evening at La Galazière's? Older, yes—by ten years—but a powerful presence, a noblewoman, and he knew of her reputation as a géomètre, physicien, and philosophe. She was lively, flirtatious, the companion of France's greatest poet, a marquise wise in the ways of the court at Versailles, a place that for Saint-Lambert could be only a distant reality. Her attention would have been flattering. Her intensity would contrast dramatically with the careful and studied games he had learned to play with the marquise de Boufflers. As Du Châtelet later wrote to him, "My exterior is always the image of my heart." Their notes to each other in March and April, when they were both in Lunéville, show them as vulnerable, untrusting, but eager to believe that they were in love. They spent an entire night talking but, despite the strong sexual attraction, did not have intercourse. They both seem to have accused each other of inconstancy, of tentativeness. Du Châtelet wanted more than a flirtation: "You are not made for my amusement, but for my happiness," she assured him, and suggested the reward, "to be my sole occupation, if you want."[47] They sent their valets back and forth with short missives, often four or five times in a day. When Saint-Lambert was ill, she prescribed remedies and advice. When he wrote verses for her, she sent back her comments.

On April, 23, 1748, Du Châtelet and Voltaire left for Paris, stopping first in Cirey so that she could deal with matters on the estate. She and Saint-Lambert continued to write to each other, but they were now dependent on the vagaries of the post and the mail coach. Though it came and went twice a week, letters were lost, and others crossed, which led to misunderstandings, to alternating expressions of eagerness and reluctance. Du Châtelet teased Saint-Lambert about his protestations of love. Prove yourself, she wrote, visit me at Cirey. He must have responded with a list of difficulties, including his obligations to his patron, the prince de Beauvau-Craon, and his inability to ride because of his health ("mal de foie," liver trouble). On the first of May she warned she could not delay much longer. Voltaire was eager to leave. Mme Denis, who preferred the excitements of the capital, awaited him. Du Châtelet also had business in Paris. She had been correcting the proofs of her translation of the Principia, completing sections of the commentary, and there was her son's marriage to arrange. She offered Saint-Lambert her analysis of their situation: he had been in love before, but never truly loved; she, in contrast, knew that this attraction, her infatuation, had become more than that: "You are the only one who has made me feel that [my heart] is still capable of loving."[48]

Voltaire must have left for Paris without her. And so, perhaps because she was now alone with only her servants, perhaps because of the novelty and excitement of a different kind of love, Saint-Lambert accepted her challenge. With her instructions in hand, he took the poste carriage to meet her at Cirey. There they had a day or two of intimacy, of sex that was more exciting than any she had known with her husband or Voltaire. On Saturday, May 11, Du Châtelet wrote to her new lover just after he had left her: "And so there I am alone in this sad château that was for me this morning the most delicious dwelling." The distance between them filled her heart with sadness: "I have not the strength to write, I only have [strength] to love." Eight days later, now at Versailles, she wrote in the glow of her newfound pleasures: "You make all my beautiful days, and without you I would never have any." The next two weeks, at Versailles and in Paris, until her return to Lorraine in July, tested their burgeoning intimacy and the future of their affair. The undependability and relative infrequency of the post again played havoc with their interchanges and their feelings. Du Châtelet's effort to number her letters did not solve these problems. She assumed he had returned to paying court to the marquise de Boufflers, burned a "dry," cruel letter she had received on the twentieth, but then wrote that he had "turned her head with the pleasure of love" on learning that he had rejected an opportunity in Tuscany in order to stay in Lorraine for her. She was full of plans to meet in July and ended with "I adore you, I adore you!"[49]

Saint-Lambert also believed that he had reason to doubt his lover's motives. The marquis's post as commander of the royal forces in Lorraine, which Du Châtelet thought she had acquired for her husband, had been announced on April 1, 1748, but suddenly became uncertain. She blamed her lover for not speaking to Boufflers for her and, worse yet, for not realizing how important this command was to her. The marquis Du Châtelet found himself potentially without any posting, which would be humiliating. To make matters worse, the marquis had not known of his wife's machinations until the announcement of his appointment. When it was lost, he and others in the Du Châtelet family were, she accepted, justly angry with her.

On the fifth of June Du Châtelet reported to Saint-Lambert that she could not eat, had a slight fever, and grew weaker each day; she could not work on "my Newton, which is a very serious and a very essential matter for me." All because of what had now become a source of le bruit and of public shame for her. In one letter to Saint-Lambert, she described her desperation: she had lost the "confidence of my husband, my lover, and my intimate friend [Voltaire]." In her letters to Saint-Lambert throughout the rest of June, she explained that there was no honorable way that she and her husband could return to Lorraine if this younger man, this Hungarian whom Stanislas had always preferred, gained the post already announced as the marquis's. Her husband could not overlook this affront to his honor. They would have to retire to Cirey, she lamented. She knew that the distance would be too much for Saint-Lambert: "I will only see you for a few moments, and your natural fickleness soon will make you disgusted with a commerce so difficult and so rare." Despite her complaints, Saint-Lambert seems to have been full of loving thoughts and hoped that they would see each other soon, perhaps in Paris, or on her return to Lorraine, or at Commercy. He asked for specific dates; he wanted her portrait. Again, she reproached him for not being as upset as she, and yet she feared that her grievances would turn him away. Then he criticized her for loving him too much, or, alternatively, for giving love only in proportion to what she received. One of his letters to her was wonderful, the next cruel. On June 16, she imagined breaking off with him altogether. "I vow that I often desire never having loved you." She would be coming to Commercy, she told him, but wanted him to understand just what this entailed. "I leave all my business affairs, and my book." She complained that he did not realize how "essential" this work was for her. "This book is awaited, promised, begun two years ago, my reputation depends on it." When new letters arrived from him reassuring her once again, she set a date for her departure from Paris. She felt "ardor"; her "blood is agitated." She reveled in her feelings of love and anticipation, but reminded him, "I cannot be happy loving you if you do not love me to excess," and "in making love, enough is never enough."[50]

On one of these early summer nights in Paris, perhaps June 22, when she was still awake at five in the morning, she finally stilled the doubts that had plagued her and kept her from enjoying all that she believed he could give her. As she had years before, when she decided to join Voltaire at Cirey, she weighed the *jetons* and found wisdom balanced on the side of love. On this night, she wrote for him the remaining section of her *Discours sur le bonheur* and in it explained her nature, her love, her doubts, and the reasoning that had finally given her peace. The echoes from her letters of March, April, May, and June are uncanny. Sentences use the same words and phrases, express the same desires, the same doubts, thoughts, and emotions of a woman considered past the age of such passions. She hoped that her lover could meet her expectations and her needs, but she was ready to risk the consequences and disappointment if he could not.[51]

These thoughts set to paper, the *Discours* finished, she turned back to her letter, which now reflected the peace she had achieved. There was ardor, but also the reflective tone of the lover who had quieted her fears and was now ready to indulge in "all the joy that I feel in thinking that I am going to see you again." Though she might still criticize his last letter, all she wanted was to love him and to tell him so. With answers formulated and consequences defined, in her last letter from Paris, Thursday, June 27, 1748, Du Châtelet gave herself up to the erotic anticipation of their reunion: "I will see only you in Commercy, my eyes will only see and search for you, and all the most indifferent of my words wanting to say that I adore you." She confessed eagerly: "I abandon myself to the pleasure of loving you, and I reproach myself no more, for I am content that your heart and your love inflame mine." She ended with the triumphant announcement "I love you à la folie and I no longer fear loving you."[52]

Saint-Lambert did not disappoint her. She and Voltaire arrived at Commercy by the beginning of July, and soon after, Saint-Lambert must have satisfied her once again. A note from the next morning could have been written by any woman in any age: "I am a lazy one. I get up. I have only a moment and I use it to say to you that I adore you, regret [that you are not here], desire you. Come, then, as soon as you can. You will eat and drink here. I hope also that you will make love here." Du Châtelet delighted in her new lover. They played together in Destouches's comedy La Fausse Agnès, she as the ingenue, he as the hero. She encouraged Saint-Lambert with his poetry and, as before, worried about his health. "Stay in your bed late. Think of me, finish Pygmalion."[53]

Too soon their duties separated them. When Stanislas traveled to Versailles to spend time with his daughter, he asked Du Châtelet to accompany Mme de Boufflers to Plombières. She could not refuse, for the king held in his hands the future of her husband, her son, and now her lover. At this point, in August 1748, no court appointment had come for her husband, her son still had no regiment, and Stanislas had never looked favorably on Saint-Lambert. Her lover wanted to join her at Plombières, but she explained that the accommodations made it impossible. She shared lodgings with fifty strangers, and only a tapestry hung from the ceiling separated one lodger from another. "I have a tax farmer sleeping in the next bed," she told him. It was at Plombières that August that Du Châtelet—inadvertently or purposely—revealed her affection for Saint-Lambert to Boufflers, who had initially encouraged their liaison. To complicate the situation, Du Châtelet now realized that "la dame volupté" had not meant for them to become serious in their passion for each other—and certainly not more ardent than the Boufflers and her own vicomte.[54]

As if to prove her love and her ability to fulfill the role of patron, Du Châtelet had already sent her lover's verses to d'Argental, just before leaving with Boufflers for Plombières. The following March, 1749, one of the *nouvellistes* published Saint-Lambert's verses on Jansenism. Du Châtelet continued to work on his behalf, particularly when she was in Paris and attending court for her family's affairs. Her letters note opportunities for a regiment, a possible diplomatic appointment to England, efforts on his behalf by a relative of d'Argenson, papers for a pension from the former duc de Lorraine that she offered to help him prepare. She worked to raise money to pay his debts, and advised him how best to cater to the prince de Beauvau-Craon, his principal patron: "One must always be on good terms with him, enjoy his charms and the ease of his company, and wait for nothing from it." Despite her teasing him about how long it took him to write, perhaps it was at her encouragement that he returned to his poetry.[55]

When Du Châtelet finally came back from Plombières in the second week of September 1748, Saint-Lambert's regimental duties kept him in Nancy. Du Châtelet was in attendance on the king at Lunéville, and then at Malgrange. She was impatient to see Saint-Lambert, and ecstatic with his new proofs of love. That summer, Saint-Lambert had worked over an elegy for Du Châtelet. Interspersed among the more formulaic bits of homage, there were images to excite and please, to call up erotic memories: a mirror, "which repeated for us the image of a thousand kisses"; the alcove where "Phyllis [Philis] gave herself over to the pleasure of being loved." He portrayed what followed in "the alcove where I paid homage":

> There, when the ecstasy of our senses had calmed,
> Waiting without being quiescent for the return of our desires,
> A delicate love varied our pleasures.

It went on, mentioning other aspects of their time together "reunited by our tastes" for study and pleasure: "Lead me in turn / From the study to pleasure, and from the arts to love." As for his writings, Du Châtelet had become "the judge, the object, and the prize."[56]

At the same time that Du Châtelet enjoyed the anticipation of their reunion, she seems to have started serious planning for their future. Living at Lunéville remained uncertain and hinged on how Boufflers treated the marquis Du Châtelet's need for an appropriate appointment at court. Yet she hated the "chains" that this implied. "I have passed my life," Du Châtelet explained to the younger man, "in independence." She only wanted "to depend on my tastes and my pleasures," and this meant a life with him. Ideally, she imagined half the year at Lunéville, and half somewhere else that did not require the constant attendance of a courtier. Was she thinking of the property that her close friend Mlle de Thil had located and purchased for her? In January 1748, de Thil had arranged all the details for Du Châtelet to own a small *hôtel* in Argenteuil. Though now part of the outer suburbs of Paris, in Du Châtelet's time it would have seemed very rural: near Paris, northwest of Versailles, but not on any of the main routes to either place.[57]

"To Risk All for All"

Devaux reported to Graffigny that, given Du Châtelet's and Boufflers's flirtations with Saint-Lambert, he could not understand how the three of them could be so friendly. He could not confirm rumors of a sexual liaison between Du Châtelet and his old friend, who referred to it as "a very strong affection." There were rumors in Paris, but on September 22, 1748, Devaux wrote to Graffigny that he still could not be sure.[58] Perhaps it was the increasing speculation that led Du Châtelet to approach King Stanislas and indirectly reveal her liaison with Saint-Lambert. With the court at Malgrange in early October, she requested an audience of fifteen minutes after *dîner*. Knowing that he worried she might importune him again about her family, she reassured the kindhearted man, "This is not about the affairs of my husband . . . but about my own, about my personal life." Stanislas had already formed a particular affection for Du Châtelet; her open, bright, and spontaneous nature would have appealed to him. "I embrace the dear Mme Du Châtelet," he wrote in sending his greetings to her in his letters to Voltaire. Du Châtelet later recounted her meeting to Saint-Lambert. He was never mentioned specifically; Du Châtelet merely asked if the name of "someone who is very much in love with me" could be added to those permitted to join the court when it moved to Commercy in a few days. Stanislas agreed, but he added that this person could not live in the château. When she pressed the king to give his permission for "other trips," he replied, "We will see." It could not have taken long for news of Saint-Lambert's new privilege to be broadcast and understood by all at the court.[59]

Voltaire probably found out just as others did, though Du Châtelet had noted his suspicions in the summer. Only the day before her audience with Stanislas, she had denied the affair when Voltaire evidently asked her. Du Châtelet reported to Saint-Lambert that the older poet was "in a great furor." The extreme reaction seemed to her out of place, given that there was not even the excuse for either of them of "the illusion of attraction and love." His rage saddened her. Saint-Lambert was upset, too; she wrote to reassure him, since he was ill: "There is nothing to do with such a character but to avoid him and to blush at having loved him."[60] As so often in the past, Voltaire resolved the difficulty with verses and subtle mockery. He made it appear as if he had been in control of the situation all the time. The gossips reported his quip, "From Richelieu to me to Saint Lambert," the mistress handed from lover to lover. In the "Epître à M. de Saint-Lambert," which he allowed to circulate in Paris in only a few months, he portrayed himself as the aging poet, no longer favored by the gods and graces, as contrasted with the young man, happy in the spring of his days. He addressed Saint-Lambert in the affectionate "tu" as if to underline his guise as the fatherly figure passing his favors on to a son. He treated Du Châtelet with similar familiarity in the language and image he created. "Our astronomical Emilie / With an old black apron, / And her hand dirty with ink again," had left her compass and her calculations, to "reclaim all her charms." Voltaire instructed the young man to "take her quickly to her *toilette*," and to sing to her on his *musette* "those beautiful airs that love repeats, / And that Newton knew not."[61]

October and November 1748 brought resolution to many of Du Châtelet's problems. The court accepted the affair and ceased to gossip about it, although the couple's obvious passion for each other annoyed some of the more jaded courtiers. Du Châtelet's husband received not the military command he hoped for—that stayed with Stanislas's compatriot from Hungary—but a civilian post, *grand maréchal des logis du roi,* grand marshall of the king's lodgings. Since her husband would now have to be in constant attendance on the monarch, arranging for his moves from palace to palace and château to château, this meant access to the king, and the secure position at court she had sought for her family had been achieved. She and Saint-Lambert finally had their reunion at Commercy, and she joked with him about their enjoyment of each other. One afternoon, she wrote, "No, you were not wrong yesterday evening to love me to the point of folly, but you again have, if it is possible, more reason [to do it] today." The affectionate banter continued on their return to Lunéville. She promised him *oeufs au bouillon,* hard-boiled eggs in gelatin. They "wait for you, and I, too, but I am not as cold as they."[62]

Voltaire, though ill again, was perhaps now reconciled with Du Châtelet. Calmer once he had been assured by the duc de Richelieu that a dreaded parody of his *Sémiramis* would not be performed at court, he finished his new comedy, *La Femme qui a raison.* Du Châtelet, in the lead role for the presentation at the end of November, must have taken particular pleasure in her last long speech, in which, as if recounting her accomplishments for her own family, she could say that she had made a "very good officer" of a young man, "married her daughter advantageously," and now "peace and pleasures reign." The Reasonable Wife, eager to prevail on her stingy husband to spend his wealth, concluded, "To be rich is nothing; all is to be happy."[63] In mid-December, as they had for so many other Christmases, Du Châtelet and Voltaire left for Cirey. The marquis had to stay behind because of his court duties. Saint-Lambert joined them later in the month. From Du Châtelet's perspective, it must have seemed idyllic.

❦

Sometime between the end of January and the middle of February 1749, Du Châtelet realized that she must be pregnant. She was as surprised as everyone else concerned. By February 18, both Saint-Lambert and the marquis knew of her condition. Perhaps Du Châtelet and Saint-Lambert had been careless in their lovemaking at Commercy; perhaps, as the gossips later suggested, it had not occurred to them that she could become pregnant. Given her age, forty-one, she was considered long past the childbearing years for women of her *état.* As the weeks had progressed, Du Châtelet with characteristic pragmatism made plans for the birth and for what she would do in the intervening months. Despite her desire to stay close to Saint-Lambert, she returned to Paris and focused her attention on her two major and as yet unfinished projects, both of which necessitated her absence from Lunéville: her collaboration with Richelieu for an advantageous marriage for her son, and consultations with Clairaut about the last parts of her *Commentaire* for Newton's *Principia*.

In those first months back in Paris, February and March 1749, Du Châtelet resumed her full round of visits to the court, to the appropriate *dîners* and late-night *soupers*. She waited until well into her fourth month, when she assumed chances of miscarriage had passed, to make her condition public. She chose Mme de Boufflers as the conduit, for, as she explained in her letter of April 3, 1749, both she and her husband wanted to have the birth at Lunéville. Neither she nor the courtiers at Lunéville could believe that the marquis was not upset. By rights, he could have had her exiled to a nunnery in disgrace. It was a measure of the marquis's character, and his affection for her, that instead he bragged of the pregnancy and cheerfully told everyone that he hoped it would be another boy, "a new support for his house," as Devaux described his reaction to Graffigny. So confident was Du Châtelet of receiving permission from Stanislas for her lying-in at his court that she even requested particular rooms, in the queen's former *appartement,* where she could look out on the gardens, rather than the aisle, the section of the palace given over to visitors and officials of the palace. Stanislas agreed, and also began to furnish one of the little garden houses for her: these were usually reserved for his favored courtiers to use in the summer months.[64]

The news spread quickly at Lunéville and in Paris. Devaux teased Saint-Lambert about his newly proven prowess. Mme de Graffigny delighted in the witticisms that accompanied the discovery of such a notable and unorthodox marquise's falling prey to the most ancient of misfortunes, an unwanted pregnancy by her lover. She reported to Devaux that the pregnancy was "the news of the day and the most complete ridicule." This would be the soldier-poet's "first masterpiece." All the sterile women, she reported, were going on pilgrimage to Saint-Lambert. By the end of April and into May, Graffigny and Devaux were hearing the same quips and riddles and sending them back and forth to each other. Devaux particularly liked the one that made Voltaire look foolish. It is, coincidentally, the interchange most often repeated in subsequent histories. The marquise announces, "I am pregnant." Her husband replies, in apparent disbelief, "You are pregnant, Madame?" Voltaire, mystified, asks, "How is that done?" Saint-Lambert, bowing and extending his arms, responds, "She wanted it." All assumed Du Châtelet's husband had long ceased to be her sexual partner; therefore,

272 EMILIE DU CHÂTELET

Voltaire became the one cuckolded. According to an old proverb repeated by the *nouvelliste* Collé, "He who leaves his place, loses it."[65]

∼✤∼

For most of 1748, Du Châtelet had made sporadic efforts to continue with her commentary. She had gone to Paris expecting to work on it but cut short her stay—exciting gossip—just to see Saint-Lambert again. Yet she wanted him to understand the significance of the project to her. She accepted that she did not need to have undertaken it, "but it is indispensable to finish it, and to do it well." She had taken her papers and books to Plombières and reported to Saint-Lambert that she worked all morning, spent a half-hour with the princesse de la Roche-sur-Yon at two, having "*café* with her" while she was in the bath taking the waters of the spa, and then worked again from three until *souper* at eight. Despite her best efforts, she had found that she could not apply herself amid so much distraction.[66]

In addition, at some point that year, she expanded her *Commentaire* once again. Now it began with the "Exposition" and went on to a two-part section that would bear the impressive title "Solution analytique des principaux problêmes qui concernent le Système du Monde [Algebraic / Analytical Solution to the principal problems which concern the System of the World]." Here she now included "problems" from Book I of the *Principia,* those mathematical and experimental idealizations relating to attraction that had been particularly contested by Newton's critics. These she recast from geometric proportions to integral calculus. This became for her, as it would have been for most *géomètres* of her day, the most difficult aspect of her project, and the part that she now struggled with in the long spring and early summer of her pregnancy. When complete, her *Commentaire* would present Newton's great work on a number of levels, in addition to the translation itself: the general description of Newton's universe in the "Exposition"; detailed explanations complete with the derivation of their most important proofs of attraction of the *Mémoires* by Clairaut and Daniel Bernoulli; and, finally, for the most sophisticated among her readers, her analytical solutions to essential propositions of Book I of the *Principia.*

In Paris, from February to early June 1749, Du Châtelet increasingly turned her attention to "my Newton," as she referred to it in her letters to Saint-Lambert. She was determined: "I will not leave until it is finished."

Even so, she acknowledged to her lover, "You are the beginning, the end, the goal, and the continual subject of all my actions and all my thoughts." She now had his portrait, and though "it is not your eyes, not your expression, . . . it resembles you and it makes me happy." The need for his support remained a constant theme as her efforts to complete the *Commentaire* became more concentrated and intense. She complained of his assumption that she stayed in Paris longer than necessary, but when he wrote less frequently so as not to "create confusion," she missed his impatience, his pressing her to leave.[67]

Du Châtelet realized by the end of April 1749 that she could not maintain her activities at Versailles and finish the analytical sections of her commentary. She had spent much of her time at the Trianon, in attendance on King Stanislas, who was enjoying one of his visits with his daughter, Queen Marie Leszczyńska. She concluded that after the king left she "would close myself off for work." Stanislas was excited about her condition and asked if she was not "delighted to be pregnant"; the old king assumed that "I already love my child *à la folie*." She admitted that, since she had arranged to give birth at Lunéville, she was less "angry with my *état*." It was, however, in this letter that she first told Saint-Lambert of her fears about the birth: that she might die. Therefore, she must be finished by that time, she must see to her "affairs." "I want to leave them in order, and take measures about my papers," she explained.[68]

By the third week in May, her husband had already begun to make plans for her return journey to Lunéville, and she hoped that Saint-Lambert might join the travelers at Troyes. She pleaded with him not to "reproach me for my *Newton*." She explained, "I have never made such a great sacrifice to reason as [I have] to stay here to finish it." In one letter, she listed the hostesses she had refused and described the regimen she had established since the departure of the king. She had resolved "to sequester myself absolutely, to risk all for all, and to do nothing else but my book." She rose at nine, "sometimes at eight, I work until three, I take my *café* at three o'clock; I resume work at four, I leave it at ten to eat a bit alone." Voltaire had also returned to Paris, and so, she continued, "I talk until midnight with M. de V, who attends me at my *souper,* and I resume work at midnight until five o'clock." Consultation with Clairaut had become essential to the completion of the project. She did not want to journey back and forth to Paris to see him after the birth. Therefore, her departure depended "on the good will of M. Clairaut and the time that he gives me." The mathematician was then in the midst of the controversy at the Académie with Euler and d'Alembert over calculations for the moon's orbit. Du Châtelet's *Commentaire* would have seemed unimportant in comparison.[69]

Du Châtelet spent these last weeks in Paris in the large bedroom of her suite in the *hôtel* on the rue Traversière that she and Voltaire shared. She kept a chafing dish, some knives, and serving spoons in her room that could be used for her late-evening meal. Here Du Châtelet could write at her *secrétaire,* a book open on the small desk lectern.[70] When Clairaut joined her, often probably after the sessions at the Académie, he read and checked the last sections of her manuscript. His careful penmanship appears in the margins of the summary she had made of his *Mémoire.* He gave more details of how a particular equation worked, clarified a phrase on one page, added some words on another. In two instances he added an entire paragraph, but overall his changes were minor. Even so, they must have reassured Du Châtelet that she had done justice to his description of the reasoning and mathematics needed to determine the shape and density of the earth.[71]

Undoubtedly, Du Châtelet also wanted Clairaut to check the new section she had decided to include that was nothing but calculations, the part of her "Solutions analytiques" in which she took some of the most controversial hypotheses of Book I of Newton's *Principia* and transformed them from geometric ratios into calculus, the new "analytical" mode that her French and continental mentors had begun to make popular. This was the project that Maupertuis had once envisioned for himself in his letters to the elder Johann Bernoulli. As Du Châtelet was the one who took on the defense of Johann Bernoulli's formula for *forces vives,* so now she took on this task as well. By the end of the eighteenth century, in the hands of mathematicians like Laplace and Lagrange, this approach had become the only way to describe the physics of the universe. Du Châtelet's excitement over the calculus is understandable: freely variable points created the possibility of a mathematics that could be used to calculate all that could be defined as taking space. For her that would have been the known universe. Only the "monad," the essential element of matter that she believed had no extension, would escape from this form of analysis.[72]

For this analytical section, Du Châtelet chose four of the most contro-

versial and complicated sections of Newton's Book I: on trajectories in relation to gravity; on the effects of attraction on spherical bodies; on spheroids
(like the earth with its flattening at the poles); and on the refraction of light
as explained by attraction. In the twentieth century, historians of science
doubted that Du Châtelet could have done this mathematics, but one only has
to study the *cahiers* she so carefully deposited with the king's librarian to know
that she was the sole author. The values for an equation run along the sides
of pages; there are notes of errors and the need to recalculate; all kinds of
markings indicate where additions were to go. One addition was on a piece
of pale-green-bordered stationery. In turn, a letter to Saint-Lambert had to be
penned on manuscript paper. The nub of her pen flattened from page after
page of numbers, letters, signs, then was sharpened again to a thin point.[73]

Death and Memory

As she had mentioned to Saint-Lambert early in her stay in Paris, Du Châtelet wished to set her affairs in order. She tied the important family papers
into more than thirty neat packages: one for the documents concerning her
marriage, another for her daughter's; one for the Trichâteau inheritance,
another for her election to the Bologna Academy; numerous leases for the
management of the lands and forges of Cirey. She also prepared an envelope
for her husband with instructions to their household intendant, De La Croix,
to give it to the marquis only in the event of her death. She returned to
Saint-Lambert the box in which he had kept her letters. She did not expect
to return to Paris for months, and so she ordered her servants to cover some
of the furniture, to put all the small decorative items away with the linens,
the tableware, and the dishes. They closed the curtains at the windows. The
routine must have been a familiar one. The clothing she did not need for
Lunéville was folded and placed neatly on the shelves of armoires and cabinets. Other clothing had to be packed for the return to Stanislas's court.[74]

On some days, Du Châtelet did not expect ever to return to Paris. The
stories she had heard of women dying in childbirth seem to have come to
mind. However, with the anticipation of seeing her lover again, she forgot
her fears and her worries about further corrections to the *Commentaire*. In
her last letter from Paris, on June 11—after much correspondence about
the route, when and where they would meet, and concerns about his fatigue

from riding in the heat—Du Châtelet admitted, "I will leave the book imperfect." She explained this uncharacteristic decision to her lover: "But it is necessary that I rejoin you or I die." He could have asked for no greater sign of her love. She concluded: "I adore you, I love you with a passion and a madness that I believe you merit, and that makes me happy."[75]

~~~

Stanislas had taken the court to Commercy as usual for the summer, but, rather than join her royal patron, Du Châtelet decided to remain at Lunéville along with Voltaire, Saint-Lambert when he could be absent from his regiment, Devaux, and the usual group of minor functionaries. Her husband and Mme de Boufflers had to be in attendance on the king. The customs surrounding Du Châtelet's condition suggested this as an appropriate decision on her part and dictated that, as the date for the birth neared, she remain most of the time in her new suite of rooms in the palace. The location could not have been better: the theater was just a few steps across the main gravel walk of the nearest part of the gardens, the king's formal rooms to the other side. Although she was increasingly uncomfortable, Devaux described her a few weeks after her return, noting that "she is not at all embarrassed by her pregnancy, she says she has not suffered from it for a moment." When together, she and Saint-Lambert "appeared in very good humor." Perhaps because she had denied herself the pleasure of late-night gatherings for so many months, she took on the responsibility for arranging the *soupers* for the group. One night they read *Alzire* in her rooms, with her taking the lead role. She played cards with Voltaire when he allowed himself time from *Catalina,* his new tragedy meant to rival that of Crébillon. With the completion of each new scene, Voltaire read to "our little society."[76]

   Du Châtelet and Saint-Lambert's love for each other continued to elicit moments of exhilaration, confusion, and reconciliation. In the glow of their first night together after so many weeks, she wrote: "You said to me yesterday things so tender and so touching that you have penetrated my heart, but love me then always the same." When he asked what she wanted to do today, she could answer with assurance: "What I want to do every day of my life: I will see you, I will love you, I will say it to you." She admitted that there was an infinite difference between the way she now idolized him and how she had loved him when she left for Paris. Today she could not imagine imposing such a privation upon herself. Despite the fears she allowed to torment her that he might come to love her less, she was sure "that no person existed as happy as me." Only in the last week or so of the pregnancy, when he had to be on duty in Nancy, or in attendance on his patron, the prince de Beauvau-Craon, did her afflictions and her presentiments make her feel desolate and discouraged.[77]

One August evening when Du Châtelet had bemoaned her condition to her lover, she sensed that she might have the baby that night, but another week passed. Then, at four in the morning on September 4, she gave birth to a daughter. The labor was probably very quick, perhaps two hours. Voltaire had been unsympathetic about the whole enterprise in these last weeks; he had declared her prospective labors less arduous than his own. The birth itself seemed so easy to Voltaire that he found himself "one hundred times more fatigued than she." After all, as he explained to the marquis d'Argenson, one of the friends he informed right away of the event, "she only had to bring the one little girl into the world who does not say a word, and for me it was necessary to make a Cicero, a Caesar, and it is more difficult to make these men speak than to make children."[78]

A number of Du Châtelet's close woman friends had gathered at Lunéville to be with her for the birth. Mlle de Thil had come from Paris, the princesse de la Roche-sur-Yon had arrived in mid-August. She and the king, acting as godparents, provided the name for the little girl, Stanislas-Adélaïde, at her baptism in the parish church just after she was born. As with her other children, Du Châtelet must have arranged a *nourrice* for her infant daughter. Custom dictated that she retire to her bed after the birth, where she was expected to rest, to receive her visitors, and to remain more or less in seclusion for the next six weeks. With everyone returned to Lunéville, this would be no hardship. The heat of the summer had not abated, but others suffered more than Du Châtelet. She had been working when she felt the labor pains, and probably went back to her papers. Four or five days later, having finished correcting the printer's proofs and the pages made by her copyist, she packaged up all of her *cahiers* and the loose sheets of her commentary and sent them to abbé Claude Salier, the royal librarian. The notaries found the receipt, dated September 10, 1749, among her other important personal and family documents. Perhaps she took this precaution because she feared another König might question her authorship.[79]

The only account of the unexpected turn of events six days after the birth comes from Longchamps, Voltaire's valet. In this instance his editor, rather than adding details, cut them short. He should have left the stark simplicity of the valet's original account. The marquise was presumed to be doing well; the "milk fever" had come as expected. Her *femme de chambre* would bind her chest, and after a few days of discomfort, her breasts would cease to produce milk. The fever added to the heat. Du Châtelet insisted that her servant bring her a barley syrup called "orgeat" poured over ice. This was the same "black syrup" that she had taken with such efficacy during her pregnancy. There was much protestation from her friends, for the luxurious entity, ice, was to them the opposite of what should be consumed when one had a slight fever. Du Châtelet had no sooner finished the drink than she was overwhelmed by "a violent headache." The king's physician was called. He ordered remedies he had given her on a similar occasion. This time, however, she seemed breathless, as if suffocating, and he feared for her life. He was right to be alarmed. Having taken to her bed after her pregnancy, it is likely that Du Châtelet had developed an embolus, a blood clot in one of the major veins in her pelvis or one of her legs. As it began to break up, pieces traveled through her circulatory system to her heart, and bits had lodged in one or more of the blood vessels of her lungs. A sharp jump in her blood pressure would explain the headache, as her heart attempted to continue its work despite the obstacles. When portions of her lungs ceased to function, she had difficulty breathing.

The royal physician sent immediately for the two most prestigious doctors from Nancy. They consulted, then gave their noble patient "drugs," after which "she seemed more tranquil." The opiates would have dilated the vessels and made it possible for the blood to flow again. Her friends who had been with her during this ordeal took the opportunity to go to their *souper*. Only Saint-Lambert, de Thil, Du Châtelet's *femme de chambre,* and history's witness, the valet Longchamps, remained behind. It was the tenth of September. Saint-Lambert went up to her bed and spoke with her for a few moments. Seeing that she was falling asleep, he left her to rest and talked a bit with Longchamps and the other servant. It was only ten minutes or so before they heard groans, a death rattle. They rushed to her side to find her unconscious, her eyes turned back in her head. They tried to revive her with vinegar, a common remedy for faintness. Saint-Lambert put his hand under the coverlet to see if her chest moved. He cried out that "she was no more."

Another piece of the clot, perhaps many bits, had closed off a major artery to the lungs, or enough smaller ones to produce the same effect. Du Châtelet had literally suffocated; she had died of pulmonary embolism. The young *femme de chambre* was sent to tell the others, who were assembled for their late-night refreshment in Mme de Boufflers's *appartement* across the inner courtyard. Did the young servant run? How must it have sounded when she blurted out that the marquise had died? As the courtiers rushed into the room, there were "cries succeeded by tears followed by a doleful silence." Who would have been delegated to tell King Stanislas? Someone led the marquis and Voltaire away. Saint-Lambert remained and was the last to leave. Perhaps it was he who closed her eyes.[80]

Longchamps did not record the subsequent rituals associated with the preparations for Du Châtelet's burial. In fact, the arrangements have an unsettling, haphazard quality. De Thil and the other women would have washed and prepared her body. Prayers must have been said throughout that night by Stanislas's priests, and perhaps by nuns from the duchy's elite convent of Remiremont. Stanislas generously gave permission for Du Châtelet to be buried in his new church of Saint-Jacques. With the hot summer to consider, the procession of carriages drawn by horses draped in black made its way to the church within a few days. A black marble slab without any identification marked her burial place, and still does today, close to the entrance to the church. When her daughter Stanislas-Adélaïde died a year and a half later, it was probably the marquis who arranged to raise the stone and to have her small body placed with her mother's. The tomb was desecrated in the Revolution of 1789, but, according to tradition, Du Châtelet's remains were eventually recovered and placed back in the tomb.[81]

The appropriate contemporary sources noted her passing. The September 20 edition of the *Gazette de France* had her age wrong, her husband's lineage and offices correct. This was significant, since the article identified her only as his wife. The *Gazette de Hollande* was more complimentary, called her "the *Sapho Moderne*," and listed her scientific writings, including the as yet unpublished translation of and commentary on Newton's *Principia*. The duc de Luynes, in his account, captured the surprise of her death after "she gave birth to a daughter very happily and very promptly." He listed her pedigree and then her accomplishments in phrases that echoed her own description of herself in the translator's preface she had written almost fifteen years before: "However often she occupied herself with frivolous things, [like] the most ignorant women, she knew much and was instructed in the most abstract sciences."[82]

The eighteenth century took the business of death seriously. Her brother, now an important member of the French clergy, and her husband authorized the appraisers and notaries to inventory and value her possessions at Lunéville, at Cirey, and in Paris. The marquis reclaimed the family diamonds. They would go to his son, perhaps at the time of his very advantageous marriage to Diane-Adélaïde de Rochechouart in 1752.[83] The best of Du Châtelet's *habits de cour,* like the two in elaborate cloth from Tuscany, would have been sold. Her old chemises made rags for the Lunéville servants. Her young *femme de chambre* packed up her remaining small but numerous personal effects, including the decorated dog-collar, two watch chains, and a broken crystal snuffbox. Perhaps Mlle de Thil supervised and assisted the family intendant with these arrangements, for she stayed on at Lunéville into the next year.[84]

Du Châtelet's manuscripts, like her possessions, were dispersed. Saint-Lambert had his copy of the *Discours sur le bonheur;* another went to a relative of the prince de Beauvau-Craon, Mme de Boisgelin. Others read it even before its publication; an eighteenth-century biographer of Voltaire complimented it as "perhaps the only one of the works on this question that was written without pretension and with entire frankness."[85] One copy of the *Examens de la Bible* stayed in the area, to be given in modern times to the local archives of the city of Troyes; another remained in Brussels, suggesting that Du Châtelet had completed the project while living in Flanders. The four drafts of her translation of Mandeville's *Fable of the Bees* were packed into one of the twenty-five cartons that Voltaire took away from Cirey. He mentioned the tears he shed "arranging the papers that speak to me of her." They found their way to St. Petersburg when Mme Denis sold his library to Catherine the Great of Russia after his own death.

And what of "my Newton"? Prault, her publisher, had the proofs, all corrected by the author and reviewed by Clairaut. As with her infant daughter, however, no one had an immediate interest in the project's survival. Quite the reverse—many had an interest in calming the notoriety that her death in such circumstances had occasioned. It took the excitement surrounding the return of Halley's comet at the end of the 1750s to revive the publisher's interest and hope for profit. An incomplete edition appeared in 1756. Then, in the winter of 1758–59, having finished his calculations for predicting the return of the comet, Clairaut once again took an interest in Du Châtelet's translation and commentary. He helped to arrange for the rest of the illustrations, and sent friends like La Condamine their long-awaited copies. Du Châtelet's "Newton," with its unique three-tiered commentary, became for a whole generation of French *physiciens* and *géomètres* their principal means of access to the *Principia*. To this day, it remains the only complete French translation.[86]

~❧~

Though Voltaire wrote of his anguish, and with eloquence of the loss not of "a mistress" but "of a friend and a great man," the events also occasioned intense protestations of devotion to his niece. While at Cirey packing his boxes of furnishings, papers, scientific instruments, paintings, and books, enough to fill two carts, he assured "my dear child," "Once again my heart, my life are for you, for you to do with as you wish."[87] Soon his letters spoke of the play she was writing, mentioning that d'Argental had read it, and of his movements from one friend's château to another. It was as if it were 1734 again and he had no fixed abode. There was the *hôtel* in Paris, but he had "an invincible repugance" for "the evil city" and "for the curious, for the chatter that must be endured." The *nouvelliste* Collé, in his *Journal historique et littéraire,* was but one of many who mocked Du Châtelet's death. "It is to be hoped that this is the last air she will put on: to die in childbirth at her age, it is to call attention to herself; it is to insist on doing nothing like other people." However, he caricatured Voltaire as well, noting that he "must ruin himself in epitaphs, *éloges,* and mortuary verses." By October, the poet had overcome his distaste for the capital enough to return and take up much of his former routine. Despite his ill health and the tragedy of his dear friend's death, he presented a reading of *Catalina* in November, and the following January, 1750, arranged to have *Electra* produced by the Comédie française. Renamed *Oreste,* perhaps to make the borrowing from Crébillon less obvious, it was not a success. The parterre knew of the competition with Pompadour's favorite and, according to Collé, called for the elder man's play rather than the one by Voltaire that they had just watched. The disaster was somewhat mitigated when Pompadour performed his *Alzire* at

Versailles. Not even the patronage of the court, however, could save his *Electra / Oreste*. When Louis XV saw it performed at court in March, the duc de Luynes reported that the king loudly exclaimed his astonishment that this and *Alzire* could be by the same author.[88]

Just as Voltaire had difficulties maintaining his aura of success at the Comédie française and at Versailles, so his relations with the noble families that had protected him worsened. Within a few months of her death, Du Châtelet's husband and Voltaire had come to serious disagreements about their shared residences and about money. Voltaire left Lunéville for Cirey only days after the burial, in theory to sort through and pack up his furniture, books, papers, and scientific instruments. He arranged for La Font, the marquis's servant, to receive the cartons, and for Denis to pay the costs.[89] The marquis and his brother were surprised to find Voltaire's wing of the château essentially empty. When Voltaire returned to Paris, he identified his possessions at their *hôtel* on the rue Traversière, including a valuable marquetry commode and a service of Sèvres porcelain. By November, the marquis's sister had become involved. Voltaire wrote a suitably respectful letter to her and to the marquis Du Châtelet. But five thousand livres was in dispute, in addition to ownership of the furniture and the dinnerware that Voltaire had listed, and three portraits of himself, one in a small diamond-decorated frame, another in a ring, and a third on a snuffbox. Perhaps as a token of good will, Voltaire, who originally had other plans, now agreed to take over the lease of the rue Traversière *hôtel,* moved his niece into Du Châtelet's former *appartement,* and offered the other to one of his young poet friends.[90]

Seven months later, at the end of June 1750, Voltaire turned away from these problems. He left Paris, his lodgings, and his niece, and accepted Frederick's invitation to join the Prussian court. He had not gone the previous summer, claiming his fears for Du Châtelet's delivery. "I am neither the maker of babies, nor doctor, nor midwife, but I am a friend, and I will not leave, even for your majesty, a woman who can die in the month of September." Assuming she did well, however, he promised "to pay his court" to Frederick in October. Now, almost a year later, Frederick's promises of "a new crown of our most beautiful laurels, a willing chambermaid for your usage, and verses in your honor" had much appeal, though Voltaire had been quick to respond that at his age he had no need of the young servant.[91]

Prussia did not give the playwright the peace or uncritical admiration he sought: instead, it became the first stop in what would be a long phase in exile. However, Voltaire's stay in Prussia has other significance. While at Frederick's court, he wrote the *éloge* for his lover and companion that set the legend of Du Châtelet and provided the memory that came to be accepted as truth. He was the admiring friend, she the favored prodigy, a marvel, "a woman who undertook and achieved [the translation of Newton] to the astonishment & the glory of her country." Her gifts exceeded those of ordinary mortals: reading "good Authors," her facility for languages, "the most lively and delicate taste for belles lettres." Her eloquence surpassed the great Newton's. Amid all of her learned activities, "she found the time not only to fulfill all the duties of society but also to seek out with eagerness all the amusements." She had no patience with the ridicule that inevitably greeted her; she believed it was a waste of her time to notice it. "Her memory has been precious to those who particularly knew her & who have been able to see the extent of her spirit [*esprit*] and her soul." He concluded with the drama of her death: she had continued to work despite her premonitions and the need to take the rest that "would have saved her."[92]

In the memoir of his own life that he wrote after he left the Prussian court, Voltaire emphasized the same themes, but now her life became an embellishment of his own. "I found in 1733 a young lady who thought a bit like me, and who resolved to come and spend several years in the countryside there to cultivate her mind [*esprit*] far from the tumult of the world." Identified first as "Madame la marquise Du Châtelet," later she was "the woman in France who had the frame of mind most disposed to all the sciences." Cirey became his and his learned visitor's; he taught her English. If one ever wanted to "give some recognition to Leibniz's ideas," it would be in her *Institutions* that "one must look for it." Voltaire then repeated his erroneous claim, first made in his *éloge* for her: "born as she was for the truth," she had abandoned these Leibnizian "systems" and returned to the Newtonian fold. He lauded her translation of the *Principia*, but he had no clear idea of the commentary beyond a portion of the "Solutions analytiques."

Voltaire's *Mémoire* rightly noted that her translation and *Commentaire* were not published, but it also proudly declared that he "was the first who had dared bring to my nation the discoveries of Newton in an intelligible language." Pages described his life at Louis XV's court with no mention of her or her husband and their protection. He depicted Du Châtelet's death, but left the causes to be surmised. This memoir, found among Voltaire's papers after his death, was copied, printed, and circulated widely. It was quoted as often as a quatrain that was supposedly by Voltaire, but which he took great pains to deny:

> The universe has lost the sublime Emilie.
> She loves pleasures, the arts, and truth.
> The gods gave her their soul and their genius
> Only keeping for themselves immortality.[93]

Voltaire became the idol of the Revolution. As his legend evolved, Du Châtelet became an integral part of his story, but more as his sexual than his intellectual companion. This portrayal of their association eclipsed all other aspects of her life. As Raynal wrote in his death notice for her in his *Correspondance littéraire,* "This lady, so famous in foreign countries, had here more censors than partisans." Her *Discours sur le bonheur,* published first in 1779 and again in 1796 and 1806, became an irresponsible justification for immorality, evidence of the betrayal of the always loyal *philosophe* by an emotional, ungrateful woman who chose a younger and lesser man. Voltaire's affair with Denis never appeared in the narratives. In contrast, as reported and embellished in the nineteenth and twentieth centuries, Du Châtelet's liaisons multiplied.[94]

As effective as these misrepresentations and omissions were in altering her memory, most dramatic was the way in which contemporaries diminished the significance of her writings or appropriated them altogether. The evidence that could fill out and correct the partial images Voltaire highlighted with his words and his verses, that could contradict the unflattering legends, receded into the background. Eventually, her work disappeared to the restricted shelves of rare-book collections and the obscurity of provincial archives. Even the eighteenth-century biographical dictionaries of "famous women," from the more accurate chronicles of her achievements such as that in the *Galerie françoise* to the hagiographical tales of women prodigies like the one quoted at the beginning of this biography, fell out of favor and out of print. As the science of the nineteenth century turned away from the metaphysical to the experimental, it became impossible to see the significance of her *Institutions,* despite its contemporary translation into Italian and

German and wide dissemination throughout the Republic of Letters. This magisterial synthesis, if mentioned at all, became nothing more than lessons for her son; the translation of Newton, when cited, only confirmed her supposed rejection of Leibniz. Both were deemed irrelevant to the central narrative of the progress of modern experimental science.[95]

Du Châtelet was neither the first nor the last woman to have her intellectual accomplishments misrepresented and forgotten. Nor was she the only one to have her works appropriated. Denis Diderot admired Du Châtelet and sought her favor. In June 1749, he had sent her and Voltaire his *Lettre sur les aveugles* (*Letter on the Blind*) and a mathematics text he had written. The next month, when he was imprisoned for the *Lettre* at Vincennes, she wrote on his behalf to her husband's cousin and helped occasion his release. In the entry on "Newtonianisme" for their *Encyclopédie,* Diderot and d'Alembert credited her for the contribution she made to knowledge of Newton with her translation and commentary. In contrast, others who wrote for them simply took whole passages from the *Institutions* for subjects as general as "Time" and "Hypothesis" and as specific as the descriptions of the metaphysical concepts of Leibniz and Wolff. Few identified the original author, and so Du Châtelet acquired the title of so many other women before and after her: she became "anonymous."[96] In the twentieth century, even this skewed acknowledgment of her abilities was taken from her. Historians of science attributed her commentary and translation to Clairaut. They ignored or neglected to look for the reviews from her own day that clearly accepted her authorship and applauded her accomplishment.[97]

Du Châtelet would have been both amused and disappointed by this negation of her achievements and her claims to *la gloire.* In her own lifetime, she had experienced derision and dismissal. She assumed that those of the next generations would have more reason and perspicacity. In her *Discours* on happiness, Du Châtelet asked for "the applause of posterity . . . from which one expects more justice than from one's contemporaries."[98] Sadly, she was mistaken. Only now have scholars begun to seek out the many facets of her history, to rewrite the narratives of Enlightenment philosophy and science. This biography, this elaborate net of a life, a mapmaker's most thoughtful re-creation, is offered as part of this effort. May it bring her the applause of new generations that she so justifiably expected.

Epilogue: 2006

Du Châtelet's unorthodox intellectual pursuits annoyed her contemporaries and made her the subject of ridicule more often than did her sexual behavior. Why, then, has her official memory been so distorted, evidence selected and analyses made that diminish her importance to our understanding of the eighteenth-century Republic of Letters and the first decades of the Enlightenment? What traditions and authorities does she challenge? For me, as a women's historian, this is a political question.[1] Did she simply fall prey to the "truisms of women's history"? Du Châtelet's history exemplifies all of the standard devices used to negate a woman's contribution to the traditional narrative of European history. Du Châtelet overcame the obstacles to women's education, but, we will be told, she allowed her responsibilities as a member of a family and her emotional attachments to take time from her intellectual pursuits. She published, but, of course, less than the men of the Republic of Letters with whom she was in an unspoken and impossible competition. Her works, when described at all, are judged derivative, dismissed as not "original."[2]

Du Châtelet's premature death, and Voltaire's incorporation of her life into his literary repertoire, facilitated this process of forgetting and remembering the marquise in stereotyped and dependent images. Was Voltaire still arguing with her in 1758, when he wrote Candide, his most famous conte? The discovery of "experimental philosophy" by Cunégonde, the central female character, made a mockery of any woman who sought knowledge. "Since the lady took a great interest in science, she watched the experiments being repeated with breathless fascination." The experiments were Dr. Pangloss (Voltaire's caricature of a Leibnizian) having intercourse with a chambermaid. "Cunégonde saw clearly the Doctor's 'sufficient reason,' and took note of cause and effect." Not surprisingly, Cunégonde, silly and misguided, "returned home filled with a desire for learning, and fancied that she could reason equally well with young Candide and he with her."[3]

Du Châtelet was not the first, nor will she be the last, exceptional woman to die too soon, and thus to leave tragic musings about what might have been. She was unique, however, in that the stories of a former lover, valets, gossips, and those who either feared or disliked her, became the principal sources for her history. Whose interests have been served by the assertions they leave us of her exaggerated sexuality? Perhaps Voltaire's. As she had protected him in life, so she now protected him in death. A nineteenth- and twentieth-century world sensitive to the mixing of sexualities could ignore his ambivalence, repeat and embellish the sexual exploits of his companion, and thus enhance his masculine identity, something that the disclosure of his letters to Denis did not accomplish. The word "incest" is never mentioned. Thus, the imagined "secrets" of Du Châtelet's life continue to protect the very real secrets of his.

What would happen to the traditional narrative of eighteenth-century intellectual history if these legends were brushed aside and Du Châtelet became an independent, honored participant in the Republic of Letters? Certainly she would achieve the deserved recognition, but others would benefit as well, particularly Saint-Lambert. For his accomplishments had to be sacrificed as he, too, became part of Voltaire's legend. In twentieth-century accounts of the events, little if any mention is made of his activities or his writings after Du Châtelet's death. Instead, he has been remembered as the favored partner not only of Voltaire's mistress, but also of the comtesse d'Houdetot, the woman Jean-Jacques Rousseau hoped to win. To spare the masculine reputations of these icons of the Enlightenment, Saint-Lambert is portrayed as little more than an eighteenth-century gigolo. In fact, he loved both women, and had a successful career first as an army officer and then as a popular member of the *salons* and of Diderot's circle of Encyclopédistes. That two very interesting and intelligent women found the officer and poet from Lorraine a more desirable lover and life companion challenges those other narratives.

Du Châtelet's death devastated Saint-Lambert. Although Devaux did not have the modern language of psychology to draw upon, his letters to Mme de Graffigny suggest a complete breakdown. Saint-Lambert's anguish, like that of Du Châtelet's husband, the marquis, seems to have been far greater than Voltaire's much-publicized misery. After Du Châtelet's burial,

Saint-Lambert sought refuge at Haroué, the Beauvau-Craon château near Luné-ville. Devaux wrote from his friend's bedside and described his condition as "pitiable," a "frightening spectacle." Saint-Lambert left Haroué for Nancy, and now "cries with his mother and sister." Devaux explained that Saint-Lambert could not eat or sleep. He just cried and kept repeating that "she died in his arms, saying to him that she loved him and thanked him for the happiness that he had provided for her since she was loved by him." With echoes of her *Discours* on happiness perhaps in his head, he remembered her saying that "she only regretted the life they had together because she was losing him." His continual cries and sobs made friends fear for his sanity. He claimed that he had "lost all." Graffigny, who had derided the affair from the beginning, now wrote, "Eh, my God, I never believed him capable of such passion."[4]

Encouraged by his friends, Saint-Lambert went to Paris, as Du Châtelet had wanted him to. For a year he stayed with his patron, the prince de Beauvau-Craon. Even so, when he returned to Lunéville the next year, he again could not stop crying. He sold his commission in the Lorraine Gardes and, through Richelieu's intervention—an indirect benefit of his association with Du Châtelet—became an officer in the Royal Infantry. Perhaps her brother the abbé was instrumental in the duc d'Orléans's awarding him a military governorship. By the time of his demission from the king's army in 1761, he had risen to aide-de-camp for the military expedition to England and be-come a chevalier de Saint-Louis. He then devoted himself exclusively to his writings and the life of a *savant*. *Les Saisons,* his long poetic evocation of a reformed and productive countryside, was finally completed and published in 1769 and became a manifesto of the economic reformers known as the Physiocrats. It won him *fauteuil* number 1 at the Académie française only a year later. He wrote numerous entries for the *Encyclopédie,* including ones that would have interested and amused Du Châtelet: on luxury, genius, taste, fantasy, and the concept of *honnête.* Writing always took him a long time. Still, he produced studies of Bolingbroke and Helvétius and a biogra-phy of the prince de Beauvau-Craon. I like to imagine the discussion Du Châtelet and he would have had over his *Analyse historique de la société,* a study of the origins of society and its rules, including his surpisingly stereo-typical portrayals of women, their roles and functions. Her influence is evi-dent in his last work, published after the Revolution, in 1806: a secular catechism that created a moral dogma to rival that of the established church.

Voltaire praised *Les Saisons* as "the best poem written in fifty years." Others were less enthusiastic. Mme Du Deffand described it as "sterile." Diderot complimented the mechanics of the language and the verse but saw his friend the poet as lacking "a soul that is tormented, a violent wit, a fiery imagination, a lyre with many chords."[5] Another of their circle noted this "singular dryness," but also sadness, and coldness. It was as if, after the shock of Du Châtelet's death, Saint-Lambert retreated into the side of his nature that she had teased him about: "half tender and half detached." He had permitted himself passion, but with disastrous results. It was as if all the tears had washed his passion away. His only other lover, and his companion for the rest of his life, the comtesse Elisabeth (Sophie) d'Houdetot, admired him as a man who lived entirely guided by reason and the principles that he espoused in his philosophical writings. He was a man without enemies, she explained, "because of his extreme modesty and especially [because he had] so little vanity [that he] never wounded anyone's pride." The *salonnière* Mme D'Epinay, Mme d'Houdetot's sister-in-law, commented on the graces of his wit, his charm, his agreeableness, and the moral appeal of his lovely soul.

This measured and moderated approach to life brought Saint-Lambert peace and success even through the turbulent years of the Revolution. He lived as part of the household of d'Houdetot and her husband and had the distinction of receiving pensions both from the king and from the governments of the Republic and the Directory. In his will, he gave specific bequests to their servants and to his, and left Plutarch's *Lives* and any other books he wanted to d'Houdetot's son. His bust of Voltaire and the pendulum clock from the prince de Beauvau-Craon were for the comtesse. Saint-Lambert asked that she put the clock in her room, so that, "in hearing it chime, she perhaps will remember sometimes that for more than fifty years I consecrated with pleasure a great part of the hours of my life to her."[6]

What would Du Châtelet have done had she survived? Are there enough bits of evidence to outline new continents on this map of a life that might have been? Certainly she would have seen to the publication of her Newton. As she indicated in one of her letters to Saint-Lambert, she planned to live at Lunéville and return to Paris for "pure society." What use did she plan for the newly purchased country property at Argenteuil? She had already paid for repairs, decorations, and furnishings. Neither she nor her husband nor Voltaire left us an explanation. Perhaps she and the marquis assumed that, when their son married, Cirey would become the young couple's official residence. Argenteuil, close to Paris and Versailles, could then be a new refuge where she and Voltaire could write, away from the "dissipation" of the courts.[7]

What would have been her next projects? She once described ambition as "insatiable."[8] Where would her extraordinary intelligence and imagination have taken her? Would she have gone on to a second volume of her *Institutions?* Most of what she planned for that book had become the "Exposition abrégée" of her commentary on the *Principia*. But she posed queries in the *Institutions* and in her letters that might represent future interests. Her study of Leibniz took her so close to the modern concepts of conservation of mass and of energy (her "force") that one has to assume she would have followed and contributed to the contemporary discussions of these as yet unexplored phenomena.[9] Bernoulli II had already encouraged her to make a submission on monads to a prize competition. With her *Principia* completed, she would have considered submitting *dissertations* on the nature of these elemental substances, if not on other subjects. In the *Institutions,* Du Châtelet had wondered how to explain the workings of attraction at the microscopic level. Her instincts about the most basic nature of matter and about the inapplicability of attraction to describe motion at that level of reality were correct, as twentieth-century quantum mechanics demonstrated. Physicists today are praised for their search for a unified theory of the universe that she assumed existed. How she would have enjoyed being part of this mathematically orchestrated world of virtual realities, atomic particles, space travel, and a plurality of universes.

Best of all, the very mathematics that she so delighted in has led to technologies that I and other scholars have used to give her back her place in the histories of science, philosophy, literature, and Biblical criticism. We discover and discuss one another's research in our e-mails. Her portraits travel on CDs from museums to publishers and illustrate the copy prepared on computers and transmitted as attachments to describe her activities for the newest article or book about her. Du Châtelet's commitment to Leibniz and Bernoulli's formula for kinetic energy won her a place in a television special on Einstein's theory of relativity. The Internet and the World Wide Web have become the means to make her works available to an international audience. When the current digitizing of her books, letters, and eventually her manuscripts is complete, all who can access the Web will simply type in "Emilie Du Châtelet" and arrive at her site. Then no one will ever again be able to suggest that the *Institutions* should be ignored, that she did not author the *Examens de la Bible,* that she did not know calculus, that she did not translate Newton's *Principia,* or that she left her commentary for someone else to finish.

꧁꧂

I first went to Paris with my aunt and my cousin. I was fourteen. We stayed at the St. James & Albany, just across from the Louvre, on the rue de Rivoli. That first night, my aunt took us walking in the Jardin des Tuileries. My most vivid memory is of the neatness and regularity of the patterns made with the pale-blue-gray and white stones that surrounded the fountains. When I returned to Paris many summers later, to begin my research on Du Châtelet's writings, I knew that the marquise had also walked in those gardens. Du Châtelet had been to the Bibliothèque du roi, now the Bibliothèque Nationale, and perhaps even sat by the same tall window I did on one of her visits to borrow books from the abbé Salier. On the days the library is closed, I like to watch the families, the young couples, and the children in the Place des Vosges, where Du Châtelet grew up. One cloudy weekday morning, I rang the bell at no. 12, the *hôtel* that had belonged to the baron de Breteuil. City officials have not marked it as they have the former residences of other famous French women and men. Du Châtelet's home became a primary school in the 1890s, so a notice board announcing the week's lunch menu, parent-teacher meetings, and children's events takes the place of a bronze plaque. The *directrice* welcomed me and gave me a tour. Two fireplaces remain, perhaps from Du Châtelet's time, but otherwise all has been altered over the century to accommodate the educational needs of the children. However, the big windows of the baron's library still look out on the *place,* the trees, the grass, the equestrian statue of a king. Ironically, one part of Breteuil's special room has been made into the library for the primary students. Carefully arranged boxes for children's stories fill one corner, inviting young readers as the book-filled cabinets and armoires of the baron's day once invited Du Châtelet and her brothers.

My aunt grew up steeped in European culture. At some point, her mother decided that they would speak together only in French. I imagine that it was her father who first introduced her to Voltaire. Perhaps he had been fascinated by the woman the great Frenchman loved and so drew her attention to Du Châtelet. There is no way to know how long or how seriously she researched. She found a collection of Voltaire's poetry and thought *Zaïre* "a lovely play." I believe my aunt saw this project as a way to make her brilliant father "proud of me," as she mentioned in one of her letters. Just as I have, she came to places where the sheer scale of the endeavor almost overwhelmed her. In Washington, D.C., just before World War II, she wrote to her parents: "I've been trying to sort over the Voltaire and in a week or so I'll send up an outline of it for you to look at—there's such a lot it's hard to know what to leave out and how to join together what there is. . . ."[10] In the end, she left it for me to make those decisions.

And Du Châtelet's appeal for both of us? There is a pastel portrait of the marquise, perhaps done in her last spring in Paris. It now hangs high on the wall beside the fireplace of the room set aside to commemorate her at the Château de Breteuil. Du Châtelet never visited this place, but the son of the current marquis believed that she came to comfort him once when, as a child, he was ill and slept here. The portrait would have been straight ahead of him as he looked up from his pillows. Du Châtelet is dressed for a morning's writing, with fichus of gauze arranged in the bodice of her dress to keep the drafts away from her chest. Her hair is pulled back and lightly powdered but with no decorative curl. The only ornamentation is a black velvet ribbon tied around her neck. Du Châtelet smiles slightly and stares straight into our eyes if we allow it. She offers us her confidence, her resolution to lead an unorthodox life, the independence she so proudly affirmed in her letter to Saint-Lambert.

In her translator's preface to Mandeville's *Fable,* Du Châtelet indirectly encouraged women to persevere despite "the invincible force on this side of a barrier," never to lack courage, and to produce a good tragedy, a beautiful painting, esteemed works of physics and history. In this pastel, it is as if she offers me, as she once may have offered my aunt, her success in answering the challenges she had posed for herself and other women. Du Châtelet succeeded because of her pleasure in study and critical, analytical questions of all varieties. She took her strength and resolve from her belief in reason, her certainty that passions can be made "to serve our happiness," and her willingness to be "susceptible" to illusion. It seems a formula written for me. Reason, passion, and illusion are the very stuff of biography.

Acknowledgments

Long ago, as a women's historian, I learned that no project of any significance can be the product of only one person's efforts and insights. This biography of the multifaceted and challenging marquise Du Châtelet is no exception. At various points in my research, my thinking, and my writing, scholars and friends supported and challenged me. These acknowledgments represent my effort to thank them for their knowledge, their interest, their excitement, and their faith.

The Dean's and Provost's Offices and the Philip and Elaina Hampton Fund of Miami University first provided the funding to travel to the archives at the Bibliothèque Nationale and then to continue my study in Paris, London, Cambridge, Troyes, and St. Petersburg. Many colleagues in the History Department encouraged me along the way and offered their expertise at key moments. I owe special thanks to Michael O'Brien, who made possible a semester as a fellow of Selwyn College, which meant my introduction to the former master of Selwyn, Sir Alan Cook, and to members of the History and Philosophy of Science Faculty—in particular, Simon Schaffer and Patricia Fara. Charlotte Goldy, the chair of the Miami History Department, facilitated leaves and teaching schedules, and was always ready to help make this book happen. My graduate and undergraduate students in my classes on the scientific revolution, the Enlightenment, and biography forced me to clarify just what it was I had to say. Marlo Troughton, Phoebe Musandu, and Emily Stimpson helped me remember why this period is so exciting. Jenny Presnell and Ed Via of the King Library staff always responded to my most pressing questions and requests. Jen Scharer and Elizabeth E. Smith negotiated and manicured the seemingly endless drafts of the manuscript. Britt Carr and his assistants prepared the illustrations.

My research began with a Mayers Fellowship to the Huntington Library, Art Collections and Botanical Gardens in San Marino, California. The National Endowment for the Humanities has supported my project in a number of ways. I first participated in an Endowment Summer Institute under the supervision of Keith Baker and John Bender. Those weeks gave me the background in the study of the Enlightenment, and introductions to generous scholars that became invaluable as I worked my way through all of the many fields into which Du Châtelet's writings led me. I then received a year-long NEH Fellowship in 2000–1 that enabled me to begin writing and to plan the biography. A collaborative fellowship under the sponsorship of Albert Rabil for his series *The Other Voice of Early Modern Europe* made possible the beginning of a translation project: a selection of the works of Du Châtelet, co-authored with Isabelle Bour, that enriched my knowledge of the wonders of eighteenth-century French and also the ways in which the marquise's mind worked.

A Camargo Fellowship (2001) allowed me to live in France for six months, to study

Racine with Mireille Lecat, and to experiment with biography in an exciting, supportive atmosphere. Imi Hwangbo and Éric Marty never lost faith; Robert Du Plessis spent hours deciphering inventories for me; Rafe Blaufarb introduced me to French military archives and history; Robert Zaretsky and Patricia Hampl treated me like a writer, and Patricia introduced me to my agent. William Monter did research trips for me; Rosellen Monter helped me complete my own.

My research in St. Petersburg would not have been possible without the efforts of Sonia Timchenko, from the moment she greeted my project with enthusiasm at a Bryn Mawr College reunion in London. Anthony Cross of Cambridge University gave me all the essential scholar's introductions. The elusive "Chef de la Réserve" of the Voltaire Library, Nicolas A. Kopanev, allowed me to work without interruption, and his assistant, Genadi Farfurian, smiled at my Russian and gave me book after precious book.

Sarah Hanley, Bonnie G. Smith, and Thomas E. Kaiser wrote numerous recommendations and thus helped me win grants and recognition, and cheered me on when the immensity of the task seemed overwhelming.

In the course of my research, I have traded on the expertise of scholars in many diverse fields. They introduced me to their specialties and to the critical study of biography. It is now my privilege to thank them for their time and their knowledge: Evelyn Lever, Bertram Eugene Schwarzbach, Olivier Courcelle, Margaret J. Osler, Craig Waff, Carson Roberts, J. B. Shank, Yves Ollivier, Susan Lancer, Dena Goodman, Nikki Shepardson, Bill Connell, Lynette Hunter, Mary Terrall, Paula Findlen, Robert Rosenstone, Alun Munslow, John Iverson, Antoinette Emch-Dériaz and Gérard Emch, J. Patrick Lee, Mordecai Feingold, Paul Veatch Moriarty, Jean-François Gauvin, W. H. Barber, Hélène Say, Ulla Kölving, Andrew Brown, and Nanette LeCoat. The modern *Emiliens*—Jane Birkenstock, Ronald K. Smeltzer, Keiko Kawashima, James Casey—were brought together through Jane's Web site, our leap from the twenty-first to the eighteenth century. From the beginning, they have eagerly awaited this biography and never wavered in their assumption that it would be well worth all of our efforts. Ronald K. Smeltzer supplied many of the illustrations from his exceptional collection of rare scientific books and initiated me into the dangerous habit of acquiring them.

Hilda L. Smith, the co-coordinator of a jointly sponsored conference on "Metaphysics into Science," was the first to take my intellectual concerns seriously and to accept my essay about Du Châtelet for a collection she was editing. A number of organizations committed to the specialized study of France and the history of Science also understood Du Châtelet's importance to the history of the Enlightenment: the Royal Society, and French Historical Studies. The Voltaire Foundation sponsored a volume of essays for its series, *Studies on Voltaire and the Eighteenth Century*, which represents the first such scholarly collection. Julie Candler Hayes coedited this collection with patience, intelligence, and good humor, despite the hours and days taken from her leave and her own projects. Certain other individuals were key to these projects: Jilliene Sellner, Jonathan Malinson, Nicholas Cronk, Janet Godden, and Rebecca Du Plessis. The editors and staff of the Graffigny Papers—J. Alain Dainard, David W. Smith, Penny Arthur, and Marion Filipiuk—gave of their time, their seemingly infinite knowledge of the period, and their precious notes and manuscripts. They provided the model of scholarly fellowship and set standards I hope I have maintained. From my first tentative letters, Jean-Daniel Candaux took the idea of a three-hundredth-birthday celebration for the marquise and, with the support of Daniel Roche and Elisabeth Badinter and the work of the Comité d'Organisation du Colloque, made it a reality. Danielle Muzerelle, Conservateur en Chef Chargé des Manuscrits of the Bibliothèque de l'Arsenal, created the exhibit and the catalogue to mark the event.

The descendants of the marquise's two families welcomed me and generously allowed me to admire and read their treasures: Henri-François de Breteuil and Séverine Decazes de Breteuil, Véronique Flacha and her family. Mme Hugues Salignac-Fénelon told me her stories of Cirey and allowed me to photograph my favorite places.

My thoughtful, energetic, wise agent, Marly Rusoff, always had the right words at the right time and the right suggestion to move the book to the next stage. Rebecca Balduff and Jennifer Ehmann Divina were also essential to the completion of the project—Becky with her patience and care with the endnotes, Jennifer with her editorial skills and understanding of how difficult cutting a manuscript can be. Both became engaged with the marquise and enthusiastic participants in those last phases of the writing. My editor at Viking, Caroline White, convinced the publisher that the biography would inspire little girls interested in mathematics. Karen Anderson at Viking fielded all of my annoying queries. Senior production editor Kate Griggs and designer Nancy Resnick turned the multicolored manuscript into an elegant book.

My friends and family helped me in more ways than one can list. For example, with a place to stay, with a kind word when I was discouraged: Antonia and Jack Grumbach, Katherine J. Zinsser, Bonnie S. Anderson, Ann Little, Carol Groneman, Dorothy O. Helly, Hester Ringnalda, Diana Byrd, Donna Stevens, and Lissa Martin. Angela V. John always understood what it meant to write this biography. Hilary Ainger read the first tentative efforts. Libby Goldby traveled the whole route with me, from my initial trip to Cirey, to reading and commenting on the entire, long version of the book. Mary Frederickson and Jennifer Morris offered me their enthusiasm and their insights. Anna Klosowska loved every new anecdote and insisted that she could not put each new chapter down, she found them so exciting. She also became my French voice for research questions and arrangements for the birthday celebrations in Paris. Without these friends, I would have floundered long ago.

Sarah K. Lippmann, Murray D. List, and Roger J. Millar bore the brunt of my complaints, confusion, exuberance, and despair. Each reminded me that I was a capable historian and a good writer, that I was meant to do this biography, that I would finish, and that they loved me without qualification. Chance has played a key role at many points in this endeavor; my greatest good fortune has been to have these three individuals in my life.

Notes

Prologue

1 #99S, Du Châtelet to Saint-Lambert, "Samedi au soir" [end of August 1749], (#485, LDC, vol. 2), pp. 242–43. The French historian Anne Soprani created a new arrangement of the letters between Du Châtelet and Saint-Lambert, which I believe more accurately reflects Du Châtelet's thinking and the course of events. I have used Soprani's edition, noted with an "S" after the letter number, as #99S here. See *Emilie Du Châtelet: Lettres d'amour au marquis de Saint-Lambert* (Paris: Editions Méditerranée, 1997). I have indicated the letter number used in the standard 1958 two-volume collection of her letters edited by Theodore Besterman in parentheses with the volume number, as, for example, (#485, LDC, vol. 2) in this instance. See *Lettres de la Marquise du Châtelet*, ed. Theodore Besterman (Genève: Institut et Musée Voltaire, 1958) (hereafter referred to as *LDC*). See also, in the Morgan Library collection in New York, N.Y., *Autograph Letters to the Marquis de Saint-Lambert*, MA2287, #97.

2 #89S, Du Châtelet to Saint-Lambert (21 [May 1749]), pp. 220, 221 (#476, LDC, vol. 2); #88S, Du Châtelet to Saint-Lambert (18 May [1749]), p. 217 (#471, LDC, vol. 2).

3 Charles Collé, *Journal [historique] et mémoires de Charles Collé . . . 1748–1772* (Paris: Didot Frères, 1868), vol. 1, p. 68; Sébastien G. Longchamps and Jean Louis Wagnière, *Mémoires sur Voltaire, et sur ses ouvrages* (Paris: Aimé André, 1826), vol. 1, p. 231.

4 #89S, Du Châtelet to Saint-Lambert (21 [May 1749]), p. 221 (#476, LDC, vol. 2).

5 As translated by Theodore Besterman, *Voltaire* (New York: Harcourt, Brace & World, 1969), p. 295 and n. 9.

6 D3995, Voltaire to d'Argental (28 Aug. 1749), in Theodore Besterman, ed., *The Complete Works of Voltaire* (hereafter referred to as *CWV*) (Genève: Institut et Musée Voltaire, 1968–), vol. 95, p. 141; D4005, Voltaire to marquis d'Argenson (4 Sept. 1749), *CWV*, vol. 95, pp. 150–51.

7 #90S, Du Châtelet to Saint-Lambert ([May 1749]), p. 225 (#470, LDC, vol. 2); #89S, Du Châtelet to Saint-Lambert (21 [May 1749]), pp. 222–23 (#471, LDC, vol. 2).

Chapter One: The Families

1 *Les Femmes célèbres,* in Pamphlets About Mme du Châtelet, Princeton University Library, 3246.766.99, vol. 1, pp. 5–6.

2 Julian Barnes, *Flaubert's Parrot* (New York: Vintage International, 1984), p. 38.

3 See René Vaillot, *Madame du Châtelet* (Paris: Albin Michel, 1978), pp. 31–35; René

Vaillot, *Avec Mme Du Châtelet, 1734–1749,* in *Voltaire en son temps,* ed. René Pomeau (Oxford: Voltaire Foundation, 1985–95), vol. 1, p. 242. For Badinter's reconstruction, see Elisabeth Badinter, *Emilie, Emilie: L'Amibiton féminine au XVIIIe siècle* (Paris: Flammarion, 1983), p. 68.

4 For this information I am indebted to Robert Du Plessis for his expertise on early modern textiles. For the description that follows I am indebted to Evelyne Lever's excellent introduction to her edition of Breteuil's memoir. Her re-creation of the interiors of his city and country residences from the inventory made in 1728 first suggested this kind of image making. See baron de Breteuil, *Mémoires,* ed. Evelyne Lever (Paris: F. Bourin, 1992), pp. 33–35.

5 On houses, see Cissie Fairchilds, *Domestic Enemies: Servants and Their Masters in Old Regime France* (Baltimore: Johns Hopkins University Press, 1984), p. 33; Charles Antoine Jombert, *Architecture moderne* (Paris, 1764); Johann Krafft, *Plans, coupes, élévations des plus belles maisons & des hôtels construits à Paris & dans les environs: 1771–1802* (Paris: Librairie d'art décoratif et industriel, G. Hue, 1909).

6 See Breteuil, *Mémoires,* ed. Lever, pp. 14, 29; Jacques Levron, *Daily Life at Versailles in the Seventeenth and Eighteenth Centuries,* trans. Claire Elaine Engel (London: George Allan, 1965), pp. 41–45. See also Charles Philippe d'Albert, duc de Luynes, *Mémoires du duc de Luynes sur la cour de Louis XV, 1735–1758,* ed. L. Dussieux and E. Soulié (Paris: Firmin Didot, 1860–65), vol. 7, pp. 113–14; vol. 6, pp. 266–67; Jean-François Solnon, *La Cour de France* (Paris: Fayard, 1987), pp. 489–90.

7 He wanted to marry conventionally, but his family did not approve of Caumartin. On his affairs and marriage, see Breteuil, *Mémoires,* ed. Lever, pp. 12–26.

8 Sara Chapman, "Patronage as Family Economy: The Role of Women in the Patron-Client Network of the Phélypeaux de Pontchartrain Family, 1670–1715," *French Historical Studies* 24, no. 1 (Winter 2001), p. 28; Breteuil, *Mémoires,* ed. Lever, pp. 29–30. See also Vaillot, *Madame du Châtelet,* pp. 23–27; baron de Breteuil, *Mémoires,* Arsenal Library, MS 3860, p. 1; Solnon, *La Cour,* pp. 493–94.

9 Breteuil, *Mémoires,* ed. Lever, p. 43. See, for example, Breteuil, *Mémoires,* MS 3859, pp. 121–22, 129, 133. The examples came from different sections of the manuscript: MS 3859, p. 411; MS 3865, p. 94; MS 3864, pp. 171–72; MS 3863, p. 161. See also MS 3862, pp. 94ff; MS 3861, pp. 149–51; MS 3861, p. 55; MS 3860, pp. 131–32; MS 3862, pp. 78–81,101; MS 3863, pp. 135–59. On the Persian ambassador, see MS 3865, pp. 151–77.

10 Breteuil, *Mémoires,* MS 3859, p. 384; MS 3859, pp. 365–487. On scheduling and arrangements, see MS 3862, pp. 2–3. On the palace of Versailles, see William R. Newton, *L'Espace du roi: La Cour de France au château de Versailles, 1682–1789* (Paris: Fayard, 2000); note map #8 c. 1709. For a typical day, see, for example, Breteuil, *Mémoires* (Tuesday, 26 Jan. 1700), MS 3860, pp. 347ff.

11 Breteuil, *Mémoires,* ed. Lever, pp. 38–39. I am grateful to Rafe Blaufarb, a historian of the eighteenth-century French military, for his patient tutelage in the intricacies of eighteenth-century military ranks and functions, and the hierarchy of companies, regiments, and royal and line service, and for introducing me to the military archives at the Château de Vincennes.

12 See Breteuil, *Mémoires,* ed. Lever, pp. 35, 33–34.

13 Marquise de Créqui, *Souvenirs de la marquise de Créqui, 1710–1803* (Paris: Michel Lévy

Frères, 1867), vol. 1, pp. 65, 69–70. Froullay was actually Créqui's *great*-aunt, and Du Châtelet her first cousin once removed.

14 See Breteuil, *Mémoires*, ed. Lever, p. 33; René Colas, *Paris qui reste: Vieux Hôtels, vieilles demeures, la Rive Gauche et l'Ile de Saint-Louis* (Paris: R. Colas, 1914), pp. 41–43. Information about the Place Royale from Antoine-Nicolas Dézallier d'Argenville, *Voyage pittoresque de Paris* (1757; Genève: Minkoff Reprints, 1972), pp. 276–77. The original statue was destroyed in the French Revolution. The current statue is a copy. On dress customs, see Madeleine Delpierre, *Dress in France in the Eighteenth Century*, trans. Caroline Beamish (New Haven: Yale University Press, 1997), pp. 29–30.

15 Breteuil, *Mémoires*, MS 3861, p. 54; MSS 3863, p. 155; Luynes, *Mémoires*, vol. 8, p. 378. On servants, see Fairchilds, *Domestic Enemies*, pp. 26–33.

16 Mark Motley, *Becoming a French Aristocrat: The Education of the Court Nobility 1580–1715* (Princeton: Princeton University Press, 1990), pp. 25–26. Fairchilds, *Domestic Enemies*, chap. 7; Breteuil, *Mémoires*, ed. Lever, pp. 31–33.

17 For these and subsequent details on aristocratic education, see Motley, *Becoming a French Aristocrat*, chap. 1, pp. 18–67 passim, especially pp. 38–39, 49–50, 54–55, 57–58; Fairchilds, *Domestic Enemies*, pp. 202–5; Elie Palairet, *La Bibliothèque des enfants . . .* (Paris: Chez Pierre Simon, 1733), pp. 10–11, 30, 38–39, 42–43; Elie Palairet, *Nouvelle méthode pour apprendre à bien écrire . . .* (La Haye: Pierre Husson, 1716); Roger Chartier, *Passions of the Renaissance*, vol. 3, *A History of Private Life*, ed. Philippe Ariès and Georges Duby (Cambridge, Mass.: Belknap Press of Harvard University Press, 1989), pp. 176–78.

18 Breteuil, *Mémoires*, ed. Lever, p. 34. See also Chartier, *Passions*, 266–70, 182–87; Motley, *Becoming a French Aristocrat*, pp. 38–42; Créqui, *Souvenirs*, vol. 1, pp. 72–74. On the *révérence*, see Emilie de Breteuil, marquise Du Châtelet, trans., *Fable of the Bees*, by Bernard Mandeville, in *Studies on Voltaire, with Some Unpublished Papers of Mme Du Châtelet*, ed. I. O. Wade (Princeton: Princeton University Press, 1947), A171v/ W147, A172/W148. I have designated the manuscript versions of Du Châtelet's preface used here as drafts A, B, and C (Voltaire Collection, St. Petersburg National Library of Russia, vol. IX, pp. 153–284v). Wade's printed text is also cited as "W" with his pagination.

19 See Solnon, *La Cour*, pp. 449–50.

20 See David Garrioch, *Neighborhood and Community in Paris, 1740–1790* (New York: Cambridge University Press, 1986), pp. 33–34. Mme du Châtelet, *Discours sur le bonheur*, ed. Robert Mauzi (Paris: Société d'Edition Belles Lettres, 1961), p. 15.

21 Martine Sonnet, *L'Education des filles au temps des lumières* (Paris: Editions du Cerf, 1987), p. 11; Sonnet, *L'Education*, pp. 27, 46, 48, 53–56, 90 (table 3). A livre was a monetary unit of accounting; you never actually saw or used a coin or a piece of paper of that denomination. See Fernand Braudel, *The Structures of Everyday Life: The Limits of the Possible*, trans. S. Reynolds (New York: Harper & Row, 1979), vol. 1, pp. 464–66, for an explanation of the monetary system. A livre was twenty sous or sols, a sou was twelve deniers, an écu was sixty-six sous, or three livres and six sous. The goals of the order quoted in Sonnet, *L'Education*, pp. 28, 196–97. Painting in Chartier, *Passions*, p. 59. Reading from Sonnet, *L'Education*, pp. 259–60. On Mme Champbonin, see L'abbé Piot, *Cirey-le-Chateau: La Marquise du Châtelet, sa liaison avec Voltaire* (Saint-Dizier: O. Godard, 1894), p. 543.

22 When a full translation by Jean Bertrand appeared in 1740, it was also banned. Du
    Châtelet, trans., *Fable*, A158v/W136, A153/W131. The statement on the *collège* is
    not included in the final version; see B222v/A158/W136.

23 Voltaire's teachers were Pierre Joseph Thoulier d'Olivet and René Joseph Tourne-
    mine. On Voltaire's education at the Jesuit *collège*, see René Pomeau, *D'Arouet à Voltaire
    (1694–1734)* in *Voltaire en son temps*, ed. René Pomeau (Oxford: Voltaire Foundation,
    1985–95), vol. 1, pp. 25–38; Robert L. Walters and W. H. Barber, Introduction to *Elé-
    ments de la philosophie de Newton* (Oxford: Voltaire Foundation, 1992), vol. 15, p. 29.
    D877, Voltaire to Tournemine ([c. June 1735]), vol. 87, p. 155. D901, Voltaire to Tour-
    nemine ([c. Aug. 1735]), vol. 87, p. 183 in *The Complete Works of Voltaire*, ed. Theodore
    Besterman (Genève: Institut et Musée Voltaire, 1968–) (hereafter referred to as *CWV*).
    See Chartier, *Passions*, p. 486. See Motley, *Becoming a French Aristocrat*, pp. 89–107, 124–
    56. A 1688 Paris guide notes the six military academies in the Saint-Germain section of
    the city (*A New Description of Paris* [London: Henry Bonwicke, 1688]), vol. 2, p. 88.

24 On the *querelle des femmes*, see Lieselotte Steinbrugge, *The Moral Sex: Woman's Nature
    in the French World*, trans. Pamela E. Selwyn (New York: Oxford University Press,
    1995), pp. 12–17, 25–34, 42–43; Ian Maclean, *Woman Triumphant: Feminism in French
    Literature 1610–1652* (Oxford: Clarendon Press, 1977), pp. 125–28; Paul Rousselot,
    Histoire de l'éducation des femmes en France. (Paris: Didier, 1883), vol. 2, pp. 207–13;
    Montaigne, *The Complete Works of Montaigne*, trans. Donald M. Frame (Stanford: Stan-
    ford University Press, 1957), 138, "Of pedantry," p. 98; "Of presumption," p. 50; "Of
    three good women," pp. 563–69; "On some verses of Virgil," pp. 685, 674.

25 Créqui, *Souvenirs*, vol. 1 pp. 64–65.

26 Voltaire, "L'Education des filles," in *Mélanges*, ed. Jacques van den Heuvel (Paris: Gal
    limard, 1961), pp. 443–45; see also Créqui, *Souvenirs*, vol. 1, pp. 72, 70.

27 #63, Graffigny to Devaux ([14 Dec. 1738]), Françoise d'Issembourg d'Happoncourt
    Graffigny, *Correspondance de Madame de Graffigny*, ed. J. A. Dainard et al. (Oxford:
    Voltaire Foundation, 1985–), vol. 1, p. 221. On convents, see Sonnet, *L'Education*,
    pp. 196–99; 206, 238–39, 259–60; Rousselot, *Histoire*, vol. 2, p. 103.

28 Lever and Vaillot suggest that Du Châtelet studied with her brothers. See Breteuil,
    Mémoires, ed. Lever, p. 38; Vaillot, *Madame du Châtelet*, chap. 1.

29 On teaching, see Palairet, *Bibliothèque des enfants*, pp. 114–18.

30 On the inventory, see Breteuil, *Mémoires*, ed. Lever, p. 32. On gambling as part of
    education, see Motley, *Becoming a French Aristocrat*, pp. 58–59.

31 See sample game in père Bernard Laurent Soumille, *Le Gran Trictrac* (1738). I am
    grateful to Denis Reynaud at the University of Lyons for alerting me to the differ-
    ences between *trictrac* and backgammon, as well as to David Levy. See Levy's Web
    site: http://pages.sbeglobal.net/david.levy/trictrac/rules/rules.htm. Note that
    education manuals recommended the game for learning multiplication; see Palairet,
    Bibliothèque des enfants, pp. 24–26, 146.

32 Breteuil, *Mémoires*, ed. Lever, pp. 33–34. For the drawing, see Chartier, *Passions*, p. 136.
    J. Patrick Lee generously allowed me to study this copybook. See J. Patrick Lee, "Le
    Recueil de Poésies de Madame Du Châtelet," in *Emilie Du Châtelet: Rewriting Enlighten-
    ment Philosophy and Science*, eds. Judith P. Zinsser and Julie Candler Hayes, *SVEC*
    (2006:1), pp. 105–23. See also a similar copybook at the Bibliothèque Municipale de
    Troyes, MS 2375–78.

33 See Carolyn Lougee, *Paradis des Femmes:Women, Salons, and Social Stratification in Seventeenth Century France* (Princeton: Princeton University Press, 1976); Dorothy Anne Liot Backer, *Precious Women: A Feminist Phenomenon in the Age of Louis XIV* (New York: Basic Books, 1974). On the eighteenth-century *salons,* see Dena Goodman, *The Republic of Letters: A Cultural History of the French Enlightenment* (Ithaca, N.Y.: Cornell University Press, 1994); Madelyn Gutwirth, *The Twilight of the Goddesses:Women and Representation in the French Revolutionary Era* (New Brunswick, N.J.: Rutgers University Press, 1992), chap. 3.

34 On Lambert, see Roger Marchal, *Madame de Lambert et son milieu* (Oxford: Voltaire Foundation, 1991), chap. 2 passim, and pp. 288–89, 487–88, 493–522, 60–63. On the members of the *salon,* the topics discussed, and Lambert's own writings, see Marchal, 13, 95, 98, 166–71, 188–94; Roger Picard, *Les Salons littéraires et la société française, 1610–1789* (Paris: Brentano's, 1943), pp. 146, 181–86.

35 See Breteuil, *Mémoires,* ed. Lever, pp. 36–37.

36 Du Châtelet, trans., *Fable,* B217, a version with slightly altered order of ideas; see the last version, A153/W131. She also suggests such an interruption to her studies indirectly in her preface to the *Institutions de physique* (Paris: Chez Prault Fils, 1740).

37 Breteuil, *Mémoires,* ed. Lever, p. 28 n. 4. The family connection to Lorraine came through Suzanne de Baudéan, who married Philippe de Montaut, duc de Navailles; their daughter married Charles de Lorraine, duc d'Elbeuf.

38 Her coat of arms: Breteuil was blue (azur) background and gold sparrow hawk; Du Châtelet, gold background, red (gules) band, and silver fleur-de-lys.

39 François-Joachim de Pierre de Bernis, *Mémoires et lettres de François-Joachim de Pierre, cardinal de Bernis,* ed. F. Masson. (Paris, 1878; reprint Paris: Société d'Editions Littéraires et Artistiques, 1903), vol. 1, pp. 128–29.

40 An ancestor accompanied Godfrey de Boullion, leader of the first crusade. See Lougee, *Paradis des Femmes,* p. 211; Guy Chaussinand-Nogaret, *The French Nobility in the Eighteenth Century: From Feudalism to Enlightenment,* trans. William Doyle (Cambridge: Cambridge University Press, 1995), p. 30; Solnon, *La Cour,* pp. 476–77; Créqui, *Souvenirs,* vol. 1, p. 61.

41 Chapman, "Patronage as Family Economy," pp. 26 n. 43, 27 n. 44; Henri Duranton, ed., *Journal de la cour de Paris* (Paris, 1836; reprint, University of Saint Etienne, 1981), p. 131. These families were also known as the *noblesse de race,* nobility of race. See Pierre Serna, in Michel Vovelle, ed., *Enlightenment Portraits,* trans. Lydia G. Cochrane (Chicago: University of Chicago Press, 1997), p. 71. See also Sarah Hanley, "Social Sites of Political Practice in France: Lawsuits, Civil Rights and the Separation of Powers in Domestic and State Government, 1580–1800," *American Historical Review,* vol. 102 (Feb. 1997), pp. 27–52.

42 Créqui, *Souvenirs,* vol. 1, p. 171; Luynes, *Mémoires,* vol. 9, p. 128.

43 For these documents, see Paris Inventory, app. D93 (hereafter referred to as Paris Inventory), in *CWV,* vol. 95, pp. 443–45. On dowries, see Vaillot, *Madame du Châtelet,* p. 38; René Vaillot, *Avec Mme Du Châtelet,* vol. 1, pp. 242–43; Marchal, *Madame de Lambert,* p. 91.

44 See Edmond Goncourt and Jules de Goncourt. *La Femme au dix-huitième siècle,* pref. Elisabeth Badiner (Paris: Flammarion, 1982), p. 65; Delpierre, *Dress in France,* pp. 78, 140.

45 For more complicated responses, see Vaillot, *Madame du Châtelet*, pp. 40–41; Badinter, *Emilie, Emilie*, p. 108.

46 Montaigne, "Of Moderation," in *Complete Works*, pp. 146–47; Du Châtelet, *Fable*, A187v/ W160, A187/ W161.

47 Jean-Paul Bertaud, "The Soldier," in Vovelle, ed. *Enlightenment Portraits*; see also the marquis's military record at Château de Vincennes #3yd724. On aristocracy's attitude, see Rafe Blaufarb, "Noble Privilege and Absolutist State Building: French Military Administration After the Seven Years' War," *French Historical Studies* 24, no. 2 (Spring, 2001), p. 239. To command a regiment meant having the rank of colonel. A regiment was made up of ten companies, but the total number varied, since a company could be eight to sixteen men.

48 See, for example, #348, Graffigny to Devaux ([9 July 1750]), in *Correspondance de Graffigny*, vol. 11, p. 1 [Penny Arthur's unpublished notes]: #88, Du Châtelet to Algarotti (11 Jan. 1737), in Emilie de Breteuil, marquise Du Châtelet, *Lettres de la Marquise du Châtelet,* ed. Theodore Besterman (Genève: Institut et Musée Voltaire, 1958), vol. 1, p. 159 (hereafter referred to as *LDC*).

49 See, for example, Voltaire's letters to Moussinot in *CWV,* vol. 88: D1299 (1737), p. 263; D1304 (1737), p. 270; D1313 (1737), p. 285. #82, Du Châtelet to d'Argental (29 Dec. 1736), *LDC*, vol. 1, p. 147. On *honnêté*, see Ian Maclean, *Woman Triumphant,* pp. 124–26.

50 Vaillot, *Madame du Châtelet,* pp. 42–46, n. 46; see also Justin Ledeuil-d'Enquin, *La Marquise du Châtelet à Semur et le passage deVoltaire* (Semur: Millon, 1892).

51 #25, Du Châtelet to d'Argental 21 ([Dec. 1734]), *LDC*, vol. 1, pp. 54–55; #82, Du Châtelet (29 Dec. 1736), #201, and #202 Du Châtelet ([c. 20/25 March 1739, c. 25 March 1739]), *LCD*, vol. 1, pp. 147–48, 349–51. On her half sister, Michelle, daughter of baron de Breteuil and Anne Bellanzini, see Breteuil, *Mémoires,* ed. Lever, pp. 26–27. See Simon Henri Dubuisson, *Lettres du Commissaire Dubuisson au marquis de Caumont, 1735–1741,* intro. A. Rouxel (Paris: Arnould, 1882), pp. 262–63.

52 See Delpierre, *Dress in France*, pp. 10–11.

53 #21, Du Châtelet to Sade (6 Sept. [1734]), *LDC*, vol. 1, p. 49; #20, Du Châtelet to Maupertuis (Sunday [Aug. 1734]), *LDC*, vol. 1, p. 49. For more on these emotions, see Du Châtelet, *Fable,* W163–4/ A190v–191, see W162–4. On the spoon, see Paris Inventory, vol. 95, p. 432.

54 Note that the daughter's and son's names vary in different documents: for example, in the Paris Inventory; Piot, *Cirey-le-Château,* pp. 541–42, 502; Gaston Maugras, *La Cour de Lunéville au XVIIIe siècle* (Paris: Plon-Nourrit, 1904), p. 38. Du Châtelet never published her commentary on the Bible; Emilie de Breteuil, marquise Du Châtelet, *Examens de la Bible,* ed. Bertram Eugene Schwarzbach (Paris: Honoré Campion, forthcoming); see Mathieu, chap. 14, pp. 7, 8, 11 (page references are to the unpublished manuscript). #63, Graffigny to Devaux (12–14 Dec. 1738), in *Correspondance de Graffigny,* vol. 1, p. 221.

55 Certificate in his file at Château de Vincennes, #11101 G.

56 See, for example, #121 Du Châtelet to Thieriot (3 April [1738]), *LCD,* vol. 1, p. 219; #112, Du Châtelet to Thieriot (23 Dec. 1737), *LDC,* vol. 1, p. 203. See Montaigne, "Learning," in *Complete Works*, p. 100. See also recommendations in Palairet, *Bibliotheque des enfants,* pp. 11–15, 62–63, Du Châtelet, preface, *Institutions,* pp. 3, 5.

57 #55, Du Châtelet to Cideville (27 Feb. 1736), *LDC*, vol. 1, p. 101; #112, Du Châtelet to Thieriot (23 Dec. [1737]), *LDC*, vol. 1, pp. 202–3; #107, Du Châtelet to Cideville (end Nov. [1737]), *LDC*, vol. 1, p. 195.

58 D1075, Linant to Cideville ([c. May 1736]), *CWV*, vol. 87, p. 446. D1075, Linant to Cideville ([May 1736]), *CWV*, vol. 87, p. 447, n. 1. #55, Du Châtelet to Cideville (27 Feb. [1736]), *LDC*, vol. 1, p. 100. #107, Du Châtelet to Cideville ([end Nov. 1737]), *LDC*, vol. 1, pp. 195, 196. See also, #109, Du Châtelet to Cideville (12 Dec. 1737), *LDC*, vol. 1, pp. 200, 199. See #110, Du Châtelet to Thieriot (12 Dec. [1737]), *LDC*, vol. 1, p. 201. #112, Du Châtelet (23 Dec. [1]737), *LDC*, vol. 1, p. 203. #119, Du Châtelet (6 Feb. 1738), *LDC*, vol. 1, p. 214. #121, Du Châtelet (3 April [1738]), *LDC*, vol. 1, p. 219. On finding a replacement see, for example, D2633, Mouhy to Marville (8 Aug. 1742), *CWV*, vol. 92, p. 228; and #281, Du Châtelet to Wolff (22 Sept. 1741), *LDC*, vol. 2, p. 73.

59 Du Châtelet, *Discours*, ed. Mauzi, p. 21.

60 The Palais Lambert still exists as no. 1 Saint-Louis-en-l'Isle. #146, Du Châtelet to d'Argental (29 Sept. 1738), *LDC*, vol. 1, p. 265. See #170, Du Châtelet to d'Argental (15 [Jan. 1739]), *LDC*, vol. 1, p. 304. #204, Du Châtelet to d'Argental (2 April [1739]), *LDC*, vol. 1, p. 354. #206, Du Châtelet to Thieriot (6 April [1739]), *LDC*, vol. 1, p. 356. *A New Description of Paris*, vol. 1, pp. 144–46. See also Dézallier D'Argenville, *Voyage pittoresque*, pp. 241–47. See D1978, Voltaire to Frederick (April 1739), *CWV*, vol. 90, p. 336. D2175, Voltaire to Fawkener (2 March 1740), *CWV*, vol. 91, p. 118. D1967, Voltaire to Moussinot (3 April [1739]), *CWV*, vol. 90, p. 321. D2067, Voltaire to Champbonin ([20 Aug. 1739]), *CWV*, vol. 90, p. 459. Paris Inventory, *CWV*, vol. 95, p. 411.

61 For the information on *hôtel* and household staff that follows, see the Plan de Turgot, 1739; René Pomeau and Christine Mervaud, *De la Cour du Jardin (1750–1759)*, in Pomeau, *Voltaire en son temps*, vol. 1, p. 3 n. 1. See Jacques Hillairet, *Dictionnaire historique des rues de Paris* (Paris: Editions de Minert, 1964), vol. 2, pp. 132–33, on the likelihood that it would have been on the other half of the rue Molière. Much of the information on the *hôtel* has been reconstructed from the Paris Inventory, *CWV*, vol. 95, pp. 414–36, 466–71. See also Daniel Roche, *A History of Everyday Things: The Birth of Consumption in France, 1600–1800*, trans. Brian Pearce (New York: Cambridge University Press, 2000), pp. 67, 97–100; Garrioch, *Neighborhood and Community*, p. 104; Fairchilds, *Domestic Enemies*, pp. 39–41; Vaillot, *Madame du Châtelet*, p. 265; Sébastien G. Longchamps, *Mémoires sur Voltaire, et sur ses ouvrages*, Bibliothèque Nationale, NAF 13006, p. 6b. This is the original manuscript version and includes the editor's changes.

62 On the city and the noble *hôtel*, see Braudel, *Structures*, vol. 1, pp. 257–58; Fairchilds, *Domestic Enemies*, p. 27. Paris Inventory, *CWV*, vol. 95, pp. 465–70. Cities information from Garrioch, *Neighborhood and Community*, especially pp. 126, 119–21. See also Roche, *Everyday Things*, p. 143; Louis Sébastien Mercier, *Tableau de Paris*, in Louis Ducros, *La Société française au XVIIIe siècle d'après les mémoires et correspondances du temps* (Paris, 1822; in English, *French Society in the Eighteenth Century*, trans. W. de Geijer [New York: Putnam's, 1927], pp. 112–14).

63 On Linant, see his letters to Cideville in *CWV*, vol. 87, pp. 348–50, D1010; D1019, pp. 361–63; D1046; p. 404. See #107, Du Châtelet to Cideville ([end Nov. 1737]), *LDC*, vol. 1, pp. 194–97. #109, Du Châtelet to Cideville (12 Dec. 1737), *LDC*, vol. 1, pp. 200–201; #192 Du Châtelet to Cideville (26 Feb. 1739), *LDC*, vol. 1, p. 338.

64 Longchamps, *Mémoires,* Bibliothèque Nationale, NAF 13006, pp. 6–7, 7v, 9v. See published version, Sébastien G. Longchamps and Jean Louis Wagnière, *Mémoires sur Voltaire* (Paris: Aimé André, 1826), especially pp. 118–23. Note that the third version of the memoir, ed. D'Albanès Havard (Paris: E. Dentu, 1863), is closer to the original manuscript in the Bibliothèque Nationale. I have used the manuscript spelling of his name throughout the biography.

65 For the expenses of her husband's company, see Blaufarb, "Noble Privilege," pp. 229–30.

66 Du Châtelet, *Discours,* ed. Mauzi, pp. 26–27, 23, 24; Du Châtelet, trans., *Fable,* W183–84 /A212–212v;W182/A211,W184/A213.; Du Châtelet, preface, *Institutions,* p. 5.

67 Chaussinand-Nogaret created figures from *capitation* tax records (see *The French Nobility,* pp. 51–53).The majority of nobles—eighteen thousand families, or 66 percent—would never see Paris or go to court, and lived on ten thousand livres per year or less. Forty-one percent lived on four thousand livres or less. See Daniel Roche, *The Culture of Clothing: Dress and Fashion in the Ancien Régime,* trans. Jean Birrell (Cambridge: Cambridge University Press, 1994), p. 94. Solnon, *La Cour,* pp. 494–95. Specific amounts taken from the Paris Inventory; others added from the marquis's file at the Château de Vincennes, and records of their notary, Bronod, at Archives Nationales, AN MC, Et. LXXXVIII.

68 Paris Inventory, *CWV,* vol. 95, p. 455. Piot, *Cirey-le-Château,* p. 121. On the negotiations for sale of a regiment, see Luynes, *Mémoires,* vol. 1, p. 162; vol. 6, p. 271.

69 On women's legal activities, see Hanley, "Social Sites," pp. 31, 33–36; Tracey Rizzo, *A Certain Emancipation of Women: Gender, Citizenship, and the Causes Célèbres of Eighteenth-Century France* (Selinsgrove, Pa.: Susquehanna University Press, 2004). On Normandy, see Du Châtelet to Cideville (14 Jan. 1742 until [c. 15 Feb. 1745]), #289, #292, #318, #336, in *LDC,* vol. 2, pp. 85, 87, 112, 132. For one settlement, see D316,Voltaire to Cideville ([12 May 1745]), *CWV,* vol. 93, pp. 242–43. On Flanders settlement, see, for example, D3647, Voltaire to marquis de Hoensbroeck (9 May 1748), *CWV,* vol. 94, p. 230; D3671,Voltaire to Johann Peter von Räsfeld (16 June [1748]), *CWV,* vol. 94, p. 255. D2558,Voltaire to Cideville (28 Oct. 1741) *CWV,* vol. 92, p. 133.

70 On notaries, see William Doyle, "The Price of Offices in Pre-Revolutionary France," *Archives Nationales, Historical Journal* 27, no. 4 (Dec. 1984), pp. 848–49. Bronod, 12 July 1725, AN MC, Et. LXXXVIII. See Paris Inventory, vol. 95, pp. 468, 475, 467, 455–56 for figures on the loans and terms of repayment. I am indebted to Robert Du Plessis for explaining this portion of the inventory to me.

71 #37, Du Châtelet to Richelieu ([c. 30 May] 1735), *LDC,* vol. 1, p. 68.

72 For information here and in subsequent sections about Paris, see especially the Plan de Turgot, 1739; *Le Guide du patrimoine: Paris* (Paris: Hachette, 1994); Louis Sébastien Mercier, *Le Paris de Louis Sébastien Mercier: cartes et index typonymique,* ed. Jean-Claude Bonnet (Paris: Mercure de France, 1994); Hillairet, *Dictionnaire historique des rues de Paris.* On daily activities, Arlette Farge, *Fragile Lives: Violence, Power and Solidarity in Eighteenth-Century Paris,* trans. Carol Shelton (Cambridge, Mass.: Harvard University Press, 1993). See Braudel, *Structures,* pp. 501–2; on prices, p. 230. See also Garrioch, *Neighborhood and Community,* pp. 119–43, 42–43; Roche, *Everyday Things,* pp. 34, 143–57. The visitor was Charles-Etienne Jordan, *Histoire d'un voyage littéraire fait en MDCCXXXIII* (The Hague: Adorren Hoetiers, 1735), p. 30. Mercier, in Ducros,

French Society, pp. 112–14. Population figures are always uncertain; these and others in the chapter are taken from Roche, *Everyday Things,* pp. 67, 69, 76, 77.

73 Lunéville Inventory, Archives Meurthe-et-Moselle. #10B411; Paris Inventory, vol. 95; routines from Goncourt and Goncourt, *La femme,* pp. 114, 116. On products, see R. Turner Wilcox, *The Mode in Costume* (New York: Scribner's, 1948), p. 198. Braudel, *Structures,* p. 138.

74 On bathing, see Chartier, *Passions,* p. 189. Paris Inventory, vol. 95, p. 437. Most of the clothing information for this and following paragraphs is from Delpierre, *Dress in France,* pp. 8–17, 21–36, 47–48, 72–73; Roche, *Clothing,* pp. 128–30, 182; Roche, *Everyday Things,* pp. 160, 211; Chartier, *Passions,* pp. 189–90, 221, 188; Wilcox, *Mode in Costume,* 198, 193–219; Lunéville Inventory.

75 For other noblewomen's inventories, see Roche, *Clothing,* p. 143. The debt in 1749 was 1,097 livres (Paris Inventory, vol. 95, pp. 468, 472). Carolyn Sargentson, *Merchants and Luxury Markets: The Marchands Merciers of 18th Century Paris* (London: Victoria and Albert Museum, in association with J. Paul Getty Museum, 1996), p. 36.

76 The amount of the bill was 5,756 livres (Bronod, 7 April 1746, Archives Nationales, AN MC, Et. LXXXVIII). See Sargentson, *Merchants,* passim.

77 Du Châtelet, trans., *Fable,* A194v/W167–68. On Hébert, see Sargentson, *Merchants,* pp. 63–68, 82–89; Paris Inventory, vol. 95, pp. 427–28, for this and subsequent descriptions. Du Châtelet, *Discours,* ed. Mauzi, p. 27.

78 See Philippe Beaussant and Patricia Bouchenot-Déchin, *Les Plaisirs de Versailles: Théâtre & musique* (Paris: Fayard, 1996), p. 130. #35, Du Châtelet to Richelieu (21 May 1735), *LDC,* vol. 1, p. 62.

79 See #32, Du Châtelet to Maupertuis (Sat. [19 Feb. 1735]), *LDC,* 1, p. 59. Goncourt and Goncourt, *La femme,* p. 135 n. 2. Ducros, *French Society,* pp. 118, 120. Lunéville Inventory, #10B411, p. 10. Du Châtelet, *Discours,* ed. Mauzi, p. 10.

80 #156, Graffigny to Devaux (Mon. [13 July 1739]), in *Correspondance de Graffigny,* vol. 2, p. 53. See composite of Du Châtelet's letters, 1733–35, in *LDC,* vol. 1, pp. 29–77.

81 See Du Châtelet, *Discours,* ed. Mauzi, pp. 15–16. On the Comédie française, see Henry Carrington Lancaster, *French Tragedy in the Time of Louis XV and Voltaire, 1715–1774* (Baltimore: Johns Hopkins Press, 1950), vol. 1, p. 598. On the look of the theater, see also pp. 4–5, 8, 595–97, fig. 707. Du Châtelet's comments come from a composite of letters, 1733–35, in *LDC,* vol. 1, pp. 29–77, but particularly those to the duc de Richelieu. See Sarah R. Cohen, *Art, Dance, and the Body in French Culture of the Ancien Régime* (New York: Cambridge University Press, 2000), p. 259, including illustrations of the patterns of steps.

82 See John Dunkley, *Gambling: A Social and Moral Problem in France, 1685–1792* (Oxford: Voltaire Foundation, 1985), chaps. 3, 5; Du Châtelet, trans., *Fable,* A197–198/W170–71; Thomas Kavanagh, *Enlightenment and the Shadows of Chance: The Novel and the Culture of Gambling in Eighteenth-Century France* (Baltimore: Johns Hopkins University Press, 1993), pp. 30–32.

83 I am grateful to Séverine de Breteuil for research on his name and the more likely explanation for its choice.

84 See Steinbrugge, *The Moral Sex,* pp. 12–20, 34, 42–43; Maclean, *Woman Triumphant,* pp. 123–28, 120–21; Lougee, *Paradis des Femmes,* pp. 85–86; Rousselot, *Histoire,* vol. 2, pp. 207, 213; Gutwirth, *Twilight of the Goddesses,* p. 58. Du Châtelet, *Discours,* ed.

Mauzi, pp. 21, 23–24. See also Du Châtelet, trans., *Fable*, B221v-222, B222v; A157v/ W135; note that she substituted "*un bon livre de physique*," a more general category than "un bon livre de géometrie," when listing the areas in which women had not written.

85 Du Châtelet, *Fable*, A198v/W171. Du Châtelet, *Discours*, ed. Mauzi, p. 16. On Semur, see Vaillot, *Madame du Châtelet*, p. 47. I am grateful to Penny Arthur of the Graffigny Papers in Toronto for information on Mlle de Thil.

86 See Vaillot, *Madame du Châtelet*, p. 47; #21, Du Châtelet to Sade (6 Sept. [1734]), *LDC*, vol. 1, p. 50.

Chapter Two: The Republic of Letters

1   See #15S, Du Châtelet to Saint-Lambert (1 May [1748]), (#372, *LDC*, vol. 2), p. 51. The French historian Anne Soprani created a new arrangement of the letters between Du Châtelet and Saint-Lambert, which I believe more accurately reflects Du Châtelet's thinking and the course of events. I have used her edition, noted with an "S" after the letter number, as #15S here. See *Emilie Du Châtelet: Lettres d'amour au marquis de Saint-Lambert* (Paris: Editions Méditerranée, 1997). I have indicated the letter number used in the standard 1958 two-volume collection of her letters edited by Theodore Besterman in parentheses with the volume number, as, for example (#372, *LDC*, vol. 2), in this instance. See *Lettres de la Marquise du Châtelet*, ed. Theodore Besterman (Genève: Institut et Musée Voltaire, 1958).

2   D4046, Voltaire to d'Aigueberre (26 Oct. 1749), Voltaire, *The Complete Works of Voltaire*, ed. Theodore Besterman (Genève: Institut et Musée Voltaire, 1968–), vol. 95, p. 184.

3   D4016, Voltaire to Du Deffand (10 Sept. [1749]), *CWV*, vol. 95. p. 161; D3851 Voltaire to Denis (18 [Jan. 1749]), *CWV*, vol. 94, p. 399; D4015, Voltaire to Denis (10 Sept. [1749]), *CWV*, vol. 95, p. 160; D4021, Voltaire to Denis (17 Sept. [1749]), *CWV*, vol. 95, p. 165. On having met previously, see also Samuel Edwards, *The Divine Mistress* (New York: David McKay, 1970), p. 65.

4   Theodore Besterman, *Voltaire* (New York: Harcourt Brace & World, 1969), p. 44; Charles Etienne Jordan, *Histoire d'un voyage littéraire fait en MOCXXXIII* (The Hague: Adorren Hoetiers, 1735), pp. 63, 64.

5   On Maupertuis's character, early life in Paris, and rise, see Elisabeth Badinter, *Les Passions intellectuelles* (Paris: Fayard, 1999), vol. 1, pp. 50–54, 62–63; Pierre Brunet, *Maupertuis* (Paris: Librairie Scientifique Albert Blanchard, 1929), pp. 178–79, 181–92; Mary Terrall, *The Man Who Flattened the Earth: Maupertuis and the Sciences in the Enlightenment* (Chicago: University of Chicago Press, 2002), chaps. 1 and 3 passim, especially pp. 27–33, 43–45. See also John Bennett Shank, *Before Voltaire: Newtonianism and the Origins of the Enlightenment in France, 1687–1734* (Ann Arbor: University of Michigan Press, 2000), pp. 516–26, 550–58.

6   One popular biographer imagines Du Châtelet dressing as a man and joining discussions at the Café Gradot. I have found no contemporary evidence for this.

7   Terrall, *Man Who Flattened the Earth*, pp. 23–25.

8   Antoine-Nicolas Dézallier d'Argenville, *Voyage pittoresque de Paris* (Paris: De Bure, 1757 [Genève: Minkoff Reprint, 1972]), p. 47.

9   Terrall, *Man Who Flattened the Earth*, p. 29, and n. 40. On the Académie, see J. L. Heil-

bron, *Elements of Early Modern Physics* (Berkeley: University of California Press, 1982), pp. 107–9; Roger Hahn, *The Anatomy of a Scientific Institution: The Paris Academy of Sciences, 1666–1803* (Berkeley: University of California Press, 1971), pp. 77–79, 98–99; David J. Sturdy, *Science and Social Status: The Members of the Académie des Sciences, 1666–1750* (Woodbridge, Suffolk: Boydell Press, 1995), pp. 343–44.

10 On Fontenelle, see Shank, *Before Voltaire*, pp. 378–83, 391–404, 465. On Maupertuis's math difficulties and choices, see Terrall, *Man Who Flattened the Earth*, pp. 10–11, 13, 15, 64–78, and, on the creation of his career generally, chaps. 1–2. See also Badinter, *Passions intellectuelles*, vol. 1, pp. 54, 63. On correspondence with Bernoulli, see Shank, *Before Voltaire*, pp. 525–26. On his health, and treatment for syphillis-Jan.–March 1729, Brunet, *Maupertuis*, pp. 178–79; Terrall, *Man Who Flattened the Earth*, p. 43 n. 28.

11 On Bernoulli, see Terrall, *Man Who Flattened the Earth*, pp. 44–47, 63–78, chap. 3 passim. See also Mary Terrall, "Vis Viva," *History of Science* 42 (2004), pp. 197–98, 207 n. 42.

12 See Shank, *Before Voltaire*, p. 521; Terrall, *Man Who Flattened the Earth*, pp. 60–64, and, on *Discours*, pp. 78–82. See also Badinter, *Passions intellectuelles*, vol. 1, p. 17.

13 Maupertuis, *Discours sur les différentes figures des astres* (Paris: De l'Imprimerie Royal, 1732), p. 21.

14 Maupertuis, *Astres*, pp. 11, 34–37. On his goal and this line of reasoning, see *Astres*, Avant Propos, pp. iv, v, 10–11, 26–27, 29–33, 37–39, 45, 81, 132, 133. See also Terrall, *Man Who Flattened the Earth*, p. 91; I. Bernard Cohen, *The Newtonian Revolution* (Cambridge: Cambridge University Press, 1980), pp. 124–27.

15 Badinter, *Intellectuelles*, vol. 1, pp. 56–57, 62–64; Terrall, *Man Who Flattened the Earth*, pp. 83–85.

16 Note that Bonnel sees nothing sexual—rather, the insistence on tutelage, Roland Bonnel, "La Correspondance scientifique de la marquise Du Châtelet: la 'lettre-laboratoire.'" *SVEC* (2000:4), pp. 86–87. For information in this and subsequent paragraphs, see *LDC*, vol. 1 passim (1734–35), especially Du Châtelet to Maupertuis: #2, #5, #8, #9, #10, #19, #27–31. See Roger Picard, *Les Salons littéraires et la société française, 1610–1789* (Paris: Brentano's, 1943), p. 245. On affectionate language, see, for example, #13, Du Châtelet to Maupertuis from Montjeu (29 April [1734]), *LDC*, vol. 1, p. 39. #9, Du Châtelet to Maupertuis (Wed [? Jan. 1734]), *LDC*, vol. 1, p. 35. #3, Du Châtelet to Maupertuis (Thursday [? Jan. 1734]), *LDC*, vol. 1, p. 31; #164, Du Châtelet to d'Argental (7 Jan. [1739]), *LDC*, vol. 1, p. 294. Note that Voltaire wrote in similarly exaggerated terms of affection. See Voltaire to Maupertuis: D515, D519, D520, *CWV*, vol. 86, pp. 212, 221; D1338, Voltaire to Moussinot, *CWV*, vol. 88, p. 323. D1445; Voltaire to Moussinot, vol. 89, p. 24; D1465, Voltaire to Berger, *CWV*, vol. 89, p. 84; D1551, Voltaire to Thieriot, *CWV*, vol. 89, p. 202; D1022, Voltaire to d'Argental, *CWV*, vol. 87, p. 366. For examples of other noblewomen, see the dauphine quoted in Charles Philippe d'Albert, duc de Luynes, *Mémoires du duc de Luynes sur la cour de Louis XV, 1735–1758*, ed. L. Dussieux and E. Soulié (Paris: Firmin Didot, 1860–65), vol. 1, p. 48 n. 2. See also Marquise Marie Du Deffand, *Correspondance complète de la marquise Du Deffand avec ses amis* (Paris: Henri Plon, 1865), Du Deffand to Chevalier de L'Isle (c. 1769), vol. 1, p. 591. Maupertuis received similar letters when he was in Berlin from the duchesses d'Aiguillon, Saint-Pierre, and Chaulnes. For their letters, see Bibliothèque Nationale, NAF 10398: Saint-Pierre, pp. 1–12;

d'Aiguillon, pp. 13–78; Chaulnes, pp. 104–33. Reference to this collection came initially from Badinter, *Passions intellectuelles,* vol. 1.

17 I am grateful to Sue Lancer for offering this approach to this aspect of their relationship. The reviewer of Fontenelle's work for the *Mercure galant* called it "inviting and provocative," as quoted in Bernard le Bovier de Fontenelle, *Conversations on the Plurality of Worlds,* ed. Nina Rattner Gelbart (Berkeley: University of California Press, 1990), p. xxi. Note that this became a trope of eighteenth-century French pornographic and erotic literature. See also Mary Terrall, "Salon, Academy, and Boudoir: Generation and Desire in Maupertuis's Science of Life," *Isis* 87, no. 2 (June 1996), pp. 217–29. Emilie de Breteuil, marquise Du Châtelet, *Institutions de physique* (Paris: Chez Prault Fils, 1740), p. 313. On Maupertuis's use of the expedition to enhance his image and advancement, see Terrall, *Man Who Flattened the Earth,* chap. 1; Mary Terrall, "Gendered Spaces, Gendered Audience: Inside and Outside the Paris Academy of Sciences," *Configurations* 2 (1994), pp. 207–32.

18 See Du Châtelet to Maupertuis, January letters, passim; #16. Du Châtelet to Maupertuis (7 June 1734), *LDC,* vol. 1, p. 44. See also, #18, Du Châtelet to Sade ([15 July 1734]), *LDC,* vol. 1, p. 46; #12, Du Châtelet (28 April [1734]), *LDC,* vol. 1, p. 37; #24, Du Châtelet to Maupertuis (23 Oct. 1734), *LDC,* vol. 1, p. 52.

19 See Judith P. Zinsser and Olivier Courcelle, "A Remarkable Collaboration: The Marquise Du Châtelet and Alexis Clairaut," *SVEC* (2003:12), pp. 107–20; see also D2106, Voltaire to Frederick ([c. 1 Nov. 1739]), *CWV,* vol. 91, p. 32.

20 On Clairaut, see Badinter, *Passions intellectuelles,* vol. 1, pp. 57–59. On de Thil, see #19, Du Châtelet to Maupertuis (Thurs. [July 1734]), *LDC,* vol. 1, p. 48.

21 Clairaut to Du Châtelet [c. Sept. 1741], in prince Baldassarre de Boncompagni, "Lettere di Alessio Claudio Clairaut," *Atti dell 'Accademia Pontificia de' Nuovi Lincei* 45 (1892), pp. 236–38. I am grateful to Craig Waff and Olivier Courcelle for giving me copies of this correspondence. Alexis-Claude Clairaut, *Elémens de géometrie* (Paris, 1741), pp. iii–iv, vii, 12, 74, 127, 131, 146, 150–51, 183. On her son's lessons, see Avertissement de l'Editeur, *Principes mathématiques de la philosophie naturelle,* trans. Emilie de Breteuil, marquise Du Châtelet, 2 vols. (1759; reprint, Sceaux: Editions Jacques Gabay, 1990), pp. ii–iii.

22 See Alexis-Claude Clairaut, *Elémens d'algèbre* (Paris: Chez les Frères Guerin, 1746), problems 1, 2, p. 73.

23 See Clairaut, *Algèbre,* pp. ix–x; xii–xiii; an example, p. 259; on shortening, p. 41; on negative numbers, pp. iv–vi, p. 37.

24 Past biographers assume Du Châtelet's sexual involvement with all of her tutors: Maupertuis, Clairaut, König, and also with the duc de Richelieu. See René Vaillot, *Madame du Châtelet* (Paris: Albin Michel, 1978), pp. 82–85, 92–93, 102–103. Elisabeth Badinter, *Emilie, Emilie: L'amibiton féminine au XVIIIe siècle* (Paris: Flammarion, 1983), pp. 218–19, and Badinter, *Passions intellectuelles,* vol. 1, pp. 130–31. Fouchy as quoted in Zinsser and Courcelle, "A Remarkable Collaboration," p. 111. In a letter to Maupertuis she wrote as if she made only one such visit, jested about the monasterylike arrangements, and sent "compliments to the superior," asking that they may "drink to my health in the refectory." See #108, Du Châtelet to Maupertuis (11 Dec. [1737]), *LDC,* vol. 1, p. 198.

25 See Patricia Fara, *Newton: The Making of Genius* (London: Macmillan, 2002), p. 197;

D. T. Whiteside, "Newton the Mathematician," in *A Norton Critical Edition: Newton*, ed. I. Bernard Cohen and Richard S. Westfall (New York: W. W. Norton, 1995), p. 410. See Shank, *Before Voltaire*, pp. 31, 42, 45; Terrall, *Man Who Flattened the Earth*, p. 44. See Clairaut's description of this process, Clairaut, *Algèbre*, pp. ii–iii.

26 As quoted in I. O. Wade, *The Intellectual Development of Voltaire* (Princeton: Princeton University Press, 1969), p. 437. See Terrall, *Man Who Flattened the Earth*, pp. 14, 32, 34, 36, 47–49, 54–55, 65.

27 #16, Du Châtelet to Maupertuis (7 June 1734), *LDC*, vol. 1, p. 44. "De finesse de calcul" in Du Châtelet, *Institutions*, pp. 327, 326. #122, Du Châtelet to Maupertuis (30 April [1738]), *LDC*, vol. 1, p. 221; #114, Du Châtelet to Maupertuis (10 Jan. 1738), *LDC*, vol. 1, p. 207.

28 #1, Du Châtelet to Sade [Dec. 1733], *LDC*, vol. 1, p. 29; #18, Du Châtelet to Sade (c. 15 July 1734), *LDC*, vol. 1, p. 47.

29 For this and the descriptions that follow, see D606, Voltaire to Cideville ([6 May 1733]), *CWV*, vol. 86, p. 330; D607, Voltaire to Du Châtelet ([c. 6 May 1733]), *CWV*, vol. 86, p. 331. D627, Voltaire to Cideville (Fri. [3 July 1733]), *CWV*, vol. 86, p. 355. D633, Voltaire to Saint-Pierre ([? July 1733]), *CWV*, vol. 86, pp. 361, 362. D676, Voltaire to Saint-Pierre ([c. 15 Nov. 1733]), *CWV*, vol. 86, p. 422.

30 D635, Voltaire to Thieriot (24 July [1733]), *CWV*, vol. 86, p. 364. Voltaire, in "On Calumny," *The Works of Voltaire* (Paris: E. R. DuMont, 1901), vol. 36, pp. 89–95. On other occasions, she was, as society dictated, "Mme Du Châtelet," as he, in her letters, was "Voltaire," or "M. de V."

31 Anne Muratori-Philip, *Le Roi Stanislas* (Paris: Fayard, 2000), p. 221.

32 D646, Voltaire to Formont ([c. 15 Aug. 1733]), *CWV*, vol. 86, p. 379. See also D637, Voltaire to Formont (26 July 1733), *CWV*, vol. 86, p. 366. D764, Voltaire to Formont (27 [June 1734]), *CWV*, vol. 87, p. 43. D672, Voltaire to Sade (3 Nov. 1733), *CWV*, vol. 86, p. 416. On the Irish teacher, D1020, Voltaire to Fawkener (22 Feb. 1736), *CWV*, vol. 87, p. 364. Note that Du Châtelet had Jacobite cousins with whom she also might have spoken English growing up.

33 Note there are two poems with the same name. Although this "Uranie" is placed second in the critical edition, because it is less explicit sexually I assume it was composed first. See Voltaire, *CWV*, vol. 14, pp. 527–30.

34 D645, Voltaire to Cideville (14 Aug. [1733]), *CWV*, vol. 86, pp. 377–78. Note that by the nineteenth century, in the *Trésor de la langue française*, "l'amitie" had acquired the meaning of the affection of one man for another. The word he used was "tempérament." D663, Voltaire to Cideville (14 Oct. [1733]), *CWV*, vol. 86, p. 405.

35 See, for example, from the summer and fall of 1733, in *CWV*, vol. 86: D637, Voltaire to Formont (26 July 1733), p. 368; D638, Voltaire to Thieriot (27 July 1733), p. 368; D641, Voltaire to Moncrif, p. 371; D684, Voltaire to Sade, p. 431; D639, Voltaire to Cideville, p. 369; D642, Voltaire to Cideville ([2 Aug. 1733]), p. 372. D686, Voltaire to Cideville ([5 Dec. 1733]), p. 434.

36 David Wootton, "Unhappy Voltaire, or 'I Shall Never Get Over It as Long as I Live,'" *History Workshop Journal* 50 (Autumn 2000), pp. 137–55; René Pomeau, *D'Arouet à Voltaire (1694–1734)*, in *Voltaire en son temps*, ed. René Pomeau (Oxford: Voltaire Foundation, 1992), vol. 1, p. 27. On Bolingbroke's circle, see Shank, *Before Volaire*, p. 572; Pomeau, *D'Arouet à Voltaire*, vol. 1, p. 40; Robert L. Walters and W. H. Barber,

introduction, *Eléments de la philosophie de Newton* (Oxford: Voltaire Foundation, 1992), vol. 15, pp. 31–32. On Paris, see also Catherine Cusset, *No Tomorrow: The Ethics of Pleasure in the French Enlightenment* (Charlottesville, Va.: University Press of Virginia, 1999), pp. 6–10.

37 D652, Voltaire to Hervey (Sept. 1733), in *CWV,* vol. 86, p. 388.

38 For Linant and Voltaire, see Simon Henri Dubuisson, *Lettres du Commissaire Dubuisson au marquis de Caumont, 1735–1741* (Paris: Arnould, 1882): Letter IX (June 1735), p. 88; Letter XI (29 July 1735), p. 113. For verses, see *Journal de la cour & de Paris,* ed. Henri Duranton (Paris, 1836; reprint: University of Saint-Etienne, 1981), 3 Oct. 1733, p. 158.

39 D644, Cideville to Voltaire and Mme Du Châtelet (11 Aug. 1733), *CWV,* vol. 86, p. 376. D648, Cideville to Voltaire and Mme Du Châtelet (23 Aug. 1733), *CWV,* vol. 86, p. 382. See also D649, Voltaire to Formont (29 Aug. 1733), *CWV,* vol. 86, p. 383. D764, Voltaire to Formont (27 [June 1734]), *CWV,* vol. 87, p. 43. D881, Voltaire to Thieriot (?), *CWV,* vol. 87, p. 161. D649, Voltaire to Sade (29 Aug. 1733), *CWV,* vol. 86, p. 384. See also D983, Cideville to Du Châtelet (7 Jan. 1736), *CWV,* vol. 87, p. 12.

40 *Journal de la cour* (3 Oct. 1733), p. 158. On the King's Library, #181, Graffigny to Devaux (8 Sept. [1739]), Françoise d'Issembourg d'Happoncourt, *Correspondance de Madame de Graffigny,* ed. J. A. Dainard et al., 10 vols. (Oxford: Voltaire Foundation, 1985–), vol. 2, p. 145, n. 3. #3190/9-306 *Histoire de la conquête de Mexique, ou de la Nouvelle Espagne* (1691). Note that this citation gives the Alekseev number first, the Voltaire Library Collection number second. The play *Alzire,* though set in Lima and ostensibly about the Incas, uses information about the Aztecs. On reading at Cirey, see D813, Voltaire to d'Argental ([10 Dec. 1734]), *CWV,* vol. 87, p. 87. On Du Châtelet's continuing involvement in the play, see D1022, Voltaire to d'Argental (26 Feb. 1736), *CWV,* vol. 87, pp. 366–67. D1076, Voltaire to Formont (May 1736), quoted in René Vaillot, *Avec Mme Du Châtelet, 1734–1749,* in *Voltaire en son temps,* ed. René Pomeau (Oxford: Voltaire Foundation, 1988), vol. 1, p. 304.

41 On Du Châtelet, see Maupertuis to La Condamine, 8 Sept. 1735, quoted in Badinter, *Passions intellectuelles,* vol. 1, p. 69 n. 5. Voltaire never explained how he arrived at his name. Voltaire scholars favor the idea that it as an anagram of "Arouet." See Vaillot, *Avec Mme Du Châtelet,* vol. 1, pp. 86–87. Note that this account of Voltaire's life before his liaison with Du Châtelet is a condensed version of information from René Pomeau, *D'Arouet à Voltaire (1694–1734).*

42 Jean-Frédéric Phélypeaux, comte de Maurepas, *Mémoires du comte de Maurepas,* 3rd ed. (Paris: Chez Buisson, 1792), vol. 4, p. 281.

43 Besterman, *Voltaire,* p. 413.

44 As quoted in Pomeau, *D'Arouet à Voltaire,* vol. 1, pp. 92–98. On the argument, see J. S. Spink, *French Free-Thought from Gessendi to Voltaire* (London: University of London, Athlone Press, 1960), pp. 204–5. See also Wade, *Intellectual Development,* pp. 6, 34–44, 142, 394, 776.

45 Jordan, *Histoire,* p. 64.

46 On Voltaire and the French theater, see Wade, *Intellectual Development,* pp. 201–2. On style and conventions, see Roger Chartier, *Passions of the Renaissance* in *A History of Private Life,* ed. Philippe Ariès and Georges Duby (Cambridge: Belknap Press of Harvard University Press, 1989), pp. 371–73. See Henry Carrington Lancaster, *French*

Tragedy in the Time of Louis XV and Voltaire, 1715–1774 (Baltimore: Johns Hopkins Press, 1950), vol. 1, pp. 608–13, on the rules and how Voltaire used them.

47   Lancaster, *French Tragedy*, vol. 1, pp. 95, 5–7. On Quinault, see Pomeau, *D'Arouet à Voltaire*, vol. 1, pp. 69–73, 76–77.

48   See Emilie de Breteuil, marquise Du Châtelet, trans. *Fable of the Bees*, by Bernard Mandeville, *Complete Works of Voltaire*, St. Petersburg National Library, vol. 9. Emilie de Breteuil, marquise Du Châtelet, trans., *Fable of the Bees*, by Bernard Mandeville, in *Studies on Voltaire, with some unpublished papers of Mme. Du Châtelet*, by I. O. Wade (Princeton: Princeton University Press, 1947). I have designated the manuscript versions of Du Châtelet's "Preface" as drafts A, B, C, and D. Hereafter, Wade's printed text is cited as "W" with his pagination. See *Fable*, preface, passim. #56, Du Châtelet to Thieriot (1 March [1736]), *LDC*, vol. 1, p. 103; #94, Du Châtelet to d'Argental (25 Jan. [1733]), *LDC*, vol. 1, p. 174.

49   See Créqui, *Souvenirs de la marquise de Créqui, 1710–1803* (Paris: Michel Lévy Frères, 1867), vol. 1, pp. 64–66, 186. Charles-Augustin Sainte-Beuve, *Causeries du lundi* (Paris: Garnier Frères, 1852–62), vol. 7, pp. 478–79. Voltaire as quoted in Badinter, *Passions intellectuelles*, vol. 1, p. 18. See also Picard, *Salons littéraires*, pp. 148, 163–64. See also Edmond Goncourt and Jules de Goncourt, *La femme au dix-huitième siècle* (Paris: Flammarion, 1982), pp. 88–114. For the clearest account of the event and the conflicting details, see Pomeau, *D'Arouet à Voltaire*, vol. 1, pp. 158–59. See also *Journal de la cour*, p. 124.

50   There were two families with similar names, which has created confusion about Goesbriand. I am grateful to Yves Olliver for unraveling the mystery in the course of his own research on his family, the Guébriants.

51   Dubuisson, *Lettres*, Letter XI (29 July 1735), p. 116; Letter V (31 March 1735), pp. 49–50. On Du Châtelet's *bruit*, see Maurepas, *Mémoires*, vol. 4, p. 173. See embellished accounts in l'abbé Piot, *Cirey-le-Château: La Marquise du Châtelet: sa liaison avec Voltaire* (Saint-Dizier: O. Godard, 1894), p. 459. Vaillot, *Madame du Châtelet*, p. 51.

52   On Goesbriand, see Voltaire letter D1343, (23 June [1737]), *CWV*, vol. 88, p. 333. Verses quoted in Vaillot, *Avec Mme Du Châtelet*, pp. 537–38.

53   Montaigne, "On Some Verses of Virgil," in *Complete Works of Montaigne*, trans. Donald M. Frame (Stanford: Stanford University Press, 1957), pp. 652, 654. Du Châtelet, trans., *Fable*, Remarks, A182v–183v/W156–W157, A184–184v/W157; see also Bernard Mandeville, *Fable of the Bees; or Private Vices, Publick Benefits* (London: J. Roberts, 1714), p. 67. Mme Du Châtelet, *Discours sur le Bonheur*, ed. Robert Mauzi (Paris: Société d'Edition Belles Lettres, 1961), p. 13.

54   See app. D26, in *CWV*, vol. 86, p. 492.

55   #14, Du Châtelet to Sade (12 May 1734), *LDC*, vol. 1, p. 41; #132, Du Châtelet to Maupertuis (17 July [1738]), *LDC*, vol. 1, p. 243; also Luynes, *Mémoires*, vol. 2, p. 249.

56   For a description of events see Pomeau, *D'Arouet à Voltaire*, vol. 1, pp. 257, 261; Shank, *Before Voltaire*, pp. 581–89; Voltaire, *CWV*, vol. 87, p. 36 n. 1. D731, Maurepas to Briffe (3 May 1734), *CWV*, vol. 87, p. 11, for the *lettre de cachet*. On these actions and attitudes, see Voltaire letters D617-D653 (June to Sept. 1733), *CWV*, vol. 86, pp. 343–90. D759, Voltaire to La Condamine (22 June 1734), *CWV*, vol. 87, p. 37. D617, Voltaire to Formont ([c. 1 June 1733]), *CWV*, vol. 86, p. 343. #13, Du Châtelet

to Maupertuis (29 April 1734), *LDC*, vol. 1, p. 38. #14, Du Châtelet to Sade (12 May 1734), *LDC*, vol. 1, p. 41.

57 #18, Du Châtelet to Sade ([c. 15 July 1734]), *LDC*, vol. 1, p. 46. See D729, duchesse de Richelieu to Cardinal Fleury (29 April 1734), *CWV*, vol. 86, pp. 469–70. See also D790, D791, *CWV*, vol. 87, pp. 66–71.

58 See D759, Voltaire to La Condamine (22 June 1734), *CWV*, vol. 87, p. 37. #14, Du Châtelet to Sade, (12 May 1734), *LDC*, vol. 1, p. 41. #18, Du Châtelet to Sade (c. 15 July 1734 [could be redated as June], *LDC*, vol. 1, p. 46. #16, Du Châtelet to Maupertuis (7 June 1734), *LDC*, vol. 1, p. 44.

59 #18, Du Châtelet to Sade ([15 July 1734]), *LDC*, vol. 1, pp. 46–47. The comments are taken from #20, Du Châtelet to Maupertuis (Sunday [Aug. 1734]), *LDC*, vol. 1, p. 49. #21 Du Châtelet to Sade (6 Sept. [1734]), *LDC*, vol. 1, p. 49. #22, Du Châtelet to Maupertuis (10 Sept. 1734), *LDC*, vol. 1, p. 51.

60 For Voltaire's comments in this and the previous paragraph, see D793, Voltaire to Champbonin ([Oct. 1734]), *CWV*, vol. 87, pp. 71–72. D800, Voltaire to La Neuville ([c. 1 Nov. 1734]), *CWV*, vol. 87, p. 77.

61 #24, Du Châtelet to Maupertuis (23 Oct. 17344), *LDC*, vol. 1, p. 53.

62 Voltaire, "Poesies," *CWV*, vol. 14, p. 517. On the manuscript, see Andrew Brown and Ulla Kölving, "Qui est l'auteur du *Traité de métaphysique?*" *Cahiers Voltaire* 2 (2003), pp. 85–93. D795, Voltaire to Maupertuis ([Oct. 1734]), *CWV*, vol. 87, p. 73.

63 #24, Du Châtelet to Maupertuis (23 Oct. 1734), *LDC*, vol. 1, pp. 52–54. D840, Formont to Cideville (5 Feb. 1735), *CWV*, vol. 87, p. 110.

64 For details see Vaillot, *Avec Mme Du Châtelet*, p. 294. For the conditions of his return to Paris, see Dubuisson, *Lettres*, Letter V, p. 47 n. 1.

65 Piot, *Cirey-le-Château*, p. 457. Bouhier quoted in Wade, *Intellectual Development*, p. 253. In 1733, the *nouvellistes* and gossips had made nothing sexual of the association. The *Journal de la cour* described Du Châtelet's relationship with Voltaire as that of protector. Not until the end of July 1735, after she had already made her decision to take up permanent residency at Cirey, did Dubuisson write of her adventure at Mont Valérien and suggest she needed Maupertuis because of Voltaire's sexual inadequacies. See *Journal de la cour* (3 Aug. 1733), p. 128. Dubuisson to Caumont ([c. 25 June 1735]), *CWV*, vol. 87, p. 165.

66 On loans to Richelieu, see Dubuisson, *Lettres*, Letter IX (June 1735), p. 86; app. D24 and app. D30, *CWV*, vol. 86, pp. 488–89, 494. See Sturdy, *Science and Social Status*, pp. 359–60. Vaillot, *Avec Mme Du Châtelet*, p. 286.

67 For play receipts, see Henry Carrington Lancaster, *The Comédie Française, 1701–1774: Plays, Actors, Spectators, Finances*, Transactions of the American Philosophical Society (Philadelphia: American Philosophical Society, 1951). D1371, Voltaire to Moussinot (14 [Sept. 1737]), *CWV*, vol. 88, pp. 372–73, p. 373 n. 1. On the lottery, see Pomeau, *D'Arouet à Voltaire*, vol. 1, p. 205. On finances, see Vaillot, *Avec Mme Du Châtelet*, p. 286; *CWV*, app. D21, vol. 86, p. 486, for investments in 1729. For later years, see appendices, *CWV*, vol. 95, pp. 386–87, 396ff, 476; app. D74, *CWV*, vol. 94, pp. 485–86, 489–91; Longchamps manuscript, Bibliothèque Nationale, NAF 13006, pp. 83v–84.

68 See for example, #1, Du Châtelet to Sade ([Dec. 1733]), *LDC*, vol. 1, p. 29; #14, Du Châtelet to Sade (12 May 1734), *LDC*, vol. 1, p. 42. #24, Du Châtelet to Maupertuis (23 Oct. 1734), *LDC*, vol. 1, pp. 52–54.

69 These and the subsequent references come from *LDC*, vol. 1, letters #35–38, Du Châtelet to Richelieu (May–June 1735, pp. 61–83; see also #17 Du Châtelet to Forcalquier (12 July [1734]), p. 45; #23 Du Châtelet to Forcalquier (14 [Sept. 1734]), pp. 51–52.

70 On similar fears, see #18, Du Châtelet to Sade [c. 15 July 1734]), *LDC*, vol. 1, p. 46.

71 Du Châtelet, *Discours,* ed. Mauzi, pp. 18, 19, 6–7, 16. Other biographies attribute her decision to an ultimatum from Voltaire. See Vaillot, *Madame du Châtelet,* pp. 106–7, and on his use of underlining to press his interpretation, p. 329 nn. 4–6.

72 For Fontenelle, see *éloge* for Carré, quoted in Charles B. Paul, *Science and Immortality: The Eloges of the Paris Academy of Sciences (1699–1971)* (Berkeley: University of California Press, 1980), p. 18. See Patricia Phillips, *The Scientific Lady: A Social History of Women's Scientific Interests 1520–1918* (New York: St. Martin's, 1990), pp. 85–86. See also John Bennett Shank, "Neither Natural Philosophy, Nor Science, Nor Literature: Gender, Writing, and the Pursuit of Nature in Fontenelle's *Entretiens sur la pluralité des mondes habités,"* in *Men, Women, and the Birthing of Modern Science,* ed. Judith P. Zinsser (DeKalb: Northern Illinois University Press, 2005); and Nina Rattner Gelbart, introduction to Bernard le Bovier de Fontenelle, *Conversations on the Plurality of Worlds,* trans. H. A. Hargreaves (Berkeley: University of California Press, 1990), p. xxviii.

73 See, for example, Fontenelle, quoted in Charles Collé, *Journal* [historique] . . . *1748–1772* (Paris: Didot, 1868), vol. 1, p. 127.

74 See Charles Jean François Hénault, *Mémoires du Président Hénault,* ed. François Rousseau (Paris: Hachette, 1911), p. 189; Jordan, *Histoire,* p. 52; Sturdy, *Science and Social Status,* p. 358.

75 See Gelbart in Fontenelle, *Conversations,* p. xix; Créqui, *Souvenirs,* vol. 1, p. 76; Sturdy, *Science and Social Status,* pp. 359–60. See also Charles Augustin Sainte-Beuve, *Causeries du Lundi* (Paris: Garnier Freres, 1852–62), vol. 3, p. 323; Collé, *Journal* [historique] (Jan. 1751), vol. 1, p. 281.

76 Du Châtelet, trans., *Fable,* 218vB.

77 Maxim quoted in Saint-Beuve, *Causeries du lundi,* vol. 3, p. 320. Her phrase is a playful reference to the *Métaphysique d'amour,* the title of one of Mme Lambert's essays.

Chapter Three: "Mon Académie"

1 Emilie de Breteuil, marquise Du Châtelet, trans., *Fable of the Bees,* by Bernard Mandeville, in *Studies on Voltaire, with some unpublished papers of Mme Du Châtelet,* by I. O. Wade (Princeton: Princeton University Press, 1947), A158/W136. I have designated the manuscript versions of Du Châtelet's "preface" used here as drafts A, B, and C (Voltaire Collection, St. Petersburg National Library of Russia, vol. IX, pp. 153–284v). Wade's printed text is cited as "W" with his pagination.

2 Du Châtelet, trans., *Fable* preface, A154/W132. See also A160/W138.

3 D866, Voltaire to Cideville ([29 April 1735]), *The Complete Works of Voltaire,* ed. Theodore Besterman (Genève: Institut et Musée Voltaire, 1968–), vol. 87, p. 135; D1022, Voltaire to d'Argental (26 Feb. [1736]), *CWV,* vol. 87, p. 367.

4 On the marquis's activities, see #114, Du Châtelet to Maupertuis (10 Jan. 1738), Emilie de Breteuil, marquise Du Châtelet, *Lettres de la Marquise du Châtelet,* ed. Theodore Besterman (Genève: Institut et Musée Voltaire, 1958), vol. 1, p. 208; D1187,

Voltaire to Champbonin ([c. 30 Oct. 1736]), *CWV*, vol. 88, pp. 100–101; D1490, Voltaire to d'Argental (3 May [1738]), *CWV*, vol. 89, p. 103; D1512, Voltaire to Moussinot (30 May [1738]), *CWV*, vol. 89, p. 137. On the wedding in Lorraine, see #96, Du Châtelet to d'Argental (30 [Jan. 1737]), *LDC*, vol. 1, p. 184.

5 #86, Du Châtelet, to d'Argental (2 [Jan. 1737]), *LDC*, vol. 1, p. 156. See also #165, Du Châtelet to d'Argental (10 Jan. 1739), *LDC*, vol. 1, p. 296. Françoise d'Issembourg d'Happoncourt Graffigny, *Correspondance de Madame de Graffigny,* ed. J. A. Dainard, et al. (Oxford: Voltaire Foundation, 1985–). #103, Graffigny to Devaux ([c. 10 March– 2 April 1739]), vol. 1, p. 379. #99, Du Châtelet to d'Argental ([1 March 1737]), *LDC,* vol. 1, p. 187.

6 See #54, 61, 66, 68, 69, 84, 98, Graffigny to Devaux (Dec. 1738–March 1739), in *Correspondance de Graffigny,* vol. 1, pp. 195, 197, 241, 250, 253, 302. See also #179, Graffigny to Devaux (3 Sept. [1739]), in vol. 2, p. 140. #54, Du Châtelet to Thieriot (20 Feb. 1736), *LDC,* vol. 1, p. 99; Voltaire to Thieriot (10 Feb. 1736), *CWV,* vol. 87, p. 345. D1115, Voltaire to Moussinot (16 July 1736), *CWV,* vol. 88, p. 19. D1155, Voltaire to Berger (25 Sept. 1736), *CWV,* vol. 88, p. 67. See #108, Du Châtelet to Maupertuis (11 Dec. 1737), *LDC,* vol. 1, p. 198. #118, Du Châtelet to Bernoulli (2 Feb. 1738), *LDC,* vol. 1, p. 213. #233, Du Châtelet to Bernoulli (11 Jan. 1740), *LDC,* vol. 2, p. 7.

7 #63, Du Châtelet to Algarotti (20 [April 1736]), *LDC,* vol. 1, p. 114; D1221, Voltaire to d'Argental ([9 Dec. 1736]), *CWV,* vol. 88, p. 149. Voltaire *Mémoires* as quoted in Theodore Besterman, *Voltaire* (New York: Harcourt Brace & World, 1969), p. 233.

8 Voltaire to d'Argental (8 May 1734), quoted in L'abbé Piot, *Cirey-le-Chateau: La Marquise du Châtelet, sa liaison avec Voltaire* (Saint-Dizier: O. Godard, 1894), p. 475. #286, Du Châtelet to d'Argental (21 Nov. 1741), *LDC,* vol. 2, p. 80. Sébastien G. Longchamps, *Mémoires sur Voltaire, et sur ses ouvrages.* Bibliothéque Nationale, NAF 13006; pp. 30b–32.

9 On distances and time see Besterman, *Voltaire,* p. 233. #92, Du Châtelet to Thieriot (16 Jan. 1737), *LDC,* vol. 1, p. 166 n. 4. For route, see #88, Graffigny to Devaux ([7 Feb. 1739]), *Correspondance de Graffigny,* vol. 1, p. 312 n. 9, and #90, Graffigny to Devaux ([11 Feb. 1739]), pp. 315, 317. #370, Du Châtelet to Saint-Lambert ([Aug. 1748]), *LDC,* vol. 2, pp. 163–64. See #272, Graffigny to Devaux (13 May 1740), *Correspondance de Graffigny,* vol. 2, p. 395, and #53, Graffigny to Devaux ([20 Nov. 1738]), vol. 1, p. 162. Longchamps, *Mémoires,* Bibliothèque Nationale NAF 13006, 30b–32.

10 Piot, *Cirey-le-Château,* p. 263.

11 *Correspondance de Graffigny,* vol. 1, p. 92 n. 70.

12 For information in this and the next paragraph, see, Piot, *Cirey-le-Château,* p. 469; Voltaire correspondence with Moussinot, 1737–38, passim: for example, D1695, Voltaire to Moussinot (18 [Dec. 1738]), *CWV,* vol. 89, p. 450; D1420, Voltaire to Moussinot (10 Jan. 1738), *CWV,* vol. 88, p. 450. On Richelieu, see D1213, Voltaire to Moussinot ([c. 30 Nov. 1736]), *CWV,* vol. 88, p. 136. The description that follows in the text represents a synthesis from Graffigny, Dec. 1738–Feb. 1739, #60–#91, in *Correspondance de Graffigny,* vol. 1, pp. 192–319; and from Du Châtelet's and Voltaire's correspondence from 1734–49. See the Cirey Web site www.visitvoltaire.com; René Vaillot, *Madame du Châtelet* (Paris: Albin Michel, 1978), p. 92; Piot, *Cirey-le-Château,* pp. 381, 264, 273 (on the forest), 198–217.

13 D800, Voltaire to Neuville ([1 Nov. 1734]), *CWV,* vol. 87, p. 77. Note I have placed the

letter in 1735, not 1734, in conjunction with Du Châtelet's move to Cirey, rather than her first brief stay. See D1196, Voltaire to Moussinot (10 [Nov. 1736]), *CWV*, vol. 88, p. 114; D1201, Voltaire to Moussinot (17 [Nov. 1736]), *CWV*, vol. 88, p. 120; D1213, Voltaire to Moussinot ([30 Nov. 1736]), *CWV*, vol. 88, p. 136. See also D1031, Voltaire to Moussinot (8 March 1736), *CWV*, vol. 87, p. 382; D996, Voltaire to Thieriot (25 Jan. [1736]), *CWV*, vol. 87, p. 330 n. 4; Piot, *Cirey-le-Château*, p. 482. The student is never mentioned by name; his mentor was Martin.

14   Daniel Roche, *A History of Everyday Things: The Birth of Consumption in France, 1600–1800*, trans. Brian Pearce (New York: Cambridge University Press, 2000), p. 178.

15   See *Correspondance de Graffigny*, #62, Graffigny to Devaux ([10 Dec. 1738]), vol. 1, p. 209. #63, Graffigny to Devaux ([14–15 Dec. 1738]), vol. 1, p. 224. #91, Desmarest to Devaux ([12 Feb. 1739]), vol. 1, p. 319.

16   See *Correspondance de Graffigny*, #61, Graffigny to Devaux ([6 Dec. 1738]), vol. 1, p. 199. #69, Graffigny to Devaux ([29 Dec. 1738]), vol. 1, p. 253.

17   Though Voltaire gave her an *écu* (three livres), a generous tip, he had her, not his valet, fired. #69, Graffigny to Devaux [(29 Dec. 1738]), *Correspondance de Graffigny*, vol. 1, p. 254. On Voltaire's need for a valet and their salaries, see D615, Voltaire to Cideville (May 1733), *CWV*, vol. 86, p. 340; D946, Voltaire to Thieriot ([c. 25 Nov. 1735]), *CWV*, vol. 87, p. 256. D966, (17 Dec. 1735), *CWV*, vol. 87, pp. 288–89. D1011, Voltaire to Thieriot ([c. 11 Feb. 1736]), *CWV*, vol. 87, p. 352 nn. D1569, Voltaire to Moussinot (2 Aug. 1738), *CWV*, vol. 89, p. 225. See also Roche, *Everyday Things*, p. 386.

18   See *Correspondance de Graffigny*, #62, Graffigny to Devaux ([11 Dec. 1738]), vol. 1, p. 211. #63, Graffigny to Devaux ([12 Dec. 1738]), vol. 1, p. 215; #65, Graffigny to Devaux ([19 or 20 Dec. 1738]), vol. 1, pp. 237–38. #82, Du Châtelet to d'Argental (30 Dec. [1736]), *LDC*, vol. 1, p. 148. Simon Henri Dubuisson, *Lettres du Commissaire Dubuisson au Marquis de Caumont, 1735–1741* (Paris: Arnould, 1882), (June 1739), p. 562 n. 1. See book plate, Voltaire Library, St. Petersburg National Library of Russia #20997/4-151.

19   On Champbonin, see D1881, Voltaire to Berger (16 Feb. 1739), *CWV*, vol. 90, p. 219; D1895, Du Châtelet to d'Argental (Feb. [1739]), *CWV*, vol. 90, p. 236. D1896, Voltaire to d'Argental (21 Feb. 1739), *CWV*, vol. 90, p. 238. #61, Graffigny to Devaux ([5 Dec. 1738]), *Correspondance de Graffigny*, vol. 1, pp. 196, 203 n. 12.

20   Also spelled "du Thiel." See Piot, *Cirey-le-Château*, p. 524. For papal maneuvers, see René Vaillot, *Avec Mme Du Châtelet, 1734–1749*, in *Voltaire en son temps*, ed. René Pomeau (Oxford: Voltaire Foundation, 1985–95), pp. 469–71; #19, Du Châtelet to Maupertuis (? July 1734), *LDC*, vol. 1, p. 48. I am grateful to Penny Arthur of the Graffigny Papers in Toronto for the details of de Thil's origins and properties.

21   D1791, Graffigny to Devaux (17 Jan. [1739]), *CWV*, vol. 90, p. 85.

22   For all the following description, see Piot, *Cirey-le-Château*, pp. 160–62, 184–85, 196, 222–35, 240–47, 249–59, 260–63, 385–406, 419–29. Champagne figure from Roche, *Everyday Things*, p. 232.

23   This information from the Paris Inventory, *CWV*, vol. 95, pp. 453, 455, 463; Piot, *Cirey-Le-Château*, pp. 122, 162.

24   Piot, *Cirey-le-Château*, pp. 269–70. #445, Du Châtelet to d'Argental (13 Jan. 1749), *LDC*, vol. 2, p. 237.

25   #148, Du Châtelet to Maupertuis ([24 Oct. 1738]), *LDC*, vol. 1, p. 267.

26 #37, Du Châtelet to Richelieu ([c. 30 May 1735]), *LDC*, vol. 1, p. 69. See D1220, Voltaire to Formont (23 Dec. [1737]), *CWV*, vol. 88, p. 431. #44, Du Châtelet to Algarotti ([c. 10 Oct. 1735]), *LDC*, vol. 1, p. 85. #95, Du Châtelet to Maupertuis (? Aug. 1735), *LDC*, vol. 1, p. 79. On Maupertuis as her Descartes, see #69, Du Châtelet to Maupertuis (18 July [1736]), *LDC*, vol. 1, p. 121. See also D1139, Voltaire to Frederick ([c. 1 Sept. 1736]), *CWV*, vol. 88, p. 45.

27 See on Du Resnel #108, Du Châtelet to Maupertuis (11 Dec. [1737]), *LDC*, vol. 1, p. 198. #166, Du Châtelet to d'Argental (10 Jan. [1739]), *LDC*, vol. 1, p. 296. D2996, Hénault to d'Argenson (9 July 1744), *CWV*, vol. 93, p. 136.

28 #66, Du Châtelet to Algarotti (15 June 1736), *LDC*, vol. 1, p. 117. Charles-Etienne Jordan, *Histoire d'un voyage littéraire fait en MDCCXXXIII* (The Hague: Adorren Hoetiers, 1735), preface, passim. #67, Du Châtelet to Algarotti (10 July 1736), *LDC*, vol. 1, p. 119. #88, Du Châtelet to Algarotti (11 Jan. 1737), *LDC*, vol. 1, p. 159. #52, Du Châtelet to "?" (3 Jan. 1736), *LDC*, vol. 1, p. 95. #43, Du Châtelet to Maupertuis (8 Oct. 1735), *LDC*, vol. 1, p. 84. #121, Du Châtelet to Thieriot (3 April [1738]), *LDC*, vol. 1, p. 219. #117, Du Châtelet to Algarotti (2 Feb. 1738), *LDC*, vol. 1, p. 211. #286, Du Châtelet to d'Argental (21 Nov. 1741), *LDC*, vol. 2, p. 80. D1140, Voltaire to d'Argens (4 Sept. 1736), *CWV*, vol. 88, p. 47. D1142, Voltaire to Berger ([5 Sept. 1736]), *CWV*, vol. 88, p. 50; D1307, Voltaire to Frederick ([c. 30 March 1737]), *CWV*, vol. 88, p. 273. D1641, Maupertuis to Bernoulli (29 Oct. 1738), *CWV*, vol. 89, p. 343. Devaux to Graffigny, *Correspondance de Graffigny*, vol. 1, p. 82 n. 32.

29 Roland Bonnel, "La Correspondance scientifique de la marquise Du Châtelet: la 'lettre-laboratoire,'" SVEC (2000:4), pp. 79–95.

30 See manuscript letters to Maupertuis, Bibliothèque Nationale, NAF 12269, #20 R (#24, Du Châtelet to Maupertuis). See also Du Châtelet manuscript letters to d'Argental. Morgan Library Collection in New York City, 1565.

31 See #92, Du Châtelet to Thieriot (16 Jan. [1737]), *LDC*, vol. 1, pp. 164, 166 n. 4. #89, Du Châtelet to d'Argental (13 Jan. [1737]), *LDC*, vol. 1, p. 160. #270, Du Châtelet to Maupertuis (2 May 1741), *LDC*, vol. 2, p. 53. #332, Du Châtelet to Maupertuis (1 Nov. 1744), *LDC*, vol. 2, p. 129. D1119, Voltaire to Berger ([c. 30 July 1736]), *CWV*, vol. 88, p. 23. D1149, Voltaire to Berger ([c. 18 Sept. 1736]), *CWV*, vol. 88, p. 55. D1151, Voltaire to Berger ([20 Sept. 1736]), *CWV*, vol. 88, p. 63. D1837, Voltaire to d'Argental (30 [Jan. 1739]), *CWV*, vol. 90, p. 165. #57, Du Châtelet to Algarotti (8 March [1736]), *LDC*, vol. 1, p. 106.

32 #92, Du Châtelet to Thieriot (16 Jan. [1737]), *LDC*, vol. 1, p. 163. See also D1155, Voltaire to Berger ([c. 25 Sept. 1736]), *CWV*, vol. 88, p. 67; D2005 Voltaire to Thieriot (7 May 1739), *CWV*, vol. 90, p. 368.

33 Fernand Caussy, *Inventaire des manuscrits de la Bibliothèque de Voltaire conservé à la Bibliothèque impériale publique de Saint-Pétersbourg* (1913; reprint, Genève: Slatkine Reprints, 1970), introduction, p. 5.

34 #73, Du Châtelet to Maupertuis (1 Dec. [1736]), *LDC*, vol. 1, p. 125.

35 See *Correspondance de Graffigny*, #61, Graffigny to Devaux ([5 Dec. 1738]), vol. 1, p. 195. #53, Graffigny to Devaux ([19 Nov. 1738]), vol. 1, pp. 158–59. D927, Algarotti to Franchini (12 Oct. 1735), *CWV*, vol. 87, pp. 227–29. For a description of the conversation, see #38, Du Châtelet to Richelieu ([15 June 1735]), *LDC*, vol. 1, p. 76.

36 D935, Voltaire to Thieriot ([Nov. 1735]), *CWV*, vol. 87, pp. 241–42. Voltaire's "le mondain" and "Défense du mondain," *Contes en vers: Oeuvres Complètes*. 52 vols. (Paris: Garnier Frères, 1877), pp. 90–93.

37 Description from *Correspondance de Graffigny*, #61, Graffigny to Devaux ([5–6 Dec. 1738]), vol. 1, pp. 198–99. Verses from Piot, *Cirey-le-Château*, p. 470.

38 See for descriptions of the *galerie* and morning *café*: #61 Graffigny to Devaux ([6 Dec. 1738]), *Correspondance de Graffigny*, vol. 1, pp. 197–99. On canaries and the parrot, see D1351, Voltaire to Moussinot (8 [July 1737]), *CWV*, vol. 88, p. 347. On the chinoiserie desk see D1303, Voltaire to Moussinot (26 March 1737), *CWV*, vol. 88, p. 269. See also D1414, Voltaire to Moussinot (Dec. 1737), *CWV*, vol. 88, p. 441; D1336, Voltaire to Moussinot (May/June 1737), *CWV*, vol. 88, p. 321. Piot, *Cirey-le-Château*, pp. 480, 480 n. 2.

39 #62, Graffigny to Devaux ([11 Dec. 1738]), in *Correspondance de Graffigny*, vol. 1, pp. 211, 213 n. 7. Historians have speculated about the name of the book by the "English dreamer." Sutton suggests Huygens's *Celestial Worlds Discovered* (Geoffrey V. Sutton, *Science for a Polite Society: Gender, Culture, and the Demonstration of Enlightenment* [Boulder, Colo.: Westview Press, 1995], p. 275). It is, however, more likely that it was a work by Christian Wolff; see D2526, Voltaire to Maupertuis (10 Aug. 1741), *CWV*, vol. 92, p. 95.

40 D1006, Voltaire to Thieriot (9 Feb. 1736), *CWV*, vol. 87, p. 342. #68, Graffigny to Devaux ([26 Dec. 1738]), *Correspondance de Graffigny*, vol. 1, p. 249. #52, Du Châtelet to "?" (3 Jan. 1736), *LDC*, vol. 1, p. 95. On misspelling, see, for example, #51, Du Châtelet to Thieriot (29 [Dec. 1735]), *LDC*, vol. 1, p. 94. #135, Du Châtelet to Richelieu (17 [? Aug. 1738]), *LDC*, vol. 1, p. 247.

41 See D838, Voltaire to Neuville ([? Jan. 1735]), *CWV*, vol. 87, p. 109–10; D808, Voltaire to Champbonin ([c. Dec. 1734]), *CWV*, vol. 87, p. 84. #62, Graffigny to Devaux ([10 Dec.] 1738), *Correspondence de Graffigny*, vol. 1, p. 209; #64, Graffigny to Devaux (16 Dec. 1738), p. 228; #89, Graffigny to Devaux ([9 Feb. 1739]), p. 313.

42 #45, Du Châtelet to Richelieu ([15 Oct. 1735]), *LDC*, vol. 1, p. 86; #52, Du Châtelet to "?" (3 Jan. 1736), *LDC*, vol. 1, p. 95; #60–62, Graffigny to Devaux (4–10 Dec. 1738), *Correspondance de Graffigny*, vol. 1, pp. 193, 207, 210; D1013, Voltaire (Feb. 1736), *CWV*, vol. 87, p. 354; D1201, Voltaire to Moussinot (17 [Nov. 1736]), *CWV*, vol. 88, p. 120; D1084, Voltaire to Moussinot (May/June 1736), *CWV*, vol. 87, p. 466; Roger Chartier, *Passions of the Renaissance, A History of Private Life*, edited by Philippe Ariès and Georges Duby (Cambridge, Mass.: Belknap Press of Harvard University Press, 1989), vol. 3, p. 292; Piot, *Cirey-le-Château*, pp. 485–86, 490; D774, Voltaire to Neuville ([end July 1734]), *CWV*, vol. 87, p. 53; D1058, Voltaire to Moussinot (12 [April 1736]), *CWV*, vol. 87, p. 428; D1690, Voltaire to Moussinot (14 [Dec. 1738]), *CWV*, vol. 89, p. 440; D2113, Voltaire to Moussinot (26 [Nov. 1739]), *CWV*, vol. 91, p. 39.

43 #162, Du Châtelet to d'Argental (31 Dec. 1738), *LDC*, vol. 1, p. 291. #62, Graffigny to Devaux ([10 Dec. 1738]), *Correspondance de Graffigny*, vol. 1, p. 207. See Sainte-Beuve, quoted in Piot, *Cirey-le-Château*, p. 477. For this and subsequent description of evening entertainments, see #63–#65, Graffigny to Devaux (12 Dec.–19 or 20 Dec. 1738), in *Correspondance de Graffigny*, vol. 1, pp. 215–39.

44 With the restoration, the places where the plaster had fallen off have been covered, and the painted scene has been changed slightly.

45 #52, Du Châtelet to "?" (3 Jan. 1736), *LDC*, vol. 1, p. 95. #62, #63, Graffigny to Devaux (10, 12 Dec. 1738), *Correspondance de Graffigny*, vol. 1, pp. 211–19. On the two versions of this play, see Besterman, introduction to *Le Comte de Boursoufle, CWV,* vol. 14, pp. 220–21 n. 42, pp. 257–58.

46 Quoted in Besterman, Introduction, *Le Comte de Boursoufle, CWV,* vol. 14, p. 227. For the dialogue and scenes, *Le Comte de Boursoufle,* Act II, scene 4, *CWV,* vol. 14, pp. 296, 333.

47 For descriptions of this forty-eight-hour period, see #86–89, Graffigny to Devaux ([2–9 Feb. 1739]) and #90–91 Desmarest and Graffigny to Devaux ([1–12 Feb. 1739]), *Correspondance de Graffigny,* vol. 1, pp. 307–20.

48 On his ill health, see Du Châtelet to Thieriot, Cideville and Formont and Moussinot (1736–1737), *LDC,* vol. 1, passim. On specific cures, see, for example, #138, Du Châtelet to Cideville (27 Aug. 1738), *LDC,* vol. 1, p. 251; #142, Du Châtelet to Moussinot (11 Sept. [1738]), *LDC,* vol. 1, p. 259; D3609, Voltaire to d'Argental (1 Feb. [1738]), *CWV,* vol. 94, p. 199. See Henri Dubuisson, *Lettres du Commissaire Dubuisson . . . 1735–1741* (Paris: Arnould, 1882), Lettre IX (June, 1735), pp. 56–57; (29 July 1735), Lettre XI, p. 113. Mme. Du Châtelet, *Discours sur le bonheur,* ed. Robert Mauzi (Paris: Société d'Editions Belles Lettres, 1961), p. 28. #5, "Pleasure" in "Discours en vers sur l'homme," *CWV,* vol. 17, p. 506. Note that Voltaire cut these lines from the final version. See other biographers on this, for example, "a great fragility of the nervous system and a chronic intestinal incontinence [diarrhea]" (Vaillot, *Madame du Châtelet,* pp. 64–65); Elisabeth Badinter, in Emilie de Breteuil, marquise Du Châtelet. *Discours sur le Bonheur,* ed. Elisabeth Badinter (Paris: Eds. Payot and Rivages, 1997), preface. See Voltaire's own admission to Cideville, of "not being highly sexed," D663, Voltaire to Cideville (14 Oct. [1733]), *CWV,* vol. 86, p. 405.

49 For this and other verses that follow, see "Miscellaneous Verses," for 1734–35, *CWV,* vol. 14, pp. 521–30. For examples in letters, see D895, Voltaire to Cideville (3 Aug. [1735]), *CWV,* vol. 87, pp. 176–77. D942, Voltaire to Formont (15 Nov. [1735]), *CWV,* vol. 87, p. 251. D1019, Voltaire to Cideville (22 Feb. 1736), *CWV,* vol. 87, p. 361. D935, Voltaire to Thieriot (3 Nov. 1735), *CWV,* vol. 87, p. 241. D1141, Voltaire to Thieriot (5 Sept. 1736), *CWV,* vol. 88, p. 49. D1225, Voltaire to Champbonin ([15 Dec. 1736]), *CWV,* vol. 88, p. 155. Dubuisson, *Lettres,* (early July 1736) Lettre VI, p. 242.

50 See #125, Du Châtelet to Algarotti (12 May 1738), *LDC,* vol. 1, p. 229, including Voltaire's additions to her letter. Voltaire, *Oeuvres Complètes* (1877 ed.), *Poésies Mêlées,* vol. 10, p. 519.

51 See D911, Voltaire to Thieriot (11 Sept. 1735), *CWV,* vol. 87, p. 196. D1173, Voltaire to Berger (18 Oct. 1736), *CWV,* vol. 88, p. 87. D1029, Voltaire to Thieriot (4 March [1736]), *CWV,* vol. 87, p. 380. D1001, Voltaire to Le Blanc ([c. Feb. 5, 1736), *CWV,* vol. 87, p. 336. D1012, Voltaire to d'Olivet (12 Feb. 1736), *CWV,* vol. 87, p. 353. D1020, Voltaire to Fawkener (22 Feb. 1736), *CWV,* vol. 87, p. 364. See also Cideville quoted in *LDC,* vol. 1, p. 61 n.

52 #46, Du Châtelet to Richelieu ([? Nov. 1735]), *LDC,* vol. 1, p. 88. #48, Du Châtelet to Richelieu ([c. 1 Dec. 1735]), *LDC,* vol. 1, p. 91. "Genius" from Du Châtelet, trans., *Fable,* preface. "Le plus honnête homme du monde" from #94, Du Châtelet to

d'Argental (25 Jan. 1737), *LDC*, vol. 1, p. 171. See also #79, Du Châtelet to d'Argental ([23 Dec. 1736]), *LDC*, vol. 1, p. 137. #66, Du Châtelet to Algarotti (15 June 1736), *LDC*, vol. 1, p. 117.

53 René Vaillot also uses "Storms in Paradise" as a chapter heading in *Avec Mme Du Châtelet*. On the coffee-cup incident and Longchamps's report, see Piot, *Cirey-le-Château*, p. 516 n. 1. See D779, Voltaire to Neuville ([? Aug. 1734]), *CWV*, vol. 87, p. 55; D781, Voltaire to Neuville ([? Aug. 1734]), *CWV*, vol. 87, p. 57; D886, Voltaire to Richelieu (30 [June 1735]), *CWV*, vol. 87, p. 168. For verses to Richelieu and Maupertuis, see *CWV*, vol. 87, pp. 168, 280–81.

54 See #37, Du Châtelet to Richelieu ([c. 30 May 1735]), *LDC*, vol. 1, p. 69. #38, Du Châtelet to Richelieu ([c. 15 June 1735]), *LDC*, vol. 1, p. 74.

55 On rumors see, Dubuisson, *Lettres* (1 Dec. 1736) Letter XIV; #586, Graffigny to Devaux (30 Aug. [1743]), in *Correspondance de Graffigny*, vol. 4, p. 360. On Du Châtelet's anxieties, see especially letters to d'Argental, Du Châtelet (1736–38), *LDC*, vol. 1, passim.

56 D935, Voltaire to Thieriot (3 Nov. [1735]), *CWV*, vol. 87, pp. 241–43. #93, Du Châtelet to d'Argental (22 [Jan. 1737]), *LDC*, vol. 1, p. 167. "Shorter Verse of 1736," *CWV*, vol. 16, pp. 47–53.

57 On the conflict, see Vaillot, *Avec Mme Du Châtelet*, pp. 297–300. D951, Voltaire to Thieriot (30 Nov. [1735]), *CWV*, vol. 87, p. 263.

58 For these interpretations of *Alzire*, see Dubuisson, *Lettres* (May 1736), Lettre IV, pp. 193, 198–99 and D909, Claude Le Pelletier to Chauvelin (1 Sept. 1735), *CWV*, vol. 87, p. 194. For the "Epître," see *Alzire, CWV*, vol. 14, pp. 109–16. On her worries, see #54, Du Châtelet to Thieriot (20 Feb. 1736), *LDC*, vol. 1, pp. 98–99. See D1072, Voltaire to Cideville (6 May [1736]), *CWV*, vol. 87, p. 443. "Ode sur la fanatisme" in *CWV*, vol. 16, pp. 425–33. Invective in #65, Du Châtelet to Algarotti ([c. 5 May 1736]), *LDC*, vol. 1, p. 116.

59 See summary in Vaillot, *Avec Mme Du Châtelet*, pp. 329–31. D1207, Voltaire to Thieriot (24 Nov. 1736), *CWV*, vol. 88, p. 127; Voltaire to d'Argental ([9 Dec. 1736]), *CWV*, vol. 88, pp. 149–50. On Du Châtelet's efforts, see #68, Du Châtelet to Cideville (18 July [1736]), *LDC*, vol. 1, p. 120; #76, Du Châtelet to d'Argental (21 Dec. 1736), *LDC*, vol. 1, p. 131; #77, Du Châtelet to duchesse de Richelieu ([? 21 Dec. 1737]), *LDC*, vol. 1, p. 133; #78, Du Châtelet to Thieriot (21 Dec. [1736]), *LDC*, vol. 1, p. 135; #81, Du Châtelet to d'Argental (28 [Dec. 1736]), *LDC*, vol. 1, p. 142. On the marquis's efforts, see #94, Du Châtelet to d'Argental (25 Jan. 1737), *LDC*, vol. 1, pp. 217, 219.

60 #82, Du Châtelet to d'Argental (29 Dec. [1736], *LDC*, vol. 1, pp. 146–48. See also #39, Du Châtelet to Marie de Fleming (5 July 1735), *LDC*, vol. 1, p. 78.

61 #82, Du Châtelet to d'Argental (29 Dec. [1736]), *LDC*, vol. 1, p. 148; #95, Du Châtelet to d'Argental (28 Jan. 1737), *LDC*, vol. 1, p. 177. #84, Du Châtelet to d'Argental (31 Dec. 1736), *LDC*, vol. 1, pp. 152, 153. #80, Du Châtelet to d'Argental (27 Dec. 1736), *LDC*, vol. 1, pp. 138–39.

62 #93, Du Châtelet to d'Argental (22 Jan. 1737), *LDC*, vol. 2, pp. 168, 169. #94, Du Châtelet to d'Argental (25 Jan. 1737), *LDC*, vol. 1, pp. 173, 175, 171. I am grateful to Véronique Flachat (a descendant of the marquis Du Châtelet) for giving me a copy of the three-page manuscript of "chapître dernier," no. 24, of Voltaire's *Eléments de la philosophie de Newton.*

63 #95, Du Châtelet to d'Argental (28 Jan. 1737), *LDC*, vol. 1, p. 179.

64 #93, Du Châtelet to d'Argental (22 Jan. 1737), *LDC*, vol. 2, p. 168. #96, Du Châtelet to d'Argental (30 [Jan. 1737]), *LDC*, vol. 1, pp. 183, 184.

65 #99, Du Châtelet to d'Argental (1 March 1737), *LDC*, vol. 1, p. 187. On the essay "Liberté," see Linda Gardiner Janik, "Searching for the Metaphysics of Science: The Structure & Composition of Madame Du Châtelet's *Institutions de physique, 1737–1740*," *SVEC* 201 (1982), pp. 85–113; Andrew Brown and Ulla Kölving, "Qui est l'auteur du *Traité de métaphysique?*" *Cahiers Voltaire* 2 (2003), pp. 85–93.

66 *Voltairomanie* was Desfontaines's response to *Le Préservatif,* Voltaire's attack against him. See #162, Du Châtelet to d'Argental (31 Dec. 1738), *LDC,* vol. 1, p. 290. Du Châtelet's "Reply to the Voltairomanie" reprinted as app. D51, in *CWV,* vol. 89, pp. 508–12.

67 #90, Du Châtelet to Graffigny (14 Jan. 1737), *LDC,* vol. 1, p. 161. See *Correspondance de Graffigny*: #80, Graffigny to Devaux ([19 Jan. 1739]), vol. 1, p. 293; #44, Graffigny to Devaux (25 Oct. 1738), vol. 1, pp. 110–14; #33, Graffigny to Devaux ([30 Sept. 1738]), vol. 1, p. 58; for "une robe honnête" see #35, Graffigny to Devaux ([4 Oct. 1738]), vol. 1, p. 65.

68 See *Correspondance de Graffigny*: #61, Graffigny to Devaux ([6 Dec. 1738]), vol. 1, p. 196; #62, Graffigny to Devaux ([9 Dec. 1738]), vol. 1, p. 205; #63, Graffigny to Devaux (15 Dec. 1738), vol. 1, p. 224. #67, Graffigny to Devaux ([25 Dec. 1738]), vol. 1, p. 245.

69 See D1686, Graffigny to Devaux, ([12 Dec. 1738]), *CWV,* vol. 89, p. 422; #64, Graffigny to Devaux ([18 Dec. 1738]), *Correspondance de Graffigny,* vol. 1, pp. 230, 231.

70 To follow the story, see *Correspondance de Graffigny*: #80, Graffigny to Devaux ([19 Jan. 1739]), vol. 1, pp. 287–97. #89, Graffigny to Devaux ([9 Feb. 1739]), vol. 1, pp. 313–14.

71 On Voltaire's reputation as a playwright, see I. O. Wade, *The Intellectual Development of Voltaire* (Princeton: Princeton University Press, 1969), pp. 375, 382; see also Henry Carrington Lancaster, *French Tragedy in the Time of Louis XV and Voltaire, 1715–1774* (Baltimore: Johns Hopkins Press, 1950), vol. 1, p. 218. See #80, Du Châtelet to d'Argental (27 Dec. 1736), *LDC,* vol. 1, p. 138. Voltaire scholars have documented Du Châtelet's collaboration on a number of projects, of which *Alzire* was only the first. For her help in his scientific studies, see Robert L. Walters and W. H. Barber, Introduction, *Eléments de la philosophie de Newton* (Oxford: Voltaire Foundation, 1992), vol. 15; Robert L. Walters, "Chemistry at Cirey," *SVEC* 58 (1967), pp. 1807–27. On Du Châtelet's essay on optics and on her contributions to the *Traité de métaphysique,* see I. O. Wade, *Studies on Voltaire, with some unpublished papers of Mme. Du Châtelet* (Princeton: Princeton University Press, 1947); Andrew Brown and Ulla Kölving, "Qui est l'auteur," pp. 85–93. See Bertram Eugene Schwarzbach's numerous articles, for example "Mme Du Châtelet's *Examens de la Bible* and Voltaire's *La Bible enfin expliquée,* in Judith P. Zinsser and Julie Candler Hayes, eds., *SVEC* (2006:1).

72 See D1169, Voltaire to Berger ([c. 15 Oct. 1736]), *CWV,* vol. 88, p. 83. D1029, Voltaire to Thieriot (4 March [1736]), *CWV,* vol. 87, p. 380. D1004, Voltaire to Pallu (9 Feb. [1736]), *CWV,* vol. 87, p. 341. D1002, Voltaire to d'Argental (26 Feb. [1736]), *CWV,* vol. 87, pp. 366–67. D1003, Voltaire to Thieriot (6 Feb. [1736]), *CWV,* vol. 87, p. 340. D991, Voltaire to d'Argental (18 and 19 [Jan. 1736]), *CWV,* vol. 87, p. 323.

D885, Voltaire to Cideville (26 June 1735), *CWV*, vol. 87, p. 166. See for this and subsequent quotations: "Epître à Madame la Marquise Du Chastelet," *CWV*, vol. 14, pp. 109–16.

73 In St. Petersburg, the Occidental manuscripts collection has an earlier version in Voltaire's own hand, with Du Châtelet's additions and corrections. See also W. H. Barber, "Critical Edition of *Traité de Métaphysique*," in *CWV*, vol. 14, pp. 71–74. #117, Du Châtelet to Algarotti (2 Feb. 1738), *LDC*, vol. 1, p. 211. See Brown and Kölving, "Qui est l'auteur," especially pp. 85–87, for the chronology of the *Traité*'s composition, and pp. 88–89, 90–94. See also Voltaire, "Discours en vers sur l'homme," written during his time at Cirey, *CWV*, vol. 17. See Voltaire's correspondence on the sequence of their composition and publication, D1441, D1471, D1468, D1484, D1483, D1621, D1937 (Feb. 1738 to March 1739), *CWV*, vols. 89–90.

74 Two drafts of her translation and four of her translator's preface have been found among Voltaire's manuscripts in St. Petersburg. Voltaire had pt. 1 of the 1724 ed. of Mandeville and pt. 2 of the 1729 ed. in his library. They are listed as #2300 and #2301 in the catalogue Voltaire, *Bibliothèque de Voltaire: Catalogue des livres*, ed. M. P. Alekseev (Moscow, 1961). For a published version of Du Châtelet's preface, see draft A, Wade, *Studies on Voltaire*, p. 28. See also I. O. Wade, *Voltaire and Madame Du Châtelet: An Essay on the Intellectual Activity at Cirey* (Princeton: Princeton University Press, 1941), pp. 26–33. Du Châtelet, trans., *Fable*, B217/W131; A155/W133; A159/W137. D1179, Voltaire to Thieriot (21 Oct. 1736), *CWV*, vol. 88, p. 93. On these ideas of her role, see Du Châtelet, trans., *Fable*, A158v/W135, A155/W133 (on "entrepreneur" [*négotiant*]), B220v; Du Châtelet underlined such phrases in Houdar de la Motte's *L'Illiade: Poème avec un discours sur Homère* (Paris, 1714), p. 145 (National Library of Russia, St. Petersburg, #1669/#6-98).

75 #383, Du Châtelet to Saint-Lambert (16 June 1748), *LDC*, vol. 2, p. 189; #67, Graffigny to Devaux ([25 Dec. 1738]), *Correspondance de Graffigny*, vol. 1, pp. 245–47. The passages Graffigny copied corresponds to W138–39, W173, W176.

76 See Du Châtelet, trans., *Fable*, A161v–162/W139. Du Châtelet drew from Descartes's *Meditations*, bks. I and II of Locke's *Essay on Human Understanding*, Pope's *Essay on Man*, Lucretius's *De rerum natura*, and Voltaire's letter #25, on Pascal, from his *Lettres philosophique*. See, for example, her *Fable*, A155v/W133. *Fable*, chap. 1, A166–166v/W142–43.

77 On the Golden Rule, see Bernard Mandeville, *Fable of the Bees* . . . (London: J. Roberts, 1714), vol. 1, pp. 42–47; Du Châtelet, trans., A168–69/W144–45, A179/W154. Du Châtelet's version is most similar to Pope in his fourth epistle of the *Essay on Man* (New York: Ronald Press Company, 1929), see pp. 145, 153.

78 On "pride," see Du Châtelet, trans., *Fable*, chap. 1, A166–166v/W142–43. *Fable*, chap. 4, A184–184v/W157; Mandeville, *Fable*, p. 67. Du Châtelet, "Liberté," St. Petersburg Voltaire Collection, vol. 9, p. 126. See also Wade, *Studies on Voltaire*, p. 93.

79 D1376, Voltaire to Frederick (15 Oct. 1737), *CWV*, vol. 88, p. 381. Voltaire, "Discours en vers," *CWV*, vol. 17, p. 520. See Du Châtelet trans., "Du Châtelet, Liberté," St. Petersburg Voltaire Library and Collection, vol. 9, p. 126. Wade, *Studies on Voltaire*, p. 93.

80 See Massimo Mazzotti, "Newton for Ladies: Gentility, Gender and Radical Culture,"

BJHS 37, no. 2 (June 2004), especially p. 130. See also Mordechai Feingold, *The New-tonian Moment: Isaac Newton and the Making of Modern Culture* (New York: Oxford University Press, 2004), p. 93.

81   This comparison occurred to contemporaries; see Jordan, *Histoire*, p. 186.

82   #52, Du Châtelet to "?" (3 Jan. 1736), *LDC*, vol. 1, p. 95. D113, Voltaire to Berger ([July] 1736), *CWV*, vol. 88, p. 16. See D950, Voltaire to d'Olivet (30 Nov. 1735), *CWV*, vol. 14, p. 375 n. 31. See also D1220, Voltaire to Cideville (8 [Dec. 1736]), *CWV*, vol. 88, p. 147.

83   Du Chatelet in this and previous paragraph, #73, Du Châtelet to Maupertuis (1 Dec. [1736]), *LDC*, vol. 1, p. 125.

84   Newton argued that the light carried the color; in fact, it is a combination of the two ideas. In the "Queries" at the end of the second edition of the *Opticks*, Newton suggested a number of hypotheses, including the concept of an "Aetherial Medium." He insisted that attraction could not be a property of bodies, but that they were subject to it. There were no vortices, but there was no void. Attraction came to be "proved" by the predictability of its effects: on the shape of the earth; in the interaction between the earth, the moon, and the tides; by the behavior of comets. For this explanation of the issues, see J. B. Shank, *Before Voltaire, Newtonianism and the Origins of the Enlightenment in France, 1687–1734* (Ann Arbor, Mich.: UMI, 2000), pp. 324–25, 315–17, especially 544–48; I. Bernard Cohen, *The Newtonian Revolution* (Cambridge: Cambridge University Press, 1980), p. 68; Rupert Hall, "Newton in France: A New View," *History of Science* 13 (1975), pp. 244–46; Walters and Barber, introduction, in *Eléments, CWV*, vol. 15. On Descartes, see Tom Sorrell, ed., *The Rise of Modern Philosophy: The Tension Between the New and Traditional Philosophies from Machiavelli to Leibniz* (Oxford: Clarendon Press, 1993), pp. 3–19, 48–49.

85   See D1113, Voltaire to Berger ([July] 1736), *CWV*, vol. 88, p. 16. D1133, Voltaire to Quinault (24 [Aug. 1736]), *CWV*, vol. 88, p. 37; D1121, Voltaire to Caumont (5 Aug. 1736), *CWV*, vol. 88, p. 125; D1141, Voltaire to Thieriot (5 Sept. 1736), *CWV*, vol. 88, p. 49. D1125, Voltaire to Thieriot (6 Aug. 1736), *CWV*, vol. 88, p. 27. D1214, Voltaire to d'Argental (1 Dec. [1736]), *CWV*, vol. 88, p. 137. On arithmetic errors, see D2497, *CWV*, vol. 92, p. 49 n. See D1204, Voltaire to d'Argens (19 Nov. 1736), *CWV*, vol. 88, p. 122. D1122, Voltaire to Cideville (5 [Aug. 1736]), *CWV*, vol. 88, p. 25. D1186, Voltaire to Quinault (29 [Oct. 1736]), *CWV*, vol. 88, pp. 99–100. D1155, Voltaire to Berger ([c. 25 Sept. 1736]), *CWV*, vol. 88, p. 67. D1208, Voltaire to Berger ([c. 25 Nov. 1736]), *CWV*, vol. 88, p. 129. #70, Du Châtelet to Cideville (10 Oct. 1736), *LDC*, vol. 1, p. 112. D1137, Voltaire to Pitot (31 Aug. 1736), *CWV*, vol. 88, p. 43.

86   Voltaire Collection, St. Petersburg, vol. 9, pp. 122–25.

87   On the order of chapters, see Walters and Barber, introduction, *Eléments*, in *CWV*, vol. 15, pp. 45–46. On her essay on color, see Wade, *Voltaire and Madame du Châtelet*, pp. 36–40; #152, Du Châtelet to Maupertuis ([c. 1 Dec. 1738]), vol. 1, pp. 273–74; #156, Du Châtelet to Thieriot (22 Dec. 1738), vol. 1, p. 279; #159, Du Châtelet to Maupertuis (c. 28 Dec. 1738), vol. 1, p. 285. #143, Du Châtelet to Du Fay (18 Sept. 1738), *LDC*, vol. 1, pp. 259–61.

88   Voltaire began each paragraph about the moon describing "her" properties with the same sentence construction: "She has her apogee. . . . She has her *noeuds*. . . . She has her equator. . . ." Yet, "in spite of all these variations . . . she follows the Earth" (*Elé-*

ments, 1738 ed.), *CWV*, vol. 15, pp. 266–67. See Du Châtelet, for example, *Eléments*, p. 85.

89	See app. D2, in *Eléments*, in *CWV*, vol. 15, p. 547. On Du Châtelet's role, see Walters and Barber, introduction, *Eléments*, *CWV*, vol. 15, p. 47 n. 40. Wade, *Studies on Voltaire*, p. 123 (summary); Wade, *Voltaire and Madame du Châtelet*, pp. 36–37. Elisabeth Badinter, *Emilie, Emilie: L'ambition féminine au XVIIIe siècle* (Paris: Flammarion, 1983), pp. 182, 279–80, suggests she might even be the "principal author." See also Linda Gardiner, "Women in Science," in *French Women and the Age of Enlightenment*, ed. Samia I. Spencer (Bloomington: Indiana University Press, 1984), p. 184. On her making it a more serious work of science, see Vaillot, *Avec Mme Du Châtelet*, vol. 1, p. 329.

90	See #118, Du Châtelet to Maupertuis (2 Feb. 1738), *LDC*, vol. 1, p. 212; #120, Du Châtelet to Maupertuis ([Feb. 1738]), *LDC*, vol. 1, p. 215. See Du Châtelet, trans., *Fable*, for changes indicating rejection of "literature" for "science": B227v, C238v, A160/W138; *Fable*, for alternate wording, A153v/W131; A158v/W135–36, B218.

91	#124, Du Châtelet to Maupertuis (9 May [1738]), *LDC*, vol. 1, p. 224.

Chapter Four: An Independent Reputation

1	Emilie de Breteuil, marquise Du Châtelet, *Discours sur le bonheur*, ed. Robert Mauzi (Paris: Société d'Edition Belles Lettres, 1961), p. 21.

2	See #78, Du Châtelet to Thieriot (Dec. [1736]), *Lettres de la Marquise du Châtelet*, ed. Theodore Besterman (Genève: Institut et Musée Voltaire, 1958), vol. 1, p. 204 n. 16.

3	On this time in Holland, see introduction to Robert L. Walters and W. H. Barber, eds., *Eléments de la philosophie de Newton* in *Complete Works of Voltaire* (Oxford: Voltaire Foundation, 1992), vol. 15, p. 64.

4	See Jean-François Gauvin, "Le Cabinet de physique du château de Cirey et la philosophie naturelle du Mme Du Châtelet et Voltaire," in Judith P. Zinsser and Julie Candler Hayes, eds., *SVEC* (2006:1). See D1503, Voltaire to Moussinot (18 May [1738]), *CWV*, vol. 89, p. 122. On what Voltaire spent, see J. L. Heilbron, *Elements of Early Modern Physics* (Berkeley: University of California Press, 1982), p. 72.

5	For the description of their "cabinet de physique" in the *galerie*, see D1550, Voltaire to Moussinot (11 July [1738]), *CWV*, vol. 89, p. 202; D1563, Voltaire to Moussinot (21 [July 1738]), *CWV*, vol. 89, p. 216; D1371, Voltaire to Moussinot (14 [Sept. 1737]), *CWV*, vol. 88, p. 372; D1957, Voltaire to Quinault (26 [March 1739]), *CWV*, vol. 90, p. 380; #108, Du Châtelet to Maupertuis (11 Dec. 1737), *LDC*, vol. 1, p. 198.

6	In the memoir of his life, Voltaire wrote that Réaumur and Mairan suggested he make this his goal. See *Mémoires . . .* , ed. Jacqueline Hellegouarc'h (Paris: Livre de Poche, 1998). See D1327, Voltaire to Pitot (17 May [1737]), *CWV*, vol. 88, p. 307. Robert L. Walters and W. H. Barber, introduction to Voltaire's *Dissertation sur la nature du feu*, *CWV*, vol. 17, pp. 21–22, 84.

7	See Isaac Newton, *Opticks: A Treatise of the Reflections, Refractions, Inflections & Colors of Light*, 4th ed. (New York: Dover, 1952), bk. III, queries 5–11, 339–45. Hermann Boerhaave, *Elementa chemiae*, in Voltaire Library and Collection, St. Petersburg National Library, Alekseev #433/8–258. Petrus van Musschenbroek, *Elmenta physicae*, in Voltaire Collection, #2538/7–38, #2540/8–238. On their views, see Walters and

Barber, introduction to *Feu*, in *CWV*, vol. 17, fnn. passim through the edition; Bernard Joly, "Les Théories du feu de Voltaire et de Mme Du Châtelet," *SVEC* (2001:11), pp. 212–37. See also Robert L. Walters, "Chemistry at Cirey," in *Studies on Voltaire and the Eighteenth Century*, ed. Theodore Besterman (Genève: Institut et Musée Voltaire, 1967).

8 On Du Châtelet's father's lucrative ironworks, see Baron de Breteuil, *Mémoires*, ed. Evelyne Lever (Paris: F. Bourin, 1992), pp. 32–33. See also Fernand Braudel, *The Structures of Everyday Life: The Limits of the Possible*, trans. S. Reynolds (New York: Harper & Row, 1979), pp. 362–69, 373–74.

9 #63, Du Châtelet to Algarotti (20 [April 1736]), *LDC*, vol. 1, pp. 10–14. See illustration in Gauvin, "Cabinet de physique." For examples of possible experiments, see Newton, *Opticks*, bk. I, pt. 2, experiments 11 and 12, pp. 144–46.

10 On experiment in France, see J. B. Shank, *Before Voltaire: Newtonianism and the Origins of the Enlightenment in France 1687–1734* (Ann Arbor, Mich.: UMI, 2000), p. 555; J. L. Heilbron, "Some Uses for Catalogues of Old Scientific Instruments," in *Making Instruments Count: Essays on Historical Scientific Instruments Presented to Gerard L'Estrange Turner*, ed. R.G.W. Anderson (Aldershot: Variorum, 1993), p. 10. Mary Terrall, *The Man Who Flattened the Earth: Maupertuis and the Sciences in the Enlightenment* (London: University of Chicago Press, 2002), pp. 319–20.

11 See Newton, *Opticks*, bk. III, pt. 1, pp. 377–83. Subsequent experimenters discovered that in "calcination" all metals gained weight, because the powder, or calx, is an oxide. Lavoisier, at the end of the eighteenth century, first perceived the effect of oxygen. See Mary Ellen Waithe, *Modern Women Philosophers, 1600–1900* (Boston: Kluwer Academic Publishers, 1991), p. 144. This confirmed the "neutrality" of fire in all but process, the position that Du Châtelet took in her essay.

12 See Voltaire, *Feu, CWV*, vol. 17, p. 10 n. 22. On procedures and conclusions, see Voltaire, *Feu, CWV*, vol. 17, pp. 76–77; see also D2519, Voltaire to 'sGraavesande (1 Aug. 1741), *CWV*, vol. 92, p. 78.

13 For the query, see D1339, Voltaire to Moussinot (18 [June 1737]), *CWV*, vol. 88, pp. 324–25. See also Voltaire to Moussinot, Thieriot, and Cousin: D1354, D1356, D1372; D1480, D1504, D1535, D1538, D1550, D1569, ([July 1737]–Aug. 1738), *CWV*, vols. 88, 89.

14 Emilie de Breteuil, marquise Du Châtelet, trans., *Fable of the Bees*, by Bernard Mandeville, in *Studies on Voltaire . . .* by I. O. Wade (Princeton: Princeton University Press, 1947); Emilie de Breteuil, marquise Du Châtelet, trans., *Fable of the Bees*, by Bernard Mandeville. Vol. 9, *Complete Works of Voltaire*, St. Petersburg National Library. The St. Petersburg citation is first, the Wade edition, second: W138/A159v. Emilie de Breteuil, marquise Du Châtelet, *Dissertation sur la nature et la propagation du feu* (Paris: Académie des sciences, 1738), pp. 136, 168. On possible rivalry with Voltaire, see Walters and Barber, introduction to *Eléments*, in *CWV*, vol. 20A, p. 220; René Vaillot, *Madame Du Châtelet* (Paris: Albin Michel, 1978), p. 149; Roland Bonnel, "La correspondance scientifique de la marquise Du Châtelet: la 'lettre-laboratoire,'" *SVEC* (2000:04), p. 81. Three versions of her essay exist. The Académie published the essay in 1739 (approximately three hundred copies), then again in 1740 in the collected *Mémoires* for the year 1738; both included her two-page list of errata. Du Châtelet's revised version of 1744 appeared with her interchange with Dortous de

Mairan about *forces vives.* The Académie version has been used here because of its more spontaneous quality, hereafter designated as "AC." Where possible, page numbers for the 1744 edition follow.

15 #129, Du Châtelet to Maupertuis (21 June [1738]), in *LDC,* vol. 1, p. 237. Du Châtelet, *Feu,* p. 34 (1744 ed.). Note that this was the conclusion of subsequent experimentation, which defines fire as similar to light and penetrable. See Du Châtelet, *Feu,* pp. 118AC, 162–63AC/128–29 (1744 ed.).

16 Du Châtelet, *Feu,* 1744 ed., p. 18; pp. 124AC, 128AC/60, 67 (1744 ed.), 141–42AC/89–92 (1744 ed.). See also pp. 128–29AC/68–69 (1744 ed.).

17 Voltaire, *Feu,* in *CWV,* vol. 17, p. 89.

18 Villefort quoted in René Vaillot, *Avec Mme Du Châtelet,* in *Voltaire en son temps,* ed. René Pomeau (Oxford: Voltaire Foundation, 1985–95), vol. 1, p. 230.

19 Du Châtelet, *Feu,* pp. 139–40AC/187 (1744 ed.), 147AC/100 (1744 ed.), 36–37 (1744 ed.), 130–31AC, 93AC/14 (1744 ed.).

20 #67, Graffigny to Devaux (25 Dec. 1738), Françoise d'Issembourg d'Happoncourt Graffigny, *Correspondance de Madame de Graffigny,* ed. J. A. Dainard, et al. (Oxford: Voltaire Foundation, 1985–) vol. 1, p. 245.

21 Du Châtelet, *Feu,* p. 151AC/107 (1744 ed.).

22 See Du Châtelet, *Feu,* pp. 44AC/78 (1744 ed.), 87AC/4 (1744 ed.), 135AC/81 (1744 ed.).

23 See Du Châtelet, *Feu,* pp. 156–59AC/115–22 (1744 ed.). Voltaire offered a brief explanation: attraction made particles cohere in the air as snow. Voltaire, *Feu,* p. 50.

24 See #129, Du Châtelet to Maupertuis (21 June 1738), *LDC,* vol. 1, p. 236.

25 Paris Inventory, app. D93, *CWV,* vol. 95, p. 462.

26 See #186, Du Châtelet to Prault (16 Feb. 1738), *LDC,* vol. 1, p. 329; Besterman gave a tentative date of 1739 for this request, but 1738 seems more appropriate and coincides with the beginning of her work on the *Institutions.* See #152, Du Châtelet to Maupertuis (1 Dec. 1738), *LDC,* vol. 1, p. 273.

27 See #88, Du Châtelet to Algarotti (11 Jan. 1737), *LDC,* vol. 1, pp. 158, 159, 159 n. 1. #63, Du Châtelet to Algarotti (20 April 1736), *LDC,* vol. 1, pp. 111–12. The portrait on which the original drawing was based has not been found. On her reactions, see #118, Du Châtelet to Maupertuis (2 Feb. 1738), *LDC,* vol. 1, p. 213; #124, Du Châtelet to Maupertuis (9 May [1738]), *LDC,* vol. 1, p. 225. On the rumors, see #66, Graffigny to Devaux (22 Dec. [1738]), *Correspondance de Graffigny,* vol. 1, p. 240. See also Elisabeth Badinter, *Les Passions intellectuelles* (Paris: Fayard, 1999), vol. 1, p. 123 n. 1.

28 See #124, Du Châtelet to Maupertuis (9 May [1738]), *LDC,* vol. 1, p. 225; #141, Du Châtelet to Maupertuis (3 Sept. [1738]), *LDC,* vol. 1, p. 258; #135, Du Châtelet to Richelieu (17 Feb. [? Aug. 1738]), *LDC,* vol. 1, p. 247. See M. Algarotti, *Le Newtonianisme pour les dames ou entretiens sur la lumière,* trans. M. Duperron de Castera (Montpellier: chez Montalant, 1738), vol. 1, pp. 68, 100; vol. 2, pp. 32, 133; vol. 2, passim Dialogue V, 183; vol. 2, pp. 213–14, 226–29, 265, 286ff, 308–9.

29 D1492, Voltaire to Thieriot (5 May [1738]), *CWV,* vol. 89, p. 106; D1505, Voltaire to Thieriot (18 May 1738), *CWV,* vol. 89, p. 125. See Voltaire's addition to her letter #125, Du Châtelet to Algarotti (12 May 1738), *LDC,* vol. 1, pp. 229, 230. D1492, Voltaire to Thieriot (5 May [1738]), *CWV,* vol. 89, p. 106.

30 On the frontispiece, see Robert L. Walters, "The Allegorical Engravings in the Ledet-Desbordes Edition of the *Eléments de la philosophie de Newton,*" in *Voltaire & His World: Studies Presented to W. H. Barber,* ed. R. J. Howells et al. (Oxford: Voltaire Foundation, 1985). Note that these portrayals are also considered demeaning in Erica Harth, *Cartesean Women: Versions and Subversions of Rational Discourse in the Old Regime* (Ithaca, N.Y.: Cornell University Press, 1992), pp. 199–205; Linda Gardiner Janik, "Searching for the Metaphysics of Science: The Structure & Composition of Madame Du Châtelet's *Institutions de physique, 1737–1740,*" *SVEC* 201 (1982); Mary Terrall, "Emilie Du Châtelet and the Gendering of Science," *History of Science* 33 (1955).

31 Voltaire, "Epître," in *Eléments, CWV,* vol. 15, pp. 186–91.

32 #237, Du Châtelet to Frederick (25 April 1740), *LDC,* vol. 2, p. 13.

33 Emilie de Breteuil, marquise Du Châtelet, *Institutions de physique* (Paris: Chez Prault Fils, 1740), preface, pp. 2–5, 13. For changes, see the two manuscript versions. Bibliothèque Nationale, Ffr. 12265, which differ, in turn, from the 1740 printed edition. See Clairaut to Du Châtelet, presumably after Sept. 1741, quoted in Judith P. Zinsser and Olivier Courcelle, "A Remarkable Collaboration: The Marquise Du Châtelet and Alexis Clairaut," *SVEC* (2003) 107–20. I am indebted to Olivier Courcelle and Craig Waff for copies of Clairaut's letters, and for generously sharing their expertise about Clairaut.

34 See #241, Du Châtelet to Bernoulli II (30 June 1740), *LDC,* vol. 2, p. 17; Du Châtelet, *Institutions,* preface, p. 7. Patricia Fara first brought my attention to this meaning of "institutions"; see her chapter on Du Châtelet in *Pandora's Breeches: Women, Science and Power in the Enlightenment* (London: Pimlico, 2004).

35 See Betty Jo Teeter Dobbs, *The Janus Face of Genius: The Role of Alchemy in Newton's Thought* (New York: Cambridge University Press, 1991), on Newton's search for a unified theory of the universe. On modern efforts to reconcile quantum mechanics with relativity, see Brian Greene, *The Elegant Universe: Superstrings, Hidden Dimensions, and the Quest for the Ultimate Theory* (New York: W. W. Norton, 1999).

36 Henri Pitot, Approbation, in Du Chatelet, *Institutions,* vol. 1. #241, Du Châtelet to Bernoulli II (30 June 1740), *LDC,* vol. 2, p. 17.

37 She retained her anonymity even though one of the reviewers, abbé Trublet, guessed that she was the author. #146, Du Châtelet to Maupertuis (29 Sept. 1738), *LDC,* vol. 1, pp. 263–64.

38 Du Châtelet, review *Journal des savants,* Sept. 1738, p. 534.

39 See Du Châtelet review, *Journal des savants,* pp. 534, 538; for disclaimer, p. 538; for her critique, pp. 538–40. See also #152, Du Châtelet to Maupertuis ([c. 1 Dec. 1738]), *LDC,* vol. 1, p. 273; #124, Du Châtelet to Maupertuis (9 May [1738]), *LDC,* vol. 1, p. 224.

40 #129, Du Châtelet to Maupertuis (21 June 1738), *LDC,* vol. 1, p. 236.

41 D1504, Voltaire to Pitot (18 May [1738]), *CWV,* vol. 89, pp. 123–24, written before he knew the names of the winners. D1525, Voltaire to Pitot ([c. 17 June 1738]), *CWV,* vol. 89, p. 157. See #126, Du Châtelet to Maupertuis (20 [or 21 May 1738]), *LDC,* vol. 1, p. 230.

42 "Avis du Libraire," *Académie Mémoires,* vol. IV (1740). See on worries #132, Du Châtelet to Maupertuis (7 July 1738), *LDC,* vol. 1, p. 243. The other three winners were Leonhard Euler, Louis-Antoine Lozeran de Fiesc, Jean-Antoine de Créquy. See

D1511, Du Châtelet to Graffigny (27 [May 1738]), *CW V,* vol. 89, p. 136. D1686, Graffigny to Devaux ([15 Dec.] 1738), *CW V,* vol. 89, p. 435.

43 See #198, Du Châtelet to Cideville (15 March 1739), *LDC,* vol. 1, p. 346. On reviews favoring Cartesians, see Walters and Barber eds., introduction to Voltaire, *Feu, CW V,* vol. 17, pp. 18–19. D1988, Maupertuis to Jurin (20 April 1739), *CW V,* vol. 90, p. 348.

44 References to *Transactions* no. 294, #193, Du Châtelet to Frederick (27 Feb. [1739]), *LDC,* vol. 1, p. 340. D1713, Jean Bernard LeBlanc to abbé de Montuzet ([c. 10 Dec. 1738]), *CW V,* vol. 89, pp. 480–81; see also #156, Du Châtelet to Thieriot (22 Dec. [1738]), *LDC,* vol. 1, p. 279. D2025, Henri du Sauzet to Voltaire (4 June 1739), *CW V,* vol. 90, p. 392.

45 For speculation on sequence of decisions, see Janik, "Searching for the Metaphysics of Science," especially pp. 99–101. Those chapters Gardiner believed Du Châtelet rewrote extensively were I, III, VI–IX, XVI, XIX, XX. The first extant reference to Du Châtelet reading in Wolff is #141, Du Châtelet to Maupertuis (3 Sept. [1738]), *LDC,* vol. 1, p. 251. On the printing history see #241, Du Châtelet to Bernoulli II (30 June 1740), *LDC,* vol. 2, p. 18. On saving Newton, see also ed. Waithe, *Modern Women Philosophers,* p. 139; Sarah Hutton, "Emilie Du Châtelet's *Institutions de physique* as a document in the history of French Newtonianism," *Studies in the History and Philosophy of Science* 35 (2004), pp. 515–31.

46 See her review in the *Journal des savants,* p. 537. #193, Du Châtelet to Frederick (27 Feb. [1739]), *LDC,* vol. 1, p. 340.

47 See #175, Du Châtelet to Maupertuis (20 [Jan.] 1739), *LDC,* vol. 1, p. 310; #216, Du Châtelet to Maupertuis (20 June [1739]), *LDC,* vol. 1, pp. 369–70.

48 In the course of the *Institutions,* she made specific reference to: Leibniz's *Théodicée,* as it was translated into French; his articles in the *Acta Eruditorum* for 1686 and 1687; his arguments as presented in Desmaizeaux's edition of his debate with Samuel Clarke; and specific chapters in Wolff's *Ontologie.* In her letters, she mentioned having read quickly Wolff's *Cosmologie* and his *Métaphysique.* See #241, Du Châtelet to Bernoulli II (30 June 1740), *LDC,* vol. 2, p. 18, where she described working with König on Leibniz's *Ontologie* and *Cosmologie.* See also #237, Du Châtelet to Frederick (25 April 1740), *LDC,* vol. 2, p. 13; #244, Du Châtelet to Frederick (11 Aug. 1740), *LDC,* vol. 2, p. 24. On Du Châtelet's approach, see Carolyn Merchant Iltis, "Madame du Châtelet's Metaphysics and Mechanics," *Studies in the History and Philosophy of Science* 8 (1977), pp. 28–48.

49 Du Châtelet, *Institutions,* preface, p. 12.

50 In a list of prose fiction from 1700 to 1750, only 14 percent of the works had been signed. On the image, see Janik, "Searching for the Metaphysics"; Du Châtelet, *Institutions,* p. 95; Julie Candler Hayes, *Reading the Enlightenment: System & Subversion* (New York: Cambridge University Press, 1999). I am indebted to the art historian Patricia Crown for her help in the identification of the engraving's figures (letter, Jan. 18, 2000).

51 Du Châtelet, *Institutions,* preface, p. 12.

52 Du Châtelet, *Institutions,* preface, pp. 5–6.

53 Du Châtelet, *Institutions,* chap. VIII, p. 157. See Desmond M. Clarke, *Descartes' Phi-*

losophy of Science (Manchester: Manchester University Press, 1982), p. 70; see also pp. 172, 199.

54 See Heilbron, *Elements of Early Modern Physics,* pp. 41–43; Walters and Barber, introduction to *Eléments de la philosophie de Newton,* in *CWV,* vol. 15, pp. 12–13. On the differences between Leibniz and Newton, see Susan James, *Passion and Actions: The Emotions in Seventeenth-Century Philosophy* (Oxford: Clarendon Press, 1997), pp. 184–86, 244–45; David Bodanis, $E=MC^2$: *A Biography of the World's Most Famous Equation* (New York: Berkley Books, 2000), p. 255 n. 65. Wolff's translator was Ulrich von Suhm, the Saxon envoy to Prussia. See Charles Augustin Sainte-Beuve, *Causeries du Lundi* (Paris: Garnier Fréres, 1852–62), vol. 7, pp. 458–73. Some of the chapters sent to Cirey were from Wolff's 1720 *Vernünfitige Gedanken von Gott, der Welt und der Seele des Menschen, auch allen Dingen überhaupt* (Reasonable Thoughts on God, the World, and Men's Soul, and All Things Generally). Note that there was a French version of Wolff published in 1743, *Cours abrégé de la philosophie Wolfienne* (Abridged Course on Wolff's Philosophy), which included summaries of his books on logic, ontology, and cosmology. The translator, Jean des Champs, was tutor to Frederick's brothers. See #129, Du Châtelet to Maupertuis (21 June [1738]), *LDC,* vol. 1, pp. 237–38; D1305, Voltaire to Chevalier Louis de Jaucourt (29 March [1737]), *CWV,* vol. 88, p. 271. See Voltaire to Frederick (Aug. 1736–Dec. 1737) passim, *CWV,* vol. 88, especially D1320, D1359, D1375. See #120, Du Châtelet to Maupertuis ([c. Feb. 1738]), *LDC,* vol. 1, pp. 216–18; Du Châtelet, *Institutions,* chap. I, p. 30.

55 Du Châtelet, *Institutions,* chap. I, pp. 18, 21; 19–20.

56 Du Châtelet, *Institutions,* chap. I, p. 22.

57 Du Châtelet, *Institutions,* chap. I, pp. 21, 23, 24, 27–28, 25. See #211, Du Châtelet to Bernoulli II (28 April 1739), *LDC,* vol. 1, p. 362. Preface to *Institutions,* p. 3; chap. IX, p. 197. Note that Einstein's general theory of relativity hinged on the concept of "sufficient reason" and the presumption that planets and stars would seek optimal paths. In contrast, modern-day chaos theory entertains just these possibilities. See ed. Waithe, *Modern Women,* vol. 3, p. 139; Bodanis, $E=MC^2$, p. 255 n. 65. I am grateful to Paul Veatch Moriarty for his comments on this section of the biography; see his article "The Principle of Sufficient Reason in Du Châtelet's *Institutions,*" *SVEC* (2006:1).

58 Du Châtelet, *Institutions,* chap. II, pp. 39–42.

59 Du Châtelet, *Institutions,* chap. II, pp. 42–44, 46–47, 51–52. See also chaps. VII, p. 142; VIII, pp. 175–76. See Catherine Wilson, *Leibniz's Metaphysics: A Historical and Comparative Study* (Princeton: Princeton University Press, 1989), p. 73. See also Terrall, "Emilie du Châtelet," p. 301. Note that Leibniz's critics perceived this reasoning as a limitation on God's power and, hence, Du Châtelet's decision to counter it.

60 See Du Châtelet, *Institutions,* chap. II, pp. 49–53.

61 Du Châtelet, *Institutions,* chap. II, pp. 50, 52, 49; chap. VIII, p. 175; see also chap. VII, p. 142. On Leibniz and ideas that Du Châtelet borrowed from the *Théodicée* and others of his works, see the descriptions of Leibniz's writings in Wilson, *Leibniz,* p. 80–95; H. Hecht, "Leibniz' Concepts of Possible Worlds & the Analysis of Motion in Eighteenth-Century Physics," in *Between Leibniz, Newton, and Kant: Philosophy & Science in the Eighteenth Century,* ed. Wolfgang Lefevre (Boston: Kluwer Academic Publishers, 2001), pp. 29–31.

62 Du Châtelet, *Institutions,* chap. VIII, pp. 175–76.

63 See Du Châtelet, *Institutions,* chap. III, pp. 62–64. Note that she called the variables "Modes."

64 Du Châtelet, *Institutions,* chap. I, pp. 24–25, 31–33; chap. XV, p. 292; chap. I, p. 33; preface, p. 3. See also chap. IX, p. 180; chap. XX, p. 409. See also D1327, Voltaire to Pitot (17 May [1737]), *CWV,* vol. 88, p. 308. Twice in the *Institutions,* she referred to Leibniz's search for a "calculus for Metaphysics similar to that which one has found for Geometry and by means of which, with the aid of certain *givens,* one arrives at knowledge of *unknowns.*" It would be like algebra, only in this instance, by the "substitution of characters, one would reach truths." (Du Châtelet, *Institutions,* preface, pp. 13–14; chap. VII, p. 151). On Locke's use of geometry for philosophy, see John Locke, *Essay on Human Understanding,* ed. Peter H. Nidditch (Oxford: Oxford University Press, 1975), bk. IV, chaps. 1 and 2. On Descartes and the example of the triangle, see Tom Sorrell, *Descartes: A Very Short Introduction* (New York: Oxford University Press, 2000), pp. 14–16, 69–70. On Leibniz, see Wilson, *Leibniz,* pp. 24–33. Note that in her reliance on mathematics, Du Châtelet was following in the Académie tradition (J. B. Shank, *Before Voltaire,* pp. 556–57).

65 Du Châtelet, *Institutions,* chap. V, p. 96.

66 Du Châtelet, *Institutions,* chap. VI, pp. 120, 121.

67 Du Châtelet, *Institutions,* chap. VI, pp. 124, 127.

68 Du Châtelet, *Institutions,* chap. VII, pp. 130–31; chap. IX, pp. 189–90. See also chap. X, pp. 202–3.

69 Du Châtelet, *Institutions,* chap. VI, pp. 122–34; #352, Du Châtelet to Bernoulli II (8 Jan. 1746), *LDC,* vol. 2, p. 149; Du Châtelet, *Institutions,* chap. VII, pp. 143–44, 146–47.

70 Du Châtelet, *Institutions,* chap. III, p. 73; chap. VIII, pp. 168–69; see also pp. 169–70. In this instance, she had to reject sense perception as proof and to point out that geometry had been misapplied in this argument, particularly in reference to the concept of infinite divisibility for nature and physical bodies. She gave the example of a watch that ceased to be a "watch" if it no longer had any of its constituent parts. (See Du Châtelet, *Institutions,* chap. IX, pp. 181–82, 185; chap. VII, pp. 131, 136, 133; chap. VIII, pp. 170–71.) On Aristotle, see Sorrell, *Descartes,* pp. 39–41; Stuart Brown, in *The Rise of Modern Philosophy: The Tension Between the New and Traditional Philosophies from Machiavelli to Leibniz,* ed. Tom Sorrell (Oxford: Clarendon Press, 1993), p. 225.

71 Du Châtelet, *Institutions,* chap. VII, p. 137–38. She also used the term *"force motrice."* Its opposite Kepler had named "inertia," or passive force, what Du Châtelet described as an entity's ability to resist movement. See also, on *force motrice* generally, chap. VIII, p. 165.

72 Du Châtelet, *Institutions,* chap. VIII, pp. 173–75; chap. VII, p. 148. See Janik, "Searching for the Metaphysics of Science," p. 107, on this synthesis. On attraction, see Du Châtelet, *Institutions,* chap. XVI, pp. 332–33. She noted with great prescience that attraction at the molecular level required more study. The inability of science to find this correlation between the workings of attraction at this level and in the universe at large resulted in quantum mechanics.

73 See Du Châtelet, *Institutions,* chap. XI, pp. 222–23, 240, 234–35. See also chap. XII, p. 259; chap. XI, pp. 221–22, 233, 241–42.

74 Du Châtelet, *Institutions,* chap. XII, p. 251. For her drawing, see Du Châtelet, *Institutions de physique,* in Bibliothéque Nationale, Ffr 12265, p. 355.

75 Du Châtelet, *Institutions,* chap. XIX, p. 394.

76 See Du Châtelet, *Institutions,* chap. XI, pp. 109–11, 216, 221. Note that she did not deal with all of the corollaries to Newton's third law of motion, but only four of them; see chap. XV, p. 278; chap. XIV, p. 277; chap. XVIII, p. 361; chap. XX, p. 405.

77 The followers of Newton, in particular, had enshrined as absolute a statement he made rejecting the practice of hypothesis in the "General Scholium" to bk. III of the *Principia:* "I imagine no hypotheses," as Du Châtelet translated it. See also Newton, *Opticks,* bk. III, query 28. I. B. Cohen agrees that Newton's "disciples" went way beyond what Newton meant. See Du Châtelet, *Institutions,* chap. IV, pp. 75–76, 81–82; preface, pp. 9–10. See also Dana Densmore, *Newton's Principia: The Central Argument—Translation, Notes, and Extended Proofs* (Santa Fe: Green Lion Press, 1995), p. 244.

78 Du Châtelet, *Institutions,* chap. IV, pp. 78, 82–87, 75; for examples, see pp. 76–81. See also Waithe, ed., *Modern Women,* pp. 146–47.

79 Du Châtelet, *Institutions,* chap. XVIII, pp. 364–68.

80 Bernoulli lost to Maclaurin in 1724, and to Mézières in 1726; see the account of the whole controversy in Terrall, "Vis Viva," *History of Science* 42 (2004): 189–209.

81 Bonnel, in his analysis of this correspondence, sees her thinking as orderly, moving from hypothesis to hypothesis (Bonnel, "La Correspondance scientifique de la marquise Du Châtelet). In contrast, I believe she must have worked on more than one chapter at a time, or that she was not writing or revising them in the same sequence as they were finally printed. See, for example, #73, #120, #122, #124, #126, #127, #129, #139, #175, Du Châtelet to Maupertuis (1 Dec. [1736]–20 Jan. 1739), *LDC,* vol. 1, pp. 125–311. For the basis of this interpretation, see Terrall, "Vis Viva"; Voltaire, introduction by David Beeson and Robert L. Walters, *Doutes sur la mesure des forces motrices et sur leur nature,* in *CWV,* vol. 20A, pp. 372–75; Thomas Hankins, "Vis Viva?," in *The History of Science in Western Civilization,* eds. L. Pearce Williams and Henry John Steffens, vol. 3, *Modern Science: 1700–1900* (Washington, D.C.: University Press of America, 1978), especially pp. 30–31, 37–39.

82 See Terrall, "Vis Viva," pp. 196–97; Terrall, *The Man Who Flattened the Earth,* p. 40.

83 Du Châtelet, *Institutions,* chap. XXI, pp. 423, 428. See also her description of Jacob Hermann's experiments, chap. XXI, pp. 434, 436–37, 439, 441.

84 Du Châtelet, *Institutions,* chap. XXI, p. 434.

85 See #124, Du Châtelet to Maupertuis (9 May [1738]), *LDC,* vol. 1, pp. 225–28; #129, Du Châtelet to Maupertuis (21 June [1738]), *LDC,* vol. 1, pp. 237–38. #127, Du Châtelet to Maupertuis (22 May 1738), *LDC,* vol. 1, p. 233. The concept of "hard bodies" had particular significance if *êtres simples* were to be impenetrable and indivisible. See Du Châtelet, *Institutions,,* chap. I, p. 34, in which, like Bernoulli, she accepted that "there are not any perfectly hard bodies in nature"—the position of modern science.

86 Du Châtelet, *Institutions,* chap. XXI, pp. 444–48. See Newton, *Opticks,* bk. III, pt. 1, query 31, pp. 375–406. On this issue and its relevance for the evolution of the "law of conservation of energy," see Carolyn Merchant Iltis, "Mme Du Châtelet's Metaphysics and Mechanics," especially, pp. 47–48.

87   See D2151, Voltaire to Bernoulli II (30 Jan. 1740), *CWV*, vol. 91, pp. 89–90; see also D2153, Voltaire to [?] ([c. 30 Jan. 1740]), *CWV*, vol. 91, p. 93. #179, Graffigny to Devaux (4 Sept. 1739), vol. 2, p. 139.

88   #211, Du Châtelet to Bernoulli II (28 April 1739), *LDC*, vol. 1, p. 363. #216, Du Châtelet to Maupertuis (20 June [1739]), *LDC*, vol. 1, p. 369; #220, Du Châtelet to Bernoulli II (3 Aug. 1739), *LDC*, vol. 1, p. 375. See especially #241, Du Châtelet to Bernoulli II (30 June 1740), *LDC*, vol. 2, pp. 18–19. D2140, Maupertuis to Bernoulli II (12 Jan. 1740, *CWV*, vol. 91, pp. 75, 76.

89   Maupertuis to Bernoulli (28 Dec. 1739), *CWV*, vol. 91, p. 55, commentary. For the story according to König, #217, Graffigny to Devaux (28 [Nov. 1739]), *Correspondance de Graffigny*, vol. 2, pp. 252–53. See also D2141, Le Blanc to Bouhier (13 Jan. 1740), *CWV*, vol. 91, pp. 76–77. Du Châtelet gave her version in her letter to Bernoulli II, 30 June 1740, #241, *LDC*, vol. 2, pp. 18–19. On König's similar accusations against Maupertuis in the 1750s, see Terrall, *The Man Who Flattened the Earth*, pp. 292–302.

90   #241, Du Châtelet to Bernoulli (30 June 1740), *LDC*, vol. 2, pp. 16–19. Du Châtelet, *Institutions*, Ffr 12265, passim.

91   See Badinter, *Passions intellectuelles*, vol. 1, p. 176 n. This review was probably written by Maupertuis.

92   Mairan to Du Châtelet, quoted in *Passions intellectuelles*, vol. 174 n. 5; D2449, Mairan to Du Châtelet ([c. 20] March 1741), *CWV*, vol. 91, p. 450.

93   Marquise de Créqui, *Souvenirs de la Marquise de Créqui, 1710–1803* (Paris: Michel Lévy Frères, 1867), vol. 3, pp. 66–67. Also reported as occurring at Geoffrin *salon* by the *philosophe* Grimm. See Badinter, *Passions intellectuelles*, vol. 1, pp. 143–44, 174 n. 5, 173, 177. #179, Graffigny to Devaux (4 Sept. 1739) *Correspondance de Graffigny*, vol. 1, p. 139. See also Nina Gelbart, introduction to *Conversations on the Plurality of Worlds*, by Bernard le Bovier de Fontenelle (Berkeley: University of California Press, 1990), p. 4.

94   See Jean-Jacques Dortous de Mairan, *Lettre à Mme*** sur la question des forces vives [en réponse]* (Paris: Académie Royale des Sciences, 1741), pp. 3–9, 12–14. Du Châtelet had summarized passages and then inadvertently presented them as if exact quotations. She had not, however, distorted or misrepresented his meaning.

95   Mairan, *Lettre*, pp. 28, 31; see also p. 37. He turned her sentences around: "Bear with me," he admonished her, using her own phrases but reversing the meaning, "the time is everything, & the speed is nothing."

96   #264, Du Châtelet to d'Argental (22 March [1741]), *LDC*, vol. 2, p. 45; #269, Du Châtelet to D'Argental (2 May [1741]), *LDC*, vol. 2, pp. 50, 51; see #272, Du Châtelet to Maupertuis (29 May 1741), *LDC*, vol. 2, pp. 56, 58; see also #273, Du Châtelet to Maupertuis (26 June [1741], *LDC*, vol. 2, p. 60. #268, Du Châtelet to Bernoulli II (28 April 1741), *LDC*, vol. 2, pp. 48, 49; #269, Du Châtelet to d'Argental (2 May [1741]), *LDC*, vol. 1, p. 50; #266, Du Châtelet to Mairan (7 April 1741), *LDC*, vol. 2, p. 47.

97   Emilie de Breteuil, marquise Du Châtelet, *Réponse de madame la marquise Du Chastelet à la lettre que m. de Mairan . . . lui a écrite le 18 février 1741 sur la question des force vives* (Bruxelles: Foppens, 1741), pp. 7–8, for example.

98   See Du Châtelet, *Réponse*, pp. 3–4, 5, 19, 6, 25, 8; note that she plays with the point he made about addition versus squaring in the formula (see pp. 6, 12, 19). Though

the sense of the passages cited is the same, she acknowledged that she had made omissions, that the quotations were not exact, but then declared with exaggerated humility, "This is an unpardonable infidelity" (the gloss, pp. 7–8). See also pp. 35, 36, 26.

99 Du Châtelet used Clairaut's critique of Mairan, as having made a "parallogism." See D2485, Clairaut to Du Châtelet ([? May 1741]), CWV, vol. 92, p. 29. Du Châtelet, *Réponse,* pp. 5, 21, 22.

100 #269, Du Châtelet to d'Argental (2 May 1741), LDC, vol. 2, p. 51. Du Châtelet, *Réponse,* pp. 6, 10–12, 34.

101 #272, Du Châtelet to Maupertuis (29 May 1741), LDC, vol. 2, p. 56; #269, Du Châtelet to d'Argental (2 May [1741]), LDC, vol. 2, p. 51.

102 See Mme d'Aiguillon's letters to Maupertuis, in Bibliothèque Nationale, NAF 10398, pp. 46, 70b. Buffon and Clairaut, quoted in Badinter, *Passions intellectuelles,* vol. 1, pp. 175–76; see also pp. 176 n. 4, 176 n. 5, 178–79.

103 #269, Du Châtelet to d'Argental (2 May [1741], LDC, vol. 2, p. 51.

Chapter Five: *Philosophe* and Courtier

1 See #273, Du Châtelet to Maupertuis (26 June [1741]), *Lettres de la Marquise du Châtelet,* ed. Theodore Besterman (Genève: Institut et Musée Voltaire, 1958), vol. 2, pp. 59–61. D2467, Cideville to Voltaire (26 April 1741), *The Complete Works of Voltaire,* ed. Theodore Besterman (Genève: Institut et Musée Voltaire, 1968–), vol. 91, p. 476.

2 D1730, Voltaire to Frederick (1 Jan. 1739), CWV, vol. 90, p. 12; see also D2477, Voltaire to d'Argental (5 May [1741]), CWV, vol. 91, p. 19 and D2585, Voltaire to Cideville (19 Jan. 1742), CWV, vol. 92, p. 163. #238, Du Châtelet to Bernoulli (27 April 1740), LDC, vol. 2, p. 15. D1675, Graffigny to Devaux (4 Dec. 1738), CWV, vol. 89, pp. 393–95; and D1677, Graffigny to Devaux (6 Dec. 1738), CWV, vol. 89, p. 401.

3 Details from Sébastien G. Longchamps and Jean Louis Wagnière, *Mémoires sur Voltaire, et sur ses Ouvrages* (Paris: Aimé André, 1826), pp. 240–41.

4 D2144, Voltaire to Champbonin ([? Jan. 1740]), CWV, vol. 91, p. 81. D1896, Voltaire to d'Argental (21 [Feb. 1739]), CWV, vol. 90, p. 238. See #216, Du Châtelet to Maupertuis (20 June [1739]), LDC, vol. 1, pp. 368, 370. D2055, Du Châtelet to Graffigny (29 July 1739), CWV, vol. 90, p. 440, suggests she learned Dutch as well. See Jeroom Vercruysse, "La M. du Chatelet prevote d'une confrérie bruxelloise," 18 SVEC (Genève: Institut et Musée Voltaire, 1961), pp. 170–71. See #215, Du Châtelet to d'Argental (1 June [1739]), LDC, vol. 1, p. 368; #217, Du Châtelet to Graffigny (27 July 1739), LDC, vol. 1, p. 371; #219, Du Châtelet to Cideville (2 Aug. 1739), LDC, vol. 1, p. 374.

5 #217, Du Châtelet to d'Argental (18 May 1741), LDC, vol. 2, pp. 54, 55. See #272, Du Châtelet to Maupertuis (29 May [1741]), LDC, vol. 1, p. 56. #274, Du Châtelet to Maupertuis (8 Aug. [1741]), LDC, vol. 2, p. 61; #286, Du Châtelet to d'Argental (21 Nov. 1741]), LDC, vol. 2, p. 81; #288, Du Châtelet to d'Argental (8 Jan. 1742), LDC, vol. 2, p. 83; D2529, Voltaire to Helvétius (14 Aug. [1741]), CWV, vol. 92, p. 99.

6 For information in this and the next paragraph, see D2443, Voltaire to comtesse d'Argental (13 March [1741]), CWV, vol. 91, pp. 443–44. D2027, Voltaire to Champ-

bonin ([c. June 1739]), *CWV,* vol. 90, p. 396. #293, Du Châtelet to d'Argental (10 Sept. 1742), *LDC,* vol. 2, pp. 87–88. #313, Du Châtelet to d'Argental (13 Nov. 1743), *LDC,* vol. 2, p. 108. #295, Du Châtelet to d'Argental (3 Oct. 1742), *LDC,* vol. 2, p. 89. See also #309, Du Châtelet to d'Argental (10 Oct. [1743]), *LDC,* vol. 2, p. 102; #331, Du Châtelet to Charlier (1744), *LDC,* vol. 2, p. 128; #334, Du Châtelet to Charlier (9 Dec. [1744]), *LDC,* vol. 2, p. 131. #342, Du Châtelet to Charlier (1 Sept. 1745), *LDC,* vol. 2, pp. 136–38; #345, Du Châtelet to Charlier (19 Sept. 1745), *LDC,* vol. 2, pp. 140–41; #348, Du Châtelet to Charlier ([? Nov. 1745]), *LDC,* vol. 2, pp. 145–46. See D3568, Du Châtelet to Aguilar (28 Aug. 1747), *CWV,* vol. 94, p. 175. See Wolff to Manteuffel (27 Nov. 1746) as quoted in H. Droysen, "Die Marquise du Châtelet, Voltaire und der Philosoph Christian Wolff," *Zeitschrift für französische Sprache und Literatur,* 35 (1910), pp. 226–48. I am grateful to John Iverson for a copy of this article, and to Erik Jensen for assurance about the translation.

7   See #76, Du Châtelet to d'Argental (21 [Dec. 1736]), *LDC,* vol. 1, p. 129. D2033, Voltaire to Frederick ([c. 20 June 1739]), *CWV,* vol. 90, p. 405. D2585, Voltaire to Cideville (19 Jan. 1742), *CWV,* vol. 92, p. 163. D2643, Voltaire to d'Argental (22 Aug. [1742]), *CWV,* vol. 92, p. 237. See, for example, D3040, Voltaire to Frederick (2 Nov. 1744), *CWV,* vol. 93, p. 183; René Vaillot, *Avec Mme Du Châtelet, 1734–1749,* in *Voltaire en son Temps,* ed. René Pomeau (Oxford: Voltaire Foundation, 1985–95), vol. 1, p. 525. Reconstruction of settlement from René Vaillot, *Madame du Châtelet* (Paris: Albin Michel, 1978), pp. 267–68. Paris Inventory, *CWV,* app. D93, vol. 95, p. 457. On Voltaire's role as mediator, see D3531, Hoensbroeck to Voltaire (29 June 1747), *CWV,* vol. 94, p. 154; D3516, Voltaire to Räsfeld (30 March 1747), *CWV,* vol. 94, p. 138. D3530, Marquis Du Châtelet-Lomont to Voltaire ([? June 1747]), *CWV,* vol. 94, p. 153. For evidence of the settlement, see D4063, Voltaire to the marquis Du Châtelet-Lomont ([15 Nov. 1749]), *CWV,* vol. 95, pp. 198–200.

8   Emilie de Breteuil Du Châtelet, *Discours sur le bonheur,* ed. Robert Mauzi (Paris: Société d'Edition Belles Lettres, 1961) pp. 37–38. *Nouvelle Bibliothèque* (July 1739), vol. III, pp. 414–22. See introduction by Robert L. Walters and W. H. Barber, in Voltaire, *Essai sur la nature du feu, CWV,* vol. 20A, pp. 194–95, 220–21. See also D2463, Voltaire to Claude Nicolas Le Cat (15 April 1741), *CWV,* vol. 91, pp. 469–71.

9   D2196, Voltaire to Pitot (5 April [1740]), *CWV,* vol. 91, pp. 144–45. D2400, Voltaire to d'Argenson (8 Jan. 1741), *CWV,* vol. 91, p. 399. D2397, Voltaire to Helvétius (7 Jan. [1741]), *CWV,* vol. 91, p. 395. D2452, Voltaire to Mairan ([24 March 1741]), *CWV,* vol. 91, pp. 453–56. D2479, Voltaire to Mairan (5 May [1741]), *CWV,* vol. 92, p. 22; D2526, Voltaire to Maupertuis (10 April 1741), *CWV,* vol. 92, p. 95. Note that Voltaire was enthusiastic when he actually met Wolff in September of 1743 (see Droysen, *Wolff,* pp. 238–40).

10 #264, Du Châtelet to d'Argental (22 March [1741]), *LDC,* vol. 2, p. 45. See Voltaire, *Métaphysique de Newton, CWV,* vol. 15, pp. 195–96, 197, 218; see chaps. 7 and 8, especially pp. 237–40, 244. On *forces vives,* see p. 250, and, on motion generally, chap. IX. For differences between the *Traité* and the *Métaphysique,* see Robert L. Walters and W. H. Barber, introduction *Eléments de la philosophie de Newton, CWV,* vol. 15, pp. 109–10, 100–3; see, David Beeson and Robert L. Walters, introduction to Voltaire, *Doutes sur la mesure des forces motrices et sur leur nature, CWV,* vol. 20A, pp. 399–400.

11 See D708, Voltaire to Mairan (1 Feb. 1734), *CWV,* vol. 86, p. 450; D1137, Voltaire to

Pitot (31 Aug. 1736), *CWV*, vol. 88, p. 42; D1195, Voltaire to Mairan (9 Nov. 1736), *CWV*, vol. 88, p. 113. See Robert L. Walters and W. H. Barber, introduction, *Eléments de la philosophie de Newton* (Oxford: Voltaire Foundation, 1992), vol. 15, pp. 49–51; and Voltaire's responses, pp. 675–76, 724–28. Voltaire had been publishing "clarifications" and explanations for the *Eléments* since it first appeared in its incomplete form from his Dutch publisher, and then in the similarly clipped together Prault version that came out in France. On reviews of the *Eléments*, see D1571, *CWV*, vol. 89, p. 232 n. 1; John Pappas, "Berthier's Journal de Trévoux and the Philosophes," *SVEC* (1957:3), p. 90; père Castel's review for the *Mémoires de Trévoux*, as quoted in Walters and Barber, introduction, *Eléments*, vol. 15, p. 87. D2433, Voltaire to d'Argental (25 [Feb. 1741]), *CWV*, vol. 91, p. 434. D2452, Voltaire to Mairan ([24 March 1741]), *CWV*, vol. 91, pp. 453–56. D2433, Voltaire to d'Argental (25 [Feb. 1741]), *CWV*, vol. 91, p. 434. On the *Doutes*, see Beeson and Walters, introduction to the *Doutes*, in *CWV*, vol. 20A, especially pp. 401–8, 426–27 n. 430 n. 19. See also Mary Terrall, "Vis Viva," *History of Science*, 42 (2004), pp. 202–9; *Mercure de France*, vol. 2 (June 1741), pp. 1247–1310. Scholars have attributed this review to Maupertuis, perhaps following Elisabeth Badinter, *Emilie, Emilie: L'amibition féminine au XVIIIe siècle* (Paris: Flammarion, 1983), p. 329. See Voltaire, *Exposition du livre des Institutions de physique, CWV*, vol. 20A, pp. 245 n. 45, 247–48, 251, 253, 261. Note that Voltaire originally accepted $f = mv^2$. See Voltaire, *Eléments*, pp. 388–89; D1974, Voltaire to Bernoulli II (April 1739), cited in Beeson and Walters, introduction, *Doutes*, in *CWV*, vol. 20A, pp. 396–97; Voltaire, *Essai sur la nature du feu, CWV*, vol. 17, p. 67 n. 3. See D1622, Voltaire to Maupertuis ([1 Oct. 1738]), *CWV*, vol. 89, p. 314 (published in 1739); D1327, Voltaire to Piot (17 May [1737]), *CWV*, vol. 88, p. 307.

12 On changes and additions, see Walters and Barber, introduction to *Eléments*, pp. 112–15, 120–21, 125–26; *Eléments*, 1741 ed., in *CWV*, vol. 15, pp. 192, 193.

13 Review in *Mémoires de Trévoux, 1701–1767*, pp. 926, 894, 895, 896, 927. See pt. 1 of the review in the *Journal des savants*, 1738. Note that this review was probably written by Maupertuis.

14 D2461, Mairan to Voltaire (8 April 1741), *CWV*, vol. 91, pp. 467–68. #265, Du Châtelet to Maupertuis (22 March 1741), *LDC*, vol. 2, p. 46. #272, Du Châtelet to Maupertuis (29 May [1741]), *LDC*, vol. 2, p. 56. See also #274, Du Châtelet to Maupertuis ([8 Aug. [1741]), *LDC*, vol. 2, p. 63. Maupertuis to Algarotti (28 June 1741), as quoted in Elisabeth Badinter, *Les Passions intellectuelles* (Paris: Fayard, 1999), vol. 1, p. 181.

15 See *Mémoires de Trevoux* (Aug. 1741), Article LXVII, pp. 1390–1402. For review of Mairan, *Mémoires de Trevoux* (Aug. 1741), Article LXVI, pp. 1381–89.

16 A version of the Loir painting exists with the marquise seated at the table, as if interrupted while reading one of the many books piled in front of her. On the compass, see Walters, "The Allegorical Engravings in the Ledet-Desbordes Edition of the *Eléments de la philosophie de Newton*," in *Voltaire & His World: Studies Presented to W. H. Barber*, eds. R. J. Howells, A. Mason, H. T. Mason, & D. Williams (Oxford: Voltaire Foundation, 1985), p. 41. On the symbols, see Gérard Le Coat and Anne Eggimann-Besançon, "Emblématique et émancipation féminine au XVIIIe siècle: Le Portrait de Madame Du Châtelet par Marie-Anne Loir," *Coloquio: Artes*, vol. 68 (March 1986), pp. 30–39. A portrait by Nattier has been lost; only a description for the 1745 salon exists.

17 #274, Du Châtelet to Maupertuis (8 Aug. [1741]), *LDC*, vol. 2, p. 63. See #273, Du Châtelet to Maupertuis (26 June [1741]), *LDC*, vol. 2, p. 59; #274, Du Châtelet to Maupertuis (8 Aug. [1741]), *LDC*, vol. 2, p. 62.

18 See, for example, Emilie de Breteuil, marquise Du Châtelet, *Dissertation sur la nature du feu* (Paris: Chez Prault Fils, 1744), pp. 31–32. See also Robert L. Walters, "Chemistry at Cirey," 58 *SVEC* (1967), especially pp. 1820–25. #287, Du Châtelet to Bernoulli II (7 Dec. 1741), *LDC*, vol. 2, pp. 82.

19 #216, Du Châtelet to Maupertuis (20 June [1739]), *LDC*, vol. 1, p. 370. #277, Du Châtelet to Bernoulli II (20 Aug. 1741), *LDC*, vol. 2, pp. 67, 68, 68 n. 2. #346, Du Châtelet to Bernoulli II (8 Oct. 1745), *LDC*, vol. 2, p. 142. See also #339, #349, #347, Du Châtelet to Bernoulli II (1745–46), *LDC*, vol. 2.

20 See #360, Du Châtelet to Jacquier (13 April 1747), *LDC*, vol. 2, p. 156. #347, Du Châtelet to Jacquier (12 Nov. 1745), *LDC*, vol. 2, pp. 143, 145 n. 2. Des Champs as quoted in H. Droysen, "Die Marquise du Châtelet, Voltaire und der Philosoph . . . ," *Zeitschrift für französische Sprache und Literatur*, 35 (1910), p. 237.

21 Clairaut's comments touched on points in chaps. XVII, XVIII, and XIX, almost all of which she incorporated; see Emilie de Breteuil, marquise Du Châtelet, *Institutions de physique* (Paris: Chez Prault Fils, 1740), 2nd edition, chap. XIX, pp. 411, 417. See his letters of May and September in (Prince Baldassarre de) Boncompagni, "Lettre de Alessio Claudio Clairaut," *Atti dell'Accademia Pontifica di Nuovi Lincei* 45 (1892), pp. 233–39. I am grateful to Olivier Courcelle and Craig Waff for their copies of these letters and for their invaluable counsel on the science and the mathematics of Clairaut's work with Du Châtelet.

22 D2504, Jurin to Voltaire (23 June 1741), *CWV*, vol. 92, p. 56. See #262, Du Châtelet to Maupertuis (24 Feb. 1741), *LDC*, vol. 2, p. 42. #273, Du Châtelet to Maupertuis (26 June [1741]), *LDC*, vol. 2, pp. 59–61. #274, Du Châtelet to Maupertuis (8 Aug. [1741]), *LDC*, vol. 2, pp. 62, 64. D2140, Maupertuis to Bernoulli II (12 Jan. 1740), *CWV*, vol. 91, pp. 75–76. For the actual letter, see #261, Du Châtelet to Jurin (17 Feb. 1741), *LDC*, vol. 2, p. 41. #281, Du Châtelet to Wolff (22 Sept. 1741), *LDC*, vol. 2, p. 73. Clairaut to Du Châtelet (? May 1741), Boncompagni, "Lettere," pp. 233–34. #324, Du Châtelet to Jurin (30 May 1744), *LDC*, vol. 2, pp. 118–22. See the more polished and corrected version, Emilie de Breteuil Du Châtelet, "Letter to Jurin," Morgan Library, MA1689 R-V Autogr Misc Fr.

23 D3457, Du Châtelet to Jacquier (4 Sept. 1746), *CWV*, vol. 94, p. 73.

24 #4, Du Châtelet to F. M. Zanotti (1 June 1746), in Mauro De Zan, "Voltaire e Mme Du Châtelet, membri e correspondenti dell'Accademia delle Scienze di Bologna," *Studi e memorie dell'Istituto per la Storia dell'Università di Bologna*, 6 (1987), appendix, pp. 157, 156. I am grateful to John Iverson for a copy of this article, and to Wietse de Boer for help with the translations. See also Count Ciambatista Suardi, *Nuovi istromenti per la descrizione di diverse curve antiche e moderne* (Brescia, 1752). I am grateful to Ronald K. Smeltzer for this reference. See *Journal universel*, 10 (1746); Paris Inventory, app. D93, *CWV*, vol. 95, p. 462.

25 #281, Du Châtelet to Wolff (22 Oct. 1741), *LDC*, vol. 2, p. 73. See Droysen, "Wolff," pp. 231–37, 229. On Gottsched, see John Iverson, "A Female Member of the Republic of Letters: Du Châtelet's Portrait in *Bilder Sal* [...]" in Judith P. Zinsser and Julie Candler Hayes, eds. *SVEC* (2006:1), p. 48 n. 35.

26 Text by Johann Jacob Brucker, with engravings by Johann Jacob Haid. The others were
    Laura Bassi, Louise Gottsched, Magdalena Sibylla Riegerin. See Iverson, "A Female
    Member," p. 46 n. 34. See *Bilder-Sal,* trans. John Iverson, *SVEC* (2006:1), pp. 52–54.
    #302, Du Châtelet to Bernoulli II (3 June 1743), *LDC,* vol. 2, p. 95; #317, Du
    Châtelet to Bernoulli II (7 Jan. 1744), *LDC,* vol. 2, p. 110; #322, Du Châtelet to
    Bernoulli II (30 May 1744), *LDC,* vol. 2, p. 116. See also Droysen, "Wolff," pp. 241,
    242 n. 31.
27 Paris Inventory, *CWV,* vol. 95, p. 426.
28 Marquis Du Châtelet, Château de Vincennes, 3yd724. I am grateful to Rafe Blaufarb,
    the military historian, for alerting me to this archive, and for his explanations of
    terms in the royal military. See D3103, Voltaire to marquis d'Argenson ([16 April
    1745]), *CWV,* vol. 93, p. 232.
29 #329, Du Châtelet to Cideville (14 Aug. 1744), *LDC,* vol. 2, p. 126. The battle the
    marquis described was Dingelfing, in Bavaria. I am grateful to David W. Smith for his
    expert assistance in learning the details of the battle. See the marquis's file at Vin-
    cennes, 3yd724.
30 See especially Voltaire, *Métaphysique de Newton,* chap. IV in *CWV,* vol. 15, p. 217.
31 See J. S. Spink, *French Free-Thought from Gassendi to Voltaire* (London: University of Lon-
    don, Athlone Press, 1960), pp. 297, 274–79. See Vaillot *Avec Mme Du Châtelet,* pp. 306–
    7; Ira O. Wade, *Voltaire and Madame du Chatelet* . . . (Princeton: Princeton University
    Press, 1941), pp. 115–22, 46–47. See also her précis of Thomas Woolston, *Six Discours
    sur les miracles de Notre Sauveur,* ed. William Trapnell (Paris: Honoré Champion, 2001).
    No part of this section on the *Examens* could have been written without the careful
    scholarship and years of study of this and other clandestine texts by Bertram Eugene
    Schwarzbach, the editor of the critical edition of the *Examens.* He generously shared
    his expertise and his writings with me. All references that follow come from the manu-
    script for his critical edition: Emilie de Breteuil, marquise Du Châtelet, *Examens de la
    Bible,* ed. Bertram Eugene Schwarzbach (Paris: Honoré Champion, forthcoming).
32 Schwarzbach, preface in Du Châtelet, *Examens,* pp. 1–2.
33 Du Châtelet, *Examens,* Jean, chap. 1, p. 86. This and the references that follow are to
    the New Testament section.
34 On Lazarus, see Du Châtelet, *Examens,* Jean, chap. 11, pp. 101, 103; note that she
    uses her précis of Woolston for many of her points about miracles. On the irrational-
    ity of the miracles, discrepancies, and contradictions, see Mathieu, chaps. 4, 9–12,
    and chap. 13, p. 27, and also chap. 28, Luc, chap. 73. On not claiming divinity, see
    Jean, chap. 19, pp. 110, 111; Luc, chap. 13, pp. 78–79, 82.
35 Du Châtelet, *Examens,* Mathieu, chap. 14, p. 30, chap. 15, p. 31; chap. 9, p. 19. On
    parables, see Mathieu, chap. 13; Luc, chap. 12; note that her précis of Woolston
    makes this point, see Du Châtelet, trans., *Six Discours,* pp. 365–66. On breaking laws,
    see Luc, chap. 17, p. 81. On avoiding questions, see Mathieu, chap. 22, and the four
    fishermen, chap. 4. On women, Jean, chap. 5, p. 93; chap. 13, p. 106. On allegories,
    see Mathieu, chap. 2, p. 7. On Jesus as a coward, see Luc, chap. 22, p. 83; as fable,
    see Actes des Apôtres, pp. 130–31, 136.
36 On the resurrection as a fraud, see Du Châtelet, *Examens;* Luc, chap. 24, p. 85; Ma-
    thieu, chap. 28: especially, pp. 58–59. She counted two nights and one day between
    his death on Friday and his apparent reappearance on Sunday.

37 Du Châtelet, *Examens,* Mathieu, chap. 12, p. 24.

38 Note that in her discussion of the Old Testament, Du Châtelet summarizes and condenses in such a way that it is not always easy to identify which particular chapter of a book in the Bible she is referring to. In these sections, it is possible to discern Voltaire's contributions. See, for example, the remarks on the Book of Job, which read like a *conte* (tale), and describe the comforters as "leibnitien." Du Châtelet, *Examens,* Genèse, chaps. 1–2, pp. 2–4; Genèse, chaps. 6, 7, 9, pp. 8–10. Exode, chaps. 7, 12, pp. 25, 28. This and subsequent references are to the Old Testament section.

39 Du Châtelet, *Examens,* Lévitique, chap. 12, p. 44.

40 Du Châtelet, *Examens,* Joël, chap. 3, p. 220.

41 See Du Châtelet, *Examens,* Psaumes, 109, p. 237. Isaïe, chap. 8, p. 209; chap. 28, p. 211.

42 See, for example, Du Châtelet, *Examens,* Proverbes, chap. 1, p. 238 and chap. 11, p. 239. Genèse, chap. 42, p. 20. See 3e and 4e Livres des rois, also premier and second Livres des rois [Samuel 1 and 2 in modern editions of the Bible], especially on Saul. See also Josué, chap. 7, p. 75 and chap. 46, p. 80. See, on human sacrifice: Juges, chap. 11, p. 88; Ruth, p. 96; Judith, p. 178.

43 Du Châtelet, *Examens,* Josué, chap. 46, p. 80; Nombres, p. 58. For contradictions see: 1st Paralipomenes, p. 140; Exode, chap. 29, p. 32. On Abraham, see Genèse, chaps. 12–15. Job, see pp. 165, 166, 169. On doing evil vs. good, see 2nd Paralipomenes, p. 147; on Adam and Eve, see Genèse, chaps. 3, 5.

44 Bertram Eugene Schwarzbach has written numerous articles on the *Examens* and established her authorship. Most recently, he has studied the possible uses made of it by Voltaire. He concludes that Voltaire took little from it. See, for example, Bertram Eugene Schwarzbach, "Mme Du Châtelet's *Examens de la Bible* and Voltaire's *La Bible enfin expliquée,*" *SVEC* (2006:1).

45 I am grateful to Clorinda Donato for this information about Bergier.

46 #252, Du Châtelet to Maupertuis (22 Oct. [1740]), *LDC,* vol. 2, p. 33. Du Châtelet, *Discours,* ed. Mauzi, p. 22.

47 Charles Philippe d'Albert, duc de Luynes, *Mémoires du duc de Luynes . . .* ed. L. Dussieux and E. Soulié (Paris: Firmin Didot, 1860–65), vol. 6, p. 372, vol. 2, p. 276.

48 *Gazette de France,* no. 34 (15 Aug. 1744); no. 36 (15 July 1744); no. 39 (19 Sept. 1744); nos. 4 and 5 (23/30 Jan. 1745).

49 Luynes, *Mémoires,* vol. 10, p. 224. See Jacques Levron, *Daily Life at Versailles in the Seventeenth and Eighteenth Centuries,* trans. Claire Elaine Engel (London: George Allan, 1965), pp. 96–98, 112–13. See William R. Newton, *L'Espace du roi: La Cour de France au Château de Versailles, 1682–1789* (Paris: Fayard, 2000), pp. 189–91; Levron, *Daily Life,* p. 47; Philippe Beaussant and Patricia Bouchenot-Déchin, *Les Plaisirs de Versailles: Théâtre & musique* (Paris: Fayard, 1996), p. 130. #128 and #130, Graffigny to Devaux (10 and 14 May 1739), Françoise d'Issembourg d'Happoncourt Graffigny, *Correspondance de Madame de Graffigny,* ed. J. A. Dainard et al. (Oxford: Voltaire Foundation, 1985–), vol. 1, p. 482–84, 489.

50 Jean-François Solnon, *La Cour de France* (Paris: Fayard, 1987), pp. 426, 509–10. On the Grand Commun on the other side of the rue de la Surintendance, see Newton, *L'Espace du roi,* pp. 189, 120. Fernand Braudel, *The Structures of Everyday Life . . .* trans. S. Reynolds (New York: Harper & Row, 1979), p. 203. Madeleine Delpierre, *Dress in*

France in the Eighteenth Century, trans. Caroline Beamish (New Haven:Yale University Press, 1997), p. 103, 110.

51 See marquise de Créqui, *Souvenirs de la marquise de Créqui, 1710–1803* (Paris: Michel Lévy Frères, 1867), vol. 1, pp. 159–60. Paris Inventory, *CWV,* vol. 95, p. 467, bill dated 30 July 1749. See Solnon, *La Cour,* p. 476.

52 On her family, see Luynes, *Mémoires,* vol. 5, p. 338; vol. 3, p. 461; vol. 6, p. 375, vol. 7, p. 123; vol. 9, pp. 193, 96, 283, 484, 505. On Breteuil's career, see Luynes, *Mémoires,* especially vols. 3 and 4; for example, see vol. 3, pp. 425, 156, 161; vol. 4, pp. 402–8, 261, 188, 296–99, 315, 381, 389. See on families and politics, Kristen Brooke Neuschel, *Words of Honor: Interpreting Noble Culture in Sixteenth-Century France* (Ithaca: Cornell University Press, 1989), pp. 97–101, 119, 130, 197–9.

53 Luynes, *Mémoires,* vol. 6, p. 290. #363, Du Châtelet to marquis d'Argenson (20 July 1747), *LDC,* vol. 2, p. 159. See Paris Inventory, *CWV,* vol. 95, pp. 433–35 for the contents of the box. See also Graffigny, *Correspondance de Graffigny,* vol. 1, p. 199. Lunéville Inventory, Archives Meurthe-et-Moselle, 10B411, p. 30.

54 See the marquis's file at Château de Vincennes, 3yd724.

55 #295, Du Châtelet to d'Argental (3 Oct. 1742), *LDC,* vol. 2, p. 89; D2744, Voltaire to d'Aigueberre (4 April 1743), *CWV,* vol. 92, p. 348; #306, Du Châtelet to Cideville (28 July 1743), *LDC,* vol. 2, p. 99. See #350, Du Châtelet to Charlier (17 Dec. [1745]), *LDC,* vol. 2, p. 148; #351, Du Châtelet to Jacquier (17 Dec. 1745), *LDC,* vol. 2, p. 148; #360, Du Châtelet to Jacquier (13 April 1747), *LDC,* vol. 2, pp. 155–56. See also D3324, Voltaire to Françoise Gabrielle-Pauline Du Châtelet, duchesse de Montenero ([Feb. 1746]), *CWV,* vol. 93, pp. 407–8; D3445, Voltaire to Algarotti (13 Aug. [1746]), *CWV,* vol. 94, p. 63. D3470, Voltaire to Algarotti (13 Nov. 1746), *CWV,* vol. 94, p. 92. Du Châtelet's daughter gave birth to at least one child but died without any heirs, and was buried in Naples.

56 #298, Du Châtelet to Cideville (21 Jan. 1743), *LDC,* vol. 2, p. 92. On the five hundred livres, see #315, Du Châtelet to Voltaire ([? 1743]), *LDC,* vol. 2, p. 109. See also, Vaillot, *Madame du Châtelet,* p. 216. On her son's career, see his file at the Château de Vincennes military archives, Arne 7475, 1101 Gen. He rose to the rank of lieutenant general, like his father, then served as ambassador, first to Vienna and then to London; commanded the Paris Gardes Françaises just before the Revolution; and died on the guillotine in 1794 leaving no direct heirs.

57 Some biographers have followed a few sentences in the memoirs of Longchamps, Voltaire's valet, and assumed more rank for Du Châtelet than she could command; the right to a *tabouret,* the stool on which some members of the nobility were allowed to sit in the king's or queen's presence. Luynes states categorically, however, that even royal titles from Lorraine carried no right to such an honor. (Longchamps, *Mémoires,* Bibliothèque Nationale, NAF, 13006, 76; Luynes, *Mémoires,* vol. 6, p. 259.)

58 Solnon, *La Cour,* pp. 477–79; Levron, *Daily Life,* p. 135. For a description of the Du Châtelet *berline* she would have used, see Paris Inventory, app. D93, vol. 95, p. 415.

59 For information in this and the next paragraph, see #916, Graffigny to Devaux (26 Oct. 1745), in *Correspondance de Graffigny,* vol. 7, p. 73; Luynes, *Mémoires,* vol. 7, pp. 78–79, 129, 424; see also vol. 8, p. 352.

60 See Louis François Armand Du Plessis; duc de Richelieu, *Mémoires du moréchal le duc de Richelieu,* èd. F. Barrière (Paris: Firmin-Didot, 1889), vol. 1, pp. 341–42. See Guy Cabourdin, *Encyclopédie illustrée de la Lorraine* (Nancy: Presses Universitaires de Nancy, 1992), p. 130. Luynes, *Mémoires,* vol. 1, pp. 28–30, 37. See also Créqui, *Souvenirs,* vol. 1, p. 323.

61 See Luynes, *Mémoires,* vol. 5, pp. 180, 225. On Easter, see #18, *Gazette de France* (24 April 1745), no. 18, p. 218; Beaussant and Bouchenot-Déchin, *Plaisirs de Versailles,* pp. 155–63, 422, 443–45, 459; Solnon, *La Cour,* pp. 458–59.

62 See Beaussant and Bouchenot-Déchin, *Plaisirs de Versailles,* pp. 130, 181; Solnon, *La Cour,* pp. 458, 482. In contrast, other playwrights enjoyed having as many as forty to fifty performances of their works.

63 #62, Graffigny to Devaux ([9 Dec. 1738]), *Correspondance de Graffigny,* vol. 1, p. 206.

64 #253, Du Châtelet to Richelieu (23 Nov. [1740]), *LDC,* vol. 2, p. 33.

65 On *Mahomet,* see D2641, Marville to Maurepas (15 Aug. 1742), *CWV,* vol. 92, p. 234. See Vaillot, *Madame du Châtelet,* p. 217; D2647, Voltaire to Frederick (29 Aug. [1742]), *CWV,* vol. 92, p. 241. Voltaire altered the Pope's bland response to indicate explicit papal approval of the play. See D3128, Voltaire to d'Argenson (30 May [1745]), *CWV,* vol. 93, pp. 257–58. D3464, François Philibert Louzeau to Benedict XIV (7 Oct. 1746), *CWV,* vol. 94, p. 82. D3192, Voltaire to Benedict XIV ([17 Aug. 1745]), *CWV,* vol. 93, p. 307; and D3193, Voltaire to Benedict XIV (Aug. 1745), *CWV,* vol. 93, p. 308; and others to cardinals, *CWV,* vol. 93, pp. 307–11; on reworking the letter see D3210, Benedict XIV to Voltaire (Sept. 1745), *CWV,* vol. 93, pp. 322–24.

66 See #294, Du Châtelet to d'Argenson (22 Sept. [1742]), *LDC,* vol. 2, p. 88; *The Works of Voltaire* (Paris: E. R. DuMont, 1901), vol. 16, pp. 5–6, vol. 19, p. 289. On government disapproval, see D2824, Maurepas to Du Châtelet (30 Aug. 1743), *CWV,* vol. 92, p. 441. See on spying, Voltaire to Jean-Jacques Amelot de Chaillou (July–Aug. 1743), *CWV,* vol. 91, passim. On effort at peace negotiations, D2830, Voltaire to Frederick ([c. 5 Sept. 1743]), *CWV,* vol. 92, p. 452–55; D2901, Voltaire to Chaillou (30 Dec. [1743]), *CWV,* vol. 93, p. 42. On court, see Luynes, *Mémoires,* vol. 5, p. 292. Note that Frederick by this time worked to create trouble for Voltaire in France. See for example, D2627, Frederick (15 July 1742), *CWV,* vol. 92, p. 216; D2813, Frederick to count von Rothenburg (17 Aug. 1743), *CWV,* vol. 92, p. 426 n., 427 n.

67 Jean-Frédéric Phélypeaux, comte de Maurepas, *Mémoires du comte de Maurepas* (Paris: Chez Buisson, 1792), vol. 2, p. 192. See on Richelieu, for example, Luynes, *Mémoires,* vol. 2, p. 86; vol. 4, pp. 278–92, 294, 299, 470; vol. 5, pp. 81 n. 1, 224–25; vol. 6, pp. 60–65. See also Charles Jean François Hénault, *Mémoires du Président Hénault,* ed. François Rousseau (Paris: Hachette, 1911), p. 124. Créqui, *Souvenirs,* vol. 1, pp. 358–60. Solnon, *La Cour,* p. 499. See Richelieu, *Mémoires,* vol. 2, pp. 147–48. Château de Vincennes Richelieu file, 2yd221. Newton, *L'Espace du roi,* pp. 63–64, on other mistresses' accommodations, see p. 172.

68 See Luynes, *Mémoires,* vol. 5, pp. 331, 339; vol. 6, p. 346. Pierre-Maurice Masson, *Madame de Tencin (1682–1749): Une vie de femme au XVIIIe siècle* (Genève: Slatkine Reprints, 1970), p. 117. On Richelieu's debt, see *CWV,* D1299, D1300, D1304, D1318, D1329, D1336, D1418, vol. 88; D1563, vol. 89; D1967, vol. 90; D2956, vol. 93; D2401, vol. 91. See Beaussant and Bouchenot-Déchin, *Plaisirs de Versailles,* pp. 140, 161. Roger Picard, *Les Salons littéraires et la société française, 1610–1789* (Paris: Brenta-

no's, 1943), p. 294. See D2968, Voltaire to Cideville (8 May [1744]), *CWV,* vol. 93, p. 103.

69 #320, Du Châtelet to d'Argental (18 April 1744), *LDC,* vol. 2, p. 114.

70 "Azile des beaux arts, solitude où mon coeur / Est toujours occupé dans une paix profonde, / C'est vous qui donnez le bonheur / Que promettoit [sic] en vain le monde." D2882, Voltaire to Champbonin ([c. 12 Nov. 1743]), *CWV,* vol. 93, p. 20; D2975, Voltaire to Podewils (14 May [1744]), *CWV,* vol. 93, p. 110; D2956, Voltaire to d'Argenson Paulmy (15 April 1744), *CWV,* vol. 93, p. 90; Voltaire to d'Argental (24 April 1744), *CWV,* vol. 93, p. 97. #326, Du Châtelet to d'Argental (8 July 1744), *LDC,* vol. 2, p. 124. For Hénault description see D2996, Hénault to d'Argenson (9 July 1744), *CWV,* vol. 93, pp. 136–37. Hénault, *Mémoires,* pp. 171–72.

71 On Voltaire's activities, see letters (June–Aug. 1744), *CWV,* vol. 93; D2999, Voltaire to d'Argental (11 July [1744]), *CWV,* vol. 93, p. 139; D2991, Voltaire to Richelieu ([June 1744]), *CWV,* vol. 93, p. 133; #327, Du Châtelet to d'Argental (10 July [1744]), *LDC,* vol. 2, p. 125. D2956, Voltaire to marquis d'Argenson (15 April 1744), *CWV,* vol. 93, p. 90. See, for example, D3073, Voltaire to Cideville (31 Jan. 1745), *CWV,* vol. 93, p. 209. Beaussant and Bouchenot-Déchin, *Plaisirs de Versailles,* pp. 139–41. On cost, see Solnon, *La Cour,* p. 504. D3076, Voltaire to d'Argental ([25 Feb. 1745]), *CWV,* vol. 93, p. 211.

72 See *Gazette de France* (Jan.–Feb. 1745), especially nos. 4–6, 9–11. See also Beaussant and Bouchenot-Déchin, *Plaisirs de Versailles,* p. 141; Solnon, *La Cour,* pp. 453–54; Lunéville Inventory, #10B411; Delpierre, *Dress in France,* p. 104.

73 See Beaussant and Bouchenot-Déchin, *Plaisirs de Versailles,* pp. 426, 453–56; Solnon, *La Cour,* pp. 453–56. Invitation as quoted from Luynes, *Mémoires,* vol. 6, p. 302. #337, Du Châtelet to Bernoulli II (9 March 1745), *LDC,* vol. 2, p. 133. See D3100, Voltaire to Denis ([April 1745]), *CWV,* vol. 93, p. 228.

74 #820, Graffigny to Devaux (Sunday, 14 March 1745), in *Correspondance de Graffigny,* vol. 6, pp. 253, 276. D3092, Voltaire to Luc de Clapiers, marquis de Vauvenargues (3 April [1745]), *CWV,* vol. 93, pp. 223, 224 n. 1.

75 Luynes, *Mémoires,* vol. 6, pp. 468–69. Passim vols. 6 and 7 (June–Aug. 1745), *CWV,* vol. 93. Maurepas as quoted in Vaillot, *Avec Mme Du Châtelet,* p. 465, see also, pp. 460–61. D3726, Voltaire to Denis (27 [July 1748]), *CWV,* vol. 94, p. 285. See D3246, Voltaire to Fawkener (21 Oct. [1745]), *CWV,* vol. 93, p. 352.

76 The courtier is Dufort de Cheverny, quoted in Colin Jones, *Madame de Pompadour: Images of a Mistress* (London: National Gallery Co., 2002), pp. 14, 29. #840, Graffigny to Devaux (30 April 1745), in *Correspondance de Graffigny,* vol. 6, p. 343; #848, Graffigny to Devaux (17 May 1745), vol. 6, p. 374. See the biography by Evelyne Lever, *Madame de Pompadour: A Life,* trans. Catherine Temerson (New York: Farrar, Strauss and Giroux, 2002). Luynes, *Mémoires,* introduction, vol. 1, p. 30.

77 See D3138, Pompadour to Voltaire (7 June [1746]), *CWV,* vol. 93, pp. 264–65. On Pompadour's activities, Lever, *Pompadour,* pp. 63, 65, 100, 134; Solnon, *La Cour,* pp. 431, 465–66. See Beaussant and Bouchenot-Déchin, *Plaisirs de Versailles,* pp. 166–69, 171–75, 177, 183, 417, 418; and Xavier Salmon, ed. *Madame de Pompadour et les arts* (Paris: Réunion des Musées Nationales, 2002), especially, Helge Siefert, "Le Raffinement et l'élégance comme maxime," pp. 36–37. See also Luynes, *Mémoires,* vol. 7, p. 424. Jones, *Pompadour,* p. 53.

78   See D3092, Voltaire to Denis ([3 April 1745]), *CWV,* vol. 93, p. 222. See D3254, Maurepas to Voltaire (7 Nov. 1745), *CWV,* vol. 93, p. 359, and D3494, Maurepas to Voltaire (26 Dec. 1746), *CWV,* vol. 94, pp. 114–15; D3081, Voltaire to d'Argenson ([5 March 1745]), and D3087 (30 March 1745), *CWV,* vol. 93, pp. 215, 219. See also #994, Graffigny to Devaux (Jan. 1746), *Correspondance de Graffigny,* vol. 7, p. 187 n. 10 and #1061, Graffigny to Devaux (9 Oct. 1746), vol. 8, p. 94 n. 7. Créqui, *Souvenirs,* vol. 3, p. 75. Karlis Racevskis, *Voltaire and the French Academy* (Chapel Hill, N.C.: Studies in the Romance Languages and Literatures, 1975), apps. A and B, pp. 131–34. Tencin to Richelieu as quoted in Vaillot, *Madame du Châtelet,* p. 219. For examples of efforts, see D2879, Maurepas to Voltaire (9 Nov. 1743), *CWV,* vol. 93, p. 18; D2718, Voltaire to Moncrif (1 Feb. [1743]), *CWV,* vol. 92, p. 328; D2723, Voltaire to Boyer ([Feb. 1743]), *CWV,* vol. 92, pp. 333–34; D2724, Voltaire to Odet Joseph de Vaue de Giry ([Feb. 1743]), *CWV,* vol. 92, p. 336. See #652, Graffigny to Devaux (Thursday, 6 Feb. 1744), *Correspondance de Graffigny,* vol. 5, p. 79; Luynes, *Mémoires,* vol. 4, pp. 452, 459. See Vaillot, *Avec Mme Du Châtelet,* p. 419. D2744, Voltaire to d'Aigueberre (4 April 1743), *CWV,* vol. 92, p. 348. Wise strategy quoted in Solnon, *La Cour,* pp. 481–83.

79   On Voltaire's efforts, see, for example, D3043, Destouches to Voltaire (15 Nov. 1744), *CWV,* vol. 93, pp. 185–86; see D3064 and D3239, Voltaire to Richelieu ([1745]) and (20 June [1745]), *CWV,* vol. 93, pp. 203, 348, 278–89. D3127, Voltaire to marquis d'Argenson (29 May [1745]), *CWV,* vol. 93, p. 256. See especially Roger Marchal, *Madame de Lambert et son milieu* (Oxford: Voltaire Foundation, 1991), pp. 247–48. See Pierre-Maurice Masson, *Madame de Tencin (1682–1749): Une Vie de femme au XVIIIme siècle* (Genève: Slatkine Reprints, 1970), pp. 49–51.

80   On Tencin and her *salon,* see Masson, *Madame de Tencin,* pp. 132–33; Picard, *Salons littéraires,* pp. 144, 188–97, 215–16, 231–32, 242–43. Tencin, quoted in Vaillot, *Madame du Châtelet,* p. 226. See D2643, Voltaire to d'Argental (22 Aug. [1742]), *CWV,* vol. 92, p. 237.

81   For information on Tencin, see Lescure, introduction, marquise Du Deffand, *Correspondance complète,* ed. m. de Lescure (Paris: Henri Plon, 1865), vol. 1, pp. viii–xx, xlvi–xlvii, xcii–c, cxii–cxxix; Picard, *Salons littéraires,* pp. 232–49. Hénault as quoted in Lescure, introduction to Du Deffand *Correspondance,* vol. 1, p. xli. See also D3165, Voltaire to Forcalquier ([c. 1745]), *CWV,* vol. 93, p. 288.

82   On Voltaire's efforts, see, for example, D3043, Destouches to Voltaire (15 Nov. 1744), *CWV,* vol. 93, pp. 185–86; D3064 and D3239, Voltaire to Richelieu ([1745]) and (20 June [1745]), *CWV,* vol. 93, pp. 203, 348, 278–79. D3127, Voltaire to marquis d'Argenson (29 May [1745]), *CWV,* vol. 93, p. 256. #28, Hénault to Du Deffand (17 July 1742), Du Deffand *Correspondance,* vol. 1, p. 67. D3005, Hénault to Voltaire (19 July [1744]), *CWV,* vol. 93, p. 148. D3205, Voltaire to Hénault ([c. 25 Aug. 1745]), *CWV,* vol. 93, p. 318. On the queen and Hénault, see Luynes, *Mémoires,* vol. 8, p. 384.

83   See D2736, Voltaire to Moncrif ([c. March 1743]), *CWV,* vol. 92, p. 344. D3125, Voltaire to Moncrif ([c. 27 May 1745]), *CWV,* vol. 93, p. 255.

84   D3342, Voltaire to d'Argental ([? 20 March 1746]), *CWV,* vol. 93, p. 420. D3353, Voltaire to Destouches (9 April [1746]), *CWV,* vol. 93, pp. 420, 433. "Je veux vivre et mourir tranquillement dans le sein de l'Eglise catholique, apostolique et romaine

sans attaquer personne," quoted in Vaillot, *Avec Mme. Du Châtelet,* p. 486. D3348, Voltaire to La Tour ([c. 1 April 1746]), *CWV,* vol. 93, pp. 423–29. #984, Graffigny to Devaux (13 April 1746), *Correspondance de Graffigny,* vol. 7, p. 353.

85 See D3358, D3364, D3365, D3368, Voltaire to Moncrif (15–23 April 1746), *CWV,* vol. 93, pp. 436–42. Vaillot, *Avec Mme. Du Châtelet,* p. 489. See #990, Graffigny to Devaux ([27 April 1746]), *Correspondance de Graffigny,* vol. 7, p. 378. D3370, Voltaire to Denis ([26 April 1746]), *CWV,* vol. 93, p. 443.

Chapter Six: The Woman of Passions and the Historians

1 On Jacquier see J. L. Heilbron, *Elements of Early Modern Physics* (Berkeley: University of California Press, 1982), p. 137. On her plans, see *Lettres de la Marquise du Châtelet,* ed. Theodore Besterman (Genève: Institut et Musée Voltaire, 1958), vol. 2, pp. 143–44. #352, Du Châtelet to Bernoulli II (8 Jan. 1746), *LDC,* vol. 2, p. 149.

2 Bertram Eugene Schwarzbach suggested using endings as part of analysis. #347, Du Châtelet to Jacquier (12 Nov. 1745), *LDC,* vol. 2, pp. 143–44. See # 352, Du Châtelet to Jacquier (8 Jan. 1746), *LDC,* vol. 2, p. 149. A partial translation was published in 1985 by Marie-Françoise Bearnais, *De philosophiae naturalis principia mathematica.* I am grateful to Antoinette Emch-Dériaz and Gérard G. Emch for this information, and to François de Gandt for explaining the extent of it. See Antoinette Emch-Dériaz and Gérard Emch, "On Newton's French Translation, How Faithful was Madame Du Châtelet?" in Judith P. Zinsser and Julie Candler Hayes eds., *SVEC* (2006:1); de Gandt (personal communication 27 Aug. 2005).

3 On the *Principia* and the many difficulties presented by Newton's choices and his manner of thinking, see I. Bernard Cohen, "A Guide to Isaac Newton's Principia," in Isaac Newton, *The Principia: Mathematical Principles of Natural Philosophy,* trans. I. Bernard Cohen and Anne Whitman, assisted by Julia Budenz (Berkeley: University of California Press, 1999), published with the modern English translation. Emch-Dériaz and Emch identified these three types of problems, see pp. 229–31. For the whole discussion of Du Châtelet's translation of and commentary on the *Principia,* I am indebted to their scholarship.

4 See Florian Cajori, "Mme Du Châtelet on Fluxions," *Mathematical Gazette* 13 (1926–27), p. 252.

5 For the manuscript of Du Châtelet's translation of Newton, see, Bibliothèque Nationale, Ffr. 12266 which includes these sections of the *Principia:* "Définitions," "Axioms," Book I on "Mouvement des Corps," Book III, "Sistème du monde"; Ffr 12267 includes: Newton's prefaces to 1st, 2nd, 3rd editions, Cotes's preface, Book II. Ffr 12268 contains only part of the *Commentaire:* the "Solution analytique" I–IV, and the "Tables des matières" for each section of the *Commentaire.* The "Table des matières" for the translation, the "Exposition abrégée," and section V of the "Solution analytique" on Daniel Bernoulli's *discours* on the tides, are missing. Emilie de Breteuil, marquise Du Châtelet, trans., *Principes mathématiques de la philosophie naturelle.* 1759; reprint Sceaux: Editions Jacques Gabay, 1990. D3580, comte d'Argenson to Du Châtelet (19 Oct. 1747), *The Complete Works of Voltaire,* ed. Theodore Besterman (Genève: Institut et Musée 1968–), vol. 94, p. 184.

6 Note that Emch-Dériaz and Emch hypothesize a clear progression of disagreement

with Newton in her translation and commentary. Du Châtelet discreetly indicated problems in the translation of the work with changes in punctuation, paragraph breaks, and such devices, while still remaining faithful to Newton's intention. In the "Exposition abrégée" of Newton's system of the world, she noted "dubious passages." In the "Solution analytique," she made her disagreement clear and presented alternative mathematics and explanations. See Emch-Dériaz and Emch, "French Translator," pp. 229–31. #347, Du Châtelet to Jacquier (12 Nov. 1745), LDC, vol. 2, pp. 144, 145 n. 4. See #361, Du Châtelet to Jacquier (1 July 1747), LDC, vol. 2, p. 157. See #351, Du Châtelet to Bernoulli II (17 Dec. 1745), and #352, Du Châtelet to Bernoulli II (8 Jan. 1746), LDC, vol. 2, pp. 148, 149.

7   #352, Du Châtelet to Bernoulli II (8 Jan. 1746), LDC, vol. 2, p. 149.

8   On the events and a different hypothesis, see Charlotte Simonin and David W. Smith, "Du nouveau sur Mme Denis. Les apports de la correspondance de Mme de Graffigny," Cahiers Voltaire 4 (2005), p. 8; #918, Graffigny to Devaux (2 Nov. 1745), Françoise d'Issembourg d'Happoncourt Graffigny, Correspondance de Madame de Graffigny, ed. J. A. Dainard, et al. (Oxford: Voltaire Foundation, 1985–), vol. 7, p. 79. The dealer who had the letters told Theodore Besterman, who arranged for their purchase by the Morgan Library.

9   Emilie de Breteuil, marquise Du Châtelet, Discours sur le bonheur, ed. Robert Mauzi (Paris: Société d'Edition Belles Lettres, 1961), pp. 31–32.

10 D2512, Voltaire to Cideville (11 July 1741), CWV, vol. 92, p. 68. See also Voltaire, "Stances [à Madame du Châtelet]," CWV, vol. 20A, pp. 563–65. The poem has also been translated into English by Ezra Pound and Robert Lowell. I am grateful to the art historian Patricia Crown for drawing my attention to the Lowell, and to W. H. Barber for identifying it.

11 Du Châtelet, Discours, ed. Mauzi, pp. 32–33. See also #313, Du Châtelet to d'Argental (13 Nov. 1743), LDC, vol. 2, p. 107. On Voltaire's explanations, see, D2618, Voltaire to Sir Everard Fawkener ([c. June 1742]), CWV, vol. 92, p. 205.

12 Du Châtelet, Discours ed. Mauzi, p. 32. Voltaire, Contes en vers: Oeuvres Complètes (Paris: Garnier Frères: 1877), vol. 10, p. 541. Note that the verses were written as if by the marquise de Boufflers.

13 D1379, Voltaire to Denis (26 Oct. 1737), CWV, vol. 88, p. 388. D1396, Voltaire to Thieriot (6 Dec. 1737), CWV, vol. 88, p. 412. See also René Vaillot, Avec Mme Du Châtelet, 1734–1749 in Voltaire en son temps, ed. René Pomeau (Oxford: Voltaire Foundation, 1985–95), vol. 1, p. 352. D1412, Voltaire to Thieriot ([23 Dec. 1737]), CWV, vol. 88, p. 435.

14 Graffigny to Devaux (10 Feb. 1750), quoted in Simonin and Smith, "Denis," p. 5.

15 See D3277, Voltaire to Denis ([27 Dec. 1745]), CWV, vol. 93, p. 378; D3300, Voltaire to Denis ([1745/1746]), CWV, vol. 93, p. 384. D3536, Voltaire to Denis ([Spring 1747]), CWV, vol. 94, p. 156; D3598, Voltaire to Denis (Wed. [1747/1748]), CWV, vol. 94, p. 192.

16 See, for example, #369, Du Châtelet to marquis d'Argenson ([March/April 1748]), LDC, vol. 2, p. 163.

17 #358, Du Châtelet to Bernoulli II (20 Nov. 1746), LDC, vol. 2, p. 154. D3491, marquis d'Argenson to Du Châtelet (22 Dec. 1746), CWV, vol. 94, p. 112. #369. Du Châtelet to marquis d'Argenson ([March/April 1748]), LDC, vol. 2, p. 163; #367,

Du Châtelet to d'Argenson (2 March [1748]), *LDC,* vol. 2, pp. 161–62. On Puisieux see #18S, Du Châtelet to Saint-Lambert (23 May [1748]), (#376, *LDC,* vol. 2), p. 60. The French historian Anne Soprani created a new arrangement of the letters between Du Châtelet and Saint-Lambert, which I believe more accurately reflects Du Châtelet's thinking and the course of events. I have used her edition, noted with an "S" after the letter number, as #18S here. See *Emilie Du Châtelet: Lettres d'amour au marquis de Saint-Lambert (*Paris: Editions Méditerranée, 1977). I have indicated the letter number used in the standard 1958 two-volume collection of her letters edited by Theodore Besterman in parentheses with the volume number, as for example (#376 *LDC,* vol. 2) in this instance.

18   D3373, Voltaire to Maupertuis (1 May [1746]), *CWV,* vol. 94, p. 11.

19   W. R. Newton *L'Espace du roi: La Cour de France au château de Versailles 1682–1789* (Paris: Fayard, 2000), pp. 334–35. I am grateful to Yves Ollivier for this reference. Voltaire transferred the lease of his palace rooms to Du Châtelet in February 1749. See, for example, D3265, Voltaire to Denis ([2 Dec. 1745]), *CWV,* vol. 93, p. 367; see also #1022, Graffigny to Devaux (Sunday, 10 July 1746), *Correspondance de Graffigny,* vol. 7, p. 505.

20   Marquise de Créqui, *Souvenirs de la Marquise de Créqui, 1710–1803* (Paris: Michel Lévy Frères, 1867), vol. 3, p. 76; D3838, Voltaire to Hénault (3 Jan. 1748 [1749]), *CWV,* vol. 94, p. 387 n. 1, p. 388.

21   Philippe Beaussant and Patricia Bouchenot-Déchin, *Les Plaisirs de Versailles: Théâtre & musique* (Paris: Fayard, 1996), p. 149. Charles Philippe d'Albert, duc de Luynes, *Mémoires,* ed. L. Dussieux and E. Soulié (Paris: Firmin Didot, 1860–65), vol. 7, p. 132. On supposed relationship, see Vaillot, *Avec Mme Du Châtelet,* p. 464; D3122, Voltaire to Pompadour ([c. 20 May 1745]), *CWV,* vol. 93, p. 253. See Russell Goulbourne, introduction to Voltaire, *L'Enfant prodigue, CWV,* 16.

22   See D2804, d'Argental to Cideville (8 Aug. 1743), *CWV,* vol. 92, p. 414.

23   D3450, Voltaire to Cideville (19 Aug. 1746), *CWV,* vol. 94, p. 66. See Vaillot, *Avec Mme Du Châtelet,* vol. 1, pp. 556–57. Originally *Catalina* was called *Rome sauvée* (Rome Saved). On continuing rivalry, see Henry Carrington Lancaster, *French Tragedy in the Time of Louis XV and Voltaire 1715–1774* (Baltimore: Johns Hopkins University Press, 1950), vol. 2, pp. 343–60.

24   See Helge Siefert, "Le reffinement et l'élégance comme maxime," in *Madame de Pompadour et les arts,* ed. Xavier Salmon (Paris: Réunion des Musées Nationales, 2002), p. 36. See also Evelyne Lever, *Madame de Pompadour: A Life,* trans. Catherine Temerson (New York: Farrar, Straus and Giroux, 2002), p. 97. For the verses see Voltaire, *CWV,* vol. 30A, pp. 426–27.

25   See Roger Picard, *Les Salons littéraires et la société française, 1610–1789* (Paris: Brentano's, 1943), pp. 165–71. Charles Augustin Sainte Beuve, *Causeries du Lundi* (Paris: Garnier Fréres, 1852–1862), vol. 3, pp. 207–28. René Pomeau, *D'Arouet à Voltaire (1694–1734)* in *Voltaire en son temps* (Oxford: Voltaire Foundation, 1985–95), vol. 1, pp. 60–66, Vaillot, *Avec Mme Du Châtelet,* vol. 1, pp. 425, 517–30.

26   Marquise Du Deffand, *Correspondance Complète de la Marquise Du Deffand . . .* (Paris, 1865), vol. 1, p. 98. See also W. H. Barber, "Penny Plan, Twopiece Colored: Longchamps's Memoire of Voltaire," in *Studies in the French Eighteenth Century presented to John Lough* (Durham: University of Durham, 1978), pp. 13–15. See Du Deffand,

Correspondance, vol. 1: #43, Staal de Launay to Du Deffand (27 Aug. 1747), p. 96; #41, Staal de Launay to Du Deffand (20 Aug. 1747), pp. 93–94; #40, Staal de Launay to Du Deffand (15 Aug. 1747), p. 92; #44, Staal de Launay to Du Deffand (30 Aug. 1747), p. 97.

27 Clairaut's Académie discourse representing the mathematical results of his trip to Lapland with Maupertuis also reworked Newton's hypothesis on the effects of attraction on the shape of the earth. See #361, Du Châtelet to Jacquier (1 July 1747), *LDC,* vol. 2, p. 157. On her plans for the commentary, see #351, Du Châtelet to Bernoulli II (17 Dec. 1745), and #352, Du Châtelet to Bernoulli II (8 Jan. 1746), *LDC,* vol. 2, pp. 148, 149; #357, Du Châtelet to Bernoulli II (6 Sept. 1746), *LDC,* vol. 2, pp. 153, 154 n. 2. D3457, Du Châtelet to Jacquier (4 Sept. 1746), *CWV,* vol. 94, p. 72.

28 #361, Du Châtelet to Jacquier (1 July 1747), *LDC,* vol. 2, p. 157. #360, Du Châtelet to Jacquier (13 April 1747), *LDC,* vol. 2, pp. 155–56. See Emilie de Breteuil, marquise Du Châtelet, *Institutions de physique* (Paris: Chez Prault Fils, 1740), chap. XV, pp. 294, 318; chap. XVIII, pp. 356, 361.

29 The chapters of her "Exposition" included an introduction on the history of astronomy; chap. I on the solar system; chap. II on the planets; chap. III on the shape of the earth; chap. IV on the precession of the equinoxes; chap. V on the tides; chap. VI on "secondary planets," especially the moon; chap. VII on comets.

30 Du Châtelet, *Commentaire,* pp. 12, 13, 25, 31, 20.

31 Du Châtelet, *Commentaire,* pp. 43, 32, 34, 37, 41.

32 Du Châtelet, *Commentaire,* see pp. 60, 62–66.

33 See Du Châtelet, *Commentaire,* pp. 74–75. See Emch-Dériaz and Emch, "French Translator," pp. 244–45. Note that I have combined Du Châtelet's description of Bernoulli's *Mémoire* on the tides in the two parts of the *Commentaire,* both the abbreviated version in the "Exposition abregée" and the separate description in the "Solution analytique." Du Châtelet, *Commentiare,* pp. 265, 267, 275, 81–82, 260. Du Châtelet also described the work of Chevalier Louville on the tides.   •

34 Du Châtelet, *Commentaire,* pp. 95, 96, 109–10, Du Châtelet, *Commentaire,* 111–13, 114. She was writing about Halley's comet, and Clairaut would labor over the calculations in the late 1750s and predict its return within a month of the actual appearance.

35 By tradition, Voltaire scholars have assumed that this was the occasion on which he sought refuge after his unfortunate comment about the queen's card-players at Fontainebleau. Du Châtelet then joined him, after quieting the storm over his remarks. For the story see Sébastien G. Longchamps, *Voltaire et Mme Du Châtelet, Révélations d'un serviteur,* ed. d'Albanès Havard (Paris: Librarie de la Société des Gens de Lettres, 1863), pp. 108–12; Vaillot, *Avec Mme Du Châtelet,* pp. 524–26.

36 D3590, Voltaire to Moncrif ([Nov./Dec. 1747]), *CWV,* vol. 94, p. 189. See Luynes, *Mémoires,* vol. 8, pp. 252–53, 253 n. 1. See also D3591, Voltaire to Denis (7 [Dec. 1747]), *CWV,* vol. 94, p. 189. See on the incident, Vaillot, *Avec Mme Du Châtelet,* pp. 530–31.

37 See on King Stanislas and his court: Jacques Charles-Gaffiot, *Lunéville: Fastes du Versailles Lorrain* (n.p., Editions Didier Carpentier, 2003), pp. 155–56, 160–64. Gaston Maugras, *La Cour de Luneville au XVIIIe Siècle* (Paris: Plon-Nourrit, 1904), pp. 177,

175 n. 2, 203 n. 1, 206–7, 213, 217–20. Stanislas's memoir written for his daughter, quoted in introduction, Luynes, *Mémoires*, vol. 1, p. 37. See also Guy Cabourdin, *Encyclopédie illustrée de la Lorraine* (Nancy: Presses Universitaires de Nancy, 1992), pp. 142–48.

38 See Maugras, *Cour de Lunéville*, pp. 230–31, 183; Picard, *Salons littéraires*, p. 301; and Charles-Gaffiot, *Lunéville*, p. 153. Voltaire verse "Le Portrait manqué, à madame la marquise de B***," in *CWV*, vol. 30A, pp. 458–59.

39 See Lunéville inventory, Archives Meurthe-et-Moselle, #10B411. See Du Châtelet's letters to d'Argental and Saint-Lambert, Voltaire's to Denis, Champbonin and d'Argental, Devaux's to Graffigny for Feb. to Sept. 1748, passim. I am grateful to the editors of the Graffigny papers at the University of Toronto for generously sharing their copies of the Graffigny-Devaux letters, both those in preparation for publication and those unpublished, their meticulous annotation, and their expertise: Alan Dainard, David W. Smith, Penny Arthur, and Marion Filipiuk. On the gardens, the palace, and the pavilions, see Martine Tronquart, *Les Châteaux de Lunéville* (Metz: Éditions Serpenoise, 1991); Charles-Gaffiot, *Lunéville*, pp. 95–97.

40 Luynes, *Mémoires*, vol. 8, p. 455. D3624, Voltaire to comtesse d'Argental (25 Feb. 1748), *CWV*, vol. 94, p. 209. See also Vaillot, *Avec Mme Du Châtelet*, p. 537.

41 Voltaire, "Parodie de la sarabande d'Issé," in *CWV*, vol. 30A, pp. 416, 416 n. 7. #1225, Devaux to Graffigny (2 March 1748), *Correspondance de Graffigny*, vol. 9, p. 28 n. 27.

42 See Devaux to Graffigny (4 April 1748–15 April 1748), *Correspondance de Graffigny*, vol. 9, passim; #1229, Devaux to Graffigny (14 April 1748), vol. 9, p. 44 n. 29. D3633, Voltaire to Champbonin ([April 1748]), *CWV*, vol. 94, p. 215. Saint-Lambert quoted in Vaillot, *Avec Mme Du Châtelet*, p. 540.

43 Voltaire, *Contes en vers: Oeuvres Completes* (Paris: Garnier Frères, 1877), vol. 10, p. 541.

44 #12S, Du Châtelet to Saint-Lambert ([25 April 1748]), p. 45 (#374 *LDC*, vol. 2).

45 See #615, Graffigny to Devaux (11 Nov. 1743), in *Correspondance de Graffigny*, vol. 4, p. 461. On Saint-Lambert's life, see Maugras, *Cour de Lunéville*, pp. 78–88; Jean-Philibert Damiron, *Mémoires sur les encyclopédistes: Saint-Lambert* (Genève: Slatkine Reprints, 1968), p. 28; Roger Poirier, *Jean-François de Saint-Lambert, 1716–1803: Sa Vie, son oeuvre* (Sarrequemines: Pierron, 2001), pp. 47–48; George Mangeot, *La Famille de Saint-Lambert, 1596–1795* (Paris: Libraire Croville-Morant, 1913), pp. 88–90. See Graffigny letters, # 26, #30, #8, in *Correspondance de Graffigny*, vol. 5, pp. 39, 84, 98. #1100, See Graffigny to Devaux (Sun., 8 Jan. 1747), in *Correspondance de Graffigny*, vol. 8, p. 197.

46 #48S, Du Châtelet to Saint-Lambert ([30 Aug. 1748]), p. 121 (#429, *LDC*, vol. 2).

47 #53S, Du Châtelet to Saint-Lambert ([Sept. 1748]), p. 133 (#419, *LDC*, vol. 2). #6S, ([?]), p. 37 (#414, *LDC*, vol. 2).

48 #14S, Du Châtelet to Saint-Lambert (29 [April 1748]), p. 48 (#371, *LDC*, vol. 2). #15S (1 May [1748]), pp. 49–51 (#372, *LDC*, vol. 2).

49 #16S, Du Châtelet to Saint-Lambert ([11 May 1748]), p. 54 (#373, *LDC*, vol. 2). #17S (19 May 1748), p. 57 (#375, *LDC*, vol. 2). #25S (16 June [17]48), p. 86 (#383, *LDC*, vol. 2). #18S (23 May [1748]), pp. 58–60 (#376, *LDC*, vol. 2). See also #21S ([30 May 1748]), pp. 66–67 (#382, *LDC*, vol. 2).

50 Du Châtelet to Saint-Lambert, #25S (16 June [17]48), p. 85 (#383, *LDC*, vol. 2). For this and the previous paragraph, see May–June 1748, #18S, #19S, #20S, #21S; on

the marquis's reaction, see #22S (5 June 1748), pp. 70–72, 74 (#376, #378, #374, #382, #379, *LDC*, vol. 2). On Newton, see #25S (16 June [17]48), pp. 82–83. #26S (19 [June 1748]), p. 88 (#385, *LDC*, vol. 2).

51 Du Châtelet, *Discours*, ed. Mauzi, pp. 28–31, 33–35; #12S ([25 Apr. 1748), p. 43 (#374, *LDC*, vol. 2); see also #23S ([6 June 1748]), p. 78 (#380, *LDC*,, vol. 2).

52 Du Châtelet, *Discours*, ed. Mauzi, pp. 36–37, 37–38. #27S (22 [June 1748]), p. 91 (#386, *LDC*, vol. 2). #28S (Thurs. [27 June 1748]), pp. 92–93 (#439, *LDC*, vol. 2).

53 #33S, Du Châtelet to Saint-Lambert ([July 1748]), p. 98 (#397, *LDC*, vol. 2). See #32S, #34S, #37S, #36S, #55–56S, (July–Oct. 1748) pp. 97, 99, 100, 101, 102, 136–38, (#408, #402, #410, #400, #395, #394, #410, *LDC*, vol. 2). #38S ([Aug. 1748]), p. 103 (#425, *LDC*, vol. 2).

54 Du Châtelet to Saint-Lambert, #45S, #46S, #47S (23–25 Aug. 1748). pp. 111–13, 118, 119 (#430, #433, #431, *LDC*, vol. 2); #49S ([2 Sept. 1748]), p. 125 (#432, *LDC*, vol. 2); #54S ([Sept. 1748]), p. 135 (#416, *LDC*, vol. 2); #50S ([5 Sept. 1748]), p. 128 (#435, *LDC*, vol. 2); #92S ([7 June 1749]), p. 228 (#474, *LDC*, vol. 2) See on similar games of Boufflers #92S (7 [June 1749]), pp. 28–29 (#474, *LDC*, vol. 2); #93S ([8 June 1749]), p. 232 (#475, *LDC*, vol. 2).

55 #388, Du Châtelet to d'Argental (30 July [1748]), *LDC*, vol. 2, p. 198. Charles Collé, *Journal [historiques] et Mémoires* (Paris: Didot, 1868) vol. 1, pp. 59–60. See Du Châtelet to Saint-Lambert, #78S, #80S, #81S, #83S, #89S, #92S (April–June 1749), passim, pp. 184–230 (#458, #463, #477, #464, #476, #474, *LDC*, vol. 2); #466, Du Châtelet to Boufflers (3 May [1749]), *LDC*, vol. 2, pp. 277–78.

56 See Du Châtelet to Saint-Lambert, #47S, #48S, #61S (Aug.–Oct. 1748), pp. 116–23, 146 (#431, #429, #415, *LDC*, vol. 2). Elegy from Soprani, ed., pp. 257–58.

57 Du Châtelet to Saint-Lambert, #53S, #54S ([Sept. 1748]), pp. 133, 135 (#419, #416, *LDC*, vol. 2). See #466, Du Châtelet to Boufflers (3 May 1749), *LDC*, vol. 2, pp. 278; Paris Inventory, *CWV*, app. D93, vol. 95, pp. 458–59, 473–75.

58 See Devaux to Graffigny (23 March 1784), Graffigny Papers, Beinecke Library, Yale University, XLII, p. 307. See also Graffigny Papers: (April 1748) XLI, p. 28. (24 May 1748) XLI, p. 153. (31 May 1748), XLI, p. 172. (2 April 1748) XLI, p. 23. (16–17 Aug. 1748), (21 Aug. 1748), (26 Aug. 1748), (22 Sept. 1748), XLII, pp. 27–30, 45, XL, p. 260.

59 Graffigny Papers: Devaux to Graffigny (19 Aug. 1748) XLII, p. 33; (12 Sept. 1748), XLII, p. 76. Du Châtelet to Saint-Lambert, #53S ([Sept. 1748]), p. 133 (#419, *LDC*, vol. 2); #56S and #57S ([3 Oct. 1748]), pp. 138, 140–41 (#394, #461, *LDC*, vol. 2). For Stanislas's affection for her, see D3874, Stanislas to Du Châtelet and Voltaire (17 Feb. 1749), vol. 49, p. 423.

60 See Du Châtelet to Saint-Lambert, #40S and 41S ([Aug. 1748]), pp. 105, 106 (#424, #426, *LDC*, vol. 2). #55S ([2 Oct. 1748]), pp. 136–37 (#395, *LDC*, vol. 2). #56S and #60S ([Oct. 1748]), pp. 139, 145 (#394 and #421, *LDC*, vol. 2).

61 Voltaire, "Epître à M. de Saint-Lambert," *CWV*, vol. 30A, pp. 441–43. By tradition, the account has been embellished. Longchamps's manuscript at the Bibliothèque Nationale does not include any stories of Voltaire's discovery of the affair. They appear in the first published edition (1826), including Voltaire's challenge of Saint-Lambert to a duel, and a bedside reconciliation between Du Châtelet and the poet. See Sébastien G. Longchamps and Jean Louis Wagnière, *Mémoires sur Voltaire et sur ses ouvrages*

(Paris: Aimé André, 1826), pp. 198–205. For the story repeated by subsequent historians, see Vaillot, *Avec Mme Du Châtelet*, pp. 575–76.

62 See #60S, #63S, #64S, Du Châtelet to Saint-Lambert ([Oct.–Nov. 1748]), pp. 145, 148, 149 (#421, #423, #398, *LDC*, vol. 2).

63 Voltaire, *La Femme qui a raison*, in *CWV*, vol. 30A, pp. 363–64.

64 #66S, Du Châtelet to Saint-Lambert (8 Feb. 1749), p. 152 (#450, *LDC*, vol. 2); #70S (24 [Feb. 1749]), p. 166 (#452, *LDC*, vol. 2). #454, Du Châtelet to Boufflers (3 April 1749), *LDC*, vol. 2, pp. 247–48. #79S, Du Châtelet to Saint-Lambert (17 [April 1749]), p. 191 (#462, *LDC*, vol. 2). See #68S (18 Feb. 1749), p. 157 (#456, *LDC*, vol. 2); Devaux to Graffigny (26 April 1749), Graffigny Papers, XLIII, p. 239.

65 See *Correspondance de Graffigny*: #1390, Graffigny to Devaux (29 April 1749), vol. 9, p. 495; #1387 (22 April 1749), vol. 9, p. 486; #1391, Devaux to Graffigny (26 April 1749), vol. 10, pp. 13–15 n; #1386, Graffigny to Devaux (16 April 1749), vol. 9, p. 483. See also Collé, *Journal [historique]* (April 1749), vol. 1, p. 68. He is also the probable source for the story that later appeared in the extended version of Longchamps's memoirs: that the marquis was summoned to Cirey in January to have intercourse with his wife once she had discovered that she was pregnant. It was necessary, so Collé told it, that "she seek out, like an honorable woman, the company of her husband." However, in January she could not have been certain that she was pregnant. See Longchamps's *Mémoires*, Bibliothèque Nationale NAF 13006, pp. 60b–61b. All probably arose from the contemporary riddle: "Why does Mme Du Châtelet suddenly want to see her husband? It is," goes the response, "one of those cravings of pregnant women."

66 #25S, Du Châtelet to Saint-Lambert (16 June [1748]), p. 83 (#383, *LDC*, vol. 2); #48S ([30 Aug. 1748]), pp. 122–23 (#429, *LDC*, vol. 2); #49S ([2 Sept. 1748]), p. 125 (#432, *LDC*, vol. 2).

67 #83S, Du Châtelet to Saint-Lambert ([22 April 1749]), p. 206 (#464, *LDC*, vol. 2); #67S ([10 Feb. 1749]), pp. 155–56 (#459, *LDC*, vol. 2); #69S ([c. 23 Feb. 1749]), pp. 160, 161 (#451, *LDC*, vol. 2); #70S ([Feb. 1749]), p. 165 (#452, *LDC*, vol. 2). On their suspicions and impatience, see #74S ([28 March 1749]), p. 172 (#473, *LDC*, vol. 2); #77S (3 [April 1749]), pp. 182, 183 (#455, *LDC*, vol. 2). See also #86S (11 May [1749]), p. 213 (#468, *LDC*, vol. 2); #88S (18 May [1749]), pp. 217, 218 (#471, *LDC*, vol. 2).

68 #83S, Du Châtelet to Saint-Lambert ([21 April 1749]), pp. 207, 205 (#464, *LDC*, vol. 2).

69 #88S, Du Châtelet to Saint-Lambert ([18 May 1749]), p. 217 (#417, *LDC*, vol. 2); #89S (21 [May 1749]), p. 220–21, 222 (#476, *LDC*, vol. 2). See #90S ([May 1749]), p. 225 (#470, *LDC*, vol. 2), on the plans for the journey. On the pressure of her routine and Clairaut's significance, see also #91S ([beginning of June 1749]), p. 226 (#446, *LDC*, vol. 2); #93S ([8 June 1749]), p. 231 (#475, *LDC*, vol. 2).

70 See Paris Inventory, app. D93, vol. 95, pp. 418–20.

71 On Clairaut's contributions, see Judith P. Zinsser and Olivier Courcelle, "A Remarkable Collaboration: The Marquise Du Châtelet and Alexis Clairaut," *SVEC* (2003:12), pp. 107–20.

72 See, for example, on the mathematics I. Bernard Cohen, "A Guide to Isaac Newton's *Principia*," in Isaac Newton, *The Principia: Mathematical Principles of Natural Philosophy*,

trans. I. Bernard Cohen and Anne Whitman, assisted by Julie Budenz (Berkeley: University of California, 1999), chap. 10. On Du Châtelet's era, see Emch-Dériaz and Emch, "French Translator," p. 238. On Maupertuis, see Mary Terrall, *The Man Who Flattened the Earth, Maupertuis and the Sciences in the Enlightenment* (London: University of Chicago Press, 2002), p. 65.

73 See, for example, in Du Châtelet, *Principia*, Bk. I, sec. 8, prop. 41; Bk. I, sec. 12, 13, 14. See Du Châtelet's *Commentaire*, Bibliothèque Nationale, Ffr. 12268, passim.

74 Paris Inventory, see app. D93; vol. 96, pp. 443–62, 415–25.

75 #93S, Du Châtelet to Saint-Lambert ([18 June 1749]), p. 232 (#475, *LDC*, vol. 2); #94S (11 [June 1749]), p. 235 (#478, *LDC*, vol. 2).

76 Devaux to Graffigny (20 July 1749), Graffigny Papers, XLV, p. 33. #97S ([Friday, Aug. 1749]), p. 238 (#480, *LDC*, vol. 2). #466, Du Châtelet to Boufflers (3 May [1749]), *LDC*, vol. 2, p. 278.

77 #95S, Du Châtelet to Saint-Lambert ([Summer 1749?]), p. 236 (#407, *LDC*, vol. 2); #97S ([Aug. 1749]), pp. 238, 239 (#480, *LDC*, vol. 2); #99S ([end of Aug. 1749]), pp. 242–43 (#485, *LDC*, vol. 2).

78 Voltaire reported the birth at two in the morning; this coupled with the official report of four o'clock, suggests the two-hour delivery. D4005, Voltaire to d'Argenson (4 Sept. 1749), *CWV*, vol. 95, p. 151.

79 Paris Inventory, app. D93, vol. 95, p. 462. Note that Clairaut and others similarly deposited papers with the Académie to establish authorship before publication.

80 Longchamps in Bibliothèque Nationale, NAF, 13006, 62b–64; see Longchamps, *Voltaire et Mme Du Châtelet,* ed. Havard pp. 174–76, including an incident on the stairs where Voltaire fell, stood up, saw Saint-Lambert and accused him of killing Du Châtelet. I am grateful to Dr. Clint Joyner for help with the explanation of the cause of Du Châtelet's death. Historians have misunderstood the phrase *fièvre de lait* and equated it with childbed (or puerperal) fever. See also Jean Hartemann, "La Malheureuse Grossesse de Madame Du Châtelet," *Mémoires de l'académie de Stanislas,* vol. 47 (1966–67), pp. 83–101.

81 See Hubert Saget, *Voltaire à Cirey* (Chaumont: Le Pythagore, 2005), p. 88.

82 *Gazette de France,* no. 39, 20 Sept. 1749, p. 480. *Gazette de Hollande,* vol. 77, (26 Sept. 1749), p. 2. Luynes, *Mémoires,* vol. 9, p. 491.

83 See Luynes, *Mémoires,* vol. 9, p. 467; vol. 12, pp. 112, 417.

84 See Paris Inventory, app. D93, vol. 96, pp. 430–31. See Devaux to Graffigny (11 July 1750), Graffigny Papers, XLIX, p. 25.

85 Condorcet, quoted in Larousse, vol. "C," p. 1085.

86 On the delays, the reasons for revived interest in connection with the comet, and Clairaut's role, see Judith P. Zinsser, "Translating Newton's *Principia:* The Marquise Du Châtelet's Revisions and Additions for a French Audience," *Notes and Records of the Royal Society of London* 55 (2001), pp. 227–45; Zinsser and Courcelle, "Remarkable Collaboration," pp. 107–20; François de Gandt, unpublished essay, p. 4. I am grateful to Simon Schafer for originally suggesting this explanation for the printer's decisions, and to Olivier Courcelle for working out the details with me.

87 D4025, Voltaire to Denis (23 Sept. [1749]), *CWV*, vol. 95, p. 168.

88 See D4032, Voltaire to Denis (5 Oct. 1749), *CWV*, vol. 95, p. 174; passim Voltaire's letters to d'Argental and others (Oct.–Nov. 1749), *CWV*, vol. 95, pp. 175–87. Collé,

Journal Historique, vol. 1 (Sept, 1749), p. 97 (Jan. 1750), p. 124. Luynes, *Mémoires,* vol. 10, p. 227.

89　D4028, Voltaire to Denis (29 Sept. 1749), *CWV,* vol. 95, pp. 170–71.

90　This could all have been part of a settlement, offered by the poet instead of the promised money toward the costs of the Argenteuil property. On plans and arrangements, see D4032, D4046; D4062, Voltaire to Marie Florence Du Châtelet ([15 Nov. 1749]), *CWV,* vol. 95, pp. 197–98; D4063, Voltaire to marquis Du Châtelet ([c. 15 Nov. 1749]), *CWV,* vol. 95, pp. 199–200. Difficulties between Voltaire and the marquis might also be related to one of Longchamps's other stories, the mysterious box of papers that Du Châtelet had instructed her husband to burn. Historians have assumed these were her love letters to Saint-Lambert. Since her husband knew of her affair, it is unlikely they would have produced the angry response described by the valet. It is more likely that this was the box in which she kept Voltaire's most dangerous writings under lock and key. If so, what would have been new and able to shock the marquis? Perhaps he did not know about the love affair with Mme Denis. Finding some of her and Voltaire's love notes, those that had so angered and hurt his wife, could have occasioned disgust and rage and brought into question Voltaire's presentation of himself as the marquise's devoted but rejected and now devastated companion. For the Longchamps account, see Bibliothèque Nationale, NAF 13006, p. 66b; see Longchamps and Wagnière, *Mémoires,* pp. 254–56; note that the incident does not appear in the Havard version.

91　D3882, Frederick to Voltaire (5 March 1749), *CWV,* vol. 95, pp. 12–13. D3952, Voltaire to Frederick (29 June 1749), *CWV,* vol. 95, p. 101.

92　Voltaire, "Éloge," *Bibliothèque impartiale,* Jan.–Feb. 1752; a slightly shorter version appeared in editions of her translation of and commentary on the *Principia;* See "Preface historique," in Du Châtelet, trans., *Principes mathématiques,* vol. 1, pp. xi–xiii.

93　See Voltaire, *Mémoires,* Jacqueline Hellegouarc'h, ed. (Paris: Livre de Poche, 1998), pp. 37–43, 73, 85, 107–11. Longchamps, in Bibliothèque Nationale, NAF, 13006, p. 64b.

94　Raynal, quoted in Elisabeth Badinter, *Emilie, Emilie: L'ambition féminine au XVIIIe siècle* (Paris: Flammarion, 1983), p. 465. Publication of a collection of her letters to d'Argental (1806), and Longchamps's memoir (1826), along with those of other contemporaries such as Maurepas, supposedly offered proof of her emotional nature and fueled suppositions about her lovers.

95　On the rediscovery of her significance, see Carolyn Merchant Iltis, "Madame du Châtelet's Metaphysics & Mechanics." *Studies in the History & Philosophy of Science* 8 (1977), pp. 46–48; Linda Gardiner Janik, "Searching for the Metaphysics of Science: The Structure & Composition of Madame Du Châtelet's *Institutions de physique,* 1737–1740." *SVEC* 201 (1982), pp. 109–10.

96　See Sonia Carboncini, "L'Encyclopédie et Christian Wolff: A propos de quelques articles anonymes," in *Autour de la philosophie Wolffienne,* ed. Jean Ecole (New York: Goerg Olms Verlag, 2001), p. 215 n. 74; I am grateful to John Iverson for this article. J. H. S. Formey is presumed to have written many of the entries in the *Encyclopédie* that used the *Institutions;* in some entries he refers readers to her book.

97　See, for example, *Le Journal encyclopédique,* vol. 6, no. 3 (Sept. 1759), pp. 3–17.

98　Du Châtelet, *Discours,* ed. Mauzi, p. 22.

Epilogue: 2006

1 In this analysis, a number of scholars have influenced my formulation: Sheila Croucher, presentation, Sept. 7, 2004, Miami University, Oxford, Ohio; Sheila Croucher, *Imagining Miami: Ethnic Politics in a Postmodern World* (Charlottesville, Va.: University Press of Virginia, 1997); Nell Irvin Painter, *Sojourner Truth: A Life, A Symbol* (New York: W. W. Norton, 1997); Felicity A. Nussbaum, *The Autobiographical Subject: Gender & Ideology in Eighteenth-Century England* (Baltimore: Johns Hopkins University Press, 1989); Jeremy D. Popkin and Bernadette Fort, eds., *The Mémoires Secrets and the Culture of Publicity in Eighteenth-Century France* (Oxford: Voltaire Foundation, 1998), p. 73.

2 Germaine Greer first composed these "truisms" for women artists. On the concept of "originality" and how it has been used to denigrate women's work, see Berenice A. Carroll, "The Politics of 'Originality': Women and the Class System of the Intellect," *Journal of Women's History* 2 (Fall 1990), pp. 136–63.

3 Voltaire, *Candide* (London: Penguin Books, 1947), pp. 20–21.

4 See David W. Smith, "Nouveaux Regards sur la brève rencontre entre Mme Du Châtelet et Saint-Lambert," in *The Enterprise of Enlightenment: A Tribute to David Williams from His Friends*, ed. Terry Pratt and David McCallam (Oxford: Peter Lang, 2004), pp. 329–43; I am particularly grateful to this scholar for bringing these letters to my attention. See Graffigny Papers collection, Beinecke Library, Yale University, Devaux to Graffigny (12[11] Sept. 1749), XLV, pp. 143–44; (13[12] Sept. 1749), XLV, p. 147; (13 Sept. 1749), XLV, p. 152; (14–15 Sept. 1749), XLV, p. 157. (13 Oct. 1749), XLV, p. 207; (29 Nov. 1749), XLV, p. 289. Note that Raynal had been spreading the story that the affair had all been part of a game fabricated by Stanislas's confessor to weaken Boufflers's authority with the king. Since the king was to turn to Du Châtelet, Boufflers supposedly set Saint-Lambert to foil the plot with his flirtation. Voltaire later presented this story in his memoirs as if true. Raynal dined with Denis and Voltaire just at this time, which suggests that the poet might have been the source of the rumor. See Voltaire's *Mémoires*, pp. 108–9. See Graffigny to Devaux (26 Nov. 1749), Graffigny Papers, XLVI, p. 25. For Devaux's denial, see Devaux to Graffigny (29 Nov. 1749), Graffigny Papers, XLV, p. 289. For the general narrative of Saint-Lambert's life, see Roger Poirier, *Jean-François de Saint-Lambert, 1716–1803: Sa Vie, son oeuvre* (Sarrequemines: Pierron, 2001); Jean-Philibert Damiron, *Mémoires sur les encyclopédistes: Saint-Lambert* (Genève: Slatkine Reprints, 1968), also describes his writings at length, and see George Mangeot, *La Famille de Saint-Lambert, 1596–1795* (Paris: Libraire Croville-Morant, 1913), pp. 88–89, for his military career. Note that Saint-Lambert began using the title of "marquis" after moving to Paris.

5 Voltaire quoted in Charles Augustin Sainte-Beuve, *Causeries du Lundi* (Paris: Garnier Fréres, 1852–1862), vol. 11, p. 125. Du Deffand and Diderot as quoted in Damiron, pp. 54–55.

6 Mme d'Houdetot, "Souvenirs et remarques sur Saint-Lambert." Morgan Library, MA 2390 RV Autograph, Misc. Fr. 1–3, 4. D'Epinay, paraphrased in Damiron, *Mémoires sur les encyclopédistes*, pp. 18–19. Saint-Lambert's will in Hippolyte Buffenoir, *La Comtesse d'Houdetot, sa famille—ses amis* (Paris: H. Leclerc, 1905), pp. 258–65.

7 On the plans for Argenteuil, see Paris Inventory, app. D93, vol. 95, in *The Complete Works of Voltaire*, ed. Theodore Besterman (Genève: Institut et Musée Voltaire, 1970),

p. 458; marquis's approval of bill to master painter, p. 475; D4063, Voltaire to marquis Du Châtelet ([c. 15 Nov. 1749]), *CWV,* vol. 95, p. 199. On plans for her year, see #93S, Du Châtelet to Saint-Lambert ([8 June 1749]), *Lettres d'Amour au Marquis de Saint-Lambert,* ed. Anne Soprani (Paris: Éditions Paris-Méditerranée, 1997), p. 231. [#475, Marquis Du Châtelet, *Lettres de la Marquise du Châtelet,* ed. Theodore Besterman (Genève: Institut et Musée Voltaire, 1958), vol. 2.]

8 #63, Du Châtelet to Algarotti (20 [April 1736]), *LDC,* vol. 1, p. 111.

9 On conservation of mass before Lavoisier, see David Bodanis, $E=MC^2$:*A Biography of the World's Most Famous Equation* (New York: Berkley Books, 2000), p. 61.

10 Gretel Zinsser Munroe to Hans Zinsser and Ruby Handforth Zinsser [?], collection of Antonia Munroe Grumbach.

Bibliography

The Bibliography lists primary texts first: those by the marquise Du Châtelet, and then those by other writers of the seventeenth and eighteenth centuries. The secondary works by modern authors are arranged topically so that readers may explore a particular area of interest; for example, "Eighteenth-Century Philosophy and Science." See the Notes to each chapter for even more specialized works about her era, her life, and her works.

1. The Works of Gabrielle Emilie le Tonnelier de Brenteuil, marquise Du Châtelet

Manuscripts and Published Works

Manuscripts in the Voltaire Collection, National Library of Russia, St. Petersburg, vol. IX, pp. 122–285. Some of the texts have been published. See in Ira O. Wade, ed. *Studies on Voltaire with some Unpublished Papers of Mme du Châtelet* (Princeton: Princeton University Press, 1947): *The Fable of the Bees* transl., version A (versions B and C exist only in manuscript); "Essai sur l'optique," "Grammaire raisonée," chaps. 6 & 8; "De la liberté," chap. 5. See also from the same collection her précis of Thomas Woolston's *Six Discours sur les miracles de notre sauveur,* ed. William Trapnell (Paris: Honoré Campion, 2004). Note that I also consulted Voltaire's Library itself, the books sold to Catherine the Great after his death in 1778. They are identified in the Notes by the Alekseev catalogue number first, and the shelf number in St. Petersburg, second.

The Occidental Manuscript Collection of the National Library of Russia, St. Petersburg, has a version of Voltaire's *Traité de métaphysique* with her annotations. For a printed version of "De la liberté," see the critical edition of the *Traité de métaphysique* and app. 1 in *The Complete Works of Voltaire* (Oxford: Voltaire Foundation, 1989), vol. 14.

Examen de la Genèse and *Examen des Livres du Nouveau Testament.* Manuscript versions exist at the Bibliothèque de Troyes and the Bibliothèque d'Académie des Sciences in Brussels. References are to the as yet unpublished critical edition by Betram Eugene Schwarzbach, *Examens de la Bible* (Paris: Honoré Campion, forthcoming).

Lettres de la marquise du Châtelet, ed. with intro. and notes by Theodore Besterman, 2 vols. (Genève: Institut et Musée de Voltaire, 1958). This edition incorporates letters published previously in 1806 and 1878, and in the article by Louise Colet, "Mme Du Châtelet: Lettres inédites au maréchal de Richelieu et à Saint-Lambert," *Revue des deux mondes,* 3 (1845), pp. 564–96. Her letters are reprinted in *The Complete Works of Voltaire: Correspondence,* ed.

Theodore Besterman, vols. 86–95 (Genève and Oxford: Voltaire Foundation, 1968–70). I also used the new edition of her letters to Saint-Lambert: *Emilie Du Châtelet: Lettres d'amour au Marquis de Saint-Lambert,* ed. Anne Soprani (Paris: Éditions Paris-Méditerranée, 1997). Note that assorted letters are scattered in the collections of her correspondents, such as Alexis Clairaut. The manuscripts of her letters to Maupertuis are at the Bibliothèque Nationale in Paris, and those to d'Argental, Jurin, and Saint-Lambert at the Morgan Library in New York, N.Y. Printed Besterman edition abbreviated in the Notes as *LDC.*

Dissertation sur la nature et la propagation du feu published in two different editions: the first version published in *Pièces qui ont remporté le prix de l'Académie royale des sciences en MDCCXXXVIII* (Paris, 1739), pp. 85–168, 218–19; *Recueil des pièces qui ont remporté le prix de l'Académie royale des sciences,* vol. 4, pp. 87–170, 220–21; the second, published with her interchange with Dortous de Mairan, *Dissertation sur la nature et la propagation du feu* (Paris: Chez Prault Fils, 1744; reprinted in the Landmarks of Science microprints).

"Reply to the *Voltairomanie,*" 1738, reprinted in *The Complete Works of Voltaire* (Oxford: Voltaire Foundation, 1969), vol. 89: app. D51, pp. 508–12.

"Lettre sur les 'Elements de la philosophie de Newton,'" *Journal des savants,* Sept. 1738, pp. 534–41.

Institutions de physique published in two editions: the first (Paris: Chez Prault Fils, 1740) reprints Amsterdam and Londres, 1741; the second was Amsterdam, 1742. Edition of 1740 reprinted in the Landmarks of Science microprints. Facsimile of 1742 ed. in Christian Wolff, *Gesammelte Werke: Materialien und Dokumente,* ed. J. Ecole, H. W. Arndt, C. A. Corr, J. E. Hofmann, M. Thormann (New York, 1988), vol. 28. Italian translation (Venice, 1743); German translation by Wolf Balthasar Adolph von Steinwehr (Leipzig, 1743). I also used the partial manuscript at the Bibliothèque Nationale.

Réponse de madame la marquise du Châtelet à la lettre que m. de Mairan lui a écrite le 18 février 1741 sur la question des forces vives (Bruxelles: Foppens, 1741). Reprinted in *Institutions* (1742 ed.) and with *Dissertation sur la nature et la propagation du feu,* 1744 ed., included with the *Dissertation,* in the Landmarks of Science microprints. Translated into Italian to accompany the Venetian edition of the *Institutions;* translated into German by L. A. Gottsched (Leipzig, 1741).

Discours sur le bonheur in five reprints with minor variations in the title and the text: *Huitième Recueil philosophique et littéraire* (Société Typographique de Bouillon, 1779); *Opuscules philosophiques et littéraires* (Paris, 1796); in *Lettres inédites de Madame la Marquise du Châtelet à M. le Comte D'Argental* (Paris, 1806). Critical edition by Robert Mauzi (Paris: Sociéte d'Edition Belles Lettres, 1961); and reprint with introduction by Elisabeth Badinter (Paris: Payot and Rivages, 1997).

Principes mathématiques de la philosophie naturelle par feue Madame la Marquise du Châtelet (Paris, editions of 1756 and 1759). Facsimile reprint of incomplete 1756 edition. Paris, 1966; of complete 1759 edition, Sceaux: Editions Jacques Gabay, 1990. This is Du Châtelet's translation of Newton's *Principia* and her accompanying *Commentaire* [Commentary].

2. Memoirs and Writings of Her Era

Archives and Unpublished Sources

Archives Nationales, Paris—Records of the *notaire* Bronod.
Arsenal, Paris—Baron de Breteuil, *Mémoires.*

Bibliography

Bibliothèque Nationale, Paris—Letters to Maupertuis from the duchess d'Aiguillon, de Chaulnes, and Saint-Pierre; Longchamps, *Mémoires*.

Château de Vincennes, Paris—Military Archives.

Morgan Library, New York—comtesse d'Houdetot *souvenirs*.

Princeton University Library, Princeton N.J.—Rare Book Collection.

Private Collections: Véronique Flachat; J. Patrick Lee.

Published Sources

Académie royale des sciences. *Mémoires* (the published versions of papers delivered at meetings of the Académie).

Algarotti, M. *Le Newtonianisme pour les dames, ou Entretiens sur la lumière*. Translated by M. Duperron de Castera. 2 vols. in 1. Montpellier: Chez Montalant, 1738.

Bernis, François-Joachim de Pierre de. *Mémoires et lettres de François-Joachim de Pierre, cardinal de Bernis*. Edited by F. Masson. 2 vols. Paris, 1878. Reprint, Paris: Société d'Editions Littéraires et Artistiques, 1903.

Bertrand, Jean, *La Fable des abeilles*. London, 1740.

Breteuil, baron de. *Mémoires*. Edited by Evelyne Lever. Paris: F. Bourin, 1992.

Clairaut, Alexis-Claude. Correspondence in [prince Baldassarre de] Boncompagni, "Lettere di Alessio Claudio Clairaut, *Atti dell'Accademia Pontificia de' Nuovi Lincei*, 45 (1892): 233—91.

———. *Elémens d'algèbre*. Paris: Chez les Frères Guerin, 1746.

———. *Elémens de géometrie*. Paris: Chez David Fils, 1741.

Collé, Charles. *Journal [historique] et mémoires de Charles Collé sur les hommes de lettres, les ouvrages dramatiques et les événements les plus mémorables du règne de Louis XV, 1748—1772*. 3 vols. Paris: Didot Frères, 1868.

Créqui, Marquise de. *Souvenirs de la marquise de Créqui, 1710—1803*. 5 vols. Paris: Michel Lévy Frères, 1867.

Descartes, René. *Discourse on Method*. Translated by John Veitch. In *The Rationalists*. Garden City, N.Y.: Dolphin Books, 1962.

Diderot, Denis *Encyclopédie: Ou, Dictionnaire raisonné des sciences, des arts et des métiers par une société de gens de lettres; mis en ordre & publié par M. Diderot . . . ; & quant à la partie mathématique par M. D'Alembert*. 35 vols. Lausanne & Berne: Les Societés Typographiques, 1778—82.

Dubuisson, Simon Henri. *Lettres du Commissaire Dubuisson au marquis de Caumont, 1735—1741*. Introduction, notes and tables by A. Rouxel. Paris: Arnould, 1882.

Ducros, Louis. *La Société française au XVIIIe siècle d'après les mémoires et correspondances du temps*. Paris, 1822. In English, *French Society in the Eighteenth Century*, translated by W. de Geijer. New York: Putnam's, 1927.

Du Deffand, Marie, marquise. *Correspondance complète de la marquise Du Deffand avec ses amis*. Edited by M. de Lescure. 2 vols. Paris: Henri Plon, 1865.

Duranton, Henri, ed., *Journal de la cour & de Paris*. Paris, 1836. Reprint, University of Saint-Etienne, 1981.

Fontenelle, Bernard le Bovier de. *Conversations on the Plurality of Worlds*. Introduction by Nina Rattner Gelbart. Translated by H. A. Hargreaves. Berkeley: University of California Press, 1990.

Graffigny, Françoise d'Issembourg d'Happoncourt. *Correspondance de Madame de Graffigny.* Edited by J. A. Dainard et al. 10 vols. Oxford: Voltaire Foundation, Taylor Institution, 1985–.

Hénault, Charles Jean François. *Mémoires du Président Hénault.* Edited by François Rousseau. Paris: Hachette, 1911.

Heuvel, Jacques van den, *Mélanges.* Paris: Gallimard, 1961.

Jordan, Charles-Etienne. *Histoire d'un voyage littéraire fait en MDCCXXXIII.* The Hague: Ador-ren Hoetiers, 1735.

Locke, John. *Essay on Human Understanding.* Edited by Peter H. Nidditch. Oxford: Oxford University Press, 1975.

Longchamps, Sébastien G., and Jean Louis Wagnière. *Mémoires sur Voltaire, et sur ses ouvrages.* Paris: Aimé André, 1826. See also, Sébastien G. Longchamps, *Voltaire et Mme Du Châtelet: Révélations d'un serviteur.* Edited by D'Albanès Havard. Paris: E. Dentu, 1863.

Luynes, Charles Philippe d'Albert, duc de. *Mémoires du duc de Luynes sur la cour de Louis XV, 1735–1758.* Edited by L. Dussieux and E. Soulié. 17 vols. Paris: Firmin Didot, 1860–65.

Mairan, Jean-Jacques Dortous de. *Lettre à Mme*** sur la question des forces vives [en réponse].* Paris: Académie Royale des Sciences, 1741.

Mandeville, Bernard. *Fable of the Bees; or Private Vices, Publick Benefits,* London: J. Roberts, 1714.

Maupertuis. *Discours sur les différentes figures des astres.* Paris: De L'Imprimerie Royal, 1732.

Maurepas, Jean Frederic Phélypeaux, comte de. *Mémoires du comte de Maurepas.* 4 vols. Paris: Chez Buisson, 1792.

Montaigne, *The Complete Works of Montaigne.* Translated by Donald M. Frame. Stanford: Stanford University Press, 1957.

Newton, Isaac. *Opticks: A Treatise of the Reflections, Refractions, Inflections & Colors of Light.* 4th ed., London, 1730. Reprint, New York: Dover, 1952.

———. *The Principia: Mathematical Principles of Natural Philosophy.* Translated by I. Bernard Cohen and Anne Whitman, assisted by Julia Budenz. Berkeley: University of California Press, 1999.

Palairet, Elie. *La Bibliothèque des enfans, ou, les premiers élémens des lettres contenant le système du bureau tipografique.* Paris: Chez Pierre Simon, 1733.

———. *Nouvelle méthode pour apprendre à bien écrire et instruction général sur tout ce qui concerne cet art.* La Haye: Pierre Hussin, 1716.

Pope, Alexander. *An Essay on Man.* In *The Best of Pope,* ed. George Sherburn. New York: Ronald Press Company, 1929. Pp. 114–54.

Richelieu, Louis François Armand Du Plessis, duc de. *Mémoires du maréchal le duc de Richelieu.* 2 vols. Edited by F. Barrière. Paris: Firmin-Didot, 1889.

Sainte-Beuve, Charles Augustin. *Causeries du lundi.* 14 vols. Paris: Garnier Frères, 1852–62.

Société archéologique de Preuilly. Pamphlet no. 85. 1985.

Soumille, père Bernard Laurent. *Le Gran Trictrac.* 1738.

Voltaire. *The Complete Works [Oeuvres complètes de Voltaire].* Edited by Theodore Besterman et al. Genève: Institut et Musée Voltaire, and Oxford: Voltaire Foundation, 1968–. Referred to as *CWV* in the Notes. (Individual works from other editions of Voltaire's works are also cited in the Notes.)

———. *Mémoires . . .* Edited by Jacqueline Hellegouarc'h. Paris: Livre de Poche, 1998.

(See the two catalogues of Voltaire's Library in St. Petersburg: *Inventaire des manuscrits de la*

Bibliothèque de Voltaire conservé à Bibliothèque impériale publique de Saint-Pétersbourg. Edited by Fernand Caussy. 1913. Reprint, Genève: Slatkine Reprints, 1970. *Bibliothèque de Voltaire: Catalogue des livres.* Edited by M. P. Alekseev. Moscow, 1961.)

3. Paris in the Eighteenth Century: Appearance and Everyday Life

Braudel, Fernand. *The Structures of Everyday Life: The Limits of the Possible.* Translated by S. Reynolds. 3 vols. New York: Harper & Row, 1979.

Colas, René. *Paris qui reste: Vieux Hôtels, vieilles demeures, la Rive Gauche et l'Ile de Saint-Louis.* Paris: R. Colas, 1914.

Dézallier d'Argenville, Antoine-Nicolas. *Voyage pittoresque de Paris.* Paris: De Bure, 1757. Reprint, Genève: Minkoff Reprint, 1972.

Fairchilds, Cissie. *Domestic Enemies: Servants and Their Masters in Old Regime France.* Baltimore: Johns Hopkins University Press, 1984.

Farge, Arlette. *Fragile Lives: Violence, Power and Solidarity in Eighteenth-Century Paris.* Translated by Carol Shelton. Cambridge, Mass.: Harvard University Press, 1993.

Garrioch, David. *Neighborhood and Community in Paris, 1740–1790.* New York: Cambridge University Press, 1986.

Le Guide du patrimoine: Paris. Paris: Hachette, 1994.

Hillairet, Jacques. *Dictionnaire historique des rues de Paris.* 2 vols. Paris: Editions de Minert, 1964.

Jombert, Charles Antoine. *Architecture moderne.* Paris, 1764.

Krafft, Johann. *Plans, coupes, élévations des plus belles maisons & des hôtels construits à Paris & dans les environs: 1771–1802.* Paris: Librairie d'art décoratif et industriel, G. Hue, 1909.

Mercier, Louis Sébastien. *Le Paris de Louis Sébastien Mercier: Cartes et index toponymique.* Edited by Jean-Claude Bonnet. Paris: Mercure de France, 1994.

A New Description of Paris. 2 vols. London: Henry Bonwicke, 1688.

The Plan de Turgot. 1739.

Roche, Daniel. *A History of Everyday Things: The Birth of Consumption in France, 1600–1800.* Translated by Brian Pearce. New York: Cambridge University Press, 2000.

4. A Noblewoman's Life: Family, Education, Interests, and Activities

Barber, W. H. "Penny Plan, Twopiece Colored: Longchamps's Mémoire of Voltaire." In *Studies in the French Eighteenth Century Presented to John Lough.* Durham: University of Durham, 1978.

Blaufarb, Rafe. "Noble Privilege and Absolutist State Building: French Military Administration After the Seven Years' War." *French Historical Studies* 24, no. 2 (Spring 2001): 223–46.

Chapman, Sara. "Patronage as Family Economy: The Role of Women in the Patron-Client Network of the Phélypeaux de Pontchartrain Family, 1670–1715." *French Historical Studies* 24, no. 1 (Winter 2001): 11–35.

Chartier, Roger. *Passions of the Renaissance.* Vol. 3, *A History of Private Life.* Edited by Philippe Ariès and Georges Duby. Cambridge, Mass.: Belknap Press of Harvard University Press, 1989.

Chaussinand-Nogaret, Guy. *The French Nobility in the Eighteenth Century: From Feudalism to Enlightenment.* Translated by William Doyle. Cambridge: Cambridge University Press, 1995.

Cusset, Catherine. *No Tomorrow: The Ethics of Pleasure in the French Enlightenment.* Charlottesville, Va.: University Press of Virginia, 1999.

Delpierre, Madeleine. *Dress in France in the Eighteenth Century.* Translated by Caroline Beamish. New Haven: Yale University Press, 1997.

Doyle, William. "The Price of Offices in Pre-Revolutionary France." *Historical Journal* 27, no. 4 (December 1984): 831–60.

Dunkley, John, *Gambling: A Social and Moral Problem in France, 1685–1792.* Oxford: Voltaire Foundation, 1985.

Goncourt, Edmond, and Jules de Goncourt. *La Femme au dix-huitième siècle.* Preface by Elisabeth Badinter. Paris: Flammarion, 1982.

Hanley, Sarah. "Social Sites of Political Practice in France: Lawsuits, Civil Rights and the Separation of Powers in Domestic and State Government, 1580–1800." *American Historical Review,* 102 (February 1997): 27–52.

Kavanagh, Thomas. *Enlightenment and the Shadows of Chance: The Novel and the Culture of Gambling in Eighteenth-Century France.* Baltimore: Johns Hopkins University Press, 1993.

Lancaster, Henry Carrington. *The Comédie Française, 1701–1772: Plays, Actors, Spectators, Finances.* Transactions of the American Philosophical Society, vol. 41. Philadelphia: American Philosophical Society, 1951.

———. *French Tragedy in the Time of Louis XV and Voltaire, 1715–1774.* 2 vols. Baltimore: Johns Hopkins Press, 1950.

Levy, David. "Rules for the Game of Trictrac." http://pages.sbcglobal.net/david.Levy/trictrac/rules/rules.htm.

Motley, Mark. *Becoming a French Aristrocrat: The Education of the Court Nobility 1580–1715.* Princeton: Princeton University Press, 1990.

Neuschel, Kristen Brooke. *Words of Honor: Interpreting Noble Culture in Sixteenth-Century France.* Ithaca, N.Y.: Cornell University Press, 1989.

Rizzo, Tracey. *A Certain Emancipation of Women: Gender, Citizenship, and the Causes Célèbres of Eighteenth-Century France.* Selinsgrove, Pa.: Susquehanna University Press, 2004.

Roche, Daniel. *The Culture of Clothing: Dress and Fashion in the Ancien Régime.* Translated by Jean Birrell. Cambridge: Cambridge University Press, 1994.

Rousselot, Paul. *Histoire de l'éducation des femmes en France.* 2 vols. Paris: Didier, 1883.

Sargentson, Carolyn. *Merchants and Luxury Markets: The Marchands Merciers of 18th Century Paris.* London: Victoria and Albert Museum, in association with J. Paul Getty Museum, 1996.

Saule, Béatrix. *Visite du musée des carrosses.* Versailles: Editions Art Lys., 1997.

Simonin, Charlotte, and David W. Smith. "Du nouveau sur Mme Denis: Les Apports de la correspondance de Mme de Graffigny." *Cahiers Voltaire* 4 (2005): 25–56.

Sonnet, Martine. *L'Education des filles au temps des lumières.* Preface by Daniel Roche. Paris: Editions du Cerf. 1987.

Vovelle, Michel, ed. *Enlightenment Portraits.* Translated by Lydia G. Cochrane. Chicago: University of Chicago Press, 1997.

5. The Republic of Letters and Its Institutions: *Académies* and *Salons*

Backer, Dorothy Anne Liot. *Precious Women: A Feminist Phenomenon in the Age of Louis XIV.* New York: Basic Books, 1974.

Badinter, Elisabeth. *Les Passions intellectuelles.* 2 vols. Paris: Fayard, 1999.

Besterman, Theodore. *Voltaire.* New York: Harcourt, Brace & World, 1969.

Buffenoir, Hippolyte. *La Comtesse d'Houdetot, sa famille—ses amis.* Paris: H. Leclerc, 1905.

Chartier, Roger. *The Cultural Origins of the French Revolution.* Translated by Lydia G. Cochrane. Durham, N.C.: Duke University Press, 1991.

Damiron, Jean-Philibert. *Mémoires sur les encyclopédistes: Saint-Lambert.* Genève: Slatkine Reprints, 1968.

Farnham, Fern. *Madame Dacier: Scholar and Humanist.* Monterey, Calif.: Angel Press, 1976.

Goldgar, Anne. *Impolite Learning: Conduct and Community in the Republic of Letters, 1680–1750.* New Haven: Yale University Press, 1995.

Goodman, Dena. *The Republic of Letters: A Cultural History of the French Enlightenment.* Ithaca, N.Y.: Cornell University Press, 1994.

Hahn, Roger. *The Anatomy of a Scientific Institution: The Paris Academy of Sciences, 1666–1803.* Berkeley: University of California Press, 1971.

Lougee, Carolyn C. *Paradis des Femmes: Women, Salons, and Social Stratification in Seventeenth Century France.* Princeton: Princeton University Press, 1976.

Lynn, Michael R. "Enlightenment in the Republic of Science: The Popularization of Natural Philosophy in Eighteenth-Century Paris." Ph.D. dissertation, University of Wisconsin, Madison, 1997.

Marchal, Roger. *Madame de Lambert et son milieu.* Oxford: Voltaire Foundation, 1991.

Marion, Michel. *Recherches sur les bibliothèques privées à Paris au milieu du XVIIIe siècle: 1750–1759.* Paris: Bibliothèque Nationale, 1978.

Masson, Pierre-Maurice. *Madame de Tencin (1682–1749): Une Vie de femme au XVIIIe siècle.* Genève: Slatkin Reprints, 1970.

O'Keefe, Cyril B. *Contemporary Reactions to the Enlightenment (1728–1762): A Study of Three Critical Journals, the Jesuit Journal de Trévoux, the Jansenist Nouvelles Ecclésiastiques, and the Secular Journal des Savants.* Genéve: Slatkine Reprints, 1974.

Pappas, John. "Berthier's Journal de Trévoux and the Philosophes." Vol. 3, *Studies on Voltaire and the Eighteenth Century* [*SVEC*]. Gènève: Institut et Musée Voltaire, 1957.

Paul, Charles B. *Science and Immortality: The Eloges of the Paris Academy of Sciences (1699–1971).* Berkeley: University of California Press, 1980.

Perry, Norma. *Sir Everard Fawkener: Friend and Correspondent of Voltaire.* Vol. 133, *Studies on Voltaire and the Eighteenth Century* [*SVEC*]. Oxford: Voltaire Foundation, 1975.

Les petites poetès du XVIIIe siècle: Morceaux choisis. Paris: La Renaissance du Livre, [1911].

Picard, Roger. *Les Salons littéraires et la société française, 1610–1789.* Paris: Brentano's, 1943.

Poirier, Roger, *Jean-François de Saint-Lambert, 1716–1803: Sa Vie, son oeuvre.* Sarrequemines: Pierron, 2001.

Pomeau, René. *Voltaire en son temps.* 2 vols. Oxford: Voltaire Foundation, 1985–95.

Popkin, Jeremy D., and Bernadette Fort, eds. *The Mémoires Secrets and the Culture of Publicity in Eighteenth-Century France.* Oxford: Voltaire Foundation, 1998.

Racevskis, Karlis. *Voltaire and the French Academy.* Chapel Hill, N.C.: Studies in the Romance Languages and Literatures, 1975.

Sgard, Jean. *Dictionnaire des journaux, 1600–1785.* Oxford: Voltaire Foundation, 1991.

Sturdy, David J. *Science and Social Status: The Members of the Académie des Sciences, 1666–1750.* Woodbridge, Suffolk: Boydell Press, 1995.

Sutton, Geoffrey, V. *Science for a Polite Society: Gender, Culture, and the Demonstration of Enlightenment.* Boulder, Colo.: Westview Press, 1995.

Terrall, Mary. "Salon, Academy, and Boudoir: Generation and Desire in Maupertuis's Science of Life." *Isis* 87, no. 2 (June 1996): 217–29.

Wade, Ira O. *The Clandestine Organization & Diffusion of Philosophic Ideas in France from 1700–1750.* Princeton: Princeton University Press, 1938.

———. *The Intellectual Development of Voltaire.* Princeton: Princeton University Press, 1969.

———. *The Search for a New Voltaire.* Philadelphia: American Philosophical Society, 1958.

Walters, Robert L. "The Allegorical Engravings in the Ledet-Desbordes Edition of the *Eléments de la philosophie de Newton.*" In *Voltaire & His World: Studies Presented to W. H. Barber,* ed. R. J. Howells, A. Mason, H. T. Mason, and D. Williams. Oxford: Voltaire Foundation, 1985.

Weil, Françoise. *Livres interdits, livres persecutés, 1720–1770.* Oxford: Voltaire Foundation, 1999.

Wolfgang, Aurora. "Les Salonnières: Reclaiming the Literary Field." *Intertexts,* 5, no. 2 (Fall 2004): 114–27.

Wootton, David. "Unhappy Voltaire, or 'I Shall Never Get Over It as Long as I Live.'" *History Workshop Journal* 50 (Autumn 2000): 137–55.

6. Eighteenth-Century Philosophy and Science

Barber, W. H. "Critical Edition of *Traité de Métaphysique.*" Vol. 14, *Complete Works of Voltaire.* Edited by W. H. Barber. Oxford: Voltaire Foundation, Taylor Institution, 1989.

Brockliss, L. W. B. "The Scientific Revolution in France." *The Scientific Revolution in National Context,* edited by Roy Porter and Mikuláš Teich. Cambridge: Cambridge University Press, 1992.

Brunet, Pierre. *L'Introduction des théories de Newton en France au XVIIIe siècle.* Paris: Libraire Scientifique Albert Blanchard, 1931.

———. *Maupertuis.* Paris: Libraire Scientifique Albert Blanchard, 1929.

Clark, William, Jan Golinski, and Simon Schaffer, eds. *The Sciences in Enlightened Europe.* Chicago: University of Chicago Press, 1998.

Clarke, Desmond M. *Descartes' Philosophy of Science.* Manchester: Manchester University Press, 1982.

Cohen, I. Bernard. "A Guide to Isaac Newton's *Principia.*" In Isaac Newton, *The Principia: Mathematical Principles of Natural Philosophy.* Translated by I. Bernard Cohen and Anne Whitman, assisted by Julia Budenz. Berkeley: University of California Press, 1999.

———. "Introduction: Scientific Method." In *A Norton Critical Edition: Newton,* edited by I. Bernard Cohen and Richard S. Westfall. New York: W. W. Norton, 1995.

———. *The Newtonian Revolution.* Cambridge: Cambridge University Press, 1980.

De Clercq, Peter. *The Leiden Cabinet of Physics: A Descriptive Catalogue.* Leiden: Museum Boerhaave Communication 271, 1997.

Densmore, Dana. *Newton's Principia: The Central Argument—Translation, Notes, and Extended Proofs.* Translated by William H. Donahue. Sante Fe: Green Lion Press, 1995.

Dobbs, Betty Jo Teeter. *The Janus Face of Genius: The Role of Alchemy in Newton's Thought*. New York: Cambridge University Press, 1991.

Fara, Patricia. *Newton: The Making of Genius*. London: Macmillan, 2002.

Feingold, Mordechai. *The Newtonain Moment: Isaac Newton and the Making of Modern Culture*. New York: Oxford University Press, 2004.

Greene, Brian. *The Elegant Universe: Superstrings, Hidden Dimensions, and the Quest for the Ultimate Theory*. New York: W. W. Norton, 1999.

Guerlac, Henry. "The Newtonianism of Dortous de Mairan." In *Essays on the Age of Enlightenment: In Honor of Ira O.Wade*. Edited by Jean Macary. Genève: Librairie Droz, 1977.

———. *Newton on the Continent*. Ithaca, N.Y.: Cornell University Press, 1981.

Hall, Rupert. "Newton in France: A New View." *History of Science* 13 (1975): 233–50.

Hankins, Thomas. *Science and the Enlightenment*. Cambridge: Cambridge University Press, 1985. Reprint, 1995.

Hecht, H. "Leibniz' Concepts of Possible Worlds & the Analysis of Motion in Eighteenth-Century Physics." In *Between Leibniz, Newton, and Kant: Philosophy & Science in the Eighteenth Century*, edited by Wolfgang Lefevre. Boston: Kluwer Academic Publishers, 2001.

Heilbron, J. L. *Elements of Early Modern Physics*. Berkeley: University of California Press, 1982.

———. "Some Uses for Catalogues of Old Scientific Instruments." In *Making Instruments Count: Essays on Historical Scientific Instruments Presented to Gerard L'Estrange Turner*, edited by R.G.W. Anderson. Aldershot: Variorum, 1993.

Hine, Ellen McNiven. "Dortous de Mairan, the 'Cartonian.'" *SVEC* (1989): 163–79.

James, Susan. *Passion and Action: The Emotions in Seventeenth-Century Philosophy*. Oxford: Clarendon Press, 1997.

Osler, Margaret J. "Mixing Metaphors: Science and Religion or Natural Philosophy and Theology in Early Modern Europe." *History of Science* 36, no. 1 (1998): 91–113.

Schaffer, Simon. "Glass Works." In *The Uses of Experiment: Studies in the Natural Sciences*, edited by David Gooding, Trevor Pinch, and Simon Schaffer. New York: Cambridge University Press, 1989.

Shank, John Bennett. *Before Voltaire: Newtonianism and the Origins of the Enlightenment in France, 1687–1734*. Ann Arbor: University of Michigan Press, 2000.

Shapin, Steven. "The House of Experiment in Seventeenth-Century England." In *The Scientific Enterprise in Early Modern Europe*, edited by Peter Dear. Chicago: Chicago University Press, 1997.

Shapin, Steven, and Simon Schafer. *Leviathan and the Air-Pump: Hobbes, Boyle and the Experimental Life*. Princeton: Princeton University Press, 1985.

Smith, George E. "The Newtonian Style in Book II of the *Principia*." In *Isaac Newton's Natural Philosophy*, edited by Jed Z. Buchwald and I. Bernard Cohen. Cambridge, Mass.: MIT Press, 2001. Pp. 244–98.

Sorrell, Tom. *Descartes: A Very Short Introduction*. New York: Oxford University Press, 2000.

———. ed. *The Rise of Modern Philosophy: The Tension Between the New and Traditional Philosophies from Machiavelli to Leibniz*. Oxford: Clarendon Press, 1993.

Spink, J. S. *French Free-Thought from Gassendi to Voltaire*. London: University of London, Athlone Press, 1960.

Terrall, Mary. *The Man Who Flattened the Earth: Maupertuis and the Sciences in the Enlightenment*. Chicago: University of Chicago Press, 2002.

———. "Vis Viva." *History of Science* 42 (2004): 189–209.

Westfall, Richard S. *The Life of Isaac Newton.* New York: Cambridge University Press, 1993.

Whiteside, D. T. "Newton the Mathematician." In *A Norton Critical Edition: Newton,* edited by I. Bernard Cohen and Richard S. Westfall. New York: W. W. Norton, 1995.

Wilson, Catherine. *Leibniz's Metaphysics: A Historical and Comparative Study.* Princeton: Princeton University Press, 1989.

Zinsser, Judith P. "The Ultimate Commentary: A Consideration of I. Bernard Cohen's Guide to Newton's Principia." *Notes and Records of the Royal Society of London* 57 (2003): 231–38.

7. Court Life: Versailles and Lunéville

Beaussant, Philippe, and Patricia Bouchenot-Déchin. *Les Plaisirs de Versailles: Théâtre & musique.* Paris: Fayard, 1996.

Cabourdin, Guy. *Encyclopédie illustrée de la Lorraine.* Nancy: Presses Universitaires de Nancy, 1992.

Charles-Gaffiot, Jacques. *Lunéville: Fastes du Versailles Lorrain.* N.p.: Editions Didier Carpentier, 2003.

Cohen, Sarah R. *Art, Dance, and the Body in French Culture of the Ancien Régime.* New York: Cambridge University Press, 2000.

Jones, Colin. *Madame de Pompadour: Images of a Mistress.* London: National Gallery Co., 2002.

Kaiser, Thomas. "Madame de Pompadour and the Theaters of Power." *French Historical Studies* 19 (1996): 1025–44.

Lever, Evelyne. *Madame de Pompadour: A Life.* Translated by Catherine Temerson. New York: Farrar, Straus and Giroux, 2002.

Levron, Jacques. *Daily Life at Versailles in the Seventeenth and Eighteenth Centuries.* Translated by Claire Elaine Engel. London: George Allan, 1965. [Originally *La Vie quotidienne à la cour de Versailles aux XVIIe et XVIIIe siècles.* Paris, 1865.]

Mangeot, George. *La Famille de Saint-Lambert, 1596–1795.* Paris: Libraire Croville-Morant, 1913.

Maugras, Gaston. *La Cour de Lunéville au XVIIIe siècle.* Paris: Plon-Nourrit, 1904.

Muratori-Philip, Anne. *Le Roi Stanislas.* Paris: Fayard, 2000.

Newton, William R. *L'Espace du roi: La Cour de France au château de Versailles, 1682–1789.* Paris: Fayard, 2000.

Salmon, Xavier, ed. *Madame de Pompadour et les arts.* Paris: Réunion des Musées Nationales, 2002.

Solnon, Jean-François. *La Cour de France.* Paris: Fayard, 1987.

Tronquart, Martine. *Les Châteaux de Lunéville.* Metz: Editions Serpenoise, 1991.

8. Women, Gender, and Learning

Äkerman, Susanna. "The Form of Queen Christian's Academies," in *The Shapes of Knowledge from the Renaissance to the Enlightenment,* edited by Donald R. Kelley and Richard H. Popkin. Boston: Kluwer Academic Publishers, 1991. Pp. 165–88.

Anderson, Bonnie A., and Judith P. Zinsser. *A History of Their Own: Women in Europe from Prehistory to the Present.* 2 vols. New York: Oxford University Press, 2000.

Bonnel, Roland, and Catherine Rubinger. *Femmes savantes et Femmes d'esprit: Women Intellectuals of the French Eighteenth Century.* New York: Peter Lang, 1994.

Carroll, Berenice A. "The Politics of 'Originality': Women and the Class System of the Intellect." *Journal of Women's History* 2 (Fall 1990): 136–63.

Fara, Patricia. *Pandora's Breeches: Women, Science and Power in the Enlightenment.* London: Pimlico, 2004.

Gutwirth, Madelyn. *The Twilight of the Goddesses: Women and Representation in the French Revolutionary Era.* New Brunswick, N.J.: Rutgers University Press, 1992.

Haraway, Donna J. "Situated Knowledges: The Science Question in Feminism and the Privilege of Partial Perspective." In *Simians, Cyborgs, and Women: The Reinvention of Nature.* New York: Routledge, 1991.

Harth, Erica. *Cartesian Women: Version and Subversions of Rational Discourse in the Old Regime.* Ithaca, N.Y.: Cornell University Press, 1992.

Hayes, Julie Candler. *Reading the Enlightenment: System & Subversion.* New York: Cambridge University Press, 1999.

Iverson, John, and Marie-Pascale Pieretti. "'Toutes Personnes [. . .] seront admises à concourir': La Participation des femmes aux concours académiques." *Dix-huitième Siècle* 36 (2004): 313–32.

Jordanova, L. J. *Languages of Nature: Critical Essays on Science and Literature.* London: Free Association Books, 1986.

Maclean, Ian. *Woman Triumphant: Feminism in French Literature 1610–1652.* Oxford: Clarendon Press, 1977.

Merchant, Carolyn. *The Death of Nature: Women, Ecology and the Scientific Revolution.* San Francisco: Harper & Row, 1980.

Mommertz, Monika. "The Invisible Economy of Science—A New Approach to the History of Gender and Astronomy at the Eighteenth-Century Berlin Academy of Sciences." Translated by Julia Baker. In *Men, Women, and the Birthing of Modern Science,* edited by Judith P. Zinsser. Dekalb: Northern Illinois University Press, 2005. Pp. 159–78.

Nussbaum, Felicity A. *The Autobiographical Subject: Gender & Ideology in Eighteenth-Century England.* Baltimore: Johns Hopkins University Press, 1989.

Phillips, Patricia. *The Scientific Lady: A Social History of Women's Scientific Interests 1520–1918.* New York: St. Martin's, 1990.

Poirier, Jean-Pierre. *Histoire des femmes de science en France du Moyen Age à la Revolution.* Paris: Pygmalion, Gérard Watelet, 2002.

Smith, Bonnie G. *The Gender of History: Men, Women and Historical Practice.* Cambridge, Mass.: Harvard University Press, 1998.

Spencer, Samia, ed. *French Women and the Age of Enlightenment.* Bloomington: Indiana University Press, 1984.

Steinbrugge, Lieselotte. *The Moral Sex: Woman's Nature in the French World.* Translated by Pamela E. Selwyn. New York: Oxford University Press, 1995.

Terrall, Mary. "Gendered Spaces, Gendered Audience: Inside and Outside the Paris Academy of Sciences." *Configurations,* 2 (1994): 207–32.

———. "Metaphysics, Mathematics, & the Gendering of Science in Eighteenth-Century France." In *The Sciences in Enlightened Europe,* edited by William Clark, Jan Golinski, and Simon Schaffer. Chicago: University of Chicago Press, 1998. Pp. 246–71.

Zinsser, Judith, ed. *Men, Women, and the Birthing of Modern Society*. DeKalb: Northern Illinois University Press, 2005.

9. Selected Works about Du Châtelet

Allen, Lydia D. *Physics, Frivolity and Madame Pompon-Newton: The Historical Reception of the Marquise du Châtelet from 1750–1996*. Ph.D. dissertation, University of Cincinnati, 1998.

Badinter, Elisabeth. *Emilie, Emilie: L'Ambition féminine au XVIIIe siècle*. Paris: Flammarion, 1983.

Bodanis, David. *E=MC²: A Biography of the World's Most Famous Equation*. New York: Berkley Books, 2000.

————. *Passionate Minds: The Great Enlightenment Love Affair*. London: Little, Brown, 2006.

Bonnel, Roland. "La Correspondance scientifique de la marquise Du Châtelet: La 'Lettre-laboratoire.'" *SVEC* (2000:4): 79–95.

Brown, Andrew, and Ulla Kölving. "Qui est l'auteur du *Traité de métaphysique?*" *Cahiers Voltaire* 2 (2003): 85–93.

Cajori, Florian. "Mme Du Châtelet on Fluxions." *Mathematical Gazette* 13 (1926–27): 252.

Carboncini, Sonia. "L'Encyclopédie et Christian Wolff: A propos de quelques articles anonymes." In *Autour de la philosophie Wolffienne*, edited by Jean Ecole. New York: Goerg Olms Verlag, 2001. Pp. 210–16.

Debever, R. "La Marquise du Châtelet traduit et commente les *Principia* de Newton." *Bulletin de la classe des sciences* 73 (5th series, 1987): 509–27.

De Zan, Mauro. "Voltaire e Mme Du Châtelet, membri e correspondenti dell'Accademia delle Scienze di Bologna." *Studi e memorie dell'Istituto per la Storia dell'Università di Bologna* 6 (1987): 141–58.

Droysen, H. "Die Marquise du Châtelet, Voltaire und der Philosoph Christian Wolff." *Zeitschrift für französische Sprache und Literatur* 35 (1909–10): 226–48.

Edwards, Samuel. *The Divine Mistress*. New York: David McKay, 1970.

Ehrman, Esther. *Mme Du Châtelet*. Oxford: Oxford University Press, 1986.

Hartemann, Jean. "La Malheureuse Grossesse de Madame Du Châtelet." *Mémoires de l'académie de Stanislas* 47 (1966–67): 83–101.

Hutton, Sarah. "Emilie du Châtelet's *Institutions de physique* as a Document in the History of French Newtonianism." *Studies in the History and Philosophy of Science* 35 (2004): 515–31.

Iltis, Carolyn Merchant. "Madame du Châtelet's Metaphysics and Mechanics." *Studies in the History and Philosophy of Science* 8, no. 1 (1977): 28–48.

Janik, Linda Gardiner. "Searching for the Metaphysics of Science: The Structure and Composition of Madame Du Châtelet's *Institutions de physique*, 1737–1740." *SVEC*, 201 (1982): 85–113.

Joly, Bernard. "Les Théories du feu de Voltaire et de Mme Du Châtelet." *SVEC* (2001:11): 212–37.

Kawashima, Keiko. "Madame Du Châtelet dans le journalisme." *LLULL*, 18 (1995): 471–91.

Le Coat, Gerard, and Anne Eggimann-Besançon. "Emblématique et émancipation féminine au XVIIIe siècle: Le portrait de Madame Du Châtelet par Marie-Anne Loir." *Coloquio: Artes* 68 (March 1986): 30–39.

Ledeuil-d'Enquin, Justin. *La Marquise du Châtelet à Semur et le passage de Voltaire*. Semur: Millon, 1892.

Locqueneux, Robert. "Les *Institutions de physique* de Madame Du Châtelet, ou un traité de paix entre Descartes, Leibniz et Newton." *Revue du nord* 77 (1995): 859–92.

Mazzotti, Massimo. "Newton for Ladies: Gentility, Gender and Radical Culture." *BJHS* 37, no. 2 (June 2004): 119–46.

Mitford, Nancy. *Voltaire in Love*. London: Hamish Hamilton, 1957.

Passeron, Irene, "Muse ou élève? Sur les lettres de Clairaut à Mme Du Châtelet." *SVEC* (2001): 187–97.

Piot, L'abbé. *Cirey-le-Château: La Marquise du Châtelet, sa liaison avec Voltaire*. Saint-Dizier: O. Godard, 1894.

Saget, Hubert. *Voltaire à Cirey*. Chaumont: Le Pythagore, 2005.

Schwarzbach, Bertram Eugene. "Les Etudes bibliques à Cirey: De l'attribution à Mme du Châtelet des *Examens de la Bible* et leur typologie." *Actes du Colloque de Joinville*, 1998.

Smith, David W. "Nouveaux Regards sur la brève rencontre entre Mme Du Châtelet et Saint-Lambert." In *The Enterprise of Enlightenment: A Tribute to David Williams from His Friends*, edited by Terry Pratt and David McCallam. Oxford: Peter Lang, 2004. Pp. 329–43.

Taton, Renée. "Mme du Châtelet, traductrice de Newton." *Archives internationales d'histoire des sciences* 22 (July–Dec. 1969): 185–209.

Terrall, Mary. "Emilie du Châtelet and the Gendering of Science." *History of Science* 33 (1995): 283–310.

Trapnell, William. "Le manuscrit 'Voltaire 80 221' de Saint-Pétersbourg." In *La Philosophie clandestine à l'âge classique*, edited by Antony McKerne and Alain Mothu. Oxford: Voltaire Foundation, 1997.

Vaillot, René. *Avec Mme Du Châtelet, 1734–1749*. Edited by René Pomeau. Vol. 1, *Voltaire en son temps*. Oxford: Voltaire Foundation, 1985–95.

———. *Madame du Châtelet*. Paris: Albin Michel, 1978.

Vercruysse, Jeroom. "La M. du Châtelet prévote d'une conférie bruxelloise." Vol. 18, *Studies on Voltaire and the Eighteenth Century* [*SVEC*]. Genève: Institut et Musée Voltaire, 1961. Pp. 169–71.

Wade, I. O. *Studies on Voltaire, with Some Unpublished Papers of Mme Du Châtelet*. Princeton: Princeton University Press, 1947.

———. *Voltaire and Madame du Châtelet: An Essay on the Intellectual Activity at Cirey*. Princeton: Princeton University Press, 1941.

Waithe, Mary Ellen. *Modern Women Philosophers, 1600–1900*. Boston: Kluwer Academic Publishers, 1991.

Walters, Robert L. "Chemistry at Cirey." *Studies on Voltaire and the Eighteenth Century* [*SVEC*], Vol. 58. Genève: Institut et Musée Voltaire, 1967.

Zinsser, Judith P. "Emilie du Châtelet: Genius, Gender, and Intellectual Authority." In *Women Writers and the Early Modern British Political Tradition*, edited by Hilda L. Smith. New York: Cambridge University Press, 1998. Pp. 168–90.

———. "Entrepreneur of the 'Republic of Letters': Emilie de Breteuil, Marquise Du Châtelet, and Bernard Mandeville's *Fable of the Bees*." *French Historical Studies* 25, no. 4 (Autumn 2002): 595–624.

———. "The Many Representations of the Marquise Du Châtelet." In *Men, Women, and the Birthing of Modern Science*, edited by Judith P. Zinsser. Dekalb: Northern Illinois University Press, 2005. Pp. 48–70.

————. "Translating Newton's *Principia:* The Marquise Du Châtelet's Revisions and Additions for a French Audience." *Notes and Records of the Royal Society of London.* 55 (2001): 227–45.

Zinsser, Judith P., and Olivier Courcelle. "A Remarkable Collaboration: The Marquise Du Châtelet and Alexis Clairaut." *SVEC* (2003: 12): 107–20.

Zinsser, Judith P., and Julie Candler Hayes, eds. *Emilie Du Châtelet: Rewriting Enlightenment Philosophy and Science. SVEC* (2006: 1).

Index